BUILDING PARALLEL, EMBEDDED, AND REAL-TIME APPLICATIONS WITH ADA

The arrival and popularity of multi-core processors have sparked a renewed interest in the development of parallel programs. Similarly, the availability of low-cost microprocessors and sensors has generated a great interest in embedded real-time programs. This book provides students and programmers whose backgrounds are in traditional sequential programming with the opportunity to expand their capabilities into parallel, embedded, real-time, and distributed computing. It also addresses the theoretical foundation of real-time scheduling analysis, focusing on theory that is useful for actual applications.

Written by award-winning educators at a level suitable for undergraduates and beginning graduate students, this book is the first truly entry-level textbook in the subject. Complete examples allow readers to understand the context in which a new concept is used, and enable them to build and run the examples, make changes, and observe the results.

JOHN W. MCCORMICK is Professor of Computer Science at the University of Northern Iowa.

FRANK SINGHOFF is Professor of Computer Science at Université de Bretagne Occidentale (University of Brest).

JÉRÔME HUGUES is Associate Professor in the Department of Mathematics, Computer Science, and Control at the Institute for Space and Aeronautics Engineering (ISAE), Toulouse.

BUILDING PARALLEL, EMBEDDED, AND REAL-TIME APPLICATIONS WITH ADA

JOHN W. MCCORMICK
University of Northern Iowa

FRANK SINGHOFF
Université de Bretagne Occidentale

JÉRÔME HUGUES
Institute for Space and Aeronautics Engineering (ISAE), Toulouse

CAMBRIDGE
UNIVERSITY PRESS

CAMBRIDGE
UNIVERSITY PRESS

University Printing House, Cambridge CB2 8BS, United Kingdom

Cambridge University Press is part of the University of Cambridge.

It furthers the University's mission by disseminating knowledge in the pursuit of education, learning and research at the highest international levels of excellence.

www.cambridge.org
Information on this title: www.cambridge.org/9780521197168

First published 2011

A catalogue record for this publication is available from the British Library

Library of Congress Cataloguing in Publication data
McCormick, John W., 1948–
Building parallel, embedded, and real-time applications with Ada / John W. McCormick,
Frank Singhoff, Jerome Hugues.
p.   cm.
Includes bibliographical references and index.
ISBN 978-0-521-19716-8 (hardback)
1. Ada (Computer program language)   2. Parallel programming (Computer science)
3. Embedded computer systems – Programming.   4. Real-time data processing.
5. Multiprocessors – Programming.
I. Singhoff, Frank.   II. Hugues, Jerome.   III. Title.
QA76.73.A35M375   2011
004´.35 – dc22   2010053214

ISBN 978-0-521-19716-8 Hardback

The photograph on the cover shows astronaut Stephen K. Robinson standing on the end of the International Space Station's robotic manipulator system, Canadarm 2. This arm, built by MacDonald, Dettwiler, and Associates Ltd for the Canadian Space Agency, is 17.6 m long when fully extended. It has seven motorized joints, each a complex embedded real-time system. Given its crucial role on the space station, the reliability of Canadarm 2 must be impeccable. The software for these joints and for the workstation that the astronauts use to control them is written in Ada. This book provides an introduction to the concepts of concurrent programming, embedded systems, and real-time constraints necessary for understanding and developing the software for such systems.

Contents

Illustrations

Tables

Foreword

The task of programming is a difficult one. Over the decades there have been many promises to eliminate this difficulty. It is interesting to recall that Fortran was first promoted on the basis that it would do away with programming, and allow scientists to enter their mathematical equations directly into the computer. Yet, the difficulty of programming has not gone away, and indeed, the task is more difficult now, especially because of the widespread introduction of parallelism into all realms of programming.

In universities today, many professors find that students shy away from difficult problems and challenges. As a result computer science programs have been made easier and "more fun," and many recent textbooks reflect this worrisome trend. What we need is not students who find easy stuff fun, we need students who find difficult challenges fun!

In this climate a textbook that tackles the most difficult area of programming, the creation of complex embedded systems in which parallelism and real-time concerns play a major role, is very welcome. We entrust our lives to such complex systems all the time these days, in cars, planes, trains, medical equipment, and many other circumstances.

This book addresses the task of teaching the complex elements required to create such systems. The choice of Ada, though unfamiliar for say the creation of simple web programs, is a natural one for two reasons. First, it is the only language in common use where tasking and parallelism play an important "first-class" citizen role (C/C++ rely entirely on external libraries for such support, and the support for such concepts in Java is very weak). Second, Ada is indeed a language of choice for building complex systems of this kind. For example, much of the avionics in the new Boeing 787 "Dreamliner" is written in Ada, as is the new air traffic control system in England. The choice of Ada as a vehicle is thus a good one, and actually makes it easier for students to grasp the critical new concepts, even though they may have been exposed to other languages previously.

This book is an important addition to the arsenal of teaching materials for a well-educated computer science graduate. It is also eminently readable, and, perhaps I can even say it is fun to read. Despite the potentially dry nature of this subject matter, it is presented in an entertaining and accessible manner that reflects the remarkable teaching skills of its authors.

Robert Dewar
AdaCore

Preface

The arrival and popularity of multi-core processors have sparked a renewed interest in the development of parallel programs. Similarly, the availability of low cost microprocessors and sensors has generated a great interest in embedded real-time programs. This book provides students and programmers with traditional backgrounds in sequential programming the opportunity to expand their capabilities into these important emerging paradigms. It also addresses the theoretical foundations of real-time scheduling analysis, focusing on theory that is useful for real applications.

Two excellent books by Burns and Wellings (2007; 2009) provide a *complete, in depth* presentation of Ada's concurrent and real-time features. They make use of Ada's powerful object-oriented programming features to create high-level concurrent patterns. These books are "required reading" for software engineers working with Ada on real-time projects. However, we found that their coverage of *all* of Ada's concurrent and real-time features and the additional level of abstraction provided by their clever use of the object-oriented paradigm made it difficult for our undergraduate students to grasp the fundamental concepts of parallel, embedded, and real-time programming. We believe that the subset of Ada presented in this book provides the simplest model for understanding the fundamental concepts. With this basic knowledge, our readers can more easily learn the more detailed aspects of the Ada language and the more widely applicable patterns presented by Burns and Wellings. Readers can also apply the lessons learned here with Ada to the creation of systems written in more complex languages such as C, C++, and real-time Java.

The first chapter gives an overview of and motivation for studying parallel, embedded, and real-time programming. The fundamental terminology of parallel, concurrent, distributed, real-time, and embedded systems is presented in the context of two cooks sharing resources to prepare food.

The first six sections of Chapter 2 provide a brief introduction to sequential programming with Ada. Only those Ada constructs relevant to the remainder of the book are presented. In conjunction with the on-line learning references provided, our students whose backgrounds did not include Ada were able to come quickly up to speed with their peers who had some previous Ada experience. Students with some Ada background found this chapter an excellent review of the language. The final section of this chapter provides detailed coverage of Ada's low-level programming constructs. These features allow the program to interact with hardware — almost always necessary in an embedded system. These features are illustrated with a complete example of a device driver for a sophisticated analog to digital converter.

Chapter 3 introduces the notion of the task, Ada's fundamental construct for parallel execution. We show how tasks are created, activated, run, and completed. We use state diagrams to illustrate the life cycle of a task. We present the parent-child and master-dependent task hierarchies. We conclude this chapter with a brief discussion of some less frequently used tasking features: abortion, identification, and programmer-defined attributes.

Chapter 4 introduces the most widely used construct for communication and synchronization between tasks — the protected object. The need for mutual exclusion, introduced with cooking examples in Chapter 1, is revisited in the context of an Ada program with multiple tasks incrementing a shared variable. After demonstrating this classic problem, we introduce encapsulation of shared data within a protected object. We illustrate the locking mechanisms provided by protected functions and procedures with several figures. The need for synchronization, again introduced with cooking examples in Chapter 1, is revisited and the solution based on the protected entry is discussed and illustrated. We provide additional practice with protected objects by developing a number of useful concurrent patterns — semaphores, barriers, and broadcasts. The use of requeue is motivated with a problem of allocating a limited number of pencils. The chapter concludes with a discussion of interrupts. We return to the analog to digital converter introduced in Chapter 2 and replace the polling logic with an interrupt handler.

Chapter 5 looks at the use of direct task interaction through the rendezvous. We begin by illustrating the behavior of simple entry calls and accepts. Then we discuss the variations of the selective accept statement that provides the server with more control over its interactions with clients. We introduce the use of both relative and absolute delays. Next we discuss the entry call options which give a client more control over its interaction with a server. We conclude this chapter with a discussion on the implementation of state machines for both passive and active objects.

Distribution is an important issue in software engineering and is the topic of Chapter 6. While it is easy to motivate the advantages of distribution, the details take more effort. We introduce middleware and discuss the major problems with distributed applications. We provide an introduction to two approaches for distributing an Ada program. The Distributed Systems Annex (DSA) provides a solution for a pure Ada application. We develop the software for a very simple distributed student information system through three examples of increasing complexity. For those who want more details, we provide information on more advanced DSA concepts. While CORBA requires a larger amount of code to implement a distributed system than the DSA, it is more commonly used in industry. Not only is there more support for CORBA than the DSA, it provides an easy integration of different programming languages in a single application. We use the same example of a distributed student information system to develop a CORBA-based solution. Again, we provide additional details for those wanting a more advanced understanding of CORBA. We introduce and use the PolyORB tool for our DSA and CORBA examples.

Chapter 7 is an introduction to the theoretical foundations of real-time scheduling analysis, focusing on theory that is useful for real applications. This presentation is independent of any programming language. We begin with an introduction of the characteristics of a task relevant to scheduling analysis. We define the characteristics of schedulers and discuss fixed priority scheduling and earliest deadline first scheduling. Ensuring that all tasks meet their deadlines is paramount to any hard real-time system. We show you how to calculate and use processor utilization factors and worst case response times to verify schedulability. We begin by analyzing examples with independent tasks. Then we add the complexities of resource sharing with different priority inheritance protocols.

In Chapter 8 we explain how to write real-time applications in Ada that are compliant with the scheduling theory discussed in the previous chapter. In particular, we show how to implement periodic tasks, activate priority inheritance protocols, and select an appropriate scheduler. The first six sections discuss how we can use Ada's Real-Time Systems Annex to implement compliant applications. The remainder of the chapter is devoted to implementing such applications with POSIX. We conclude with a comparison of the two approaches.

Our Ada applications do not run alone. They execute within a run-time configuration consisting of the processor and the environment in which the application operates. Our final chapter introduces the reader to run-time environments. We discuss three variants of the GNAT run-time: ORK+, MaRTE, and RTEMS. We examine the effect of the run-time on the analysis of schedulability and the determination of task characteristics such as worst case execution time. The schedulability tools MAST and Cheddar are also introduced.

Resources

A website with the complete source code for all examples and some of the exercises in the book may be found at www.cambridge.org/9780521197168.

Solutions to all of the exercises are available to qualified instructors. Please visit www.cambridge.org/9780521197168.

Acknowledgments

We would like to thank the many individuals who have helped us with this project. The comments, corrections, and suggestions made by our technical reviewers, Alexander Mentis and Pat Rogers, have enormously improved and enriched this book. We are grateful to them both. In addition to providing many useful comments and corrections, Dan Eilers compiled many of our examples with the ICC Ada compiler to ensure we did not use any GNAT-specific constructs.

It is sometimes difficult for those of us with years of experience to write for those who are just beginning. The students in the Real-Time Systems class at the University of Northern Iowa did not hesitate to point out those portions of the manuscript, including the exercises, they felt needed further explanation.

Anyone who has written a textbook can appreciate the amount of time and effort involved and anyone related to a textbook author can tell you at whose expense that time is spent. John thanks his wife Naomi for her support and understanding.

Frank would like to thank all his Master's students who have for the past 10 years tested his courses and exercises on real-time systems. In 2002, we began work on Cheddar, a simple tool whose goal is to provide students with a better understanding of real-time scheduling. We were helped by different partners and contributors: special thanks to Pierre Dissaux, Alain Plantec, Jérôme Legrand, Laurent Pautet, Fabrice Kordon, Peter Feiler, Jérôme Hugues, Yvon Kermarrec and all the others that are listed on the Cheddar website. Finally, many thanks Magali for your patience during all my busy days off!

Jérôme would like to thank all his friends and colleagues for the memorable years he spent working on PolyORB at Telecom ParisTech: Laurent Pautet, Fabrice Kordon, and all our Master's students that helped us at that time; Bob Duff and Thomas Quinot from AdaCore; and Vadim Godunko for all his personal contributions to the project. Participating in such a large project, and seeing it now as a project used in the industry, is a great pleasure. Finally, I'd like to thank Alice for letting me write this book near the fireplace over the long winter nights!

John W. McCormick
University of Northern Iowa
mccormick@cs.uni.edu

Frank Singhoff
Université de Bretagne Occidentale
singhoff@univ-brest.fr

Jérôme Hugues
Institute for Space and Aeronautics
Engineering (ISAE), Toulouse
jerome.hugues@isae.fr

1

Introduction and overview

The arrival and popularity of multi-core processors have sparked a renewed interest in the development of parallel programs. Similarly, the availability of low-cost microprocessors and sensors has generated a great interest in embedded real-time programs. Ada is arguably the most appropriate language for development of parallel and real-time applications. Since it was first standardized in 1983, Ada's three major goals have remained:

- Program reliability and maintenance
- Programming as a human activity
- Efficiency

Meeting these goals has made Ada remarkably successful in the domain of mission-critical software. It is the language of choice for developing software for systems in which failure might result in the loss of life or property. The software in air traffic control systems, avionics, medical devices, railways, rockets, satellites, and secure data communications is frequently written in Ada. Ada has been supporting multiprocessor, multi-core, and multithreaded architectures as long as it has existed. We have nearly 30 years of experience in using Ada to deal with the problem of writing programs that run effectively on machines using more than one processor. While some have predicted it will be another decade before there is a programming model for multi-core systems, programmers have successfully used the Ada model for years. In February 2007, Karl Nyberg won the Sun Microsystems Open Performance Contest by building an elegant parallel Ada application (Nyberg, 2007). The parallel Ada code he wrote a decade earlier provided the foundation of this success.

It is estimated that over 99% of all the microprocessors manufactured these days end up as part of a device whose primary function is not computing (Turley, 1999). Today's airplanes, automobiles, cameras, cell phones,

GPS receivers, microwave ovens, mp3 players, tractors, and washing machines all depend on the software running on the microprocessors embedded within them. Most consumers are unaware that the software in their new washing machine is far more complex than the software that controlled the Apollo moon landings. Embedded systems interact with the world through sensors and actuators. Ada is one of the few programming languages to provide high-level operations to control and manipulate the registers and interrupts of these input and output devices.

Most programs written for embedded systems are real-time programs. A real-time program is one whose correctness depends on both the validity of its calculations and the time at which those calculations are completed (Burns and Wellings, 2009; Laplante, 2004). Users expect that their wireless phone will convert and transmit their voice quickly and regularly enough that nothing in their conversation is lost. Audio engineers quantify "quickly" into the maximum amount of time that the analog to digital conversion, compression, and transmission will take. They specify a set of deadlines. A deadline is a point in time by which an activity must be completed. Software engineers have the responsibility of ensuring that the computations done by the software are completed by these deadlines. This responsibility is complicated by the parallel nature of most real-time embedded software. One embedded processor may be responsible for a number of related control operations. Our wireless phone should not lose any of the video it captures simultaneously with our talking. The software engineer must ensure that all of the tasks competing for processor cycles finish their computations on time.

1.1 Parallel programming

A parallel program is one that carries out a number of operations simultaneously. There are two primary reasons for writing parallel programs. First, they usually execute faster than their sequential counterparts. The prospect of greater performance has made parallel programming popular in scientific and engineering domains such as DNA analysis, geophysical simulations, weather modeling, and design automation. There are theoretical limits on how much speedup can be obtained by the use of multiple processors. In 1967, Gene Amdahl published a classic paper (Amdahl, 1967) that showed that if P is the fraction of a sequential program that can be run in parallel on N processors, the maximum speedup is given by the formula

$$\frac{1}{(1 - P) + \frac{P}{N}}$$

Thus, for example, if 80% of our program can be run in parallel, the maximum speedup obtained with four processors is

$$\frac{1}{(1 - 0.8) + \frac{0.8}{4}} = 2.5$$

The second reason for writing parallel programs is that they are frequently better models of the processes they represent. More accurate models are more likely to behave in the manner we expect. As the real world is inherently parallel, embedded software that interacts with its environment is usually easier to design as a collection of parallel solutions than as a single sequential set of steps. Parallel solutions are also more adaptable to new situations than sequential solutions. We'll show you some examples later in this chapter where the parallel algorithm is far more flexible than the sequential version. Before beginning our discussion of parallel programming, let's take a brief look at the hardware on which such programs execute.

1.1.1 Flynn's taxonomy

Michael Flynn (1974) described a simple taxonomy of four computer architectures based on data streams and instruction streams. He classifies the classic Von Neumann model as a Single stream of Instructions executing on Single stream of Data (SISD). An SISD computer exhibits no parallelism. This is the model to which novice programmers are introduced as they learn to develop algorithms.

The simplest way to add parallelism to the SISD model is to add multiple data streams. The Single stream of Instructions executing on Multiple streams of Data (SIMD) architecture is often called array or vector processing. Originally developed to speed up vector arithmetic so common in scientific calculations, an SIMD computer applies a single instruction to multiple data elements. Let's look at an example. Suppose we have the following declarations of three arrays of 100 real values.

```
subtype Index_Range is Integer range 1..100;
type Vector is array (Index_Range) of Float;

A, B, C : Vector;    -- Three array variables
```

We would like to add the corresponding values in arrays B and C and store
the result in array A. The SISD solution to this problem uses a loop to apply
the add instruction to each of the 100 pairs of real numbers.

```
for Index in Index_Range loop
   A (Index) := B (Index) + C (Index);
end loop;
```

Each iteration of this loop adds two real numbers and stores the result in
array A. With an SIMD architecture, there are multiple processing units for
carrying out all the additions in parallel. This approach allows us to replace
the loop with the simple arithmetic expression

```
A := B + C;
```

that adds all 100 pairs of real numbers simultaneously.

The Multiple stream of Instructions executing on a Single stream of Data
(MISD) architecture is rare. It has found limited uses in pattern matching, cryptology, and fault-tolerant computing. Perhaps the most well-known
MISD system is the space shuttle's digital fly-by-wire flight control system (Knoll, 1993). In a fly-by-wire system, the pilot's controls have no direct
hydraulic or mechanical connections to the flight controls. The pilot's input
is interpreted by software which makes the appropriate changes to the flight
control surfaces and thrusters. The space shuttle uses five independent processors to analyze the same data coming from the sensors and pilot. These
processors are connected to a voting system whose purpose is to detect and
remove a failed processor before sending the output of the calculations to
the flight controls.

The most common type of parallel architecture today is the MIMD (Multiple stream of Instructions executing on Multiple streams of Data) architecture. Nearly all modern supercomputers, networked parallel computers,
clusters, grids, SMP (symmetric multiprocessor) computers and multi-core
computers are MIMD architectures. These systems make use of a number
of independent processors to execute different instructions on different sets
of data. There is a great variety in the ways these processors access memory and communicate among themselves. MIMD architectures are divided
into two primary groups: those that use shared memory and those that use
private memory.

The simplest approach to shared memory is to connect each processor
to a common bus which connects them to the memory. The shared bus
and memory may be used for processors to communicate and to synchronize their activities. Multi-core processors reduce the physical space used by
placing multiple processors (cores) on a single chip. Each core usually has its

own small memory cache and shares a larger on-chip cache with its counter-parts. In more complicated schemes, multiple processors may be connected to shared memory in hierarchical or network configurations.

When each processor in an MIMD system has its own private memory, communication among them is done by passing messages on some form of communication network. There are a wide variety of interconnection networks. In static networks, processors are hardwired together. The connections in a static network can be made in a number of configurations including linear, ring, star, tree, hypercube, and so on. Dynamic networks use some form of programmable switches between the processors. Switching networks may range from simple crossbar connections between processors in a single box to the internet-connecting processors on different continents.

1.1.2 Concurrent programming

With the many different organizations of parallel hardware available, it might seem that a programmer would need a detailed understanding of the particular hardware they are using in order to write a parallel program. As usual in our discipline, we are saved by the notion of abstraction. The notion of the concurrent program as a means for writing parallel programs without regard for the underlying hardware was first introduced by Edsger Dijkstra (1968). Moti Ben-Ari (1982) elegantly summed up Dijkstra's idea in three sentences.

Concurrent programming is the name given to programming notation and techniques for expressing potential parallelism and solving the resulting synchronization and communication problems. Implementation of parallelism is a topic in computer systems (hardware and software) that is essentially independent of concurrent programming. Concurrent programming is important because it provides an abstract setting in which to study parallelism without getting bogged down in the implementation details.

When a sequential program is executed, there is a single thread of control. The instructions are executed one at a time in the order specified by the program. A concurrent program is a collection of sequential processes.[1] Each of these processes has its own thread of control that executes its instructions one at a time, its own set of registers, and its own stack for local variables, parameters, etc. Given adequate hardware, each process may execute on its own processor using shared or private memory. A concurrent program may

---

[1] The term process has specific and sometimes different meanings in the context of particular operating systems. The term process in the context of concurrent programming is a general term for a sequence of instructions that executes concurrently with other sequences of instructions.

also execute on a single processor system by interleaving the instructions
of each process. Between these extremes is the more common situation of
having N processes executing on M processors where $N > M$. In this case,
the execution of instructions from N processes is interleaved among the M
processors.

If the processes in a concurrent program are independent, we can write
each process in the same manner in which we write a sequential program.
There are no special concerns or requirements that the programmer must
address. However, it is rare that the processes in a concurrent program are
truly independent. They almost always need to share some resources or
communicate with each other to solve the problem for which the concurrent
program was written. Sharing and communication require programming language constructs beyond those needed in sequential programs. In this chapter we introduce the problems that we must resolve in concurrent programs
with interacting processes. Later, we present the Ada language features and
techniques for solving them.

Synchronization is a problem faced in any activity involving concurrent
processing. For example, suppose that Horace and Mildred are cooperating
in the cooking for a dinner party. They expect that the work will go faster
with two people (processors) carrying out the instructions in the recipes. For
the preparation of scalloped potatoes, Horace has taken on the responsibility
of peeling the potatoes while Mildred will cut them into thin slices. As it is
easier to peel a whole potato rather than remove peels from individual slices
of potato, the two have agreed to synchronize their operations. Mildred will
not slice a potato until Horace has peeled it. They worked out the following
algorithms:

Horace's scalloped potato instructions
>   **while** there are still potatoes remaining **do**
>   Peel one potato
>   Wait until Mildred is ready for the potato
>   Give Mildred the peeled potato
>   **end while**

Mildred's scalloped potato instructions
>   **loop**
>   Wait until Horace has a peeled potato
>   Take the peeled potato from Horace
>   Slice the potato
>   Place the potato slices in the baking dish
>   Dot the potato slices with butter
>   Sprinkle with flour
>   Exit loop when Horace has peeled the last potato
>   **end loop**

Communication among processes is another activity present in nearly all concurrent activities. **Communication** is the exchange of data or control signals between processes. In our cooking example, Horace communicates directly with Mildred by handing her a peeled potato (data). Further communication is required to let Mildred know that he has peeled the last potato (a control signal).

What happens when Mildred's potato slicing is interrupted by a phone call? When Horace finishes peeling a potato, he must wait for Mildred to complete her phone call and resume her slicing activities. Horace's frustration of having to hold his peeled potato while Mildred talks to her mother can be relieved with a more indirect communication scheme. Instead of handing a peeled potato directly to Mildred, he can place it in a bowl. Mildred will take potatoes out of the bowl rather than directly from Horace. He can now continue peeling potatoes while Mildred handles the phone call. Should Horace need to answer a knock at the front door, Mildred may be able to continue working on the potatoes that he piled up in the bowl while she was on the phone. The bowl does not eliminate all waiting. Mildred cannot slice if there is not at least one potato in the bowl for her to take. She must wait for Horace to place a peeled potato into the bowl. Horace cannot continue peeling when the bowl is completely full. He must wait for Mildred to remove a potato from the bowl to make room for his newly peeled potato.

Our concurrent scalloped potato algorithm is an example of the producer-consumer pattern. This pattern is useful when we need to coordinate the asynchronous production and consumption of information or objects. In Chapter 4 we'll show you how Ada's protected object can provide the functionality of the potato bowl and in Chapter 5 you will see how Ada's rendezvous allows processes to communicate directly with each other.

Mutual exclusion is another important consideration in concurrent programming. Different processes typically share resources. It is usually not acceptable for two processes to use the same resource simultaneously. **Mutual exclusion** is a mechanism that prevents two processes from simultaneously using the same resource. Let's return to our cooking example. Suppose that Mildred is currently preparing the cake they plan for dessert while Horace is preparing the marinade for the meat. Both require use of the 5 ml (1 teaspoon) measuring spoon. Mildred cannot be measuring salt with the spoon at the same time Horace is filling it with soy sauce. They must take their turns using the shared spoon. Here are the portions of their cooking algorithms they worked out to accomplish their sharing:

Horace's marinade instructions

Wait until the 5 ml measuring spoon is on the spoon rack

Remove the 5 ml measuring spoon from the rack
Measure 10 ml of soy sauce
Wash and dry the 5 ml measuring spoon
Return the 5 ml measuring spoon to the spoon rack

Mildred's cake instructions

Wait until the 5 ml measuring spoon is on the spoon rack
Remove the 5 ml measuring spoon from the rack
Measure 5 ml of salt
Wash and dry the 5 ml measuring spoon
Return the 5 ml measuring spoon to the spoon rack

This example illustrates a set of steps for using a shared resource. First, some **pre-protocol** is observed to ensure that a process has exclusive use of the resource. In our cooking example, Horace and Mildred use the fact that the rack on which they hang their measuring spoons cannot be accessed by two people at the same time in their small kitchen. Second, the resource is used for a finite amount of time by a single thread of control (a person in our cooking example). This stage of mutual exclusion is called the critical section. A **critical section** is a sequence of instructions that must *not* be accessed concurrently by more than one thread of execution. In our example, the critical section is the use of the 5 ml measuring spoon. After the critical section, the fourth and final step, the post-protocol, is carried out. The **post-protocol** signals an end of the exclusive use of the shared resource. In our example, the post-protocol consists of cleaning the measuring spoon and returning it to the spoon rack.

Mutual exclusion is a static safety property (Ben-Ari, 1982). The requirement that each critical section excludes other processes from using the resource (Mildred and Horace cannot both be filling the 5 ml spoon) does not change during the execution of the instructions. It is possible to have safety features that adversely affect the dynamic behavior of a system. For example, we could make a hand-held electric power saw completely safe by cutting off the power cord. However, such a drastic safety measure precludes us from using the saw for its primary purpose. The safety provided by mutual exclusion can also disrupt our system so that its goals remain unfulfilled. Returning to our cooking example, Mildred and Horace have devised the following algorithms for sharing two different measuring spoons.

Horace's deadly embrace

Wait until the 5 ml measuring spoon is on the spoon rack
Remove the 5 ml measuring spoon from the rack
Wait until the 15 ml measuring spoon is on the spoon rack
Remove the 15 ml measuring spoon from the rack
Measure 20 ml of soy sauce

Wash and dry the 15 ml measuring spoon
Return the 15 ml measuring spoon to the spoon rack
Wash and dry the 5 ml measuring spoon
Return the 5 ml measuring spoon to the spoon rack

Mildred's deadly embrace

Wait until the 15 ml measuring spoon is on the spoon rack
Remove the 15 ml measuring spoon from the rack
Wait until the 5 ml measuring spoon is on the spoon rack
Remove the 5 ml measuring spoon from the rack
Measure 20 ml of salt
Wash and dry the 5 ml measuring spoon
Return the 5 ml measuring spoon to the spoon rack
Wash and dry the 15 ml measuring spoon
Return the 15 ml measuring spoon to the spoon rack

These steps certainly prevent Horace and Mildred from using the same measuring spoon simultaneously. The cooking for most dinner parties goes without problem. However, one day, when the guests arrive they find no meal and Horace and Mildred waiting in the kitchen. This is an example of deadlock. **Deadlock** means that no process is making progress toward the completion of its goal. Can you see what happened in the kitchen that fateful day?

Use of scenarios is a common way to uncover the potential for deadlock in a concurrent program. A **scenario** is one possible sequence of events in the execution of a concurrent set of instructions. Here is one scenario that results in the deadlock observed in the kitchen.

1. Mildred finds that the 15 ml measuring spoon is available
2. Mildred removes the 15 ml measuring spoon from the rack
3. Horace finds that the 5 ml measuring spoon is available
4. Horace removes the 5 ml measuring spoon from the rack
5. Horace finds that the 15 ml measuring spoon is not available and waits
6. Mildred finds that the 5 ml measuring spoon is not available and waits

Our two cooks become deadlocked when each of them holds the measuring spoon that the other needs to continue. This problem may arise any time that a process requires multiple resources simultaneously. How is it possible that previous dinner parties have come off without problem? Here is a scenario in which everything goes smoothly with the sharing of the measuring spoons.

1. Mildred finds that the 15 ml measuring spoon is available
2. Mildred removes the 15 ml measuring spoon from the rack
3. Mildred finds that the 5 ml measuring spoon is available
4. Mildred removes the 5 ml measuring spoon from the rack

5. Horace finds that the 5 ml measuring spoon is not available and waits
6. Mildred measures 20 ml of salt
7. Mildred washes and dries the 5 ml measuring spoon
8. Mildred returns the 5 ml measuring spoon to the spoon rack
9. Horace finds that the 5 ml measuring spoon is available
10. Horace removes the 5 ml measuring spoon from the rack
11. Horace finds that the 15 ml measuring spoon is not available and waits
12. Mildred washes and dries the 15 ml measuring spoon
13. Mildred returns the 15 ml measuring spoon to the spoon rack
14. Horace finds that the 15 ml measuring spoon is available
15. Horace removes the 15 ml measuring spoon from the rack
16. and so on ... *Each cook has used both spoons successfully*

The simplest solution to the form of deadlocking seen in the first scenario is to forbid the simultaneous use of multiple resources. In our kitchen we could restructure the two algorithms so that each cook takes one measuring spoon, uses it, and returns it before taking the second spoon. There is no reason that each cook needs both measuring spoons at a given time. However, there are times when processes do need multiple resources simultaneously. For example, a cook may need both a measuring spoon and a bowl to complete a particular mixing chore. A common solution for avoiding deadlock in this situation is to require that all processes obtain the resources in the same order. If our two cooks are required to obtain the 5 ml spoon before obtaining the 15 ml spoon, they will avoid deadlock. The first cook to take the 5 ml spoon will be able to obtain the 15 ml spoon as well. The second cook will wait for the 5 ml spoon to be returned to the rack and will not, in the meantime, try to obtain the 15 ml spoon.

Now that you understand scenarios, you may notice another potential problem in our mutual exclusion examples. Suppose one cook observes that the 5 ml measuring spoon is on the rack. But before they remove it, the other cook also observes that the spoon is on the rack and removes it. The first cook is now baffled by the disappearance of the spoon they recently observed. Our pre-protocol consisted of two separate steps: observing and removing. For this example and for all other mutual exclusion protocols to succeed, the pre-protocol must be completed as an atomic action. An **atomic action** is an action that cannot be interrupted. The observation of the spoon must be immediately followed by its removal. Fortunately for our cooks, the kitchen is so small that when one cook is checking the spoon rack, there is no room for the other cook to approach it. Our observe and remove is done as an atomic action.

Liveness is an important dynamic property of concurrent programs. **Liveness** means that every process in a concurrent program makes progress toward its goals. Deadlock is the most serious violation of liveness. Starvation is a more localized violation of liveness. **Starvation** is the indefinite postponement of some of the processes in a concurrent program while others do make progress toward their goals. Let's look at an example of starvation in our kitchen example. Suppose Horace and Mildred need to repeatedly use the 5 ml measuring spoon. It is possible, though unlikely, that every time Horace checks for the 5 ml measuring on the rack he finds it is not there. Mildred has managed to beat him to the spoon each time. Every time she replaces the spoon, she returns to take it again before Horace gets the opportunity to check for it. Horace's starvation violates our human concept of fairness. In a real kitchen, Horace and Mildred would certainly take turns using the spoon so that each of them makes progress towards their goals. **Fairness** in a concurrent program means that each process has an equal opportunity to move forward toward its goal. As we will see later, we often assign different priorities to different tasks making a conscious decision to be unfair.

You now have a basic understanding of some of the problems associated with concurrent programming. In Chapter 3 you'll learn how to create processes (called tasks) in an Ada program. Chapters 4 and 5 describe solutions to Ada task synchronization and communication necessary to construct a concurrent program in Ada.

1.2 Distributed programming

A distributed program is one whose concurrent processes are assigned to different computers connected by a network. There is a distributed version of the dinner party called a potluck. In this version of dinner, each person or couple is expected to cook one dish at their home and bring it to a central location for the dinner. Some communication is necessary between homes to coordinate the dishes — most people would not want a dinner of eight desserts and no other courses. Each participant uses the resources in their own home to prepare their dish.

Distributed programming usually requires abstractions beyond those needed for non-distributed concurrent programming. These abstractions provide the tools necessary for dealing with heterogeneous environments, network connections of varying response times, and potential network failures. A main goal of distributed programming is to provide a more powerful application than is possible on a single machine. Scalability, the property of a design to be easily enlarged, is a highly desirable property for distributed applications. Two well-known distributed processing systems are SETI@home, which uses over 300,000 active computers to analyze radio telescope data to find evidence of intelligent signals from space, and Folding@home, which uses over 200,000 computers to simulate protein folding to better understand biological systems. The processors in both of these distributed systems are connected by the internet. It is also common to use a private network for communication among processors making up a distributed system. The National Ignition Facility at the University of California Lawrence Livermore National Laboratory uses a private network to connect the 300 front-end processors that control the 192-beam, 1.8-Megajoule, 500-Terawatt laser used for inertial confinement fusion and high-energy-density experimental studies (Carey *et al.*, 2003). The control software at the facility is a mixed language environment of Ada (for functional controls) and Java (for user interface and database back end). CORBA (discussed in Chapter 6) is used to communicate between languages and processors.

The great potentials of distributed applications come with additional risks. Distributed programs are best suited for applications that do not require large amounts of communication between processes. The delay (latency) between the time a message is sent to a process and the time a response is received is much greater going through a network than over a local bus. If the distributed program is not well designed, failure of a small number of computers in the network can completely disrupt the application. Diagnosing problems in distributed applications is usually more difficult than in non-distributed applications as the analysis may require connections to a widely dispersed set of computers.

Chapter 6 describes two approaches to building a distributed Ada program. The first approach uses features from the Distributed Systems Annex (DSA) in the Ada library. The second describes the use of the CORBA middleware for communication between the distributed processes.

1.3 Real-time systems

There are many definitions of a real-time system but, as you would expect, all include the concept of time. A particular activity must be completed within a specified time limit, its deadline. A non-real-time program is considered correct when the output is that described in the program's specification. You have probably spent a good deal of time verifying programs you have written by testing them with various input values. You may have even used proof checkers such as the one available with SPARK Ada (Barnes, 2003) to verify a program mathematically. A real-time program's correctness depends on both the correctness of the outputs and their timeliness (Stankovic, 1988). A real-time program that calculates the correct answer after the deadline has passed is not correct.

You may have noticed that our earlier discussions were on concurrent programming while this section discusses real-time systems. The only time-related property of a concurrent program is liveness. Liveness is concerned with every process making progress toward its goal. It makes no assumptions concerning the absolute or relative speeds at which the processes execute their instructions. A concurrent program is independent of the hardware on which it is executing. In order to determine whether or not our software can meet its real-time deadlines, we must have a good understanding of the hardware on which it executes. We must consider the entire system (hardware and software) in our analysis of real-time applications.

1.3.1 Classification of real-time systems

Don't all programs have deadlines? A monthly billing program needs to complete the printing of invoices before they can be mailed at the end of the month. The automated teller machine should dispense cash to a customer immediately after their request. In both of these cases, missing the deadline is not a failure of the software, but a degradation of the service it provides. We will still get the invoices to our customers and the bank customer may be a little annoyed for having to wait longer than they would like. We call a system whose performance is only degraded by a missed deadline a **soft real-time system**. A soft real-time system need only produce the correct answers; missing deadlines is only an inconvenience. Of course, such inconveniences in a commercial application may result in sluggish sales. A **hard real-time system** is one in which a single missed deadline leads to complete failure of the system. The fly-by-wire system described earlier is an example of a hard real-time system. The aircraft will likely crash if the system does not complete current calculations required for moving the control surfaces by a deadline. The deadline in this case is imposed by the aircraft's aerodynamics. Control systems for automobile engines, chemical plants, oil refineries, and nuclear power plants are all hard real-time systems. Some people (Burns and Wellings, 2009; Laplante, 2004) include a third category of real time systems. A **firm real-time system** is one in which a few missed deadlines are acceptable, but missing more than a few may lead to system failure. A video analysis application may miss deadlines on a few frames and still be acceptable. How many missed deadlines are acceptable depends on the quality of service (QoS) expected by the users of the system.

It is really the system requirements that characterize a particular system as soft, firm, or hard real-time. The specification for a payroll processing program does not generally contain a requirement such as "an employee's taxes must be calculated within 53 milliseconds of obtaining their gross pay and number of deductions." A specification for an automated teller machine may state that the system should respond to customer requests in a timely manner without specifying an exact number of seconds. The specification for a video analysis program may specify some acceptable level of quality but say nothing about a deadline for completing the processing of one video frame. On the other hand, the specification for software running an engine control unit inside a race car will specify strict deadlines for the computations that determine the quantity of fuel injected into each cylinder. If the computations are not completed within that deadline, the engine could experience a catastrophic failure.

The desired behaviors of real-time systems are sometimes different than those for a concurrent program. For example, starvation, which is generally seen as something to avoid in a concurrent program, may be expected in a real-time system.

A common myth equates real-time systems and fast systems. The deterministic nature of real-time systems is the defining characteristic, not the speed at which they execute. It is true that many deadlines specified for real-time systems are short. And a specification with many short deadlines certainly challenges the designer and implementer to create efficient, fast code. So it is not difficult to see why people equate real-time and fast. But, keep in mind that it is possible to have a slow real-time system.

1.3.2 Embedded systems

You may have noticed that all of the examples of hard real-time systems given in the last section are embedded systems. The engine control computer in our race car is a component of that car that is no less important to winning a race than its tires. Similarly, the fly-by-wire aircraft, chemical plant, oil refinery, and nuclear power plant all use computers to produce results that are more than computations. An embedded system interacts with its environment through sensors (input devices) and actuators (output devices). Each embedded system must respond to sensor events and meet deadlines imposed by its environment. The engine control unit's deadlines are imposed by the movements of the mechanical parts making up that engine. Because deadlines are imposed by environmental constraints, it might be argued that all hard real-time systems are embedded systems.

You might think that in order to meet short deadlines, an embedded system would benefit from the use of multiple processors. However, many embedded systems are mass market products. The economy of scale is an incentive to manufacture many units of a particular model car or cellular phone. In such a manufacturing environment, a great deal of money can be saved by shaving a few cents off the cost of each individual unit. So most such embedded systems are implemented with a single processor that has the minimum performance required for the application. Running a concurrent program on a single processor requires the interleaving of instructions from each process. Switching the processor from executing the instructions of one process to those of another process is known as a **context switch**. A context switch requires the processor to save its current state (typically the values of all the registers) and restore the state of the process being resumed. The time required for the context switches may be a significant fraction of the total execution time. So you might assume that sequential programming would be far more common than concurrent programming in embedded systems. But just the opposite is usually true. Because the real world is a parallel system, it is easier to design an embedded system using concurrent rather than sequential programming techniques. The cost of context switching is small in relation to the reduction in development and maintenance efforts.

Let's look at an example. Our cooks, Horace and Mildred, have started a small commercial venture to manufacture their popular tomato apple chutney. They have purchased a large pressure cooker with an embedded microprocessor. The cooker has a sensor called a thermocouple that is used to measure the internal temperature. The electronics associated with the thermocouple produce a voltage that is proportional to the temperature at the tip of the probe. The output of the thermocouple is connected to an *analog to digital converter* (ADC) that converts the analog voltage to a 12-bit unsigned integer which can be read by the processor. A second sensor produces a voltage that is proportional to the pressure within the cooker. It is connected to a second ADC. The cooker is heated by a gas flame whose intensity is set by a valve connected to a rotary actuator. A voltage sent to the actuator determines the setting of the gas valve. Our processor is connected to the actuator through a *digital to analog converter* (DAC) which converts a 12-bit unsigned integer to a voltage. The cooker has a vent to relieve excess pressure. The amount of venting is controlled by a second valve/actuator that is connected to a second DAC. Figure 1.1 is a representation of the pressure cooker system.

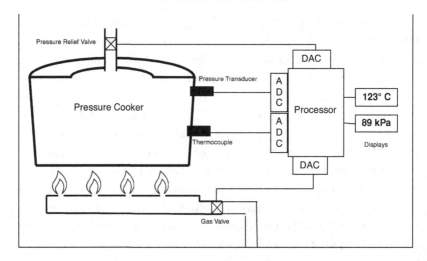

Figure 1.1 An example of an embedded system

Mildred develops the following algorithm to maintain optimal cooking conditions for their chutney:

Initial sequential control algorithm for cooking tomato apple chutney

loop

Input the pressure value from the ADC connected to the pressure transducer
Calculate a new relief valve setting
Output the new relief valve setting to the DAC connected to the relief valve
Display the pressure

Input the temperature value from the ADC connected to the thermocouple
Calculate a new gas valve setting
Output the new gas valve setting to the DAC connected to the gas valve
Display the temperature

Wait until 5 seconds have elapsed from the start of the loop iteration
end loop

This simple algorithm adjusts the relief valve and gas valve every five seconds. The input, calculations, and output must be completed within this five-second window. Failure to meet this deadline may result in a catastrophic event. Now after running a few tests, our cooks discover that the pressure fluctuates beyond acceptable limits. They consult with a friend who is a control engineer. He suggests that they decrease the period for pressure regulation from five seconds to two seconds and decrease the period for temperature regulation from five seconds to four seconds. Here is Mildred's second algorithm.

Final sequential control algorithm for cooking tomato apple chutney

   loop

      Input the pressure value from the ADC connected to the pressure transducer
      Calculate a new relief valve setting
      Output the new relief valve setting to the DAC connected to the relief valve
      Display the pressure

      Input the temperature value from the ADC connected to the thermocouple
      Calculate a new gas valve setting
      Output the new gas valve setting to the DAC connected to the gas valve
      Display the temperature

      Wait until 2 seconds have elapsed from the start of the last pressure input

      Input the pressure value from the ADC connected to the pressure transducer
      Calculate a new relief valve setting
      Output the new relief valve setting to the DAC connected to the relief valve
      Display the pressure

      Wait until 2 seconds have elapsed from the start of the last pressure input
   end loop

The loop in this algorithm has a period of four seconds. The temperature is adjusted once during that time and the pressure is adjusted twice. This second algorithm provides adequate control of the cooking conditions for their tomato apple chutney recipe. However, they find that with these periods, the pressure control is unstable when they use it to cook an experimental batch of mango chutney. After analyzing the fluctuations, their control engineer friend suggests that mango chutney requires a pressure adjustment every 1.5 seconds and a temperature adjustment every 2.5 seconds. It takes a lot of trial and error for Mildred to develop her sequential algorithm for mango chutney.

Sequential control algorithm for cooking mango chutney

   loop

      Input the pressure value from the ADC connected to the pressure transducer
      Calculate a new relief valve setting
      Output the new relief valve setting to the DAC connected to the relief valve
      Display the pressure

      Input the temperature value from the ADC connected to the thermocouple
      Calculate a new gas valve setting
      Output the new gas valve setting to the DAC connected to the gas valve
      Display the temperature

      Wait until 1.5 seconds have elapsed from the last pressure input

      Input the pressure value from the ADC connected to the pressure transducer
      Calculate a new relief valve setting
      Output the new relief valve setting to the DAC connected to the relief valve
      Display the pressure

Wait until 1.0 seconds have elapsed from the last pressure input

Input the temperature value from the ADC connected to the thermocouple
Calculate a new gas valve setting
Output the new gas valve setting to the DAC connected to the gas valve
Display the temperature

Wait until 0.5 seconds have elapsed from the last temperature input

Input the pressure value from the ADC connected to the pressure transducer
Calculate a new relief valve setting
Output the new relief valve setting to the DAC connected to the relief valve
Display the pressure

Wait until 1.5 seconds have elapsed from the last pressure input

Input the pressure value from the ADC connected to the pressure transducer
Calculate a new relief valve setting
Output the new relief valve setting to the DAC connected to the relief valve
Display the pressure

Wait until 0.5 seconds have elapsed from the last pressure input

Input the temperature value from the ADC connected to the thermocouple
Calculate a new gas valve setting
Output the new gas valve setting to the DAC connected to the gas valve
Display the temperature

Wait until 1.0 seconds have elapsed from the last temperature input

Input the pressure value from the ADC connected to the pressure transducer
Calculate a new relief valve setting
Output the new relief valve setting to the DAC connected to the relief valve
Display the pressure

Wait until 1.5 seconds have elapsed from the last pressure input
end loop

The loop in this algorithm has a period of 7.5 seconds. The temperature is adjusted three times during this period and the pressure is adjusted five times. This algorithm seems quite complicated for such a seemingly simple task. It is fortunate that the two sensor periods had the common factor of 0.5 seconds or the algorithm could have been even longer. This simple embedded system controls just two process variables. Imagine the complexity of the sequential software if we were to expand our system to include the control of pH and sugar content of the chutneys.

Now let's look at a concurrent version of the pressure cooker control algorithm. We create one process for each of our control variables. The processor will execute these two processes concurrently.

Control pressure for mango chutney
loop
    Input the pressure value from the ADC connected to the pressure transducer
    Calculate a new relief valve setting
    Output the new relief valve setting to the DAC connected to the relief valve
    Display the pressure
    Wait until 1.5 seconds have elapsed from the last pressure input
end loop

Control temperature for mango chutney
loop
    Input the temperature value from the ADC connected to the thermocouple
    Calculate a new gas valve setting
    Output the new gas valve setting to the DAC connected to the gas valve
    Display the temperature
    Wait until 2.5 seconds have elapsed from the last temperature input
end loop

The concurrent algorithm for cooking the mango chutney is significantly shorter and easier to understand than the sequential one. Another advantage of this approach is that we can use the same program for all of our pressure cooker recipes. With the sequential approach, we had to write different algorithms for our two chutneys, each with its own set of customized delays. In our concurrent version, we simply replace the delay time in the last statement of each process with a variable whose value could be entered from a keypad. Because the interleaving of the instructions in the two processes is non-deterministic, the concurrent approach requires significantly more effort to show that each of the deadlines can be met. Chapters 7 and 8 describe how to demonstrate that our concurrent Ada programs will meet all their deadlines. But before that, you will learn the sequential and concurrent features of Ada necessary for writing real-time applications.

Summary

- Ada is arguably the most appropriate language for development of parallel and real-time applications.
- Over 99% of processors manufactured are used in embedded systems.
- A parallel program is one that carries out a number of operations simultaneously.
- Flynn's taxonomy categorizes parallel architectures into four simple groups: SISD, SIMD, MISD, and MIMD.
- Concurrent programming provides notations and techniques for writing parallel programs without the need to understand the details of the underlying architecture.

- Synchronization is the coordination of processes to reach a common goal.
- Communication is the exchange of data or control signals between processes.
- A scenario is one possible sequence of events in the execution of a concurrent set of instructions.
- Mutual exclusion is a mechanism that prevents two processes from simultaneously using the same resource.
- An atomic action is an action that cannot be interrupted.
- Liveness is a property of concurrent programs that indicates that every process is making progress toward its goal.
- Deadlock is the state in which no process is making progress toward the completion of its goal.
- Starvation is the indefinite postponement of some of the processes in a concurrent program.
- A distributed program is one whose concurrent processes are assigned to different computers connected by a network.
- A deadline is a point in time by which an activity must be completed.
- A soft real-time system need only produce the correct answers; missing a deadline is only an inconvenience.
- A hard real-time system fails when a single deadline is missed.
- A firm real-time system may miss a few deadlines, but missing more than a few may lead to system failure.
- An embedded system interacts with its environment through sensors (input) and actuators (output).
- Most embedded systems are hard real-time systems — they must respond to sensor events and meet deadlines imposed by their environment.
- Concurrency provides a simpler programming model for embedded systems than sequential programming.

Exercises

1.1 Suppose that 75% of a particular sequential program can be run in parallel. Use Amdahl's equation to determine the amount of speedup obtained by running this program on 8 processors. On 16 processors.

1.2 Cluster computing and grid computing are two forms of MIMD computing. Search the internet to find out more about these two hardware configurations. What is the primary difference between these systems? For what sorts of applications is each most suited?

1.3 Name two reasons for using parallel programming rather than sequential programming.

1.4 What is the relationship between parallel and concurrent programming?

1.5 Rewrite the algorithms that Horace and Mildred followed for peeling and slicing potatoes to incorporate a bowl to hold the potatoes that Horace has peeled. Be sure to handle the cases of the empty bowl and the completely full bowl.

1.6 Define the term *scenario*.

1.7 Write a scenario for the algorithms you wrote for Exercise 1.5. Assume that the bowl holds a maximum of three potatoes. Just after slicing the first potato, Mildred is called away to answer the phone. She spends more time on the phone than it takes to peel four potatoes. There are a total of five potatoes to prepare.

1.8 Modify the scenario you wrote for Exercise 1.7. This time, while Mildred is on the phone, Horace is called away to answer the front door. Mildred returns to resume slicing before Horace returns to the kitchen.

1.9 Define the terms *pre-protocol*, *post-protocol*, *critical section*, and *atomic action*.

1.10 Define the terms *deadlock*, *liveness*, *starvation*, and *fairness*.

1.11 Search the internet for a definition of the term *livelock*.

1.12 We gave one scenario for the deadly embrace algorithms that did not result in a deadlock. Write a different scenario that also does not result in a deadlock. Remember that checking for a spoon and removing it from the rack are done as an atomic action.

1.13 We gave one scenario for the deadly embrace algorithms that resulted in a deadlock. Write a different scenario that also results in a deadlock. Remember that checking for a spoon and removing it from the rack are done as an atomic action.

1.14 Rewrite the algorithms that Horace and Mildred followed for obtaining and using two measuring spoons. Eliminate the possibility of deadlock by removing the need for one cook to have the two spoons simultaneously. Remember that checking for a spoon and removing it from the rack are done as an atomic action.

1.15 Rewrite the algorithms that Horace and Mildred followed for obtaining and using two measuring spoons. Eliminate the possibility of deadlock by ensuring that each cook obtains the two spoons in the same order. Remember that checking for a spoon and removing it from the rack are done as an atomic action.

1.16 Distributed systems can be implemented with CORBA. Most of CORBA architectures are client-server oriented. Search the internet for a description of client-server architectures.

1.17 Differentiate between soft real-time systems and hard real-time systems.

1.18 List some examples of software that have no deadlines.

1.19 Can you think of an embedded system that is not a hard real-time system? Conversely, can you think of a hard real-time system that is not an embedded system?

1.20 Define the term *context switch*.

1.21 Search the internet for examples of processors which are typically used in embedded systems. Look for low-cost and high-quality processors.

1.22 Name some items in your home that might be embedded systems.

1.23 Write a sequential algorithm for the pressure cooker example that adjusts the pressure relief valve every 1.2 seconds and the gas control valve every 1.8 seconds.

1.24 To ensure that all deadlines of our pressure cooker example are met, we must determine the worst case execution time (WCET) of each statement of the sequential algorithm. Search the Internet for a definition of worst case execution time and some methods for determining worst case execution times. We'll make use of WCET in Chapters 7, 8, and 9.

2

Sequential programming with Ada

In this chapter we will introduce you to the basic sequential features of the Ada programming language. You may find it useful to skim this chapter on first reading and then return to it when you encounter an unfamiliar language feature in later chapters. One chapter is not adequate to discuss all aspects of sequential programming with Ada. We discuss those that are most relevant to concurrent, embedded, and real-time programming and the examples used in this book. Barnes (2006) presents a comprehensive description of the Ada programming language. Ben-Ari (2009) does an excellent job describing the aspects of Ada relevant to software engineering. Dale *et al.* (2000) provide an introduction to Ada for novice programmers. You can find Ada implementations of the common data structures in Dale and McCormick (2007). There are also many Ada language resources available online that you may find useful while reading this chapter including English (2001), Riehle (2003), and Wikibooks (2010a). We will often refer you to the ARM, the Ada Reference Manual (Taft *et al.*, 2006), which is available in both print and electronic forms.[1]

DeRemer and Kron (1975) distinguished the activities of writing large programs from those of writing small programs. They considered large programs to be systems built from many small programs (modules), usually written by different people. It is common today to separate the features of a programming language along the same lines. In the first part of this chapter we present the aspects of Ada required to write the most basic programs. Then we'll discuss some of Ada's features that support the development of large programs. Finally, we'll look at those features that allow our Ada program to interact directly with hardware. Let's start with a simple example that illustrates the basic structure of an Ada program. The

---

[1] `http://www.ada-auth.org/arm.html` provides the ARM in multiple formats.

following program prompts the user to enter two integers and displays their average.

```ada
with Ada.Text_IO;
with Ada.Integer_Text_IO;
with Ada.Float_Text_IO;
procedure Average is
-- Display the average of two numbers entered by the user
   A : Integer;
   B : Integer;
   M : Float;
begin
   Ada.Text_IO.Put_Line (Item => "Enter two integers.");
   Ada.Integer_Text_IO.Get (Item => A);
   Ada.Integer_Text_IO.Get (Item => B);
   M := Float (A + B) / 2.0;
   Ada.Text_IO.New_Line;
   Ada.Text_IO.Put (Item => "The average of your integers is ");
   Ada.Float_Text_IO.Put (Item => M,
                          Fore => 1,
                          Aft  => 2,
                          Exp  => 0);
   Ada.Text_IO.New_Line;
end Average;
```

The bold words in all our examples are reserved words. You can find a list of all 72 reserved words in section 2.9 of the ARM. The first three lines of the program are **context clauses**. The *with clauses* specify what library units our program requires. In this example, we use input and output operations from three different library units: one for the input and output of strings and characters (**Ada.Text_IO**), one for the input and output of integers (**Ada.Integer_Text_IO**), and one for the input and output of floating point real numbers (**Ada.Float_Text_IO**). Following the context clauses is the specification of our program. In this example the specification consists of the name **Average** and no parameters. The name is repeated in the last line that marks the end of this program unit. The line that begins with the two adjacent hyphens is a comment. Comments start with two adjacent hyphens and extend to the end of the line.

Following the program unit's specification is the **declarative part**. In our example, we declare three variables. Variables **A** and **B** are declared to be of type **Integer**, a language-defined whole number type with an implementation-defined range. Variable M is declared to be of type **Float**, a language-defined floating point number type with an implementation-defined precision and range. The initial value of all three variables is not defined.

All but one of the executable statements in our example are calls to procedures (subprograms) in various library packages. In the first statement, we call the procedure Put_Line in the library package Ada.Text_IO. Ada allows us to overload subprogram names. The use of the library package name as a prefix makes it perfectly clear which put procedure we are calling. Some Ada programmers prefer to eliminate these package name prefixes by including an additional context clause called the use clause. We'll show you examples of the use clause and positional parameter association at the end of this section.

Except for procedure New_Line, all of the procedures called in the example require parameters. Ada provides both *named* and *positional* parameter association. You are probably very familiar with positional parameter association in which the formal and actual parameters are associated by their position in the parameter list. With named parameter association, the order of parameters in our call is irrelevant. Our example uses named association to match up the formal and actual parameters. To use named association, we give the name of the formal parameter followed by the arrow symbol, =>, followed by the actual parameter. In our call to procedure Put_Line, the formal parameter is Item and the actual parameter is the string literal of our prompt. When there is but a single parameter, named parameter association provides little useful information. But when there are multiple parameters, as in the call to Ada.Float_Text_IO.Put, named parameter association provides information that makes both reading and writing the call easier. The formal parameters Fore, Aft, and Exp in this call supply information on how to format the real number. Details on the formatting of real numbers are given in section A.10.9 of the ARM.

The only statement in our example that is not a procedure call is the assignment statement that calculates the average of the two integers entered by the user. The arithmetic expression in this assignment statement includes three operations. First, the two integers are added. Then the integer sum is explicitly converted to a floating point number. Finally, the floating point sum is divided by two. The explicit conversion (casting) to type Float is necessary because Ada makes no implicit type conversions. The syntax of an explicit type conversion is similar to that of a function call using the type as the name of the function.

Here is a shorter version of our example that illustrates the use of *use clauses* and positional parameter association. Throughout the remainder of this book we will make use of prefixing and named parameter association when it makes the code clearer.

```
with  Ada.Text_IO ;           use  Ada.Text_IO ;
with  Ada.Integer_Text_IO ;   use  Ada.Integer_Text_IO ;
with  Ada.Float_Text_IO ;     use  Ada.Float_Text_IO ;
procedure  Average  is
--  Display  the  average  of  two  numbers  entered  by  the  user
    A :  Integer;
    B :  Integer;
    M :  Float;
begin
    Put_Line  ("Enter  two  integers." );
    Get  (A);
    Get  (B);
    M :=  Float  (A + B) / 2.0;
    New_Line;
    Put  ("The  average  of  your  integers  is  " );
    Put  (M,  1,  2,  0);
    New_Line;
end  Average;
```

2.1 Control structures

Ada provides two statements for making decisions: the if statement and the case statement. Section 5.3 of the ARM gives the details of the if statement and section 5.4 gives the details of the case statement. Ada provides a loop statement with several different iteration schemes. These schemes are described in detail in section 5.5 of the ARM. In this section we'll provide examples of each control structure.

2.1.1 If statements

Here are some examples of various forms of the if statement.

```
if  A < 0  then
    Put_Line  ("A  is  negative" );
end  if;

if  A > B  then
    Put_Line  ("A  is  greater  than  B" );
else
    Put_Line  ("A  is  not  greater  than  B" );
end  if;

if  A = B  then
    Put_Line  ("A  and  B  are  equal" );
elsif  A > B  then
    Put_Line  ("A  is  greater  than  B" );
else
```

```
      Put_Line ("A is less than B" );
end if;

if A > B and A > C then
   Put_Line ("A is greater than both B and C" );
elsif B > A and B > C then
   Put_Line ("B is greater than both A and C" );
elsif C > A and C > B then
   Put_Line ("C is greater than both A and B" );
end if;
```

While these examples show only one statement for each choice, you may use a sequence of statements. Ada provides the following equality, relational, and logical operators commonly used in the Boolean expressions of if statements.

Equality operators

=	equal
/=	not equal

Relational operators

<	less than
<=	less than or equal to
>	greater than
>=	greater than or equal to

Logical operators

not	logical negation
and	logical conjunction
or	logical disjunction
xor	exclusive or
and then	short circuit and
or else	short circuit or

Boolean expressions which include both **and** and **or** operators must include parentheses to indicate the desired order of evaluation. Section 4.5 of the ARM gives a complete listing and description of all of Ada's operators and the six precedence levels.

2.1.2 Case statement

The case statement selects one of many alternatives based on the value of an expression with a discrete result. Here is an example of a case statement.

```
case Ch is
   when 'a' .. 'z' =>
      Put_Line ("Ch is a lowercase letter");
   when 'A' .. 'Z' =>
      Put_Line ("Ch is an uppercase letter");
   when '0' .. '9' =>
      Put_Line ("Ch is a digit");
   when '.' | '!' | '?' =>
      Put_Line ("Ch is a sentence termination character");
   when others =>
      Put_Line ("Ch is some other character");
end case;
```

The case selector may be any expression that has a discrete result. In our example the expression is the character variable Ch. Variable Ch is of the language-defined type **Character**, a character type whose 256 values correspond to the 8-bit Latin-1 values. Ada also provides 16-bit and 32-bit character types which are described in section 3.5.2 of the ARM.

Our example contains five case alternatives. The determination of which alternative is executed is based on the value of the case selector. While our example shows a single executable statement for each alternative, you may use a sequence of statements. Each alternative is associated with a set of discrete choices. In our example, these choices are given by ranges (indicated by starting and ending values separated by two dots), specific choices (separated by vertical bars), and the final choice, **others**, which handles any selector values not given in previous choice sets. The **others** alternative must be given last. Ada requires that there be an alternative for every value in the domain of the discrete case selector. The **others** alternative is frequently used to meet this requirement.

2.1.3 Loop statements

Ada's loop statement executes a sequence of statements repeatedly, zero or more times. The simplest form of the loop statement is the infinite loop. While it may at first seem odd to have a loop syntax for an infinite loop, such loops are common in embedded software where the system runs from the time the device is powered up to when it is switched off. Here is an example based on our pressure cooker temperature control algorithm from Chapter 1.

```
loop
   ADC.Read (Temperature);    -- Read the temperature from the ADC
   Calculate_Valve
            (Current_Temp => Temperature,    -- Calculate the new
             New_Setting  => Valve_Setting); -- gas valve setting
```

```
DAC. Write ( Valve_Setting );    -- Change the valve setting
    delay 1.5;                   -- Wait 1.5 seconds
end loop;
```

We use an exit statement within a loop to terminate the execution of that loop when some condition is met. The exit statement may go anywhere in the sequence of statements making up the loop body. Here is a loop that reads and sums integer values until it encounters a negative sentinel value. The negative value is not added to the sum.

```
Sum := 0;
loop
    Get ( Value );
    exit when Value < 0;
    Sum := Sum + Value;
end loop;
```

There are two iteration schemes that may be used with the loop statement. The *while* iteration scheme is used to create a pretest loop. The loop body is executed while the condition is true. The loop terminates when the condition is false. The following loop uses a while iteration scheme to calculate the square root of X using Newton's method.

```
Approx := X / 2.0;
while abs (X - Approx ** 2) > Tolerance loop
    Approx := 0.5 * (Approx + X / Approx);
end loop;
Put ("The square root of ");
Put (Item => X, Fore => 1, Aft => 5, Exp => 0);
Put (" is approximately ");
Put (Item => Approx, Fore => 1, Aft => 5, Exp => 0);
New_Line;
```

This program fragment uses two operators not found in some programming languages. abs returns the absolute value of its operand and ** is used to raise a number to an integer power.

The *for* iteration scheme is used to create deterministic counting loops. Here is a simple example of this scheme.

```
for Count in 5..8 loop
    Put (Count);
    New_Line;
end loop;
```

As you can probably guess, this loop displays the four integers 5, 6, 7, and 8. Let's look at the details underlying the for iteration scheme. The variable Count in this example is called the **loop parameter**. The loop parameter is not defined in a declarative part like normal variables. Count is defined only for the body of this loop. The range 5..8 defines a discrete subtype with four values. The body of the loop is executed once for each value in this discrete subtype. The values are assigned to the loop parameter in increasing order. Within the body of the loop, the loop parameter is treated as a constant; we cannot modify it. To make our loops more general, we can replace the literals 5 or 8 in our example with any expression that evaluates to a discrete type. We'll revisit this topic when we discuss types and subtypes later in this chapter.

If we add the reserved word **reverse** to the for loop, the values are assigned to the loop parameter in decreasing order. The following for loop displays the four numbers in reverse order.

```
for Count in reverse 5 .. 8 loop
    Put (Count);
    New_Line;
end loop;
```

Reversing the order of the values in our example range creates a subtype with a *null range* — a subtype with no values. A for loop with a null range iterates zero times. Such a situation often arises when the range is defined by variables. Each of the following for loops displays nothing.

```
A := 9;
B := 2;
```

```
for Count in A .. B loop          -- With a null range, this
    Put (Count);                  -- loop iterates zero times
    New_Line;
end loop;
```

```
for Count in reverse A .. B loop   -- With a null range, this
    Put (Count);                   -- loop iterates zero times
    New_Line;
end loop;
```

2.2 Subprograms

A subprogram is a program unit whose execution is invoked by a subprogram call. Ada provides two forms of subprograms: the *procedure* and the *function*. We use a procedure call statement to invoke a procedure. You saw examples of procedure call statements in the program **Average** at the beginning of this chapter. We invoke a function by using its name in an expression. A function returns a value that is used in the expression that invoked it. The definition of a subprogram can be given in two parts: a declaration defining its signature and a body containing its executable statements. Alternatively, we can skip the subprogram declaration and use the specification at the beginning of the body to define the signature. We will take this second approach in this section and use separate declarations when we discuss packages later in this chapter. Section 6 of the ARM provides the details on Ada's subprograms.

2.2.1 Procedures

Let's start with an example that illustrates the major features of a procedure. Here is a program called **Example**. For the time being, ignore the shading in this program listing. We will use the shading later in our discussion of scope.

```ada
with Ada.Text_IO;          use Ada.Text_IO;
with Ada.Integer_Text_IO;  use Ada.Integer_Text_IO;
procedure Example is

   Limit : constant Integer := 1_000;

   procedure Bounded_Increment (Value   : in out Integer;
                                Bound   : in     Integer;
                                Changed :    out Boolean) is
   begin
      if Value < Bound then
         Value   := Value + 1;
         Changed := True;
      else
         Changed := False;
      end if;
   end Bounded_Increment;

   Value    : Integer;
   Modified : Boolean;

begin
   Put_Line ("Enter a number");
   Get (Value);
   Bounded_Increment (Bound   => Limit,
                      Value   => Value,
                      Changed => Modified);
   if Modified then
      Put ("Your number was changed to ");
      Put (Item => Value, Width => 1);
      New_Line;
   end if;
end Example;
```

The first thing you might notice is that our program is itself a procedure. It is called the main procedure. We defined another procedure called

Bounded_Increment in the main subprogram's declarative part. Execution of our program begins with the call to procedure Put_Line that displays the prompt "Enter a number." The program then obtains a value from the user, calls procedure Bounded_Increment, and finally, based on the actions of the procedure just called, it may display a message.

Now that we have shown you the order of execution in this program, let's look at some other features. The declarative part of procedure Example contains four definitions: the named constant Limit, the procedure Bounded_Increment, and the variables Value and Modified. Named constants are assigned values which we may not change. This program also introduces the language-defined type Boolean with possible values True and False.

Now let's look at some of the details needed to write procedures.

Parameter modes

Many programming languages require that programmers assign parameter passing mechanisms such as pass-by-value and pass-by-reference to their parameters. Ada uses a higher level means based on the direction of data flow of the parameter rather than the passing mechanism. Procedure Bounded_Increment illustrates all of the three different modes we can assign to a parameter.

in   Used to pass data from the caller into the procedure. Within the procedure, an in mode parameter is treated as a constant. The actual parameter may be any expression whose result matches the type of the formal parameter. In our example, parameter Bound is assigned mode in.

out   Used to pass results out of the procedure back to its caller. You should treat the formal parameter as an uninitialized variable. The actual parameter must be a variable whose type matches that of the formal parameter. In our example, parameter Changed is assigned mode out.

in out   Used to modify an actual parameter. A value is passed in, used by the procedure, possibly modified by the procedure, and returned to the caller. It is like an out mode parameter which is initialized to the value of the actual parameter. Since a value is returned, the actual parameter must be a variable. In our example, parameter Value is assigned mode in out.

A common mistake made by novice Ada programmers is to select mode in out for all parameters regardless of the data flow requirements of their application. By using the most appropriate mode, the Ada compiler can provide additional feedback on potential errors in our programs. While the three parameter modes are defined in terms of use rather than passing mechanism, section 6.2 of the ARM provides the details of the mechanisms actually used to implement the mode abstractions.

Scope

The scope of an identifier determines where in the program that identifier may be used. We have already seen one example of scope in our discussion of the for loop. The scope of a loop parameter is the body of the loop. You may not reference the loop parameter outside the body of the loop. The scope of most every other identifier in an Ada program is based on the notion of **declarative regions**. Each subprogram defines a declarative region. This region is the combination of the subprogram declaration and body. A declarative region is more than the declarative part we defined earlier.

Let's look at the declarative regions defined in program `Example` on page 31. The declarative region of procedure `Example` begins after its name and ends with its end keyword. We used a light gray box to highlight this declarative region. Similarly, the declarative region for procedure `Bounded_Increment` begins just after its name and ends with its end keyword. The darker gray box highlights this declarative region. These gray boxes make it easy to see that `Bounded_Increment`'s declarative region is nested within the declarative region of `Example`. Notice that this declarative region contains the definition of `Bounded_Increment`'s three parameters.

Where a particular identifier may be used is determined from two rules.

- The scope of an identifier includes all the statements following its definition, within the declarative region containing the definition. This includes all nested declarative regions, except as noted in the next rule.
- The scope of an identifier does not extend to any nested declarative region that contains a locally defined *homograph*.[2] This rule is sometimes called *name precedence*. When homographs exist, the local identifier takes precedence within the procedure.

Based on these rules, the variables `Value` and `Modified` may be used by the main procedure `Example` but not by procedure `Bounded_Increment`. The constant `Limit` could be used in both procedure `Example` and procedure `Bounded_Increment`. Because `Limit` is declared within procedure `Example`'s declarative region, `Limit` is said to be *local* to `Example`. As `Limit`

---

[2] A different identifier with the same name.

is declared in procedure Bounded_Increment's enclosing declarative region, Limit is said to be *global* to Bounded_Increment. The three parameters, Value, Bound, and Changed, are local to procedure Bounded_Increment.

While global constants are useful, the use of global variables is usually considered a bad practice. We use the style of always declaring variables after procedures so that the variables may not be accessed by those procedures. Section 8.2 of the ARM provides the complete description of the scope of declarations.

2.2.2 Functions

Functions return a value that is used in the expression that invoked the function. While many programming languages restrict return values to scalars, an Ada function may return a composite value such as an array or record. All function parameters must be mode *in*.[3] This mode restriction encourages programmers to create pure functions — functions that have no side effects. Here is an example of a function that is given a real value and acceptable error tolerance. It returns an approximation of the square root of the value.

```
function Sqrt (X : in Float; Tolerance : in Float) return Float
    Approx : Float;   -- An approximation of the square root of X
begin
    Approx := X / 2.0;
    while abs (X - Approx ** 2) > Tolerance loop
        Approx := 0.5 * (Approx + X / Approx);
    end loop;
    return Approx;
end Sqrt;
```

The signature of this function includes its parameters and the type of the value that it returns. Approx is a local variable that holds our approximation of the square root of X. Execution of the return statement completes the execution of the function and returns the result to the caller. Should control reach the end of a function without encountering a return statement, an exception is raised. You may have multiple return statements in a function. Should you need to calculate a square root in your programs, it would be better to use the function Sqrt in the Ada library package Ada.Numerics.Elementary_Functions than our example code.

---

[3] This restriction will be removed in Ada 2012.

2.3 The Ada type model

A type is defined by a set of possible values (its domain) and a set of primitive operations on those values. In all of our previous examples we used language-defined types such as Integer, Float, and Boolean. Ada allows us to define our own simple and complex types. Ada's type model is perhaps the single feature that gives Ada a significant advantage over other programming languages. It allows us to create accurate models of the real world and provide valuable information to the compiler so it can identify errors before the program is executed. Four principles govern the type system (Wikibooks, 2010a):

- **Strong typing** Types are incompatible with one another. It is not possible to mix apples and oranges. We can, however, use explicit type conversions to cast a value of one type to another type when we do need to combine values of different types.

- **Static typing** Types are checked by the compiler allowing type errors to be found earlier in the development life cycle.

- **Abstraction** Types model the real world or the problem at hand. The Ada programmer need not be concerned about how the computer represents the data internally. But, as we shall see later, we may use representation clauses to specify exactly how a type is represented at the bit level. We can map specific types to specific hardware.

- **Name equivalence** Two types are compatible if and only if they have the same name — not if they just happen to have the same size or bit representation (structural equivalence). You can declare two floating point types with the same precision and ranges that are totally incompatible.

Let's look at an example program with an obvious error.

```
with Ada.Float_Text_IO;   use Ada.Float_Text_IO;
procedure Bad_Types is
    Room_Length      : Float;    -- length of room in feet
    Wall_Thickness : Float;    -- thickness of wall in inches
    Total            : Float;    -- in feet
begin
    Get (Room_Length);
    Get (Wall_Thickness);
    Total := Room_Length + 2.0 * Wall_Thickness;
    Put (Item => Total, Fore => 1, Aft => 1, Exp => 0);
end Bad_Types;
```

In this example we have defined three variables, each of which holds a real number. The programmer ignored the comments given with each of these variable declarations and neglected to convert the wall thickness measurement from inches to feet before adding it to the room length measurement. While the error in this short program is obvious, finding similar errors in large programs requires a great deal of effort in testing and debugging. Ada's type model helps to eliminate a wide class of errors from our programs. But, as the example illustrates, we can still have such errors in our Ada programs when we do not take full advantage of the type system to model our values.

Figure 2.1 shows the relationships among Ada's various types. The hierarchy in this figure is similar to a class inheritance hierarchy. Type Boolean is an enumeration type. An enumeration type is a discrete type. The types whose names are in italics in Figure 2.1, such as *Ada data types*, are abstract entities used to organize the classification of types. The set of operations available for all Ada types[4] include assignment (:=) and equality testing (= and /=).

Figure 2.1 shows that types are divided into two groups: atomic and composite. A composite type is one whose values may be decomposed into smaller values. A string type is a composite type. A string value is composed of characters. We can access and use the individual characters making up a string. An atomic type is one whose values cannot be decomposed into smaller values. A character type is an atomic type. A character value cannot be decomposed into smaller values. Integers and real numbers are also atomic types.

2.3.1 Scalar types

A scalar type is an atomic type with the additional property of ordering. We can compare scalar values with the relational operators (<, <=, >, and >=). Characters, integers, and real numbers are all scalar types.

One of the principles of object-oriented programming is the development of classes that accurately model the objects in the problem. We can apply this same approach to the design of our scalar types. By using scalar types that more accurately reflect the nature of the data in a problem we are solving, we can write better programs. One research study on the nature of costly software faults indicates that poor models of scalar quantities were responsible for nearly 90% of the errors in the cases studied (Eisenstadt, 1997; McCormick, 1997). Ada allows programmers to define their own scalar data types that accurately model the scalar values in the problem domain.

---

[4] Assignment and equality testing are not available for Ada's limited types; types for which copying is not allowed. A limited type is a type that includes the reserved word limited, synchronized, task, or protected in its definition or in the definition of a component of a composite type.

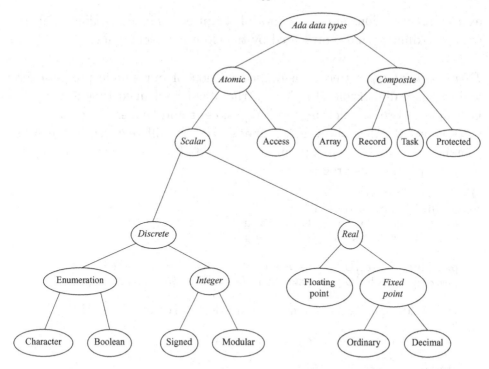

Figure 2.1 The Ada type hierarchy

Although we won't say that using well-designed scalar types will eliminate 90% of costly faults, they certainly give us a valuable tool for the production of quality software.

Figure 2.1 shows that there are two kinds of scalar types. Real types provide the mechanisms for working with real numbers. A discrete type is a scalar type with the additional property of unique successors and predecessors. We'll look at specific real and discrete types in the next sections.

Real types

The storage and manipulation of real numbers is the substance of the discipline of numerical analysis. The underlying problem with computations involving real numbers is that very few real numbers can be represented exactly in a computer's memory. For example, of the infinite number of real numbers in the interval between 1.0 and 2.0, only about 1016 are represented exactly in the IEEE 754 single precision representation. The numbers with

exact representations are called **model numbers**. The remaining numbers
are approximated and represented by the closest model number.

Floating point types Here is a revised version of our simple program for
adding room dimensions. In place of the language-defined type `Float`, we
have defined two new floating point types: `Feet` and `Inches`. Since the variables `Room_Length` and `Wall_Thickness` are now different types, the Ada
compiler will catch the inappropriate addition of feet and inches we had in
our earlier erroneous program.

```ada
with Ada.Text_IO;
procedure Good_Types is
    type Feet   is digits 4 range 0.0 .. 100.0;
    type Inches is digits 3 range 0.0 .. 12.0;

    package Feet_IO is new Ada.Text_IO.Float_IO (Feet);
    package Inch_IO is new Ada.Text_IO.Float_IO (Inches);

    function To_Feet (Item : in Inches) return Feet is
    begin
        return Feet (Item) / 12.0;
    end To_Feet;
    pragma Inline (To_Feet);

    Room_Length    : Feet;
    Wall_Thickness : Inches;
    Total          : Feet;
begin
    Feet_IO.Get (Room_Length);
    Inch_IO.Get (Wall_Thickness);
    Total := Room_Length + 2.0 * To_Feet (Wall_Thickness);
    Feet_IO.Put (Item => Total, Fore => 1, Aft => 1, Exp => 0);
end Good_Types;
```

The addition of feet and inches requires that we convert a value from one
unit to another. We have included a function that makes this conversion.
The function **To_Feet** first does an explicit type conversion (three inches is
converted to three feet) which is then divided by twelve to complete the unit
conversion.

Our two new floating point types are defined by the type definitions at
the beginning of the program. To define a new floating point type, we must
specify the minimum number of decimal digits we require in the mantissa
in the floating point numbers. This number follows the word "digits" in
the type definition. The specification of a range for a floating point type is
optional. If the range is omitted, the compiler will create a floating point
type with the widest range possible.

We select the minimum number of digits in the mantissa based on the expected precision of our largest value. For our room length, we selected 100 feet as the upper bound of our domain. We estimated that the precision of a measurement of a 100 foot long room is a tenth of a foot. Therefore, we need four digits of precision to represent 100.0 — three account for the digits to the left of the decimal point and one for the digit to the right of the decimal point. Should we use a laser range finder with a precision of a thousandth of a foot in place of a tape measure, we would increase the number of digits of precision to six, three on each side of the decimal point. Similarly we estimated that the precision of a measurement of a twelve inch thick wall is a tenth of an inch. So we need a total of three digits of precision for our wall thickness type. The precisions we select are minimums we will accept. The Ada compiler will select the most efficient floating point representation available on the hardware with at least the precision we specify. The most common representations used are those specified by the IEEE 754 standard for floating point representation. We usually consider the precisions specified in our floating point type definitions as documentation on the precision of our actual data.

We cannot use the procedures in the library package `Ada.Float_Text_IO` to do input and output with values of type **Feet** and **Inches**. Ada provides a generic library package that may be instantiated to obtain packages for doing input and output with our own floating point types. You can see the two instantiations for packages **Feet_IO** and **Inch_IO** immediately following the definitions of our two floating point types. We prefixed our get and put procedure calls with the names of these newly created packages so you can clearly see that we are not calling procedures from the library.

The program **Good_Types** includes the pragma Inline. A **pragma** is a compiler directive. There are language-defined pragmas that give instructions for optimization, listing control, etc. Pragma Inline, requests that the subprogram be expanded inline, thereby eliminating the overhead of a subprogram call. In our example, we get the advantage of abstraction without the usual cost of a function call.

Fixed point types As illustrated in Figure 2.1, Ada provides support for two representations of real numbers: fixed point and floating point. Fixed point numbers provide a fixed number of digits before and after the radix point. When we write a real number on paper, we usually use a fixed point format such as

12.75   0.00433   1258.1

In a floating point number, the radix point may "float" to any location. Floating point is the computer realization of scientific notation. A floating point value is implemented as two separate numbers, a mantissa and an exponent. The following are all valid representations of 1258.1.

$$.12581 \times 10^4 \qquad 1.2581 \times 10^3 \qquad 12.581 \times 10^2$$
$$125.81 \times 10^1 \qquad 1258.1 \times 10^0 \qquad 12581. \times 10^{-1}$$

Floating point is by far the more commonly used representation for real numbers. In most programming languages, floating point is the only type available for representing real numbers. Floating point types support a much wider range of values than fixed point types. However, fixed point types have two properties that favor their use in certain situations. First, fixed point arithmetic is performed with standard integer machine instructions. Integer instructions are typically faster than floating point instructions. Some inexpensive embedded microprocessors, microcontrollers, and digital signal processors (DSPs) do not support floating point arithmetic. In such cases, fixed point is the only representation available for real numbers.

The second advantage of fixed point is that the maximum representational error is constant throughout the range of the type. The maximum representational error for a floating point type depends on the magnitude of the number. This difference is a result of the distribution of model numbers in each of the representations. The distance between model floating point numbers varies through the range; it depends on the value of the exponent. The distance between model fixed point numbers is constant throughout the range.

Figure 2.2 illustrates the difference in model number distributions. Figure 2.2a shows the model numbers for a very simple floating point representation. There are ten model numbers between 1.0 and 10.0, ten model numbers between 0.1 and 1.0, and ten model numbers between 0.01 and 0.1. Figure 2.2b shows the model numbers for a simple fixed point representation. The distance between model numbers is constant throughout the range. The representational error for a particular real number is equal to the difference between it and the model number used to represent it. Figure 2.2 shows that the representational error for a floating point number gets larger as the number gets larger while the representational error for a fixed point number is constant throughout its range.

Does the choice of real number representation really make a difference in our applications? "On February 25, 1991, a Patriot missile defense system operating at Dhahran, Saudi Arabia, during Operation Desert Storm failed to track and intercept an incoming Scud [missile]. This Scud subsequently

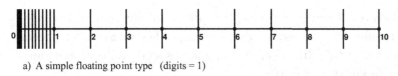

a) A simple floating point type (digits = 1)

b) A simple fixed point type (delta = 0.25)

Figure 2.2 Distribution of model numbers

hit an Army barracks, killing 28 Americans" (Blair *et al.*, 1992). The Patriot battery failed because of a software problem related to the storage and use of floating point numbers. The system stored time, in tenths of a second, in a floating point variable. Table 2.1, taken from the Government Accounting Office report, shows the magnitude of the error in representing this time as a floating point value. As with all floating point representations, the magnitude of the error increases with the magnitude of the value.

Time		Absolute inaccuracy (seconds)	Approximate shift in missile range gate (meters)
Hours	Seconds		
0	0.0	0.0	0
1	3600.0	0.0034	7
8	28800.0	0.0275	55
20	72000.0	0.0687	137
48	172800.0	0.1648	330
72	259200.0	0.2472	494
100	360000.0	0.3433	687

Table 2.1 *Magnitude of range gate error when modeling time as a floating point real number*

Table 2.1 shows that the floating point representation error grows as the number grows. After 20 hours, the time is off enough that the target is outside the range gate and the Patriot missile fails to launch against a threat. After the tragedy, the software was corrected by replacing the floating point time variables with fixed point variables. Let us note that Ada's predefined type **Duration** is a fixed point type for seconds.

To declare a fixed point type, we specify the maximum distance between model number that we are willing to accept. The maximum representational error is half of this distance. We may also specify an optional range for the type. Here are two examples.

```
type Thirds is delta 1.0 / 3.0  range 0.0 .. 100_000.0;
type Volts  is delta 2.0**(-12) range 0.0 .. 5.0;
```

Thirds is a fixed point type with a specified distance of $\frac{1}{3}$ (0.33333...) between model numbers and Volts is a fixed point type with a specified distance of $\frac{1}{4096}$ (0.000244140625) between model numbers.

Both of these types are called *ordinary fixed point types*. The actual distance between model numbers in our fixed point type may be smaller than our request. The actual distance between model numbers is the largest power of two that is less than or equal to the value given for delta. So while we specified a delta value of $\frac{1}{3}$ for Thirds, the actual delta used is the power of two, $\frac{1}{4}$ (2^{-2}). The delta we specified for Volts is a power of two so it is used directly. Because the distance between model numbers is some power of two, ordinary fixed point types are sometimes called *binary fixed point types*.

Neither floating point nor ordinary fixed point types are appropriate for currency calculations. Neither is capable of accurate storage of decimal fractions that are so important in commercial applications. Ada's *decimal fixed point types* are the more appropriate choice for such values. Here is an example.

```
type Dollars is delta 0.01 digits 12;
```

For decimal fixed point types, we must specify both a delta that is a power of ten and the number of decimal digits. A range is optional. A value of type Dollars contains twelve decimal digits. Since the distance between model numbers is 0.01, two of these digits are to the right of the decimal point leaving ten digits for the left side of the decimal point.

We use the generic packages Ada.Text_IO.Fixed_IO and Ada.Text_IO. Decimal_IO to instantiate packages for the input and output of ordinary and decimal fixed point types. You may find the details for the available I/O operations in section A.10.9 of the ARM. Here are the instantiations for our example types.

```
package Thirds_IO is new Ada.Text_IO.Fixed_IO (Thirds);
package Volts_IO  is new Ada.Text_IO.Fixed_IO (Volts);
package Dollar_IO is new Ada.Text_IO.Decimal_IO (Dollars);
```

Ada's rules that prevent the mixing of different types are more relaxed for fixed point type multiplication and division. Multiplication and division are allowed between any two fixed point types. The type of the result is determined by the context. So, for example, if we assign the result of multiplying a Volts value and a Thirds value to a Volts variable, the result type of the multiplication would be Volts. Similarly, if we assign the same product to a Thirds variable, the result type of the multiplication would be Thirds. Additionally, a fixed point value may be multiplied or divided by an integer yielding the same fixed point type.

2.3.2 Discrete types

Recall that a scalar type is an atomic type with the additional property of ordering. A discrete type is a scalar type with the additional property of unique successors and predecessors. The language-defined types Boolean, Character, and Integer are all discrete types. In the next sections we'll look at defining our own discrete types.

Enumeration types

An enumeration type provides a means for defining a type by enumerating (listing) all the values in the domain. The following program illustrates the definition and use of three enumeration types.

```
with Ada.Text_IO;          use Ada.Text_IO;
with Ada.Integer_Text_IO;  use Ada.Integer_Text_IO;
procedure Enum_Example is

   type Day_Type is (Monday, Tuesday, Wednesday, Thursday,
                     Friday, Saturday, Sunday);
   type Traffic_Light_Color is (Red, Green, Yellow);
   type Pixel_Color        is (Red, Green, Blue, Cyan,
                               Magenta, Yellow, Black, White);

   package Day_IO is new Ada.Text_IO.Enumeration_IO (Day_Type);

   function Next_Day (Day : in Day_Type) return Day_Type is
   begin
      if Day = Day_Type'Last then
         return Day_Type'First;
      else
         return Day_Type'Succ (Day);
      end if;
   end Next_Day;

   Today     : Day_Type;
   Tomorrow  : Day_Type;
   Count     : Integer;
```

```ada
begin
    Put_Line ("What day is today?");
    Day_IO.Get (Today);
    Tomorrow := Next_Day (Today);
    Put ("Tomorrow is ");
    Day_IO.Put (Item  => Tomorrow,
                Width => 1,
                Set   => Ada.Text_IO.Lower_Case);
    New_Line;

    if Today > Tomorrow then
        Put_Line ("Today must be Sunday");
    end if;
    New_Line;

    Put_Line ("The week days are ");
    for Day in Monday .. Friday loop
        Day_IO.Put (Day);
        New_Line;
    end loop;
    New_Line (2);

    for Color in Traffic_Light_Color loop
        Put_Line (Traffic_Light_Color'Image (Color));
    end loop;
    New_Line (2);

    Count := 0;
    for Color in Pixel_Color range Red .. Yellow loop
        Count := Count + 1;
    end loop;
    Put (Item => Count, Width => 1);
end Enum_Example;
```

Each of our three enumeration types is defined by listing literals for all of the values in the domain. These literals are case insensitive. We could also have typed MONDAY or monday for the first value of Day_Type. Notice that the Red is both a Pixel_Color literal and a Traffic_Light_Color literal.

We may instantiate packages for the input and output of enumeration values. In our example program, we instantiated the package Day_IO to allow us to get and put day values. You may find the details of the input and output operations available for enumeration values in section A.10.10 of the ARM. Like the defining literals, the input values are not case sensitive. For output, we may select between all uppercase or all lowercase values. The first portion of the main procedure in our example calls procedures get and put in package Day_IO to get a day and display the next day.

Our main subprogram calls the function Next_Day to determine the day that follows the day entered by the user. This function has our first use of attributes. An **attribute** is an operator that yields a characteristic of a type or object. Some attributes require parameters. Here are the most common attributes for scalar types.

'First	Returns the lower bound of the type
'Last	Returns the upper bound of the type
'Image	Returns a string equivalent to the given value

And here are two additional attributes available for discrete types.

'Succ	Returns the successor of the given value
'Pred	Returns the predecessor of the given value

Let's look at the attributes used in program `Enum_Example`. The expression `Day_Type'Last` (read day type *tick* last) in the if statement of our function uses the attribute `'Last` to determine the last (largest) value in the domain of the type. As you might expect, the attribute `'First` returns the first (smallest) value in the domain of the type. The attribute `'Succ` requires a parameter. It returns the successor of the value passed to it. Because there is no successor for the value `Sunday` in type `Day_Type`, passing `Sunday` to the successor attribute function raises an exception (a run time error) that would halt this flow of execution. The purpose of the if statement in function `Next_Day` is to avoid this exception by returning the first day of our type (`Monday`) for the one case where the successor function fails. The attribute `'Pred` returns the predecessor of a value passed to it. An exception is raised on an attempt to use this function to determine the predecessor of the smallest value in the type's domain. You may find descriptions of the attributes available for all scalar types in section 3.5 of the ARM. Additional attributes for all discrete types are described in section 3.5.5. Sections 3.5.8 and 3.5.10 describe attributes available for all floating point and fixed point types.

The next portion of the main subprogram of our example illustrates the use of relational operators with enumeration values. These operators use the order of the literals in each enumeration type definition. `Day_Type` defines an order of days in which `Monday` is the smallest day and `Sunday` is the largest day. The if statement that asks whether `Today` is greater than `Tomorrow` is true only when `Today` is `Sunday`.

The remainder of our example program illustrates additional variations of the for loop. Our previous for loop examples used only integer loop parameters. A loop parameter may be of any discrete type. Recall that a loop parameter is not declared before the loop. It takes its type from the discrete subtype following the reserved word `in`. The loop parameter `Day` in the first for loop in our example program takes its type, `Day_Type`, from that of the range `Monday..Friday`.

The second loop in our example program uses a type name rather than a range. This loop iterates through all three values of type `Traffic_Light_Color` displaying each value. We used another approach for displaying the traffic light colors in this loop. The `'Image` attribute function returns an uppercase string equivalent to the enumeration parameter. We then used `Ada.Text_IO.Put_Line` to display this string. The advantage of the `'Image` attribute is its simplicity. However, it does not provide the control available for formatting enumeration values available in the put procedures created in instantiations of enumeration I/O packages.

The final loop illustrates a solution to a typical problem with duplicate enumeration literals. The range `Red..Yellow` could be either type `Traffic_Light_Color` or type `Pixel_Color`. We explicitly indicated the type desired, `Pixel_Color`, for the loop parameter in this for loop.

The language-defined types `Boolean`, `Character`, `Wide_Character`, and `Wide_Wide_Character` are all enumeration types. You can see their definitions in section A.1 of the ARM. Because all three character types share common literals, the type of a character range is usually ambiguous. Here is a for loop with a syntax error resulting from the ambiguity of the type of the range.

```
for Letter in 'a' .. 'z' loop
```

```
***ERROR*** ambiguous character literal
```

We resolve the ambiguity by giving the range an explicit type.

```
for Letter in Character range 'a' .. 'z' loop
```

Integer types

Most programmers use the integer type defined in their language for all variables that hold whole numbers. As we saw earlier, in our room length example, using the same type for different quantities may result in logic errors requiring debugging effort. By again using different and appropriate types for our integers, we can have more confidence in our software. In the next sections we'll look at Ada's two different integer types.

Signed integers To define a new signed integer type, we need only specify the range. Here are the definitions of three signed integer types and the declaration of a variable of each of those types.

```
type Pome      is range    0 ..  120;
type Citrus    is range  -17 ..  30;
type Big_Range is range  -20 ..  1_000_000_000_000_000_000;
```

```
Apples  : Pome;
Oranges : Citrus;
Fruit   : Big_Range;
```

The range of each type is specified by a smallest and largest value, not by some storage unit size such as a byte or word. Should we assign a value to **Apples** that is outside of the range constraint given for **Pome**, the Ada run-time system will raise a **Constraint_Error** exception. Because they are different types, a comparison of **Apples** and **Oranges** is illegal. Of course, should you really want to combine apples and oranges in an expression, you can use explicit type conversions as in

```
Fruit := Big_Range (Apples) + Big_Range (Oranges);
```

Operations available for signed integers include +, -, *, /, **, abs, rem, and mod. The rem (remainder on division) and mod (the mathematical modulo operation) operators return the same result when both of their operands are positive. Should one of your operands be negative, you should consult the formal definitions of these two similar operators given in section 4.5.5 of the ARM. The attributes 'First, 'Last, 'Succ, 'Pred, and 'Image discussed for enumeration values are also available for signed integers.

To do input and output of our own integer types we need to instantiate a package from the generic integer I/O package available in the Ada library. Here are the instantiations for the three integer types we defined.

```
package Pome_IO   is new Ada.Text_IO.Integer_IO (Pome);
package Citrus_IO is new Ada.Text_IO.Integer_IO (Citrus);
package Big_IO    is new Ada.Text_IO.Integer_IO (Big_Range);
```

Modular integers Modular integer types are unsigned integer types that use modular arithmetic. The value of a modular integer variable wraps around after reaching an upper limit. To define a modular integer type we need only specify a modulus. Here are some modular integer type definitions and variable declaration.

```
type Digit  is mod 10;      -- range is from 0 to 9
type Byte   is mod 256;     -- range is from 0 to 255
type Nybble is mod 16;      -- range is from 0 to 15
type Word   is mod 2**32;   -- range is from 0 to 4,294,967,295
```

```
Value : Nybble;
```

The following assignment statement illustrates the modular nature of this type.

```
Value := 12 + 8;     -- Value is assigned 4
```

In addition to the usual arithmetic operators, the logical operators **and**, **or**, **xor**, and **not** are available for modular integer types. These operators treat the values as bit patterns. The result of the **not** operator for a modular type is defined as the difference between the high bound of the type and the value of the operand. For a modulus that is a power of two, this corresponds to a bit-wise complement of the binary representation of the value of the operand.

Again, we must instantiate packages to do input and output with the types we define. You can find the details on these packages and the get and put procedures in section A.10.8 of the ARM. Here are the instantiations for our four modular types.

```
package Digit_IO   is new Ada.Text_IO.Modular_IO (Digit);
package Byte_IO    is new Ada.Text_IO.Modular_IO (Byte);
package Nybble_IO  is new Ada.Text_IO.Modular_IO (Nybble);
package Word_IO    is new Ada.Text_IO.Modular_IO (Word);
```

2.3.3 Subtypes

By defining our own types, we make our programs easier to read, safer from type errors, and allow range checking at run time. In some cases, values with different constraints are related so closely that using them together in expressions is common and desired. Although explicit type conversion allows us to write such expressions, Ada provides a better solution — the subtype. Subtypes allow us to create a set of values that is a subset of the domain of some existing type. Subtypes inherit the operations from their base type. Subtypes are compatible with the type from which they were derived and all other subtypes derived from that type. A subset is defined by specifying an existing type and an optional constraint. Let's look at some examples.

```
subtype Lowercase is Character range 'a' .. 'z';
subtype Negative  is Integer   range Integer'First .. -1;

type    Day_Type is (Monday, Tuesday, Wednesday, Thursday,
                     Friday, Saturday, Sunday);
subtype Weekday is Day_Type range Monday .. Friday;
subtype Weekend is Day_Type range Saturday .. Sunday;

type    Pounds      is digits 6 range 0.0 .. 1.0E+06;
subtype UPS_Weight  is Pounds   range 1.0 .. 100.0;
```

```
subtype FedEx_Weight is Pounds    range 0.1 .. 1.0;

subtype Column_Number is Ada.Text_IO.Count;  -- A synonym

Total    : Pounds;
Box      : UPS_Weight;
Envelope : FedEx_Weight;
```

The domain of the subtype **Lowercase** is a subset of the domain of the language-defined type **Character**. Objects of subtype **Lowercase** may be combined with or used in place of objects of type **Character**. Similarly, the domain of the subtype **Negative** is a subset of the domain of the language-defined type **Integer**. The domain of subtypes **Weekday** and **Weekend** are both subsets of the programmer-defined type **Day_Type**. The following assignment statement illustrates the combining of subtypes with the same base type.

```
-- Adding two different subtypes with same base type
Total := Box + Envelope;
```

Subtype definitions may also be used to create synonyms — subtypes with the same domain as their base type. Synonyms are often used to provide a more problem-specific name for a type whose name is more general or to eliminate the need to prefix a type name defined in a package. The subtype **Column_Number** is an example of such a synonym.

There are two commonly used language-defined subtypes defined in Ada. **Positive** is a subtype of Integer with a range that starts at one. **Natural** is a subtype of Integer with a range that starts at zero.

2.3.4 Array types

Arrays are composite types whose components are the same type. We access a specific component by giving its location via an index. Defining an array type requires two types: one type or subtype for the component and one type or subtype for the index. The component may be any type. The index may be any discrete type. Here are some examples of array definitions.

```
type Index_Type      is range 1..1000;
type Inventory_Array is array (Index_Type) of Natural;

subtype Lowercase is Character range 'a' .. 'z';
type    Percent    is range 0..100;
type    Frequency_Array is array (Lowercase) of Percent;

type Day_Type is (Monday, Tuesday, Wednesday, Thursday,
                  Friday, Saturday, Sunday);
```

```
type On_Call_Array is array (Day_Type) of Boolean;

Inventory  :  Inventory_Array;
Control    :  Frequency_Array;
Unknown    :  Frequency_Array;
On_Call    :  On_Call_Array;
```

Variable **Inventory** is an array of 1000 natural numbers indexed from 1 to 1000. **Control** and **Unknown** are arrays of 26 percentages indexed from a to z. **On_Call** is an array of seven Boolean values indexed from **Monday** to **Sunday**.

Ada provides a rich set of array operations. Let's start with a selection operation. We use indexing to select a particular component in an array. We can use indexing to obtain a value from an array or change a value in an array. Here are some examples using the variables we just defined.

```
Inventory (5)      := 1_234;
Control ('a')      := 2 * Control ('a');
On_Call (Sunday) := False;

Total_Days := 0;
for Day in Day_Type loop
    if On_Call (Day) then
        Total_Days := Total_Days + 1;
    end if;
end loop;
```

Assignment is another operation available with arrays. As usual, strong typing requires that the source and target of an assignment statement be the same type. The following assignment statement makes the array **Unknown** a copy of the array **Control**.

```
Unknown := Control;
```

We can use the equality operators to compare two arrays of the same type. If the array components are discrete values, we can also compare two arrays with any of the relational operators. The relational operators are based on lexicographical order (sometimes called dictionary order) using the predefined order relation of the discrete component type. We frequently use relational operators with arrays of characters (strings). Here is an example that uses two of the array variables we defined earlier.

```
if Control = Unknown then
    Put ("The values in the two arrays are identical");
elsif Control < Unknown then
    Put ("The values in Control come lexicographically " &
         "before those in Unknown");
end if;
```

Slicing is another selection operation. It allows us to work with sub-arrays. We use slicing to read a portion of an array or write a portion of an array. A range is used to specify the portion of interest. Here are two examples of slicing.

```
-- Copy elements 11-20 into locations 1-10
Inventory (1 .. 10) := Inventory (11 .. 20);

-- Copy elements 2-11 into locations 1-10
Inventory (1 .. 10) := Inventory (2 .. 11);
```

Our second example illustrates slice assignment with overlapping ranges. Such assignments are useful in shuffling the components in an array when inserting or deleting components in an array-based list.

While indexing and slicing both access components, their results are quite different. The indexing operation accesses a single component. The slicing operation accesses an array. So while the expressions `Inventory(5)` and `Inventory(5..5)` are very similar, their result types are very different. `Inventory(5)` is a natural number while `Inventory(5..5)` is an array consisting of one natural number.

Our slicing examples also illustrate the sliding feature of array assignment. The index ranges of the source and target of these assignments are different. The ten values in the source array slide into the target array. The ranges of the indices of the source and target may be different. The two restrictions for array assignment are that the target and source be the same type and that the number of components is the same.

We define multidimensional arrays by defining multiple indices. The following examples illustrate two ways to define an array in which we use two indices to locate a component.

```
type Row_Index is range  1 .. 1000;
type Col_Index is range -5 .. +5;

type Two_D_Array is array (Row_Index, Col_Index) of Float;

type One_Row is array (Col_Index) of Float;
type Another_2D_Array is array (Row_Index) of One_Row;

Canary : Two_D_Array;        -- A 2 dimensional array variable
Finch  : Another_2D_Array; -- An array of arrays variable
```

The syntax for indexing a two-dimensional array is different from that for indexing an array of arrays. Here are examples of each kind.

```
-- Assign zero to row 12, column 2 of the 2-D array
Canary (12, 2) := 0.0;
```

```
-- Assign zero to the second component of the 12th array
Finch (12)(2)  := 0.0;
```

Slicing is limited to one-dimensional arrays. We cannot slice the array variable **Canary**. However, we can slice an array in our array of arrays variable **Finch**.

Constrained and unconstrained array types

All the previous array examples were of constrained arrays. A constrained array type is an array type for which there is an index range constraint. An unconstrained array type definition provides only the type of the index, it does not specify the range of that type. Here is an example.

```
type Float_Array is array (Positive range <>) of Float;
```

This statement defines the unconstrained array type **Float_Array**. The components of this array type are type **Float** and the index of this array is subtype **Positive**. We did not specify the range of the positive index. The box symbol, <>, indicates that this is the definition of an unconstrained array type. Since there is no range constraint for this array type, we cannot use an unconstrained array type to declare an array variable because the compiler cannot determine how much memory to allocate to such an array variable.

```
Illegal : Float_Array;   -- This declaration will not compile
```

The two important uses of unconstrained array types are as a base for a constrained array subtype and for the type of a formal parameter. Here are examples of constrained array subtypes.

```
subtype Small_Array is Float_Array (1 .. 10);
subtype Large_Array is Float_Array (1000 .. 9999);

Small : Small_Array; -- An array of 10 Float values
Large : Large_Array; -- An array of 9,000 Float values
```

Since the arrays **Small** and **Large** have the same base type, we can combine them in expressions like these.

```
Large (1001 .. 1010) := Small;           -- Copy 10 values
if Small /= Large (2001 .. 2010) then    -- Compare 10 values
   -- Copy 21 values
   Large (2001 .. 2021) := Small & 14.2 & Small;
end if;
```

The second assignment statement in the above example illustrates another array operation, **concatenation**. The & operator may be used to concatenate two arrays, an array and a component, or two components. The result in all cases is an array. In our example, we created a 21-component array by concatenating a copy of array Small with the value 14.2 and a second copy of Small.

Here is an example of a subprogram specification with an unconstrained array parameter.

```
function Average (Values : in Float_Array) return Float is
```

The formal parameter Values will match any actual parameter that is a constrained array subtype of Float_Array. The formal parameter will take on the index constraint of the actual parameter. Here are some calls to function Average using our two previously defined array variables.

```
Avg := Average (Small);              -- Average of 10 values
Avg := Average (Large);              -- Average of 9,000 values
Avg := Average (Large (2001..2010)); -- Average of 10 values
Avg := Average (Large & Small);      -- Average of 9,010 values
```

Array attributes

As you just saw, we can pass different size arrays to function Average. We do not need to pass the size of the array or its starting or ending indices. The function makes use of attributes to obtain the properties of the actual array parameter. Earlier we introduced some of the most commonly used attributes for discrete types. There are attributes for array types as well. The attributes most commonly used with arrays are

'First	Returns the lower bound of the index range
'Last	Returns the upper bound of the index range
'Length	Returns the number of components in the array ('Last – 'First + 1)
'Range	Returns the index range of the array ('First .. 'Last)

Here is the complete code for function Average which uses two of these attributes.

```
function Average (Values : in Float_Array) return Float is
   Sum : Float;
begin
   Sum := 0.0;
   for Index in Values'Range loop
      Sum := Sum + Values (Index);
   end loop;
   return Sum / Float (Values'Length);
end Average;
```

When working with unconstrained array parameters, you should not make any assumptions about the first or last index values. While many arrays use 1 as a starting index, you should use the attributes rather than make such an assumption.

Section 3.6 of the ARM provides the details on array types and attributes. There you may also find how to use attributes with multi-dimensional arrays.

Strings

We conclude our discussion of unconstrained arrays with a very brief discussion of Ada's predefined fixed-length string type. Type **String** is predefined as an unconstrained array of characters with a positive index.

```ada
-- Type String is defined in Ada.Standard as
type String is array (Positive range <>) of Character;
```

Here is a complete program that uses type **String** to illustrate constrained array subtypes, slicing, unconstrained array parameters, and array attributes.

```ada
with Ada.Text_IO;   use Ada.Text_IO;
procedure Palindrome is

    function Is_Palindrome (Item : in String) return Boolean is
    begin
        if Item'Length <= 1 then
            -- All strings of length 0 and 1 are palindromes
            return True;
        elsif Item (Item'First) /= Item (Item'Last) then
            -- The first and last letter of the string are different
            return False;
        else
            -- First and last characters match, check the remaining
            return Is_Palindrome (Item (Item'First + 1 .. Item'Last - 1));
        end if;
    end Is_Palindrome;

    Max_Length : constant Positive := 100;
    subtype Line_Type is String (1 .. Max_Length);

    Line  : Line_Type;   -- Characters entered by user
    Count : Natural;     -- Number of characters entered

begin
    Put_Line ("Enter a line. I'll tell you if it is a palindrome.");
    -- Get_Line reads characters to end of line
    -- Last is the index of the last character read
    Get_Line (Item => Line,  Last => Count);
    -- Slice off garbage before calling Is_Palindrome
    if Is_Palindrome (Line (1 .. Count)) then
        Put_Line ("is a palindrome");
    else
        Put_Line ("is not a palindrome");
    end if;
end Palindrome;
```

In addition to the predefined fixed-length string, the Ada library defines bounded varying-length strings and unbounded varying-length strings. See section A.4 of the ARM for details on the wealth of string operations available.

2.3.5 Record types

Arrays are homogeneous composite data types — the components are all of the same type. Records are heterogeneous composite types — the components may be different types. In an array we access a specific component by giving its position in the collection. We access a specific component in a record by giving its name. The following declarations define a simple record type for an inventory system.

```
subtype Part_ID is Integer range 1000 .. 9999;
type    Dollars is delta 0.01 digits 7 range 0.0 .. 10_000.0;

type Part_Rec is
    record
        ID       : Part_ID;
        Price    : Dollars;
        Quantity : Natural;
    end record;

Part     : Part_Rec;
Discount : Dollars;
```

There are three components (fields) defined in type **Part_Rec**. Each component is identified by a name. The name is used with the variable name to select a particular component in the record. Here are some examples that illustrate component selection.

```
Part.ID       := 1234;
Part.Price    := 1_856.25;
Part.Quantity := 597;
Discount      := 0.15 * Part.Price;
```

Record aggregates

In the above example, we used three assignment statements to give the record variable **Part** a value. We can use a record aggregate to assign a value to a record variable with a single assignment statement. A record aggregate is a record value written as a collection of component values enclosed with parentheses. The association of values in the aggregate and the record field may be given by position or by name. Here are examples of each.

```
Part := (1234, 1_856.25, 597);  -- Assign values by position

Part := (ID        => 1234,     -- Assign values by name
         Quantity => 597,
         Price    => 1_856.25);
```

When using named association in a record aggregate, we can order the fields as we like.

Discriminants

We often parameterize record types with one or more discriminants. A discriminant is a record component on which other components may depend. The following declarations use a discriminated record to define an array-based list of inventory records. The discriminant, **Max_Size**, is used to define the index constraint of the array component.

```
type Part_Array is array (Positive range <>) of Part_Rec;

type Inventory_List (Max_Size : Positive) is
    record
        Size  : Natural := 0;
        Items : Part_Array (1.. Max_Size);
    end record;
```

When we use a discriminated record in the declaration of an object, we supply an actual value for the discriminant. The following declaration defines an inventory list that holds a maximum of 1000 part records.

```
Inventory : Inventory_List (Max_Size => 1000);
```

Inventory is a record with three components: **Max_Size**, **Size**, and **Items**. The last component is an array of part records. Here is some code that accesses the information in this data structure.

```
-- Append a new part to the inventory list
if Inventory.Size = Inventory.Max_Size then
    Put_Line ("The inventory list is full");
else
    Inventory.Size := Inventory.Size + 1;
    Inventory.Items (Inventory.Size) := New_Part;
end if;
```

The declaration of the record type **Inventory_List** also illustrates the use of optional initial values for record components. Whenever an object of type **Inventory_List** is created, its **Size** component is set to zero. As no initial value was specified for the array component **Items**, its initial value is undefined.

While ordinary record components can be any constrained type, discriminants are limited to discrete types and access (pointer) types. We'll use discriminants again in later chapters to parameterize task-related composite types. Section 3.7 of the ARM gives the complete details of discriminants.

2.3.6 Derived types

Subtypes allow us to define subsets of existing types whose values may be combined with any other subtype that shares the same base type. Sometimes we would like to create a new type that is similar to an existing type yet is a distinct type. Here is an example of a definition of a derived type.

```
-- Define a floating point type
type Gallons is digits 6 range 0.0 .. 100.0;
-- Define a new type derived from Gallons
type Imperial_Gallons is new Gallons;
```

Type `Imperial_Gallons` is a derived type. `Gallons` is the *parent* of `Imperial_Gallons`. Derived types are not limited to scalar types. We can derive types from array and record types as well. The domain of the derived type is a copy of the domain of the parent type. But since they are different types, values of one type may not be assigned to objects of the other type. We may use explicit type conversions to convert a value of one type to a value of the other type.

The most common use of derived types is in the creation of class hierarchies associated with object-oriented programming. A detailed discussion of classes and inheritance is not in the scope of this book. We will provide a brief introduction to these topics in Section 2.6. You can find the details of object-oriented programming with Ada in the references given at the beginning of this chapter. We will find another use for derived types in our discussion of low-level programming features at the end of this chapter.

2.3.7 Access types

An access value holds the location of some other value. Access types are often called pointers. There are two kinds of access types, those that designate objects and those that designate subprograms. In this section, we restrict our discussion to access types that designate objects. We'll look at access types that designate subprograms in Chapter 5. When we define an access type, we explicitly state what type of object the access value designates. Here are the definitions of two different access types and a variable of each of those types.

```
type Integer_Ptr  is  access  Integer;
type String_Ptr   is  access  String;

N :  Integer_Ptr;
S :  String_Ptr;
```

N contains the location of an integer object and S contains the location of a string object. The initial value of all access variables is `null`. Null is a nonexistent location used to indicate that the access value is not currently designating an object. Figure 2.3a shows the initial values of N and S.

a) Initial values of N and S

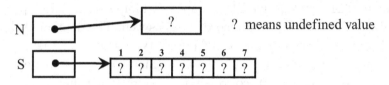

? means undefined value

b) After execution of the assignment statements
```
        N := new Integer;
        S := new String (1..7);
```

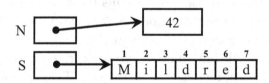

c) After execution of the assignment statements
```
        N.all := 42;
        S.all := "Mildred";
```

Figure 2.3 Access variables

The operations on access values are limited to assignment, equality testing, and dereferencing. As usual in Ada, we cannot mix values of different types so we cannot assign the value of N to S.

We use the allocator **new** to allocate memory for a designated object. Section 4.8 of the ARM provides the details of allocators. The following assignment statements obtain memory for an integer and a string and assign the location of this memory to the access variables.

```
N := new Integer;          -- Obtain memory for an integer
S := new String (1..7);    -- Obtain memory for a string
```

The first assignment statement requests enough memory to store one integer and assigns its location to N. The second statement requests enough memory to store a string of seven characters and assigns that location to S. Note that in order to allocate memory for the unconstrained type String, we had to supply an index constraint. Figure 2.3b illustrates the results of these two assignment statements. The question marks in this figure indicate that the contents in the designated objects are undefined.

We may use the access variables to assign values to these objects. We use the dereferencing operator .all to access the object from the access variables. The following two statements assign values to our designated objects.

```
-- Assign 42 to the memory designated by N
N. all := 42;
-- Assign "Mildred" to the memory designated by S
S. all := "Mildred";
```

The results of these two assignment statements are shown in Figure 2.3c. We may also include a initial value when we use the new allocator to obtain memory. The following two assignment statements combine the steps shown in Figure 2.3b and 2.3c into a single step.

```
-- Obtain memory for an integer with initial value
N := new Integer '(42);

-- Obtain memory for a string with initial value
S := new String '("Mildred");
```

Let's look at a more realistic use of access types. The following declarations define a stack implemented as the linked list illustrated in Figure 2.4.

```
type Node_Type;      -- Incomplete type definition

type Node_Ptr is access Node_Type;

type Node_Type is   -- Complete type definition
   record
      Info : Character;
      Next : Node_Ptr;
   end record;

Top : Node_Ptr;   -- Designates the top node in the stack
```

As the definition of type Node_Ptr uses Node_Type, the scope rules require that Node_Type be declared first. But since the record Node_Type uses Node_

Figure 2.4 A linked list implementation of a stack of characters

`Ptr`, the scope rules require that `Node_Ptr` be declared first. To solve this circularity problem, we make use of an incomplete type declaration of `Node_Type`. We then declare `Node_Ptr`. Finally we give the complete definition for `Node_Type`.

Making use of the allocator and an initial value for the node memory, it takes only one assignment statement to push a new character onto the stack.

```
-- Push 'd' onto the stack
Top := new Node_Type'( Info => 'd',
                       Next => Top );
```

The execution of this assignment statement begins with the evaluation of the expression on the right — memory for a node is allocated, the `Info` component of the node is initialized to `'d'`, and the `Next` component of the node is initialized to designate the current top node of the stack. The location of this new node is then copied into `Top` so it now designates our latest node.

It takes a few more lines to pop a value from our stack.

```
 -- Pop a character from the stack
To_Recyle := Top;           -- Make To_Recyle an alias of Top
Value := Top.all.Info;  -- Copy the info from the top node
Top    := Top.all.Next;  -- Unlink top node from the list
Free (To_Recyle);       -- Deallocate the node's memory
```

Ada does not have a predefined operator for deallocating memory.[5] The procedure `Free` we used is instantiated from a generic procedure in the Ada library. Here is the required instantiation.

```
procedure Free is new Ada.Unchecked_Deallocation
                      ( Object => Node_Type, -- The object type
                        Name   => Node_Ptr ); -- The pointer type
```

Since Ada is strongly typed, we must instantiate a deallocation procedure for every pointer type we use. Unchecked programming requires care. It is the responsibility of the programmer to ensure that the memory they deallocate

---

[5] The Ada standard allows implementations to support garbage collection. Currently, no implementation provides garbage collection.

is not designated by other access variables. To avoid memory leaks, we must be sure to deallocate all memory that is no longer needed.

General access types and aliased objects

The access types we have described allow us to manipulate objects created through execution of the allocator **new**. The memory that an allocator obtains for an object comes from a *storage pool*,[6] an area of memory used to hold dynamically allocated objects. Because they designate objects in a storage pool, the access types we defined and used in the previous section are called **pool-specific access types**.

We may also define access types that can designate objects in places other than storage pools. These types are called **general access types**. We include the word **all** in the type declaration to specify a general access type. For example the two declarations

```
type G_String_Ptr is access all String;

Flower : G_String_Ptr;
```

define the general access type **G_String_Ptr** and the variable **Flower** that designates a string.

Two common uses of general access types are the designation of declared objects and the designation of remote objects. We'll look at remote objects in Chapter 6. In order to designate a declared variable, that variable must be marked as **aliased** as in the following declaration of a string variable:

```
Weed : aliased String := "Dandelion";
```

We use the 'Access attribute to assign the location of the declared variable Weed to the access variable Flower. Then we can access the string variable Weed through the access variable Flower.

```
Flower := Weed'Access;   -- Assign the location of Weed to Flower
Put_Line (Flower.all);   -- Displays Dandelion
Flower.all := "Pissenlit"; -- Change the value of Weed
Put_Line (Weed);          -- Displays Pissenlit
```

Like pool-specific access types, general access types may designate objects in a storage pool. Here is an example.

```
Flower := new String'("Daffodil");
Put_Line (Flower.all);
Free (Flower); -- Free instantiated from Unchecked_Deallocation
```

The use of a general access type rather than a pool-specific access type comes with a potential trap. When using general access types, you must not

---

[6] Many programming languages refer to the storage pool as the *heap*.

attempt to use a procedure instantiated from Unchecked_Deallocation to deallocate the memory of a declared variable.

The Ada compiler automatically associates a standard storage pool with each pool-specific access type. It is possible for us to define our own storage pools and associate different access types with different storage pools. Defining our own storage pools provides more control over the allocation and deallocation of memory of dynamic objects. Defining new storage pools is beyond the scope of this book. See Barnes (2006) or Cohen (1996) for details.

2.4 Blocks and exceptions

Pointers are the source of many errors in programs. In fact, pointers are sometimes prohibited or severely limited in use in certain safety-critical applications. Pointers are frequently used to create and manage collections whose size is not known at compile time. For example, suppose we need a collection of integers whose size is specified by the user at run time. With pointers, after getting the size from the user, we can allocate the necessary memory on the heap. Ada's block structure allows us to dynamically allocate objects on the stack, avoiding the need for pointers in many situations. Here is an example program that uses a block to dynamically allocate memory on the stack for an array.

```ada
with Ada.Text_IO;          use Ada.Text_IO;
with Ada.Integer_Text_IO;  use Ada.Integer_Text_IO;
procedure Block_Example is
   type Int_Array is array (Positive range <>) of Integer;
   Count : Positive;
begin
   Put_Line ("How many numbers are in your data set?");
   Get (Count);

   declare     -- beginning of the block statement
      subtype List_Array is Int_Array (1 .. Count);
      List   : List_Array;
   begin
      Put_Line ("Enter your" & Positive'Image (Count)
                               & " numbers");
      for Index in List_Array'Range loop
         Get (List (Index));
      end loop;
      -- processing of the values in List would go here
   end;     -- of the block statement
end Block_Example;
```

The first thing that happens when procedure `Block_Example` begins its execution is the elaboration of its declarations. **Elaboration** is the run-time processing of declarations. This processing includes allocating memory and providing initial values for objects. In `Block_Example`, the memory for `Count` is allocated on the stack. After elaboration of its declarations, execution continues with the prompting of the user and getting the size from them. Next the block statement is executed. The block statement includes an optional declarative part and a sequence of statements. In our example, the declarative part of our block contains two declarations: the definition of a constrained array subtype whose index constraint was obtained from the user, and an array variable. When these declarations are elaborated, memory for the array is allocated on the stack. We use this dynamically allocated array in the block's sequence of executable statements. When we reach the end of the block. the memory allocated on the stack for the block's variables is released. Blocks give us the advantage of dynamic memory allocation without the dangers of pointers.

We could have used a procedure to accomplish the same dynamic allocation of memory. With this approach, we pass the procedure the size of the desired array. The size parameter is used in the procedure's declarative part to define the same constrained array type and variable we have in our block. When we return control to the caller, the memory for the procedure's local array is deallocated from the stack. A block is sometimes called an inline procedure. Blocks, functions, and procedures dynamically allocate memory during the elaboration of their declarations and deallocate that memory when their execution is complete.

Several times in this chapter we have said that if something goes wrong during the execution of an Ada program, then an exception will be raised. An **exception** is an abnormal condition that requires special processing. We briefly mentioned two exceptions: `Constraint_Error` and `Program_Error`. There are four predefined exceptions.

- **Constraint_Error** is raised during an attempt to assign a value to an object if the value does not satisfy a defined limitation. Limitations include range constraints on scalar types and index constraints on array types. Attempting to dereference a null pointer or dividing by zero also raises this exception.

- **Program_Error** is raised when our program violates a control structure in some way. Reaching the end of a function's sequence of statements without executing a return statement is one situation that raises this exception. Other situations involve tasking and the elaboration of packages.

- **Storage_Error** is raised when our program requires more memory than is available.
- **Tasking_Error** is raised in situations involving problems with task activation or communication.

There are a number of other exceptions defined in the Ada library. For example the library package `Ada.IO_Exceptions` (section A.13 of the ARM) defines eight exceptions related to abnormal conditions with input and output. We may also define and raise our own exceptions.

An **exception handler** is a segment of code that executes when an exception occurs. Exception handlers allow us to recover from abnormal conditions. They may be included in any begin/end construct, including procedures, functions, and block statements. Here is a procedure with three exception handlers — two at the end of a block statement and one at the end of the procedure.

```
subtype Count_Range is Integer range 0 .. 10;

procedure Get_Count (Prompt  : in   String;
                     Count   : out  Count_Range) is
begin
   loop     -- Data validation loop
      Put_Line (Prompt);
      begin
         Ada.Integer_Text_IO.Get (Count);
         exit;
      exception
         when Constraint_Error =>
            Put_Line ("Value must be between 0 and 10");
         when Ada.IO_Exceptions.Data_Error =>
            Put_Line ("Value must be a number");
            Ada.Text_IO.Skip_Line;
      end;
   end loop;
exception
   when Ada.IO_Exceptions.End_Error =>
      Count := 0;
end Get_Count;
```

`Get_Count` is a robust procedure that obtains an integer value from the keyboard. Let's begin by tracing a successful read of an integer. After the prompt is displayed, the procedure gets a valid integer from user, control exits the loop, the procedure is completed and control returned to the caller.

Now let's trace the execution with some exceptions. Suppose after the prompt is displayed, the user enters the number 42. As this value is outside of the domain of `Count`, the Ada run-time system raises `Constraint_Error`.

Control is transferred to the exception handler for `Constraint_Error` at the end of the block. The handler displays an appropriate message. Execution continues with the statement following the block statement — the enclosing loop statement. The prompt is displayed a second time. Suppose this time the user enters the string *hello*. The get procedure, expecting a number, raises the exception `Data_Error`. Control is transferred to the exception handler which displays an appropriate message. When the data is not an integer, `Ada.Integer_Text_IO.Get` does not consume it. So we call `Skip_Line` to skip over the erroneous input. We return to the top of the loop, repeat the prompt and make another attempt to obtain valid data from the user.

Let's see how the remaining exception handler might be invoked. Suppose after the prompt, the user types the control code that signals the end of file. When the get procedure encounters the end of file while attempting to read a number, it raises the exception `End_Error`. There is no handler for this exception associated with the block statement. Control is transferred to the statement following the block statement and the `End_Error` is re-raised. There is an exception handler in the enclosing block (the procedure). This handler assigns zero to the out parameter and control is returned normally to the caller.

In a final example of exception handling, suppose that there is a hardware failure in the keyboard while the user is typing their value and the Ada run-time system raises the exception `Device_Error`. There is no handler for this exception in the block or the procedure. The exception is propagated back to the caller of the procedure.

Section 11 of ARM is devoted to the facilities for dealing with errors and other exceptional situations that arise during program execution.

2.5 Programming in the large

To facilitate the construction of large programs, Ada makes use of library units. An Ada program consists of a main subprogram that uses services provided by library units. A **library unit** is a separately compiled program unit. We have already made use of many predefined library units in our examples. The *with clause* provides access to a library unit. The *use clause* provides direct visibility to the public declarations within a library unit. A library unit is a subprogram (a procedure or function), a package, or a generic unit. The main subprogram is itself a library unit. In the following sections we'll introduce you to the package and to generic units. Generally, we use a compiler and linker to create an executable from a collection of library units. In Chapter 6 we'll show you how to distribute the library units making up a program across a network.

2.5.1 Packages

Information hiding and encapsulation are the cornerstones of programming in the large. Information hiding is what we do in the design process when we hide the decisions that are most likely to change. We hide information in order to protect the other portions of our design from changes to that decision. Information hiding does not mean that the information is not available; it is just kept out of sight when not required. The *module*, a collection of related objects and operations, is the key component of hiding information. Encapsulation is the implementation of information hiding; the programming language features that allow a compiler to enforce information hiding.

The package is Ada's implementation of the module. The package supports abstract data types, encapsulation, separate compilation, and reuse. We write packages in two parts: the package declaration and the package body. The declaration specifies the resources the package can supply to the rest of the program. These resources may include types, subtypes, constants, variables, and subprograms. The package body provides the implementation of the subprograms defined in the package declaration.

Although there are many different ways to define and use packages, we can usually place packages into one of three categories: definition packages, service packages, and data abstraction packages. This classification scheme is neither strict nor inclusive. In the next sections we'll look at an example from each category.

Definition packages

A definition package groups together related constants and types. Such packages are useful when the same types must be used in several different programs or by different programmers working on different parts of one large program. Here is an example of a definition package.

```ada
with Ada.Numerics;
package Common_Units is

    type Degrees is digits 18 range 0.0 .. 360.0;
    type Radians is digits 18 range 0.0 .. 2.0 * Ada.Numerics.Pi;

    type Volts is delta 1.0 / 2.0**12 range -45_000.0 .. 45_000.0
    type Amps  is delta 1.0 / 2.0**16 range -1_000.0 .. 1_000.0;
    type Ohms  is delta 0.125         range 0.0 .. 1.0E8;
```

```
type Light_Years is digits 12 range 0.0 .. 20.0E9;

subtype Percent is Integer range 0 .. 100;
end Common_Units;
```

This package defines six types and one subtype. It uses the value of π from the Ada library definition package **Ada.Numerics**. Since definition packages have no subprograms, there is nothing to implement. In fact, the compiler will give us an error should we try to compile a body for it. Here is a short program that uses our definition package.

```
with Common_Units;  use type Common_Units.Ohms;
with Ada.Text_IO;   use Ada.Text_IO;
procedure Ohms_Law is

   package Ohm_IO  is new Fixed_IO (Common_Units.Ohms);
   package Amp_IO  is new Fixed_IO (Common_Units.Amps);
   package Volt_IO is new Fixed_IO (Common_Units.Volts);

   A  : Common_Units.Amps;
   R1 : Common_Units.Ohms;
   R2 : Common_Units.Ohms;
   V  : Common_Units.Volts;
begin
   Put_Line ("Enter current and two resistances");
   Amp_IO.Get (A);
   Ohm_IO.Get (R1);
   Ohm_IO.Get (R2);
   V := A * (R1 + R2);
   Put ("The voltage drop over the two resistors is ");
   Volt_IO.Put (Item => V,
                Fore => 1,
                Aft  => 2,
                Exp  => 0);
   Put_Line (" volts");
end Ohms_Law;
```

This program also illustrates the *use type clause*. When we declare a type, we define its domain and a set of operations. As type **Ohms** is a fixed point type, the operations include all of the standard arithmetic operators. In order to add two resistance values, we use the plus operator. But since this operator is defined in package **Common_Units**, we must either prefix the plus operator with the package name or include a use clause to access the operator directly. A *use clause* makes all of the resources in the named package available without prefixing. A *use type clause* is more specific — it allows us to use operators[7] of the given type without prefixing.

---

[7] Ada's operators are **and, or, xor, =, /=, <, <=, >, >=, +, − , &, *, /, rem, mod, **, abs,** and **not.**

Service packages

A service package groups together the constants, types, subtypes, and subprograms necessary to provide some particular service. The library package **Ada.Numerics.Elementary_Functions** is a service package that includes 29 mathematical functions such as square root, trigonometric functions, and logarithms for Float values. Here is the declaration of a service package that provides three operations for control over output displayed on a screen.

```ada
package Display_Control is

   procedure Bold_On;
   -- Everything sent to the screen after this procedure
   -- is called will be displayed in bold characters

   procedure Blink_On;
   -- Everything sent to the screen after this procedure
   -- is called will be blinking

   procedure Normal;
   -- Everything sent to the screen after this procedure
   -- is called will be displayed normally

end Display_Control;
```

The implementation of these three operations depends upon the display hardware. Having encapsulated this dependency in a package body allows us to use the operations without knowledge of that hardware. Here is a body for this package with the implementation for a display that supports ANSI escape sequences. It includes one procedure body for each procedure declared in the package specification.

```ada
with Ada.Text_IO;
with Ada.Characters.Latin_1;   -- Characters in the
                               -- ISO 8859-1 character set
package body Display_Control is

-- Assumes that the display accepts and processes American
-- National Standards Institute (ANSI) escape sequences.

   -- Code to start an ANSI control string (the Escape
   -- control character and the left bracket character)
   ANSI_Start : constant String :=
                   Ada.Characters.Latin_1.ESC & '[';

   procedure Bold_On is
   begin -- "ESC[1m" turns on Bold
      Ada.Text_IO.Put (ANSI_Start & "1m");
      -- Send any buffered characters to the display
      Ada.Text_IO.Flush;
```

```
end  Bold_On ;

procedure  Blink_On  is
begin  --  "ESC[5m"  turns  on  Blink
    Ada . Text_IO . Put  ( ANSI_Start  &  " 5m" );
    Ada . Text_IO . Flush ;
end  Blink_On ;

procedure  Normal  is
begin  --  "ESC[0m"  turns  off  all  attributes
    Ada . Text_IO . Put  ( ANSI_Start  &  " 0m" );
    Ada . Text_IO . Flush ;
end  Normal ;

end  Display_Control ;
```

This package body uses resources from two library packages. While not necessary in this package body, bodies may include additional subprograms. These helper subprograms are local to the package body; they may not be called from outside.

Data abstraction packages

We use the data abstraction package to create abstract data types (ADTs). An **abstract data type** consists of a set of data values and associated operations that are specified independent of any particular implementation. The abstract data type is a fundamental concept of Ada (Barnes 2006; Ben-Ari 2009; Dale and McCormick 2007). Our example is an abstract data type that we will make use of in later chapters — the bounded queue. Here is the queue package declaration for a bounded queue whose elements are integers.

```
package  Bounded_Queue_V1  is
--  Version  1,  details  of  the  queue  type  are  not  encapsulated

    subtype  Element_Type  is  Integer ;

    type  Queue_Array  is  array  ( Positive  range  <>)  of  Element_Type ;
    type  Queue_Type  ( Max_Size  :  Positive )  is
        record
            Count  :  Natural   :=  0;    -- Number  of  items
            Front  :  Positive  :=  1;    -- Index  of  first  item
            Rear   :  Positive  :=  Max_Size ;   -- Index  of  last  item
            Items  :  Queue_Array  (1  ..  Max_Size );   -- The  element  array
        end  record ;

    Overflow   :  exception ;
    Underflow  :  exception ;
```

```ada
   procedure Clear (Queue : in out Queue_Type);

   procedure Enqueue (Queue : in out Queue_Type;
                      Item  : in     Element_Type);
   -- Overflow is raised on attempt to Enqueue an element
   --           onto a full queue.  Queue is unchanged.

   procedure Dequeue (Queue : in out Queue_Type;
                      Item  :    out Element_Type);
   -- Underflow is raised on attempt to dequeue an element
   --           from an empty Queue.  Queue remains empty.

   function Full (Queue : in Queue_Type) return Boolean;

   function Empty (Queue : in Queue_Type) return Boolean;
end Bounded_Queue_V1;
```

This package defines a queue type as a record with five components and five queue operations. The initial values assigned to three of the record components ensure that every queue object is initialized to empty when it is elaborated. The package declaration also contains the declaration of two programmer-defined exceptions. The comments with the enqueue and dequeue operations document which of these exceptions they might raise. Here is a very short program that illustrates the use of our abstract queue data type.

```ada
with Bounded_Queue_V1;  use Bounded_Queue_V1;
with Ada.Text_IO;       use Ada.Text_IO;
procedure Bounded_Queue_Example_V1 is
-- Uses the first version of the bounded queue package

   My_Queue : Bounded_Queue_V1.Queue_Type (Max_Size => 100);
   Value    : Integer;

begin
   for Count in 17 .. 52 loop
      Enqueue (Queue => My_Queue, Item => Count);
   end loop;
   Dequeue (Queue => My_Queue, Item => Value);
   Put_Line (Integer'Image (Value));
   Clear (My_Queue);
   Dequeue (Queue => My_Queue, Item => Value);
   Put_Line (Integer'Image (Value));
exception
   when Underflow | Overflow =>
      Put_Line ("An exception was raised");
end Bounded_Queue_Example_V1;
```

The first declaration in this example program defines a bounded queue with a maximum size of 100. After the loop enqueues 36 values, the program dequeues one value and displays it. After clearing the queue, it attempts to dequeue another element which raises an underflow exception that is handled by the exception handler.

Here is the package body with the implementation of the five operations defined in the package declaration.

```ada
package body Bounded_Queue is

   procedure Enqueue (Queue  : in out Queue_Type;
                      Item   : in      Element_Type) is
   begin
      if Queue.Count = Queue.Max_Size then
         raise Overflow;
      else
         Queue.Rear := Queue.Rear rem Queue.Max_Size + 1;
         Queue.Items (Queue.Rear) := Item;
         Queue.Count := Queue.Count + 1;
      end if;
   end Enqueue;

   procedure Dequeue (Queue  : in out Queue_Type;
                      Item   :     out Element_Type) is
   begin
      if Queue.Count = 0 then
         raise Underflow;
      else
         Item := Queue.Items (Queue.Front);
         Queue.Front := Queue.Front rem Queue.Max_Size + 1;
         Queue.Count := Queue.Count - 1;
      end if;
   end Dequeue;

   function Full (Queue : in Queue_Type) return Boolean is
   begin
      return Queue.Count = Queue.Max_Size;
   end Full;

   function Empty (Queue : in Queue_Type) return Boolean is
   begin
      return Queue.Count = 0;
   end Empty;

   procedure Clear (Queue : in out Queue_Type) is
   begin
      Queue.Count := 0;
      Queue.Front := 1;
      Queue.Rear  := Queue.Max_Size;
   end Clear;

end Bounded_Queue;
```

The only new feature in the package body is the use of the raise statement to raise the overflow and underflow exceptions.

2.5.2 Private types

The declaration of the queue record type in our bounded queue package declaration is a form of information hiding. But while the details of the queue type are hidden, they remain accessible to the application using this package. A programmer could manipulate the record components directly rather than call the defined queue operations. Such direct access could leave a queue object in an inconsistent state. And, should we need to modify the definition of the queue type later, we would need to locate and modify all instances of direct access. We need to encapsulate the queue type so that its details are not accessible. We use private types to encapsulate the details of abstract data types. Here is a second version of our queue package declaration in which we use a private type to encapsulate our queue record.

```
package Bounded_Queue_V2 is
-- Version 2, details of the queue type are encapsulated

    subtype Element_Type is Integer;

    type Queue_Type (Max_Size : Positive) is limited private;

    Overflow  : exception;
    Underflow : exception;

    procedure Clear (Queue : in out Queue_Type);

    procedure Enqueue (Queue : in out Queue_Type;
                       Item  : in      Element_Type);
    -- Overflow is raised on attempt to Enqueue an element
    --          onto a full queue.  Queue is unchanged.

    procedure Dequeue (Queue : in out Queue_Type;
                       Item  :     out Element_Type);
    -- Underflow is raised on attempt to dequeue an element
    --          from an empty Queue.  Queue remains empty.

    function Full (Queue : in Queue_Type) return Boolean;

    function Empty (Queue : in Queue_Type) return Boolean;

private

    type Queue_Array is array (Positive range <>) of Element_Type
    type Queue_Type (Max_Size : Positive) is
```

```
   record
      Count : Natural  := 0;       -- Number of items
      Front : Positive := 1;       -- Index of first item
      Rear  : Positive := Max_Size;  -- Index of last item
      Items : Queue_Array (1 .. Max_Size);  -- The element array
   end record;
```

end Bounded_Queue_V2;

This package declaration is divided into two portions by the word **private** found a little more than three quarters of the way down. Everything defined above this word is public and may be accessed by any unit that withs this package. Definitions below **private** are accessible only by the package body. The public definition of type Queue_Type is not a record. It is a limited private type. The operations available for limited private types are limited to those defined in the package. An application may use the type Queue_Type and a value for Max_Size to declare queue variables. But that application is limited to the five queue operations defined in the package. Program Bounded_Queue_Example did not directly access the queue record components. So it will work fine with the second version of our queue.

For each private type defined in the public portion of our package declaration we must have a complete definition in the private portion.[8] In our queue package, the complete definition is the record we used in our first version. As the package body has full access to the details defined in the private portion, we need not make any changes to our original package body to receive the benefits of encapsulation.

2.5.3 Generic packages

The abstract queue data types we developed in the previous sections were restricted to queues whose components were integers. By defining Element_Type as a synonym for Integer, we made it relatively easy to create new queue packages whose components are other types. However, Ada provides a mechanism that can make this substitution for us — the generic package. Earlier, we used generic packages to do input and output with programmer-defined types. In each use we instantiated a package from the generic package and supplied the type. We can write our own generic packages and generic subprograms. Here is a generic queue package declaration.

---

[8] The full information in the private part allows us to compile program units that use the package before its body is even written. Of course, we must complete the package body before we can link our program.

```ada
generic
    type Element_Type is private;
package Bounded_Queue is
-- Final version, encapsulated generic queue

    type Queue_Type (Max_Size : Positive) is limited private;

    Overflow  : exception;
    Underflow : exception;

    procedure Clear (Queue : in out Queue_Type);

    procedure Enqueue (Queue : in out Queue_Type;
                       Item  : in      Element_Type);
    -- Overflow is raised on attempt to Enqueue an element onto
    --          a full queue.  Queue is unchanged.

    procedure Dequeue (Queue : in out Queue_Type;
                       Item  :     out Element_Type);
    -- Underflow is raised on attempt to dequeue an element from
    --          an empty Queue.  Queue remains empty.

    function Full (Queue : in Queue_Type) return Boolean;

    function Empty (Queue : in Queue_Type) return Boolean;

private

    type Queue_Array is array (Positive range <>) of Element_Type;
    type Queue_Type (Max_Size : Positive) is
        record
            Count : Natural  := 0;          -- Number of items
            Front : Positive := 1;          -- Index of first item
            Rear  : Positive := Max_Size;   -- Index of last item
            Items : Queue_Array (1 .. Max_Size);   -- The element arr.
        end record;

end Bounded_Queue;
```

A generic package declaration begins with the reserved word **generic**, followed by zero or more generic formal parameters, followed by a normal package declaration. We have removed the subtype **Element_Type** from the previous version and added it as a generic formal parameter.

The reserved word **private** is used for two different purposes in this package. It is used in the definition of the generic formal parameter **Element_Type** to specify that the actual formal parameter may be any type that is not limited. Since the application may use nearly any type, the writer of the package body is restricted to operations that are available for all non-limited types: assignment and equality testing. Since our original queue package body used only assignment with its queue components, no changes are necessary. The second use of private in our generic package declaration is in the definition of Queue_Type. As before, this type restricts the operations that can be used in an application to those defined in the package. In both situations, private restricts access to details. In a generic formal parameter definition, it restricts the writer of the package body. In a type definition, it restricts the application using the type. When we instantiate a queue package from this generic package, we supply an actual parameter that is the type of the desired queue component. Here is our earlier queue application with the addition of the instantiation.

```
with Bounded_Queue;
with Ada.Text_IO;    use Ada.Text_IO;
procedure Bounded_Queue_Example is

    package Int_Queue is new Bounded_Queue
                             (Element_Type => Integer);
    use Int_Queue;

    My_Queue : Int_Queue.Queue_Type (Max_Size => 100);
    Value    : Integer;

begin
    for Count in 17 .. 52 loop
        Enqueue (Queue => My_Queue, Item => Count);
    end loop;
    Dequeue (Queue => My_Queue, Item => Value);
    Put_Line (Integer'Image (Value));
    Clear (My_Queue);
    Dequeue (Queue => My_Queue, Item => Value);
    Put_Line (Integer'Image (Value));
exception
    when Underflow | Overflow =>
        Put_Line ("An exception was raised");
end Bounded_Queue_Example;
```

Ada's generic facilities are a powerful tool for creating safe reusable code. We have covered a very small part of these facilities. You can find additional details in section 12 of the ARM and in the references mentioned at the beginning of this chapter.

2.5.4 Child packages

We end our discussion of packages with a brief discussion of child packages. Child packages provide a hierarchical structure to organize modules. Without explaining the concept of child packages, we have been making use of them since the beginning of this chapter. All standard packages are organized under three parent packages: `Ada`, `Interfaces`, and `System`. The package named `Ada` serves as the parent of most other standard library packages. Resources for combining Ada code with code written in other programming languages are found in the package `Interfaces` and its children. Finally, package `System` and its children provide the definitions of characteristics of the particular environment in which the program runs.

We use dot notation to identity a particular package in the hierarchy. For example, the standard package `Elementary_Functions` is a child of package `Numerics` which is a child of package `Ada`. We use the syntax `Ada.Numerics.Elementary_Functions` to name this package.

The most common use of child packages in applications is in the creation of class hierarchies associated with object-oriented programming. A class may be defined in Ada by a package that contains a tagged type and a set of operations. Subclasses, which inherit the methods and member data of their parent class, are usually defined in child packages. We'll take a brief look at this topic next.

2.6 Object-oriented programming

Object-oriented (OO) is a software development paradigm based on objects and their interactions. A full explanation of object-oriented programming in Ada is beyond the scope of this book. In this section we will cover those OO features used in later chapters. Among the fundamental concepts of OO are:

Object an entity that has state, behavior, and identity. An object is an instance of a class.

Class represents a set of objects that share common characteristics (attributes) and behaviors (methods). In Ada, a class is implemented as a tagged record type (containing the attributes) and a set of subprograms encapsulated within a package.

Attribute a named property of a class that describes a value held by each object of the class.

Method an operation on an object. In Ada, methods are procedures and functions associated with classes.

Association a physical or conceptual connection between classes. The statement "students enroll in courses" defines the association *enroll* between the classes *student* and *course*.

Generalization a special association between one class, called the *superclass*, and one or more *subclasses* derived from the superclass. The superclass holds common attributes and methods. Each subclass *inherits* the attributes and methods of its superclass. The subclasses usually have additional attributes and/or methods that make them more specialized than the superclass. Generalization is often called the "is a" association since each instance of a subclass is also an instance of the superclass.

There are three majors uses of generalization. First, it provides a method to structure a description of objects. The taxonomy developed by biologists is a prime example of this use. Second, generalization provides the support for polymorphism (see below) — our major use of generalization in this book. The third, and least important, use of generalization is to provide a means for reusing code.

Polymorphism is the property that an operation may behave differently on different classes. You can call an operation defined for the superclass and have that call redirected to the code for the correct subclass.

Abstract class a class that can have no direct instances. We inherit from them to produce *concrete* classes from which we can create instances. Abstract classes are used to represent abstract concepts that by themselves are incomplete. The incomplete features of the abstract class may be shared by a group of subclasses which add different variations of the missing pieces.

Let's look at an example. The three most common commercial oven types used in restaurants are convection, conveyor, and microwave. A convection oven is a conventional oven that incorporates a fan to circulate the air around the food being cooked. The operator can adjust the temperature in a range from about 200 to 550 degrees Fahrenheit. You may have seen conveyor ovens in your favorite sandwich or pizza place. The food is placed on a conveyor belt which moves it through the oven. The operator of a conveyor oven can adjust both the temperature and the amount of time that the food remains in the oven. We do not set a microwave oven's temperature. However, we can set the power of the microwave generator.

Figure 2.5 is a UML class diagram for these three commercial ovens. We have used an abstract class, `Oven`, to hold the two attributes (`On` and `Fuel`) and four operations (`Create`, `Turn_On`, `Turn_Off`, and `Fueled_By`) common to all three of our oven types. The three concrete subclasses `Convection`, `Conveyor`, and `Microwave` extend the abstract superclass.

We encapsulate the resources (types and operations) of each of the classes in Figure 2.5 in a package. Each subclass is encapsulated in a child package

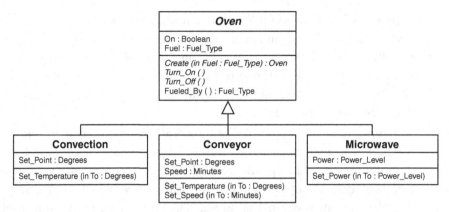

Figure 2.5 Class diagram for commercial ovens

of the package used to encapsulate its superclass. The abstract class Oven is the root of our hierarchy. Here is the specification of the package that implements it.

```
package Ovens is

    type Oven_Type is abstract tagged private;
    type Oven_Ptr  is access Oven_Type'Class;

    type Fuel_Type is (Electric, Natural_Gas, Propane);

    function Create (Fuel : in Fuel_Type) return Oven_Type
              is abstract;
    procedure Turn_On   (Oven : in out Oven_Type) is abstract;
    procedure Turn_Off  (Oven : in out Oven_Type) is abstract;
    function  Fueled_By (Oven : in Oven_Type) return Fuel_Type;

private
    type Oven_Type is abstract tagged
        record
            On   : Boolean := False;
            Fuel : Fuel_Type;
        end record;
end Ovens;
```

Type Oven_Type defines our abstract class. It should come as no surprise that the reserved word *abstract* specifies that this type may not be used in the declaration of objects (variables and constants). The reserved word *tagged* indicates that this type may be extended. In most object-oriented languages, classes may be extended unless the programmer includes something to specifically prohibit inheritance. Ada takes a different approach. The default is *no* inheritance. We must include *tagged* in a type definition in order to allow inheritance. The reserved word *private* in our type definition is used to encapsulate the data as described in Section 2.5.2.

Following the declaration of our class type is a declaration of a pointer type. The definition of type `Oven_Ptr` uses the attribute `'Class`. The target type, `Oven_Type'Class`, in this context allows the pointers to designate any object in the class hierarchy rooted at `Oven_Type`. A variable of type `Oven_Ptr` can at different times designate a convection oven, a conveyor oven, and a microwave oven.

The type `Fuel_Type` is defined next. We use this type to define an attribute for the oven class that indicates the type of fuel used by a particular oven.

The next group of declarations define the four methods available for our oven class. The first three operations are labeled as *abstract*. The implementation of abstract subprograms is done in each of the three subclasses that inherit from the oven class. The `Fueled_By` method is not abstract. We must implement this function in `Ovens'` package body. We'll show you this package body shortly.

Finally, the private section of our oven class specification contains the data (attributes) that we determined was common for all of our concrete subclasses. A record with the descriptors *abstract* and *tagged* holds the private data.

Here is the complete body for our abstract class oven. The only code we need to write for the oven class is our one concrete operation.

```
package body Ovens is
   function Fueled_By (Oven : in Oven_Type) return Fuel_Type is
   begin
      return Oven.Fuel;
   end Fueled_By;
end Ovens;
```

Let's look next at the specification of one of our oven subclasses. Here is the specification of the child package that defines the conveyor oven subclass.

```
package Ovens.Conveyor is

   type Degrees is range 200 .. 500;
   type Minutes is range 1 .. 10;

   type Conveyor_Oven is new Oven_Type with private;

   overriding function Create (Fuel : in Fuel_Type)
                        return Conveyor_Oven;
   overriding procedure Turn_On  (Oven : in out Conveyor_Oven);
   overriding procedure Turn_Off (Oven : in out Conveyor_Oven);

   procedure Set_Temperature (Oven : in out Conveyor_Oven;
                              To   : in      Degrees);
```

```
   procedure Set_Speed (Oven : in out Conveyor_Oven;
                         To   : in      Minutes );
private
   type Conveyor_Oven is new Oven_Type with
      record
         Set_Point : Degrees;
         Speed     : Minutes;
      end record;
end Ovens.Conveyor;
```

After defining the types **Degrees** and **Minutes** for conveyor oven attributes, we define the conveyor oven class type **Conveyor_Oven** as an extension of the superclass **Oven_Type**. **Conveyor_Oven** inherits all of the attributes and operations of its superclass. The **with private** clause indicates that this class has additional attributes that are defined in the private section.

The next three declarations define conveyor oven class operations that override (replace) the operations defined in its superclass. We then define two additional operations for conveyor ovens: **Set_Temperature** and **Set_Speed**.

Finally, the private section of this package specification defines the attributes for a conveyor oven. We inherit the two attributes **On** and **Fuel** from the superclass and add the attributes **Set_Point** and **Speed**.

The body of child package **Conveyor** contains the subprogram bodies that implement the three overridden operations and the two new operations. You can see these bodies on our web site. The other two subclasses, **Convection_Oven** and **Microwave_Oven** are implemented as child packages similar to that for **Conveyor_Oven**. These packages are also available on our web site.

Now that we can implement classes with inheritance, let's look at how we use them. All of the following code fragments may be found in the program **Ovens_Demo** on our web site. Let's start with some simple variable declarations for three different ovens.

```
Main_Oven  : Convection_Oven := Create (Electric);
Pizza_Oven : Conveyor_Oven   := Create (Natural_Gas);
Quick_Oven : Microwave_Oven  := Create (Electric);
```

In each declaration, we called the function **Create** to construct the object. With tagged types we can use either of two different syntaxes to invoke an object's operation. We may use the standard subprogram call syntax. Here, for example, is a standard call to the function **Fueled_By** which returns the type of fuel that heats our main oven.

```
-- Function call syntax
The_Fuel := Fueled_By (Main_Oven);
```

The second syntax for invoking an object's method is called the distinguished receiver syntax. This syntax is commonly referred to as *object dot method* syntax. To use this approach, the first parameter of the functions and procedures defined for a class must be an instance of the class. Here is the same function call with object dot method syntax.

```
-- Distinguished receiver (object dot method) syntax
The_Fuel := Main_Oven.Fueled_By;
```

Using references (pointers) to objects rather than simple object variables provides the flexibility required for many object-oriented programming patterns. Here is a simple example to illustrate the creation and use of a dynamically created oven object.

```
Portable_Oven : Oven_Ptr;   -- A pointer to any oven type

-- Create a new oven
Portable_Oven := new Microwave_Oven '( Create ( Electric ));

-- Function call syntax
The_Fuel := Fueled_By (Oven => Portable_Oven.all );
-- Object dot method syntax
The_Fuel := Portable_Oven.all.Fueled_By;
```

We used the option of giving an initial value to the newly created oven object. You may wish to review the simpler examples of the allocation operator **new** in Section 2.3.7.

Finally, let's look at an example that demonstrates how we can use polymorphism to solve a simple problem. We have a collection of ovens that we would like to turn on when our cooks arrive for work. Such a collection could be stored in an array or linked list. Here are the declarations for an array-based list of five ovens.

```
type Oven_Array is array (1 .. 5) of Oven_Ptr;
Oven_List : Oven_Array;
```

As our list is heterogeneous, the array elements are pointers to ovens rather than the ovens themselves. Here is the code to create the five ovens, turn them all on, and then turn them all off.

```
Oven_List (1) := new Convection_Oven '( Create ( Natural_Gas ));
Oven_List (2) := new Convection_Oven '( Create ( Electric ));
Oven_List (3) := new Microwave_Oven '( Create ( Electric ));
Oven_List (4) := new Conveyor_Oven '( Create ( Electric ));
Oven_List (5) := new Conveyor_Oven '( Create ( Propane ));

for Index in Oven_List 'Range loop
    -- Procedure call syntax
    Ovens.Turn_On (Oven => Oven_List (Index).all );
```

```
end loop;

for Index in reverse Oven_List 'Range loop
    -- Object dot method syntax
    Oven_List (Index). all. Turn_Off;
end loop;
```

The loop in which we turn on all of the ovens uses standard procedure call syntax. Notice that the Turn_On procedure called is the one defined in our abstract class Ovens. When the call is made, we have no idea of what kind of oven our pointer is designating. The call to the abstract procedure is dispatched at run time to the appropriate method for the referenced oven. While the polymorphism is not explicit in the object dot method syntax used to turn all five ovens off, the same dynamic dispatching to the appropriate oven method is done.

While we will not be using any sophisticated object-oriented patterns in the remainder of this book, we will make use of type extension (inheritance) and polymorphism in later chapters. See the references at the beginning of this chapter for more information on Ada's rich set of object-oriented features.

2.7 Low-level programming

A key characteristic of embedded software is the use of specialized input and output (I/O) devices. Our computers are electrical devices. Yet the environments with which embedded systems interact are usually not electrical. There are other important forms of energy and forces that our systems must sense and control. A **transducer** is a device that converts one form of energy into another form. A photovoltaic cell converts light energy into electrical energy and a piezoelectric buzzer converts electrical energy into sound energy. Embedded systems obtain their input through **sensors** — transducers that transform some physical stimulus (light, temperature, pressure, magnetism, acceleration, etc.) into an electrical signal. The output of an embedded system is often generated by an **actuator** — transducers that transform an electrical signal into some other form (light, sound, motion, heat, etc.).

Electrical signals can be classified as either analog or digital. Most sensors provide an analog electrical signal. A thermocouple produces a voltage that is proportional to its temperature. An analog signal, like most everything in nature, is continuous; there are no jumps or singularities over time. The temperature of a batch of mango chutney goes through an infinite number of temperatures as we heat it from room temperature to boiling. A digital signal is quantized; it has a finite number of possible states. The light given off by a lamp with a three-way bulb has only four possible values. You might think of an analog value as a real number and a digital value as an integer. The former can take on any value while the latter is restricted to whole numbers. As our computers work with digital data, we must convert the analog input signals to digital values and the digital output signals to analog values. Digital signal processing is an important engineering discipline that is beyond the scope of this book. Our task is to describe how to implement the algorithms developed by control engineers.

The code that interacts directly with an I/O device is called a **device driver**. A device driver provides an abstraction between the gate or register level logic of the device hardware and the application that uses that device. The temperature control algorithm for our pressure cooker example in Chapter 1 included the step "Input the temperature value from the ADC ...." The loop example on page 28 implements this algorithm. It calls a read procedure in package ADC to obtain the temperature. Package ADC is a device driver; it has code to access the registers of the analog to digital converter and return a number that our temperature control application can use. In the next sections we'll look at some features Ada provides for accessing device registers and writing device drivers.

2.7.1 Representations

The driving force of the evolution from machine instructions to assembly languages to high-level languages is a desire to abstract away the details of the machine on which our program executes. Today we concentrate on modeling the problem domain rather than manipulating computer hardware. When we define a data type, the compiler decides how values of that type will be represented as sequences of bits that we can manipulate. While such abstraction is extremely useful for the majority of projects, writing device drivers requires some knowledge of how data is represented. You have probably studied the representations of some of the more common types. Today, most signed integer values are represented with two's complement. One's complement and sign and magnitude are less commonly used representations for signed integers. The IEEE 754 standard for floating point numbers defines five basic representations. You are probably familiar with the two commonly called single and double precision.

Ada's enumeration values are stored by their position in the list of enumeration literals that defines the type. Given the type definition

type Pixel_Color **is** (Red, Green, Blue, Cyan,
                            Magenta, Yellow, Black, White);

Red is represented as 000_2, Green as 001_2, Blue as 010_2, Cyan as 011_2, Magenta as 100_2, Yellow as 101_2, Black as 110_2 and White as 111_2.[9]

We can override this default representation scheme and specify our own bit pattern for each value. Let's look at an example where defining a different representation scheme makes sense. Suppose we are writing the software embedded within a digital alarm clock. The user may set up to five different alarms. Each alarm may be assigned to a particular day of the week, all five weekdays, both weekend days, or all seven days of the week. When setting an alarm, the clock displays the days of the week for which that alarm is active. The day display is controlled by an 8-bit register. Setting a bit to one turns on the appropriate day light and setting it to zero turns it off. Setting multiple bits turns on multiple lights.

Figure 2.6 shows the association between register bits and lights. The most significant bit of the display register is not connected to anything. To turn on the weekend lights, we need to set bits 0 and 6. To turn on all five weekday lights, we need to set bits 1 through 5. Your first thought might be to model this register as an integer with a range from 1 to 127. However, this representation allows for illegal displays. For example, storing 5 in the display register illuminates both Sunday and Tuesday, an illegal combination.

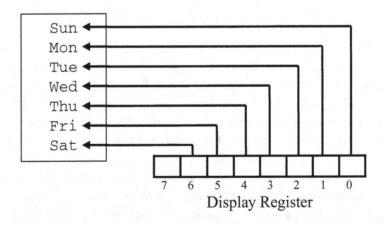

Figure 2.6 Association between register bits and enunciation lights

There are ten legal combinations of lights. By enumerating these possibilities, we limit the possible values that can be assigned to the display register.

---

[9] The subscript 2 indicates base-2 (binary) numbers.

Here is the specification of a package to handle the clock display. We have included only the portions necessary for our day enunciation.

package Clock_Display **is**

    type Day_Type **is** (Sun, Mon, Tue, Wed, Thu, Fri,
                        Weekdays, Sat, Weekend, Everyday);

    procedure Display_Days (Days : **in** Day_Type);

    -- A real clock display package would include
    -- additional display procedures

private
    for Day_Type **use** (Sun   => 2#00000001#,
                     Mon   => 2#00000010#,
                     Tue   => 2#00000100#,
                     Wed   => 2#00001000#,
                     Thu   => 2#00010000#,
                     Fri   => 2#00100000#,
                     Weekdays => 2#00111110#,
                     Sat   => 2#01000000#,
                     Weekend => 2#01000001#,
                     Everyday => 2#01111111#);
    for Day_Type'Size **use** 8;
end Clock_Display;

The enumeration type **Day_Type** defines our ten possible display values. The order of the literals in this enumeration type definition may not seem logical. We'll explain that shortly. Procedure **Display_Days** takes one of these ten values and illuminates the appropriate light(s).

The private portion of this package contains an **enumeration representation clause**. Enumeration representation clauses allow us to specify the binary representation of each value in the domain of an enumeration type. In our example, we assign the numeric value that represents each of the ten enumeration values. We have written these numbers as base-2 literals rather than normal decimal literals. Using base 2 provides a clearer association between the value and the register bits. We may use any base from 2 to 16 for a numeric literal. The following three lines are equivalent.

                         Weekdays => 2#00111110#,   *-- base 2*
                         Weekdays => 62,   *-- base 10*
                         Weekdays => 16#3E#,   *-- base 16*

The order of the literals defining the enumeration type are constrained; their numeric values must be in ascending order. This constraint explains why we did not list **Sat** immediately after **Fri** in the definition of our enumeration type. Saturday's value, 1000000_2, is greater than the value 0111110_2 required for all weekdays. So `Sat` must follow `Weekdays` in the definition of `Day_Type`.

The values we assign to the different enumeration literals have no effect on the normal operations available with enumeration types. The relational operators are still based on the order of the literals in the type definition. The attributes 'First, 'Last, 'Image, 'Succ, and 'Pred also function as defined earlier in this chapter.

While we did not discuss them earlier, the attributes 'Pos and 'Val also operate the same whether or not we use enumeration representation clauses. These attributes provide a mapping between enumeration values and position numbers. Both require arguments.

'Pos	Returns the position number of the given value
'Val	Returns the value at the given position number

In our example, `Day_Type'Pos(Tue)` returns 2 and `Day_Type'Pos(Everyday)` returns 9. `Day_Type'Val(3)` returns `Wed` and `Day_Type'Val(0)` returns `Sun`.

In addition to specifying the values that represent each of our enumeration literals, we can specify the amount of storage the compiler will allocate for objects of a type. The final line in the private portion of the package is an **attribute definition clause**. Attribute definition clauses allow us to control certain implementation-dependent characteristics (attributes) of objects and types. The 'Size clause specifies that objects of type `Day_Type` should occupy *no less* than 8 bits, the size of our register. If the size specified is inadequate for the values, the compiler will reject the program. We need at least 7 bits to support our largest value, 1111111_2.

Memory mapped I/O

Now let's look at the body of package `Clock_Display`. Here we need to declare the actual register object. Normally we allow the compiler to determine where in memory an object is stored. I/O device registers are located at specific locations. Our program must specify those locations to the compiler. Accomplishing this task requires a knowledge of our embedded system's organization. There are two general ways to organize input and output devices. With **memory mapped I/O**, the device registers are treated exactly the same as other memory locations — the same address bus is used for both device registers and memory. The PowerPC and ARM processors are examples of processors that use memory mapped I/O.

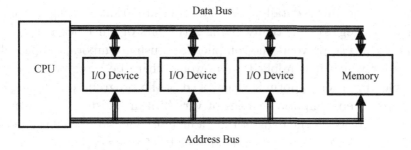

Figure 2.7 Memory mapped input/output

Figure 2.7 illustrates a memory mapped organization. We can access the device registers just as we would for any variable. We just need to tell the compiler the actual addresses of the registers. Here is the body for package Clock_Display as it could be written for a memory mapped I/O system.

```
with System.Storage_Elements;   use System.Storage_Elements;
package body Clock_Display is
-- Implementation for a memory mapped I/O system

    Day_Register : Day_Type;
    for Day_Register'Address use To_Address (16#600080FA#);
    for Day_Register'Size use 8;
    pragma Volatile (Day_Register);

    procedure Display_Days (Days : in Day_Type) is
    begin
        Day_Register := Days;
    end Display_Days;

end Clock_Display;
```

This package body encapsulates the variable Day_Register. On this particular system, the day register is located at address $600080FA_{16}$. Type Address is a private type defined in package System. We use the To_Address function found in the child package Storage_Elements to convert an integer into an address. We use the attribute definition clause, 'Address, to specify the actual address of the variable used for the day register. You can find the details on addresses and the conversion we used in sections 13.7 and 13.7.1 of the ARM. We have also used the attribute definition clause 'Size to specify the *exact* amount of storage used for our register. Used with a type, this attribute specifies the minimum storage. Used with an object, it specifies the exact amount of storage. In either use, the compiler will give an error if the size constraint cannot be met. See section 13.3 of the ARM for the details on the 'Size attribute.

There is one more detail necessary to ensure that writing a value to variable `Day_Register` actually changes the bits of our clock register. The pragma `Volatile` prevents the compiler from using temporary copies of the variable for which it is applied. Why would there be a temporary copy of a variable? In order to optimize the speed of the program, optimizing compilers often keep temporary copies of variables in registers. It is generally much faster to access the register than a memory location. It is even possible that since we never read the value of variable `Day_Register`, the compiler sees it as an unused variable and optimizes it away completely. Pragma `Volatile` ensures that the compiler does not optimize this variable — all values written to it go directly to memory.

Now that we have set the characteristics of global package variable `Day_Register`, the body of procedure `Display` is very simple. We just assign the desired value to `Day_Register` to illuminate the desired lights on the clock face.

Port mapped I/O

The second approach for organizing input and output uses two different address buses. One is used for accessing memory and the other for accessing input/output devices. This method is called **port I/O** or **port mapped I/O**. The x86 architecture introduced by Intel uses port mapped I/O. Figure 2.8 illustrates the organization of a port mapped I/O system. We must use special machine instructions to access the registers of a port mapped I/O device. For example, the x86 instruction set includes the instruction `IN` for transferring data from a device register to a processor register and `OUT` for transferring data the opposite direction. We can't use the approach of declaring a variable and using an assignment statement to set it as we did with memory mapped I/O. To use the `IN` and `OUT` instructions, we need to write some assembly language code. We will show how to do that in Section 2.7.4.

2.7.2 A device driver for an analog to digital converter

Our day display register can be represented as a simple discrete value. Most input/output devices have more complex registers. Frequently, a register is divided into a number of different fields, each of which uses a few bits of the register. Let's look at an example. The analog to digital converter (ADC) that we introduced in the pressure cooker example in Chapter 1 is a common input device for embedded systems. The ADC converts an analog voltage into a digital number. Here is a package specification for a fictitious ADC.

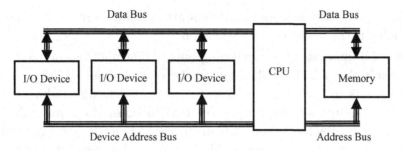

Figure 2.8 Port mapped input/output

```
with  Common_Units;
package ADC is
-- Specification of a make-believe analog to digital converter

    type     Channel_Number  is range 0 .. 31;
    subtype  Input_Volts      is Common_Units.Volts range 0.0 .. 5.0;
    type     Gain_Choice      is (One, Two, Four);

    Over_Range : exception;

    procedure Read (Channel : in   Channel_Number;
                    Gain    : in   Gain_Choice;
                    Value   : out  Input_Volts);
    -- Returns the voltage on the given channel
    -- Potentially blocking (executes a delay statement)
    -- Raises Over_Range if the amplified voltage exceeds 5 volts

private
    for  Channel_Number'Size use 5;
    for  Gain_Choice use (One => 2#001#, Two => 2#010#,
                          Four => 2#100#);
    for  Gain_Choice'Size use 3;
end ADC;
```

The **Read** procedure returns the value of the voltage on one of 32 possible
analog inputs (channels). Our ADC also has the ability to amplify the input
voltage. The amplifier gain may be set to one (no amplification), two, or
four. Our ADC can handle a voltage range, after amplification, of 0.0 to 5.0
volts. The procedure raises the exception **Over_Range** when the amplified
voltage exceeds 5.0 volts. We'll discuss the representation clauses in the
private portion of our package specification once we have gone through the
hardware details.

Our fictitious ADC has two 16-bit registers: a control and status register
and a data register. The control and status register allows us to set up

a voltage conversion and monitor the status of that conversion. The data register holds the result of the conversion.

Figure 2.9 illustrates the three components that make up our ADC. The analog multiplexer (MUX) allows us to choose one of our 32 different channels. Five bits in the control and status register determine which channel is used. The amplifier (Amp) may be used to boost the input voltage by one of three gain factors. Three bits in the control and status register determine the amount of amplification. The output of the amplifier goes into the converter which does the actual conversion. An analog voltage between 0.0 and 5.0 volts is converted into an integer that ranges from 0 to 4095. This conversion takes some time. As is common in many ADCs, our fictitious converter requires more time to convert higher voltages. In the worst case (5 volts) our converter takes 10 milliseconds. There are four bits that control the converter component.

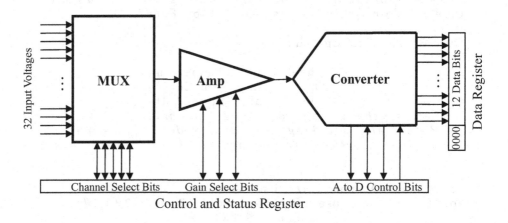

Figure 2.9 Example digital to analog converter

The double-ended arrows connected to the control and status register in Figure 2.9 indicate read/write bits. We can write a value to a read/write bit and then, later, read it back to see what we originally wrote. Single-ended arrows into a register indicate read-only bits. Writing to a read-only bit is not illegal, but has no effect on the bit. Single-ended arrows out of a register indicate write-only bits. The result of reading such a bit is undefined. If you need to know what values you wrote to write-only bits, you should keep a copy of the register in a regular variable. This copy is commonly called a **shadow register**.

Bit	Name	Meaning
0	Start	Set to 1 to start a conversion (Write only)
1	Done	0 = conversion not finished (device is busy) 1 = conversion finished (Read only)
2	Interrupt Enable	Set to 0 to disable interrupt when conversion is complete Set to 1 to enable interrupt when conversion is complete (Read/Write)
3	Overflow	0 = voltage is in range 1 = voltage range exceeded (Read only)
8–10	Gain	001 = gain of 1 010 = gain of 2 100 = gain of 4 (Read/Write)
11–15	Channel	Channels are numbered 0 to 31 (Read/Write)

Table 2.2 *The layout of the control status register*

Table 2.2, taken from the hardware manual for the ADC, specifies how the 16-bit control and status register is structured. Bit 0 is the least significant bit in this register. Bits 4 through 7 are not used.

Now you can see the origins of the size clauses in the private portion of the ADC package specification. The sizes come directly from the number of bits allocated to the corresponding field in the register. We elected to use an enumeration type for the gain rather than an integer type to better match the three distinct gains available in our hardware. An integer type with a range from 1 to 4 would include the illegal value 3. The enumeration representations come from the gain control bits defined by the hardware of our ADC.

Record representation clauses

How do we read or write individual bits in our control and status register? You may recall using the logical **and**, **or**, and **xor** operators with bit masks in your assembly language, C, C++, or Java programs to clear, set, and toggle individual bits. As we mentioned earlier in this chapter, these operators are also available for Ada's unsigned (modular) integer types. Programming with bit masks is tedious and error-prone. Ada provides a higher-level abstraction for bit manipulation — the record with a representational clause.

A record is a collection of heterogeneous components. We access the individual components by name. A **record representational clause** allows us to associate component names with bit positions. Here are the declarations for a record type that matches the hardware definitions of our control and status register.

```
type CSR_Rec is   -- Type for the control and status register
   record
        Start       : Boolean ;
        Done        : Boolean ;
        Int_Enable  : Boolean ;
        Overflow    : Boolean ;
        Gain        : Gain_Choice ;
        Channel     : Channel_Number ;
   end record ;

for CSR_Rec use   -- First of two equivalent versions
   record
        Start       at 0 range 0 .. 0;
        Done        at 0 range 1 .. 1;
        Int_Enable  at 0 range 2 .. 2;
        Overflow    at 0 range 3 .. 3;
        Gain        at 0 range 8 .. 10;
        Channel     at 0 range 11 .. 15;
   end record ;

for CSR_Rec'Size use 16;
for CSR_Rec'Bit_Order use System.Low_Order_First ;
```

We used type Boolean for the single-bit fields in the register. Boolean is an enumeration type defined in package Standard with values False and True (section A.1 of the ARM). The default representations of these two enumeration values are their positions, 0 and 1.

Following the definition of our record is a record representation clause. This clause allows us to map the record's component names to individual bits. The ranges in this clause come directly from the register description given for the hardware.

The **at** 0 portion of the record representation clause needs further explanation. But first, we need to define some terms. Most machine instructions work on small values called **machine scalars**. Bytes, words, and long words are all examples of machine scalars. The **storage unit** of a particular system is the smallest addressable unit of memory. The constant System.Storage_Unit (section 13.7 of the ARM) is the number of bits in the storage unit on our system. On typical architectures, the storage unit is the 8-bit byte. Larger machine scalars are composed of several storage units. For example, the word on a PowerPC is made up of 4 bytes.

The **at** part of the record representation allows us to specify the location of a record component's bits in two different ways. We can simply use **at** 0 and give the offsets from the beginning of the record of the first and last bit of the component. That is the approach we took in the representation clause for **CSR_Rec**. We specified that the **Gain** field occupy bits 8 through 10 of the record. Alternatively, we can specify the location of a bit using a combination of storage unit offset and bit offset. With this approach, we specify that the **Gain** field occupy bits 0 through 2 of the second storage unit of our 16-bit register. We use the **at** part to specify the storage unit offset. The first storage unit is offset 0 and the second is offset 1. The following record representation clause uses this second approach to describe the bit layout of our control and status register.

```
--  This  record  representation  is
--  equivalent  to  our  first  version
for  CSR_Rec  use
    record
        Start          at  0  range  0  ..  0;
        Done           at  0  range  1  ..  1;
        Int_Enable     at  0  range  2  ..  2;
        Overflow       at  0  range  3  ..  3;
        Gain           at  1  range  0  ..  2;  --  Bits  8  to  15  in
        Channel        at  1  range  3  ..  7;  --  the  16  bit  register
    end  record;
```

This record representation is equivalent to our first version. We recommend that you use the approach that more closely matches the description in your device's hardware specification.

Following the first version of our record representation clause is an attribute definition clause specifying that the record objects should use no less than 16 bits. Should this value conflict with our record representation clause, the program will not compile. A second attribute definition clause specifies the order of bit numbers in the record. In our example, we specified that the low order bit come first, a bit numbering scheme sometimes called little-endian. This endian choice matches the hardware specification that bit 0 is the least significant bit in the register.

Now that we have a record type that matches our hardware definitions, we can use record component selection to access the desired bits in our register. For example, suppose we have the following declaration of a register variable.

```
Control_Status_Register  :  CSR_Rec;
```

The following statements change the bit fields for gain and channel number and examine the overflow bit.

```
Control_Status_Register.Gain      := Two;
Control_Status_Register.Channel := 28;

if Control_Status_Register.Overflow then
    raise Over_Range;
end if;
```

The declarations required for the read-only 16-bit data register are far simpler. The bits in positions 0 to 11 contain the output of our converter. Bits 12 to 15 are always zero. All we need is a 16-bit integer with a range from 0 to 4095 as defined by the following declarations.

```
type Data_Type is range 0 .. 4095; -- Type for the data register
for Data_Type'Size use 16;
```

We are finally ready to write the code for our **Read** procedure. The first step is to set the channel number and gain to the values given by the parameters. We can simultaneously start the conversion by setting the start bit to **True**. Then we wait until the done bit is **True**. We use a loop to repeatedly check this bit, a technique known as **polling**. After exiting the polling loop, we raise **Over_Range** if the overflow error bit is set. If the conversion is successful, we obtain the integer value from the data register and convert it into a fixed point voltage. Here is the complete body of our ADC package for a system using memory mapped I/O.

```
with System.Storage_Elements;  use  System.Storage_Elements;
package body ADC is

    use Common_Units;   -- For operators on Volts

    -- Addresses of the ADC's two registers (memory mapped I/O)
    CSR_Address   : constant System.Address :=
                            To_Address (16#60008010#);
    Data_Address : constant System.Address :=
                            To_Address (16#60008012#);

    -- Ten milliseconds
    Max_Conversion_Time : constant Duration := 10 * 1.0E-3;

    type CSR_Rec is   -- Type for the control status register
        record
            Start        : Boolean;
            Done         : Boolean;
            Int_Enable : Boolean;
            Overflow    : Boolean;
            Gain          : Gain_Choice;
            Channel     : Channel_Number;
        end record;

    for CSR_Rec use
```

```
record
   Start         at 0 range  0 ..  0;
   Done          at 0 range  1 ..  1;
   Int_Enable    at 0 range  2 ..  2;
   Overflow      at 0 range  3 ..  3;
   Gain          at 0 range  8 .. 10;
   Channel       at 0 range 11 .. 15;
end record;

for CSR_Rec'Size use 16;
for CSR_Rec'Bit_Order use System.Low_Order_First;

type Data_Type is range 0 .. 4095; -- for the data register
for Data_Type'Size use 16;

-- The two device registers

Control_Status_Register : CSR_Rec;
for Control_Status_Register'Address use CSR_Address;
for Control_Status_Register'Size use 16;
pragma Volatile (Control_Status_Register);

Data_Register : Data_Type;
for Data_Register'Address use Data_Address;
for Data_Register'Size use 16;
pragma Volatile (Data_Register);

------------------------------------------------

procedure Read (Channel : in   Channel_Number;
                Gain    : in   Gain_Choice;
                Value   : out  Input_Volts) is
   Shadow : CSR_Rec;
begin
   -- Set up for the conversion (use a record aggregate)
   Shadow := (Start       => True,   Done      => False,
              Int_Enable  => False,  Overflow  => False,
              Gain        => Gain,   Channel   => Channel);
   -- Start the conversion (by setting the start bit)
   Control_Status_Register := Shadow;
   -- Wait until the conversion is complete
   loop
      delay Max_Conversion_Time / 10;
      exit when Control_Status_Register.Done;
   end loop;
   if Control_Status_Register.Overflow then
      raise Over_Range;
   end if;
   -- Convert whole number data to a fixed point voltage
   Value := 5 * Volts (Data_Register) / 4095;
end Read;

end ADC;
```

Our read procedure loop contains a delay statement. While this delay is not necessary in a program with a single process, leaving it out in a concurrent program might result in the loop starving other processes. Picking the amount of time to delay between each status check has tradeoffs. Making it very small uses additional CPU time while making it larger may decrease the response time of the read operation. We selected a delay value that is one tenth the maximum conversion time. In Chapter 4 we'll examine another approach to handling the unknown time between the start of a conversion and its completion — interrupts. As you might expect, the interrupt enable bit plays an important role in this alternative to polling.

2.7.3 Unchecked conversions

Conversion is the changing of a value of one type to a value of a different type. The example program given at the very beginning of this chapter illustrated the use of explicit type conversion. The assignment statement

```
M := Float (A + B) / 2.0;
```

in that program uses an explicit type conversion to convert an integer sum into a floating point number. This conversion requires some data manipulation to transform a two's complement integer representation into an IEEE 754 floating point representation. Not all explicit type conversions require changing bits. The explicit type conversions we made to combine apples and oranges during our discussion of signed integer types

```
Fruit := Big_Range (Apples) + Big_Range (Oranges);
```

involve converting one signed integer type to another signed integer type. As both values are stored as two's complement integers, these conversions require no modification of bits; the bits are simply interpreted as a different type.

Explicit type conversions are available only between related types. While we can convert any numeric type to any other numeric type, explicit type conversion is not allowed between a numeric type and a character type. The following conversion attempt will not compile.

```
Num := Integer ('a');   -- Illegal explicit conversion
```

When writing software for embedded systems, there are times when we want to interpret a bit pattern in different ways. We may, for example, want to interpret a byte as a number in one part of our program and as a record in another part. Unchecked conversions allow us to change our interpretation of a group of bits at will. The Ada library includes a generic function called

Ada.Unchecked_Conversion which may be used to copy bits from objects of one type to objects of another type. Here is an example that illustrates its use.

```
with Ada.Unchecked_Conversion;
with Ada.Text_IO;            use Ada.Text_IO;
with Ada.Integer_Text_IO;  use Ada.Integer_Text_IO;
procedure Unchecked_Example is

    type Bit_Array is array (0 .. Integer'Size - 1) of Boolean;
    for Bit_Array'Component_Size use 1;
    for Bit_Array'Size use Integer'Size;

    function To_Bits is new Ada.Unchecked_Conversion
                            (Source => Integer,
                             Target => Bit_Array);
    Num  : Integer;
    Bits : Bit_Array;
    for Bits'Size use Integer'Size;

begin
    loop
        Put_Line ("Enter an integer");
        Get (Num);
        -- Perform an unchecked conversion (copy the bits)
        Bits := To_Bits (Num);
        Put_Line ("The bits are");
        for Index in reverse Bits'Range loop
            if Bits (Index) then
                Put ('1');
            else
                Put ('0');
            end if;
        end loop;
        New_Line;
    end loop;
end Unchecked_Example;
```

Type **Bit_Array** is an array of Booleans whose index range is determined by the number of bits ('Size) used by type **Integer**. While it takes only one bit to represent a Boolean object, the compiler will typically use an entire storage unit for that object. The expense of the extra storage is justified by the faster time to access the object. So an array of 32 Boolean values will typically use 32 bytes of memory rather than 32 bits of memory. We used the 'Component_Size clause to specify that only one bit be used for each Boolean component. With this attribute definition clause, the compiler will pack 32 Booleans into 4 bytes. We also included the 'Size clause to specify that the array be stored in no less memory than an **Integer**. The *exact* amount of storage for **Bits** is set with another 'Size clause.

The function **To_Bits** is instantiated from the generic library function **Ada.Unchecked_Conversion**. The instantiation requires two generic parameters: the type for the source of the bits and the type of the target of the bit copying. In the body of the program, we prompt for and get an integer from the user. This integer is converted into an array of Booleans by the function **To_Bits**. Unchecked conversions do no manipulation of bits. They simply copy the bits from the source, **Num**, to the target, **Bits**. The loop displays the Boolean values in the array as 1's and 0's allowing us to view the bit pattern used to represent the number.

As you are giving up the safety of Ada's type system, use unchecked conversions with caution. Be sure that the size of the source and target types are the same.[10] We will see another example of unchecked conversion in the next section.

2.7.4 Machine code insertion

While writing code at the machine or assembly level is error-prone, there are situations for which it is necessary. Earlier we mentioned that port mapped I/O required special instructions to access the device registers. These special machine instructions have no counterparts in high-level languages such as Ada. One way to use such instructions is to include them in assembly language subroutines and call those subroutines from our Ada program. An alternative approach is to insert machine instructions directly into our Ada program. Other than stating that machine code insertion can be achieved by a call to a subprogram of "code statements," section 13.8 of the ARM provides no details on how to accomplish the task. The Ada standard leaves it up to the individual compiler vendors to determine the syntax of these code statements. In this section we'll give an example of the use of machine code insertion for two different compilers. First, we give the specification of a package for doing input and output with Intel x86 ports.

```
with Interfaces;
package Port_IO  is

-- This package provides access to I/O ports. It provides the
-- Ada programmer with the Intel x86 IN and OUT instructions.

   -- Port addresses
   type Address_Range is new Interfaces.Unsigned_16;
```

---

[10] Most Ada compilers issue a warning when the sizes differ.

```
-- Data for IN and OUT instructions
type Byte is new Interfaces.Unsigned_8;
type Word is new Interfaces.Unsigned_16;

-- The following procedures write a byte or word to a port
procedure Out_Byte (Address : in Address_Range;
                    Data    : in Byte);
procedure Out_Word (Address : in Address_Range;
                    Data    : in Word);

-- The following functions read a byte or word from a port
function In_Byte (Address : in Address_Range) return Byte;
function In_Word (Address : in Address_Range) return Word;
end Port_IO;
```

Package **Interfaces** is the parent of several library packages that declare types and other entities useful for interfacing to other programming languages. It also contains some implementation-defined types that are useful for interfacing to assembly language. We derive our port address type and data types from the types for 8 and 16-bit unsigned integers defined in that package. We derived new types rather than use the unsigned integer types directly to ensure that we do not inappropriately mix address values and data values.

The following package body is written for the GNAT Ada compiler. We won't explain the features in this package body. This code is presented only as an example to demonstrate that we can include assembly language statements in an Ada program. Consult section 12.1 of the GNAT Reference Manual (2010) for the necessary details.

```
with System.Machine_Code; use System.Machine_Code;
package body Port_IO is

    -- The x86 IN and OUT instructions are accessed through
    -- the ASM function found in package System.Machine_Code.

    -- For all routines, we use register DX to hold the port
    -- address. This avoids the hassles of determining if the
    -- value is in 0..255, where we can use immediate mode.

procedure Out_Byte (Address : in Address_Range;
                    Data    : in Byte) is
begin
    System.Machine_Code.Asm
       (Template => "outb %%al, %%dx",
        Outputs  => No_Output_Operands,
        Inputs   => (Byte'Asm_Input ("a", Data),
                    Address_Range'Asm_Input ("d", Address)),
```

```
            Clobber  => "",
            Volatile => True );

      end Out_Byte;

      procedure Out_Word (Address : in Address_Range;
                          Data    : in Word) is
      begin
         System.Machine_Code.Asm
            (Template => "outw %%ax, %%dx",
             Outputs  =>  No_Output_Operands,
             Inputs   => (Word'Asm_Input ("a", Data),
                          Address_Range'Asm_Input ("d", Address)),
             Clobber  => "",
             Volatile => True );

      end Out_Word;

      function In_Byte (Address : in Address_Range) return Byte is
         Result : Byte;
      begin
         System.Machine_Code.Asm
            (Template => "inb %%dx, %%al",
             Outputs  => Byte'Asm_Output ("=a", Result),
             Inputs   => Address_Range'Asm_Input ("d", Address),
             Clobber  => "",
             Volatile => True );

         return Result;
      end In_Byte;

      function In_Word (Address : in Address_Range) return Word is
         Result : Word;
      begin
         System.Machine_Code.Asm
            (Template => "inw %%dx, %%ax",
             Outputs  => Word'Asm_Output ("=a", Result),
             Inputs   => Address_Range'Asm_Input ("d", Address),
             Clobber  => "",
             Volatile => True );

         return Result;
      end In_Word;
end Port_IO;
```

As an example to show how machine code insertion is compiler-dependent, here is the code for the **Out_Byte** procedure written for the Rational Apex Ada compiler.

```
procedure Out_Byte (Address : in Address_Range;
                    Data    : in Byte) is
```

```
begin
   Code_2 '(Mov,  Dx,  Address 'Ref);
   Code_2 '(Mov,  Al,  Data 'Ref);
   Code_2 '(Out_Op,  Dx,  Al);
end Out_Byte;
```

As you can see, a good knowledge of the assembly language is needed to insert machine code into an Ada program.

Earlier we presented the package body for our fictitious ADC on a memory mapped computer. We can use the **Port_IO** package and modify our ADC code for a port mapped I/O computer. First we'll need some unchecked conversion functions to copy bits between our control and status record and Port_IO's word type.

```
function To_CSR   is new Ada. Unchecked_Conversion
                              (Source => Port_IO .Word,
                               Target => CSR_Rec);
function To_Word is new Ada. Unchecked_Conversion
                              (Source => CSR_Rec,
                               Target => Port_IO .Word);
```

Instead of reading and writing memory mapped variables, we use the IN and OUT instructions available through **Port_IO** to read and write the device registers. We keep copies of the two registers in local variables. Here is the code for the ADC read procedure revised for the port mapped machine. The entire package body is available on our web site.

```
procedure Read (Channel : in   Channel_Number;
                Gain     : in   Gain_Choice;
                Value    : out  Input_Volts) is

-- Port mapped I/O implementation

   Shadow    : CSR_Rec;          -- Copy of control status register
   for Shadow'Size use 16;
   Data_Reg : Port_IO .Word;   -- Copy of data register
   for Data_Reg'Size use 16;
begin
   -- Set up for the conversion (using a record aggregate)
   Shadow := (Start         => True,   Done     => False,
              Int_Enable => False,  Overflow => False,
              Gain          => Gain,   Channel  => Channel);
   -- Start the conversion (by setting the start bit)
   -- Note conversion of record to word
   Port_IO .Out_Word (Address => CSR_Address,
                      Data    => To_Word (Shadow));
   -- Wait until the conversion is complete
   loop
      delay Max_Conversion_Time / 10;
```

```
      -- Get the CSR word from the port
      -- and convert it to a record
      Shadow := To_CSR (Port_IO.In_Word (CSR_Address));
      exit when Shadow.Done;
   end loop;
   if Shadow.Overflow then
      raise Over_Range;
   end if;
   -- Get and convert whole number data to a
   -- fixed point voltage
   Data_Reg := Port_IO.In_Word (Data_Address);
   Value    := 5 * Volts (Data_Reg) / 4095;
end Read;
```

Summary

- Ada provides all of the control structures expected in a high-level programming language.
- Ada provides two kinds of subprograms: procedures and functions.
- Parameter passing modes are based on direction of data flow, not on the underlying passing mechanism.
- The nested structure of an Ada program provides a powerful mechanism for controlling the scope of identifiers.
- Ada's type model is perhaps the most important feature giving Ada a significant advantage over other programming languages.
- Programmer-defined scalar types allow us to more accurately model the problem we are solving.
- Ada provides both floating point and fixed point representations for real numbers.
- Ada provides both signed and unsigned (modular) representations for integer numbers.
- Enumeration types allow us to create types by listing all possible values in the domain.
- Attributes provide information about a type or object.
- Subtypes allow us to create a set of values that is a subset of the domain of some existing type.
- We may index our arrays with any discrete data type; we are not limited to integer indices.
- Indexing allows us to access an element of an array.
- Slicing allows us to access a portion of an array; a slice is an array.
- Unconstrained array types allow us to define formal array parameters that match any size actual array parameter.

- Records are heterogeneous composite data types.
- Access types are strongly typed pointers.
- Exceptions allow us to separate normal processing from error processing.
- Packages provide the framework for information hiding and encapsulation in Ada.
- A class may be defined by a package containing a type with the attributes and functions and procedures for the operations.
- We may use child packages to build a class hierarchy.
- A key characteristic of embedded software is the use of specialized input and output devices.
- Enumeration representation clauses allow us to specify the representation of the values defining an enumeration type.
- Attribute definition clauses allow us to specify some property of a type or object such as size, location in memory, and bit order.
- Record representation clauses allow us to specify the bit layout of an object.
- Memory mapped I/O and port mapped I/O are two common approaches for organizing input and output devices.
- Unchecked conversion allows us to copy bits from one object to another without any type constraints.
- We can insert machine code instructions directly into our Ada program. The exact method is compiler-dependent.

Exercises

2.1 Write an if statement that checks three integer variables, A, B, and C, and displays one of the three messages: "Two of the values are the same," "All three values are the same," or "All of the values are different."

2.2 Write a loop that displays all of the integers between 0 and 100 that are evenly divisible by 3.

2.3 Write a procedure that swaps the contents of its two integer parameters.

2.4 Write a function that returns the larger of its two real parameters.

2.5 Write a for loop that uses the 'Image attribute to display all of the values in type Day_Type (declared on page 43).

2.6 Why did we not have to declare the variable Day used in the for loop of our enumeration example program on page 44?

2.7 What property makes a discrete type more specialized than a scalar type?

2.8 Write a loop that uses an exit statement rather than a for iteration scheme to display all of the values in type `Day_Type` (declared on page 43). You will need to use the attributes `'Image`, `'First`, `'Last`, and `'Succ`.

2.9 Declare an array type whose components are positive whole numbers indexed by `Pixel_Color` (defined on page 43).

2.10 Given the following unconstrained array type

   type Int_Array **is array** (Character **range** <>) **of** Integer ;

   complete the following function that returns the value of the largest value in the array.

   function Max (Items : **in** Int_Array) **return** Integer **is**

2.11 Rewrite program `Palindrome` on page 54 using the unbounded, varying length string type `Ada.Strings.Unbounded.Unbounded_String` defined in section A.4.5 of the ARM in place of the subtype `Line_Type`. Input and output operations for unbounded varying length strings are defined in package `Ada.Text_IO.Unbounded_IO` described in section A.10.12 of the ARM.

2.12 Why is an access type not a scalar type?

2.13 Define the terms *elaboration, exception,* and *exception handler.*

2.14 Download the definition package `Common_Units` and the program *Ohms_Law* from our web site. Compile and run the program. Then delete the *use clause* for `Common_Units` from the program. Recompile and explain the error message.

2.15 Using the generic queue package on page 74 as an example,

   1. Write the package declaration for an array-based stack.
   2. Write the package body for your stack.

2.16 Write the specification for the class `Convection_Oven` which is a subclass of `Oven_Type` defined on page 89. After you are done, download our specification from the web site and compare it to your work.

2.17 Download all of the files for the oven class hierarchy from our web site. Compile and run program `Ovens_Demo`. Add a new subclass of microwave oven that includes a heating element to brown food. Include operations to switch this heating element on and off. Write a body similar to that of the other oven packages. Add the necessary code to program `Ovens_Demo` to test your code.

2.18 Define the terms *transducer, sensor,* and *actuator.*

2.19 What is a device driver?

2.20 What is an enumeration representation clause? What is an attribute definition clause?

2.21 Add another enumeration value, **None**, to the enumeration type **Day_Type** used in the alarm clock example on page 85. When this value is sent to procedure **Display_Days**, all of the seven lights are extinguished.

2.22 Add another enumeration value, **Midweek**, to the enumeration type **Day_Type** used in the alarm clock example on page 85. When this value is sent to procedure **Display_Days**, the lights for **Tue**, **Wed**, and **Thu** are illuminated.

2.23 Differentiate between *memory mapped I/O* and *port mapped I/O*.

2.24 What is a record representation clause?

2.25 The attribution definition clause **'Size** may be applied to both types and variables. What is the difference between applying this clause to a type and applying it to a variable?

2.26 Write a program fragment that calls procedure **ADC.Read** on page 89 and displays the channel number and voltage of all 32 channels. Use a gain of one. You'll need to instantiate a package to output voltage values.

2.27 Modify the program fragment you wrote for the previous question. Instead of using a gain of one, use the highest gain possible for each channel. You will need to handle possible over-range exceptions and lower the gain when necessary.

2.28 Given the following package declaration for a digital to analog converter

```
with  Common_Units;
package DAC is
-- Specification of a make-believe digital to analog converter

    type     Channel_Number is range 0..7;
    subtype  Output_Volts    is Common_Units.Volts range 0.0 .. 5.0;

    procedure Write (Channel : in Channel_Number;    -- Which channel
                     Value   : in Output_Volts);     -- Output value
    -- Sets the voltage on the given channel
end DAC;
```

write a program that sets each of the 8 channels to a voltage equal to half the channel number. For example, channel 5 is set to 2.5 volts. Compile your work to check your syntax.

2.29 Complete the package body for the package declared in the previous question. The digital to analog converter has eight 16-bit data registers.

There is no control or status register. Like the analog to digital example in this chapter, only the low-order 12 bits of the data registers are used. To output a voltage, you simply write a value between 0 (for 0.0 volts) and 4095 (for 5.0 volts) to the appropriate register. The data register for channel zero is memory mapped to address $FFFAA0_{16}$. Each of the other data registers follow at two-byte intervals. Compile your work to check your syntax.

3
Task basics

In Chapter 1 we demonstrated the effectiveness of concurrent algorithms. Together, Horace and Mildred can prepare a meal faster than one of them alone. The concurrent algorithm for controlling the process of chutney cooking provides a simpler and more reusable solution than the original sequential algorithm. Now that you have a basic understanding of sequential programming with Ada we are ready to create concurrent Ada programs.

Ada is a concurrent programming language — it provides the constructs needed to support the creation of programs with multiple threads of control. Ada's task is an implementation of Dijkstra's (1968) process. An Ada program is composed of one or more tasks that execute concurrently to solve a problem. In this chapter we examine the Ada task as an independent entity. In the next two chapters, we'll examine the facilities that allow tasks to communicate, synchronize, and share resources.

3.1 Defining tasks

As with packages, the definition of a task has two parts: a declaration and a body. We can define a task type from which we can create multiple tasks that execute the same sequence of statements. Alternatively, we can define a singleton task that ensures that only one task executes the sequence of statements in the body. Let's look at a program that illustrates both alternatives.

```ada
with Ada.Text_IO;   use Ada.Text_IO;
procedure LED_Task_Examples is

   type Color_Type is (Red, Green, Yellow, Blue);

   procedure Turn_On_LED (Color : in Color_Type) is
```

```
   begin
      Put_Line (Color_Type'Image (Color) & " on");
   end Turn_On_LED;

   procedure Turn_Off_LED (Color : in Color_Type) is
   begin
      Put_Line (Color_Type'Image (Color) & " off");
   end Turn_Off_LED;

   ----------------------------------------------------------------

   task Flash_Red_LED;                -- Declare a singleton task

   task body Flash_Red_LED is -- Body of the task
   begin
      loop
         Turn_On_LED (Red);
         delay 0.5;
         Turn_Off_LED (Red);
         delay 0.5;
      end loop;
   end Flash_Red_LED;
   ----------------------------------------------------------------

   task type Flash_LED (Color  : Color_Type; -- A task type
                        Period : Natural);
   task body Flash_LED is                    -- Body of the task
   begin
      loop
         Turn_On_LED (Color);
         delay Duration (Period) / 2;
         Turn_Off_LED (Color);
         delay Duration (Period) / 2;
      end loop;
   end Flash_LED;
   ----------------------------------------------------------------

   -- Two task objects (variables)
   Yellow_LED : Flash_LED (Color  => Yellow,
                           Period => 4);
   Green_LED  : Flash_LED (Color  => Green,
                           Period => 3);
   -- A pointer to a task object
   type Flash_Ptr is access Flash_LED;
   Blue_LED : Flash_Ptr;

begin
   Put_Line ("Flashing LEDs");
   Blue_LED := new Flash_LED (Color  => Blue,
                              Period => 8);
   Put_Line ("Main task is done");
end LED_Task_Examples;
```

When this program executes, five tasks run concurrently to display the state (on or off) of four different-colored light-emitting diodes (LEDs). You can download this program from our web site, build it, and run it to see the output displayed by the five tasks.

It takes only a single line to declare the singleton task `Flash_Red_LED`. This declaration provides only the task's name. The body contains the sequence of instructions executed by the task. In this case, our task body contains an infinite loop that alternatively calls a procedure to turn on the red LED and a procedure to turn it off.

The declaration of task type `Flash_LED` includes two discriminants. As with record discriminants, we supply an actual value when we use the type to declare an object. The declarations of variables `Yellow_LED` and `Green_LED` illustrate the use of these discriminants. The values we gave to the discriminants `Color` and `Period` are used by the task body. Looking at the body for task type `Flash_LED`, you may wonder why we declared the discriminant `Period` to be an integer subtype rather than `Duration`. That would save us the trouble of converting the whole number to a `Duration` value. Task discriminants, like record discriminants, are limited to discrete types and access types. Being a real type, `Duration` discriminants are illegal.

We have shown two ways to create a task: defining a singleton task or defining a task type and declaring task variables. Tasks may also be created dynamically using access types. Our program declares the access type `Flash_Ptr` that designates a `Flash_LED` task and an access variable that holds the location of a `Flash_LED` task. Like all access objects, the initial value of `Blue_LED` is null. In the main subprogram we use the allocator **new** to create a new `Flash_LED` task and assign its location to `Blue_LED`. We supplied appropriate values for the two discriminants when we allocated the task.

Unlike a package, a task cannot be written and compiled by itself. The task declaration and body must exist within some other program unit such as a package or subprogram. All of the example tasks are written within the declarative part of the program `LED_Task_Examples`.

3.2 The task life cycle

A task passes through several different states during its lifetime. The state diagram in Figure 3.1 shows the basic states and transitions that define the behavior of a task. In the next sections we'll look at each of the different states in this diagram.

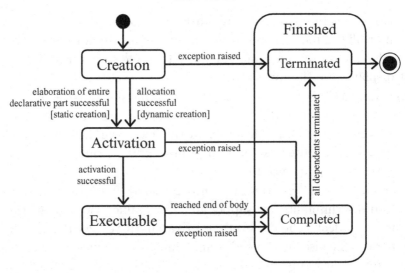

Figure 3.1 The basic states of a task

3.2.1 Task creation

Our LED examples demonstrated the two approaches for creating task objects. **Static creation** is done when we define a singleton task or we declare a variable of a task type. **Dynamic creation** uses the allocator operation to assign a location to an access variable that designates a task. Static creation is done through elaboration, the run-time processing of declarations. The elaboration of ordinary variables includes allocation of memory for them on the stack and the assignment of any initial values. The elaboration of a task object (singleton task or task variable) also allocates memory. This memory includes a *task control block* and a *run-time stack* where the task's local variables and subprogram call frames are stored. Since each task has its own run-time stack, tasks of the same type have their own separate copies of any local objects defined in the task body. Tasks created dynamically obtain their memory when the allocator operator is invoked.

In program LED_Task_Examples, tasks Yellow_LED and Green_LED are created when those variables are elaborated. The task designated by the pointer Blue_LED is not created until it is assigned a value from the allocator when the assignment statement in the main subprogram is executed.

The amount of memory allocated to each task for its task control block and run-time stack is determined by a default value in the compiler. This amount may be insufficient for tasks that require large amounts of storage for local variables and/or are highly recursive. On the other hand, the default stack size may be overly large for a program with many tasks each requiring little stack space. We can use the pragma `Storage_Size` to specify the amount of memory allocated for each singleton task and for each stack object created from a task type. This pragma is given in the declaration of the singleton task or the declaration of the task type. The following task declarations include pragmas to set the memory available for our four flashing tasks to 1000 storage units.

```
task Flash_Red_LED is
   pragma Storage_Size (1_000 );
end Flash_Red_LED;

task type Flash_LED (Color   : Color_Type;
                     Period : Natural)    is
   pragma Storage_Size (1_000 );
end Flash_LED;
```

Comparing this code to our original declarations of these tasks in program `LED_Task_Examples`, you'll notice that we needed to include end clauses in the declarations. Later we'll include other task items in task declarations.

It is possible that an exception is raised during the elaboration of the declarative region containing task definitions. For example, the constant declaration

```
-- calling function LED_Count to initialize Count
Count : constant Positive := LED_Count;
```

would raise a `Constraint_Error` exception when it is elaborated if the function `LED_Count` returns zero. Any tasks that were created prior to this failed constant elaboration become terminated. A wise programmer will avoid declarations that could raise exceptions during elaboration.

3.2.2 Task activation

During this phase of a task's life cycle, the declarative part of the task body is elaborated. Space is allocated for any local variables on the task's run-time stack. The task body's declarative part could include the definition of another task which is created as part of the task's elaboration.

A dynamically created task is activated immediately after a successful allocation. The activation of static tasks is deferred until the elaboration of the declarative region in which they are defined is complete. In our example program, the tasks `Flash_Red_LED`, `Yellow_LED`, and `Green_LED` are activated after the elaboration of program `LED_Task_Examples` is complete. They are activated before the execution of the first executable statement in the program.

Should the elaboration of the task body's declarative part raise an exception, the task becomes completed. Again, the wise programmer will avoid complex declarations that might raise exceptions during their elaboration.

3.2.3 Task execution

A task enters the executable state immediately after a successful activation. In this state the statements in the task's body are executed. The executable state does not mean that the task is actually executing statements. If there are more tasks than processors, some of the tasks must wait until a processor is available. A task may also need to suspend executing its statements until some resource is available. For example, a task calling `Get` to read information will be blocked until the input is available. We'll discuss resources in the next two chapters. Executing a delay statement is another way a task may block itself. Figure 3.2 shows the substates of a task within the executable state.

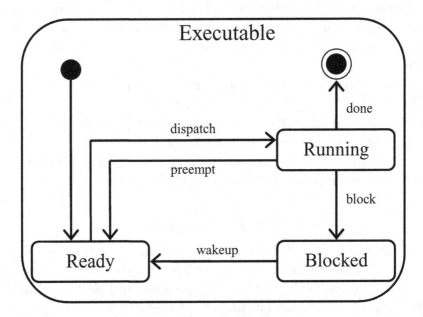

Figure 3.2 The substates of executable

When a task first becomes executable, it starts off in the ready state. Tasks in the ready state have all of the resources they need to run except for a processor. When a processor becomes available the task scheduler dispatches the task to the running state. In this state the task executes its sequence of statements. Should the running task execute a delay statement or need some resource that is not currently available, it relinquishes the processor and moves to the blocked state. When the delay expires or the required resource becomes available, the task is awoken by moving it to the ready state. A running task is done when it has finished execution of the statements in its body or raised an exception.

The replacement of the running task with a ready task is called a **context switch**. When there is more than one task in the ready state, the scheduler must select one of them. We'll discuss the scheduler in detail in Chapters 7 and 8. For now we'll mention that the set of ready tasks is usually stored in either a FIFO queue or priority queue. The scheduler simply picks the task at the front of the queue. Figure 3.2 also includes a transition from running to ready labeled *preempt*. In many scheduling schemes, a task may be preempted by the scheduler because a higher priority task is now ready or the task has used up its allotment of processor time.

3.2.4 Task finish

A finished task is either in the completed state or the terminated state. For most purposes, it makes little difference which of these two states a finished task is in. There are two ways an executable task moves to the completed state. Completion of all of the statements in the task body is the normal way. An exception handled by the task body provides another expected way to complete the task. An unhandled exception in the task body also sends a task to the completed state. As we mentioned in our discussion of activation, should an exception be raised during the elaboration of the task body, it will go directly to the completed state.

A task moves from completed to terminated when all its dependent tasks are terminated. To understand this state transition requires an understanding of the master-dependent relationship. We'll discuss that in the next section.

3.3 Task hierarchies

While the sequential programs we discussed in Chapter 2 defined no task objects, a task was still part of their execution. Sequential programs have a single thread of control carried out by a predefined task called the environment task. The **environment task** provides the thread of control that executes the main subprogram. Before it calls the main subprogram, the environment task carries out the elaboration of the bodies of packages that are part of the program. Elaboration of a package body consists of the elaboration of any declarations followed by the execution of the optional package body initialization sequence.

Each task is part of two hierarchical relationships. The **parent-child hierarchy** is most relevant to task creation. The **master-dependent hierarchy** is most relevant to the finishing of tasks.

3.3.1 Parent-child

A task that is directly responsible for creating another task is called the parent of the task, and the task it creates is called the child. A parent task may create a child statically through the elaboration process or dynamically through use of the allocator. In program LED_Task_Examples (page 107), the environment task is the parent of the four child tasks created by the main subprogram.

When a parent task creates a child, it is suspended until that child completes its activation. When that activation is complete, both parent and child execute concurrently. Ada's block structure allows us to declare task objects in any block, including within a task body. Such task nesting can give rise to a hierarchy of suspensions. For example, while a parent task is suspended for the activation of a child task, that child task may have its activation suspended while a task it created activates. The environment task is at the top of the parent-child hierarchy.

Program LED_Task_Examples is suspended three times during its elaboration to create the three child tasks Flash_Red_LED, Yellow_LED, and Green_LED. The program is suspended a fourth time during its execution when it uses the allocator to create task Blue_LED.all. Figure 3.3 adds the suspended state to the basic task state diagram we illustrated in Figure 3.1.

3.3.2 Master-dependent

Every task depends on a master. The concept of master is more complicated than that of parent. The *direct* master of a task is a block structure. Block structures can be task bodies, block statements, subprogram bodies, or library packages. Determining the direct master of a task depends on how the task was created. The direct master of a statically created task is the block in which the task object is declared. The direct master of a dynamically allocated task is the block in which the access *type* is declared (not the block in which the task pointer *variable* is declared). If the direct master is a block statement or a subprogram, then this master is dependent on the

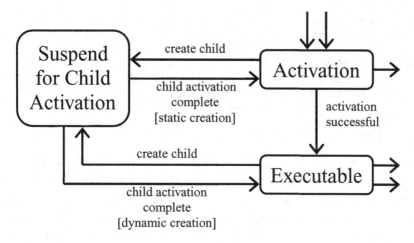

Figure 3.3 Parent tasks are suspended during the activation of a child task

task executing the block. Therefore, a task may have multiple masters, the block or subprogram acting as its direct master, and the task that executes the block as an indirect master.

An important property of the master-dependent relationship is that a master may not terminate until all of its dependents have terminated. Figure 3.1 illustrates this property for the case in which a master is a task. A task moves from completed to terminated when all of its dependents have terminated. When the direct master of a task is a block statement or subprogram, the task executing that block may not exit the block until all of that block's dependent tasks have terminated. Procedure LED_Task_Examples is the master of all four tasks in that program. Control does not leave this procedure after executing its three statements. The environment task must wait until the dependents of the main subprogram terminate. As these tasks contain infinite loops, the main subprogram never terminates. Let's look at another example. The following procedure is passed an array of real numbers and returns the sum and the product of all the numbers in that array.

```
procedure Math (Values  :  in   Float_Array;
                Sum      :  out  Float;
                Product  :  out  Float)  is
    task  Multiply;

    task body  Multiply  is
    begin
        Product  :=  1.0;
        for  Index  in  Values 'Range loop
            Product  :=  Product  *  Values (Index);
```

```
        end loop;
    end Multiply;

begin  -- Math
    Sum := 0.0;
    for Index in Values'Range loop
        Sum := Sum + Values (Index);
    end loop;
end Math;
```

The singleton task `Multiply` is declared locally within procedure `Math`. The task whose thread of control called procedure `Math` is the parent of task `Multiply`. The scope rules described in Chapter 2 apply to all identifiers, including tasks. As task `Multiply` is nested within procedure `Math`, it has global access to procedure `Math`'s parameters. Task `Multiply` is activated during the elaboration of procedure `Math`. After task `Multiply` completes its activation, the code in its body executes concurrently with the code in the body of procedure `Math`. Procedure `Math` is the *direct master* of task `Multiply`. The task whose thread of control called procedure `Math` is an *indirect master* of task `Multiply`. Should procedure `Math` complete the calculation of `Sum` before task `Multiply` completes the calculation of `Product`, `Math`'s thread of control will be suspended until the dependent task is terminated. Should task `Multiply` complete the calculation of `Product` before procedure `Math` completes its calculation of `Sum`, task `Multiply` will become completed. As task `Multiply` has no dependent tasks, it will then immediately move to the terminated state. The main point in this example is that control does not leave a block while that block is the master of a task that is not terminated.

Let's look at another example. The following procedure sorts an array of real numbers. It uses two tasks to accomplish its objective. One task sorts the first half of the array and the other sorts the second half. Each task calls a sequential sort procedure to do the actual sorting. We call a merge function to combine the two sorted slices into a single sorted array.

```
procedure Concurrent_Sort (Values : in out Array_Type) is
    Split : constant Integer := Values'First + Values'Length / 2;
begin
    declare  -- a block statement
        task type Worker_Task (First : Positive;
                               Last  : Positive);
        task body Worker_Task is
        begin
            -- Call a sequential sort to sort the assigned slice
            Sort (Values (First .. Last));
        end Worker_Task;
```

```
            -- Declare  two  worker  tasks
      Low_Part    :  Worker_Task  (First  => Values 'First ,
                                    Last   => Split - 1);
      High_Part :  Worker_Task  (First  => Split ,
                                    Last   => Values 'Last );
   begin    -- executable  part  of  block  statement
         -- do  nothing  (wait  for  the  worker  tasks  to  terminate )
         null;
   end;     -- of  block  statement

   -- Call  a  function  to  merge  the  two  sorted  halves;
   Values := Merge (Values (Values 'First .. Split - 1),
                    Values (Split .. Values 'Last ));
end Concurrent_Sort;
```

We cannot merge the two array halves until the worker tasks have completed their work. To ensure that we don't call the merge function before the two array halves are sorted, we declared the worker tasks in a block statement. We used two task discriminants to assign a different slice of the array to each of our worker tasks. The block statement is the direct master of the two worker tasks. Control will not exit this block until both worker tasks have terminated. Thus we are guaranteed that the merge function will not be called until both halves of the array are sorted. The executable portion of the block contains only a **null** statement. As an alternative, we could have divided the array into three pieces giving one third to each of the worker tasks and one third to the calling task. For the most efficient sort, we would have as many concurrent tasks sorting as there are processors in our system. You can find a complete program, `Concurrent_Sort_Demo`, on our web site that demonstrates procedure `Concurrent_Sort`.

You can find more details on the termination of tasks in section 9.3 of the ARM. Section 7.6.1 of the ARM discusses completion of masters including masters that include controlled types. A controlled type allows us to write destructor code for objects. Dale and McCormick (2007) provide simple examples that use controlled types to reclaim memory used by dynamic data structures.

3.4 Exceptions

When a sequential program running under a typical operating system raises an exception for which it has no exception handler, the exception is propagated to the operating system, which displays a message. When a task raises an exception for which it has no exception handler, the exception is not propagated; the task dies silently.[1] We recommend including an `others` handler with every task body that will inform us of an unhandled exception. The following task body includes such a handler.

```
task body Bad_Logic is
   subtype Dozen_Range is Integer range 1 .. 12;
   Dozen : Dozen_Range;
begin
   Dozen := 1;
   loop
      Dozen := Dozen + 1;
      exit when Dozen > 12;
   end loop;
exception
   when Except : others =>
      Put_Line
         (File => Standard_Error,
          Item => "Task Bad_Logic died with the exception " &
                  Ada.Exceptions.Exception_Name (Except));
end Bad_Logic;
```

This code includes an exception feature we did not discuss in Chapter 2. The package `Ada.Exceptions` (section 11.4.1 of the ARM) provides the type `Exception_Occurrence` and a number of operations for exceptions. The handler for `others` includes the `Exception_Occurrence` choice parameter `Except`. This parameter is assigned the occurrence information on the exception that this handler caught. We use this parameter in the call to `Exception_Name` to obtain the name of the exception. Our call to `Put_Line` writes this information to the standard error file. Here is the output from this handler.

```
Task Bad_Logic died with the exception CONSTRAINT_ERROR
```

Such an exception handler will not handle exceptions raised in the task body's declarative part. These exceptions must be handled in an enclosing scope. It is usually better to simplify declarations (e.g. use an executable statement to give an initial value to an object rather than in its declaration) than to handle exceptions.

Handling exceptions that are raised during the creation or activation of a task is a complex matter. We recommend keeping declarations simple (for example, avoid using function calls to initialize declared constants and variables). Burns and Wellings (2007) provide additional details on exceptions and tasking.

---

[1] Package `Ada.Task_Termination` provides mechanisms we may use to identify a protected procedure that is called by the implementation when a task terminates. We discuss protected procedures in Chapter 4.

3.5 The implementation of Ada tasking

Many programmers have their first introduction to the concept of the process in a class on operating systems. All modern operating systems provide the facilities for creating processes. The term process has specific and sometimes different meanings in the context of particular operating systems. Many operating systems support different levels of sequential processes. For example, Linux uses the word *process* for an instance of an executing program. We might run a word processing program and a spreadsheet program simultaneously on a Linux machine, each executing as a process. Each process has its own private address space. One process may not access another process's address space. In order for processes to communicate, they must use inter-process communication mechanisms provided by the operating system. Linux uses the word *thread* to refer to a sequential "subprogram" executing concurrently within the context of a process. The threads within a process share that process's address space. Within our word processing program, a spell checking thread may execute concurrently with a thread that takes our input from the keyboard. Since they share the same memory space, these threads may access the same variables. The terms heavyweight and lightweight are often used with process and thread. A process is said to be heavyweight because it takes significantly more effort to create a process with its new address space than a thread in an existing address space.

An Ada task executes within a memory space shared by all tasks in the program. The usual scope rules determine which objects a task can access. So the task is more like a Linux thread than a process. If our Ada program is running under Linux, it is very likely that the Ada run-time support system maps the Ada tasks to operating system threads. Alternatively, it is possible that the Ada program might have its own tasking support system making it invisible to the operating system. We may also use such a tasking support system for running concurrent Ada programs on bare (no operating system) hardware. In practice, you rarely need to know the underlying implementation of the task. We'll give more details on the implementation of Ada tasks in our discussions of run-time systems in Chapter 9.

3.6 Other task features

In this section we'll introduce some less commonly used Ada tasking features of tasks. You can find more details in the ARM and in Burns and Wellings (2007).

3.6.1 *Aborting tasks*

The abort statement allows us to halt one or more tasks. The following statement aborts the task named `Yellow_LED` and the task that the pointer `Blue_LED` designates.

abort Yellow_LED , Blue_LED . **all** ;

These tasks were defined in the program `LED_Task_Examples` on page 107. The execution of an abort statement results in the named tasks becoming *abnormal*. Tasks that are dependent on a task named in an abort statement also become abnormal.

The use of an abort statement may have catastrophic effects upon the entire program. It is a means of last resort. We, like many others (Burns and Wellings, 2007; Taft *et al.*, 2006; Wikibooks, 2010b), strongly discourage using the abort statement.

You can abort a task any time after its creation. Aborting an abnormal task or a completed task has no effect. The execution of the abort statement is finished once the named task and all of its dependents become abnormal. Abnormal tasks that were not running when they were aborted move immediately from the abnormal state to the completed state. Abnormal tasks that were running when they were aborted may not move to the completed state immediately. Such tasks may continue to execute until they reach an *abort completion point*. Section 9.8 of the ARM lists these points. Many of the points involve concepts we cover in Chapters 4 and 5. It is possible that a task may never reach an abort completion point and continue its execution, further corrupting the program. A program making use of the Real-Time Systems Annex (discussed in Chapter 8) will have an upper bound on the time it takes for an abnormal task to complete. To make the task abortion issue even more complicated, there are a number of *abort-deferred operations* which must be allowed to complete before an abnormal task completes. These operations are also listed in section 9.8 of the ARM.

3.6.2 *Task identification*

In most circumstances a task name or pointer that designates a task is all we need to reference that task. You may find in some circumstances that it is useful to have a unique identifier rather than a name. The package `Ada.Task_Identification` (section C.7.1 of the ARM) defines unique identifiers for tasks. This package includes the private type `Task_ID`, an equality operator for comparing IDs, a function for converting an ID into a string, and a function that returns the ID of the calling task. Here is a revised version of the task body in program LED_Task_Examples that calls function Current_ Task to obtain the ID of the task that calls it and function Image to convert the ID to a string.

```
task body Flash_LED is
   use Ada. Task_Identification;
   My_ID : Task_Id;
begin
   My_ID := Current_Task;
   Put_Line (Color_Type'Image (Color) &
            "'S ID is " & Image (My_ID));
   loop
      Turn_On_LED (Color);
      delay Duration (Period) / 2;
      Turn_Off_LED (Color);
      delay Duration (Period) / 2;
   end loop;
end Flash_LED;
```

The output produced by the Put_Line statement in the three tasks executing this body is

```
YELLOW'S ID is yellow_led_003E7110
GREEN'S ID is green_led_003EA160
BLUE'S ID is blue_led_003ED2E8
```

Package Ada.Task_Identification also provides the attribute 'Identity which returns the identity of the task. For example, the assignment statement

```
My_ID := Flash_Red_LED 'Identity;
```

assigns the value of the singleton task Flash_Red_LED's ID to the variable My_ID.

3.6.3 Task attributes

The generic package Ada.Task_Attributes (section C.7.2 of the ARM) allows you to create, set, and query your own attributes for tasks. Once you create an instance of this package, the attribute is added to each task. You use the task IDs defined in package Ada.Task_Identification to specify the task for which you want to query or set your attribute.

Summary

- A task is a program unit that executes concurrently with other tasks.
- The definition of a task includes two parts: a declaration and a body.

- We use a task type declaration to create multiple tasks that execute the same sequence of statements.
- Each instance of a task type has its own run-time stack and therefore its own copies of variables defined in the task body.
- We use a singleton task declaration when we want to ensure that there is only one task executing a sequence of statements.
- Tasks may be created statically (through elaboration of declarations) or dynamically (through use of an allocator).
- Each task passes through several different states during its lifetime.
- During task creation, memory is allocated for the task control block and run-time stack.
- During task activation, the task body is elaborated.
- When a task is executable, it may be in one of three substates: Ready, Running, and Blocked.
- The task scheduler is responsible for deciding which tasks run at a given time.
- The environment task provides the thread of control for the main subprogram.
- The parent-child hierarchy is most relevant to task creation. A parent task is suspended while its child activates.
- The master-dependent hierarchy is most relevant to task finalization.
- A master may be a block statement, subprogram, or package.
- Control will not exit a block statement or subprogram as long as it has a dependent that has not terminated. This feature allows us to synchronize some concurrent activities.
- A task is complete when the execution of the sequence of statements in its body is complete or it raises an exception.
- A completed task is terminated when all its dependents are terminated.
- A task usually dies silently when it raises an unhandled exception.
- The abort statement provides a means for halting tasks. We strongly discourage its use.
- The package `Ada.Task_Identification` defines unique identifiers for tasks.
- The generic package `Ada.Task_Attributes` allows you to create, set, and query your own attributes for tasks.

Exercises

3.1   Obtain a copy of the program `LED_Task_Examples` (page 107) from our web site. Build and run it. Do you get the same output each run? Why?

3.2 Obtain a copy of the program LED_Task_Examples (page 107) from our web site. Rewrite the specification of task type Flash_LED so that the discriminant Period is a pointer to a duration value rather than an integer.

3.3 Obtain a copy of the program LED_Task_Examples (page 107) from our web site. Delete the singleton task definition. Delete the variables Yellow_LED, Green_LED, and Blue_LED. Declare an array type indexed by Color_Type with Flash_Ptr components. Write a for loop in the main subprogram that dynamically creates a flashing task for each of the four colors with periods of 1, 2, 3, and 4 seconds. You'll find the attribute 'Pos useful in calculating the periods in the loop.

3.4 Write a program with a task type called Put_Name that has a discriminant that is a pointer to String. The task body should display the designated name five times, waiting one second between each display. Declare the task variable Name_Writer as an instance of type Put_Name. Within this declaration, use the new operator to obtain the memory containing a string with your first name and assign its location to the task discriminant. The main task should simply display the word *Hello*. Build and execute your program.

3.5 Obtain a copy of the program Master_Demo from our web site. This program calls procedure Math (page 115). Add a Put_Line statement after the for loop in task Multiply that displays "Product Computed." Add a Put_Line statement after the for loop in procedure Math that displays "Sum Computed." Increase the size of the array to 10. Build and run the program. Which calculation was completed first? Does that calculation always complete first?

3.6 Obtain a copy of the program Concurrent_Sort_Demo from our web site. Rewrite procedure Concurrent_Sort (page 116) so that the array is divided into four chunks. Three of these chunks are sorted by three worker tasks while the fourth is sorted by procedure Concurrent_Sort. You'll need to carry out three merges.

3.7 Given the following program which is available on the web site:

```
with Ada.Text_IO;                  use Ada.Text_IO;
with Ada.Numerics.Float_Random;    use Ada.Numerics.Float_Random;
procedure Exercise is

   Generator : Ada.Numerics.Float_Random.Generator;

   task type Do_Nothing (Letter : Character);
   task body Do_Nothing is
      Period : Duration;
```

```
      begin
          Period := Duration (Random (Generator)) / 10;
          if Letter = 'W' or Letter = 'X' then
              Period := 2 * Period;
          end if;
          for Count in 1 .. 10 loop
              Put (Letter);
              delay Period;
          end loop;
      end Do_Nothing;

      type A_Ptr is access Do_Nothing;

      procedure Do_Nothing_More is
          type B_Ptr is access Do_Nothing;
          X : A_Ptr;
          Y : B_Ptr;
      begin
          X := new Do_Nothing (Letter => 'X');
          declare
              Z : Do_Nothing (Letter => 'Z');
          begin
              for Count in 1 .. 10 loop
                  Put ('-');
                  delay 0.008;
              end loop;
          end;
          Y := new Do_Nothing (Letter => 'Y');
      end Do_Nothing_More;

      W : Do_Nothing (Letter  => 'W');

  begin
      New_Line;
      Put_Line ("Calling  Do_Nothing_More");
      Do_Nothing_More;
      New_Line;
      Put_Line ("Returned  from  Do_Nothing_More");
  end Exercise;
```

1. How many tasks are in this program?

2. What is the parent of each of these tasks?

3. What is the direct master of each of these tasks?

4. Are we guaranteed that nothing is displayed on the screen by this program before the phrase *Calling Do_Nothing_More*? Why or why not?

5. Are we guaranteed that the last thing displayed on the screen by

this program is the phrase *Returned from Do_Nothing_More*? Why or why not?

6. Are we guaranteed that no "Y" will be displayed before a "Z"? Why or why not?

7. Are we guaranteed that no "Y" will be displayed before an "X"? Why or why not?

3.8 Obtain a copy of the program `Handler_Demo` from our web site. This program includes the task `Bad_Logic` whose body is on page 118. Build and run it. Now add a definition for the exception `My_Exception` to this program. Add a raise statement that raises `My_Exception` after the fourth iteration of the loop in the body of task `Bad_Logic`. Build and run the revised program.

3.9 Extend the state diagram in Figure 3.1 with the state "Suspend for Child Activation" from Figure 3.3 and a state "Waiting Dependent Termination" to indicate that a master is waiting for its dependents to terminate.

3.10 Extend the state diagram in Figure 3.1 with the state "Abnormal."

4

Communication and synchronization based on shared objects

In Chapter 3 we introduced the task. The tasks in all of the examples in that chapter were independent. They did not share any resources nor did they communicate with each other. As suggested by the cooking examples of Chapter 1, the solution to most parallel problems requires cooperation among tasks. Such cooperation involves communication, mutual exclusion, and synchronization. **Communication** is the exchange of data or control signals between processes. **Mutual exclusion** is a mechanism that prevents two processes from simultaneously using the same resource. **Synchronization** ensures that multiple processes working on a job complete the steps of that job in the correct order. There are two approaches for communication among processes. In this chapter we look at indirect communication via shared objects. In Chapter 5, we'll look at direct communication via Ada's rendezvous mechanism.

4.1 Mutual exclusion

Let's start with a simple example that illustrates the need for mutually exclusive access to a resource used by multiple tasks. A small but popular museum has a limited capacity. When that capacity is reached, the sale of tickets must be suspended until space is made available by the departure of some visitors. Recently, the museum has installed turnstiles at each of its four entrances and hired a programmer to write the software to monitor the turnstiles and keep count of the number of visitors currently in the museum. Here is the specification of the package that provides the input from the turnstile sensors at the museum's four entrances.

```
package Turnstile is

-- This package provides an interface to the
-- Museum's turnstile sensors

   -- The Museum has four doors
```

```
type Entrance_Type  is (North, South, East, West);
-- A person can enter or leave through a turnstile
type Direction_Type is (Enter, Leave);

procedure Get (Entrance  : in  Entrance_Type;
               Direction : out Direction_Type);
-- The caller of this procedure is blocked until a
-- person passes through the turnstile at the given
-- entrance.  Its return value indicates whether the
-- person has entered or left the Museum.

end Turnstile;
```

This package encapsulates the code that monitors the turnstiles at the four museum entrances. Procedure **Turnstile.Get** waits until someone passes through the designated turnstile. It then returns the direction in which the person passed. Here is the first version of a program that uses the information from the turnstiles to track the current number of visitors in the museum.

```
with Turnstile;          use Turnstile;
with Ada.Exceptions;
with Ada.Integer_Text_IO;  use Ada.Integer_Text_IO;
with Ada.Text_IO;          use Ada.Text_IO;
procedure Museum_V1 is

-- This program uses a global variable shared by five tasks
-- to monitor the number of visitors inside a museum
--
-- This version works "most of the time"
--
--     Sometimes at closing time, it indicates that
--     the museum is not empty when indeed it is empty
--
--     Sometimes an entrance monitor task terminates with
--     the exception Constraint_Error

   Maximum    : constant := 100; -- Museum capacity
   Population  : Natural  := 0;  -- Current number of visitors

   -- A task type for monitoring turnstiles
   task type Entrance_Monitor
             (My_Entrance : Turnstile.Entrance_Type);

   task body Entrance_Monitor is
      Direction : Turnstile.Direction_Type;
   begin
      loop
         -- Wait until someone passes through my turnstile
         Turnstile.Get (My_Entrance, Direction);

         -- Update the number of people in the Museum
```

```ada
        case Direction is
          when Turnstile.Enter =>
            Population := Population + 1;
          when Turnstile.Leave =>
            Population := Population - 1;
        end case;
      end loop;
  exception
    when Except : others =>
        Put_Line
          (File => Standard_Error,
           Item => Entrance_Type'Image (My_Entrance) &
            " turnstile task terminated with exception "
            & Ada.Exceptions.Exception_Name (Except));
  end Entrance_Monitor;

  -- One task to monitor each of the four museum doors
  North_Door : Entrance_Monitor (Turnstile.North);
  South_Door : Entrance_Monitor (Turnstile.South);
  East_Door  : Entrance_Monitor (Turnstile.East);
  West_Door  : Entrance_Monitor (Turnstile.West);

  Museum_Full : Boolean := False;

begin
  loop
    Put ("Current number of visitors is ");
    Put (Item => Population, Width => 1);
    New_Line;

    -- Check for change in ticket selling status
    if not Museum_Full and Population >= Maximum then
        Put_Line ("The Museum is full. " &
                  "Suspend ticket sales.");
        Museum_Full := True;
    elsif Museum_Full and Population < Maximum then
        Put_Line ("The Museum is no longer full. " &
                  "Resume ticket sales.");
        Museum_Full := False;
    end if;

    delay 1.0;  -- Update status every second
  end loop;
end Museum_V1;
```

The program uses the global variable **Population** to track the current number of visitors. Four tasks monitor the turnstiles at the museum's four entrances. The body of these tasks contains a loop that gets information from its turnstile and either increments or decrements the global variable **Population**. A fifth task executes the main subprogram which contains a loop that queries the global variable `Population`, displays the current number of visitors, and displays an appropriate message when ticket sales should be suspended or resumed. The four monitor tasks communicate with the display task indirectly through the global variable `Population`.

As the comments in this program indicate, it operates correctly most of the time. Perhaps once a month the visitor count displayed is greater than zero at closing time even through the museum docents have confirmed that all visitors have left. Also occasionally, one of the four turnstile monitor tasks displays an error message indicating that it has terminated because of a Constraint_Error. We suspect that the task attempted to make the `Natural` variable `Population` negative.

In Chapter 1 we introduced the scenario as a tool for discovering the potential for deadlock when multiple tasks share a resource. The same technique may be used to debug the problem in this application. This time, it is a computer executing instructions rather than humans. While we may see and think of instructions written in Ada, we must remember that the computer is executing machine language instructions. An assignment statement is usually translated by the Ada compiler into several machine instructions. For example, the Ada statement to increment `Population` might be translated into three machine language instructions as follows:

`Population := Population + 1;`

    Copy the value of `Population` from memory to a CPU register
    Increment the CPU register
    Replace the value of `Population` in memory with the value of the CPU register

With this insight, it isn't difficult to find a scenario that fails when two people enter through the East and North turnstiles around the same time.

1. The East task copies the value of `Population` (say it is 52) into its CPU register
2. The North task copies the value of `Population` (52) into its CPU register
3. The North task increments its register (it becomes 53)
4. The North task replaces the value of `Population` in memory with the value of its register (53)
5. The East task increments its register (it becomes 53)
6. The East task replaces the value of `Population` in memory with the value of its register (53)

Each of the two tasks incremented the original value (52) of the shared variable. We need to find a way to delay one of the tasks from carrying out the update of the variable until the other has completed its update. Each task requires exclusive access to the shared variable `Population` while it completes all the necessary machine instructions to increment or decrement that variable.

4.2 The protected object

Ada's protected object provides a safe and efficient mechanism for multiple tasks to share data. The protected object encapsulates the data allowing access only through protected operations. Ada ensures that these operations are executed with mutually exclusive access to the encapsulated data. We can declare singleton protected objects or define a protected object type from which we can declare multiple protected objects. As with packages and tasks, a protected unit has a specification and body. Let's look at a complete example. Here is a correct version of our museum visitor counting program that encapsulates a shared variable, Count, within the protected object Population.

```ada
with Turnstile;            use Turnstile;
with Ada.Exceptions;
with Ada.Integer_Text_IO;  use Ada.Integer_Text_IO;
with Ada.Text_IO;          use Ada.Text_IO;
procedure Museum is

-- This program uses a protected object shared by five
-- tasks to monitor the number of visitors inside a museum

   Maximum : constant := 100;   -- The Museum capacity

   protected Population is -- The current number of visitors
      procedure Increment;
      procedure Decrement;
      function Current return Natural;
   private
      Count : Natural := 0;
   end Population;

   protected body Population is
      procedure Increment is
      begin
         Count := Count + 1;
      end Increment;

      procedure Decrement is
      begin
         Count := Count - 1;
      end Decrement;

      function Current return Natural is
      begin
         return Count;
      end Current;
   end Population;
```

```ada
-- A task type for monitoring turnstiles
task type Entrance_Monitor
        (My_Entrance : Turnstile.Entrance_Type);

task body Entrance_Monitor is
    Direction : Turnstile.Direction_Type;
begin
    loop
        -- Wait until someone passes through my turnstile
        Turnstile.Get (My_Entrance, Direction);

        -- Update the number of people in the Museum
        case Direction is
            when Turnstile.Enter =>
                Population.Increment;
            when Turnstile.Leave =>
                Population.Decrement;
        end case;
    end loop;
exception
    when Except : others =>
        Put_Line
            (File => Standard_Error,
             Item => Entrance_Type'Image (My_Entrance) &
                " turnstile task terminated with exception "
                & Ada.Exceptions.Exception_Name (Except));
end Entrance_Monitor;

-- One task to monitor each of the four museum doors
North_Door : Entrance_Monitor (Turnstile.North);
South_Door : Entrance_Monitor (Turnstile.South);
East_Door  : Entrance_Monitor (Turnstile.East);
West_Door  : Entrance_Monitor (Turnstile.West);

Museum_Full   : Boolean := False;
Current_Count : Natural;

begin
    loop
        Current_Count := Population.Current;
        Put ("Current number of visitors is ");
        Put (Item => Current_Count, Width => 1);
        New_Line;

        -- Check for change in ticket selling status
        if not Museum_Full and Current_Count >= Maximum then
            Put_Line ("The Museum is full. " &
                    "Suspend ticket sales.");
            Museum_Full := True;
        elsif Museum_Full and Current_Count < Maximum then
```

```
        Put_Line ("The Museum is no longer full.   " &
                 "Resume ticket sales.");
        Museum_Full := False;
    end if;

    delay 1.0;   -- Update status every second
  end loop;
end Museum;
```

The specification of a protected object such as `Population` has a public part and a private part. The public part of `Population` includes the procedures `Increment` and `Decrement` and the function `Current`. These are the protected operations of the protected object. The private part of `Population` contains the data that the object is protecting from simultaneous access. The body of a protected object contains the implementation for each of the operations defined in the specification. These operation bodies can access the data defined in the private part of the specification. In our example, procedures `Increment` and `Decrement` and the function `Current` all access the encapsulated variable `Count`.

In Chapter 1 we demonstrated the need for a protocol to prevent erroneous simultaneous use of a shared resource. The beauty of a protected object is that it provides, through ordinary-looking functions and procedures, sophisticated pre-protocols and post-protocols for safe and efficient use of shared data. We simply place the critical sections of code in the bodies of these subprograms. A protected procedure may examine and modify the encapsulated data. A protected procedure provides mutually exclusive read/write access to the data. When one task is executing the body of a protected procedure, all other tasks are locked out of the object. A protected function may examine the encapsulated data but not modify it. This restriction allows multiple tasks to safely examine the shared data simultaneously.

Let's look at a model that illustrates how protected objects operate. A locking mechanism provides the protection of shared data. Each protected object has two associated locks: a *read lock* and a *read/write lock*. Only one of these locks may be active at any time. Initially both locks are inactive. Both locks must be inactive before a task is allowed to start a protected procedure. The read/write lock becomes active when a task starts a protected procedure. The read/write lock returns to inactive when the task completes execution of the body of the protected procedure. A task may not start a protected function when the read/write lock is active — that lock indicates that a procedure is modifying the shared data. Figure 4.1 illustrates this situation. The protected object is represented by the rectangle containing the protected variables. The large circle around the protected object with the lock symbol represents a lock; the read/write lock in this example. Tasks are represented by small circles. The open circles represent tasks executing or wanting to execute a protected function. Currently all of these tasks are delayed by the read/write lock protecting the data. The small circles with diagonal lines represent tasks executing or wanting to execute a protected procedure. One such task is shown within the protected object indicating that task is currently executing the body of a protected procedure. The double-ended arrow between this task and the encapsulated variables indicates that the task may read and write the protected data. The other seven tasks in this figure are delayed by the read/write lock.

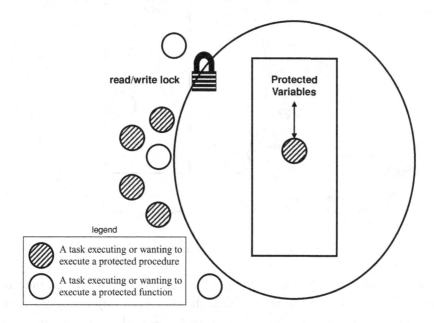

Figure 4.1 The read/write lock

When the task currently executing within the protected object completes the body of the protected procedure, it will leave the object and the read/write lock will become inactive. At that point one of the other tasks will start its desired operation and activate a lock. Which of those many delayed tasks is selected is not defined by the core language.

A task may start a protected function when both locks are inactive or when the read lock is active. The read lock becomes active when a task starts the protected function. Since protected functions cannot change the protected data, any number of tasks may be executing protected functions when the read lock is active. Figure 4.2 illustrates the read lock. In this example, three tasks are executing protected functions within the protected object. The arrows between the encapsulated variables and the tasks currently executing the protected functions indicate that each task may only read the protected data. A fourth task wanting to start a protected function is shown passing through the read lock. The tasks wanting to execute protected procedures are delayed behind the lock. The read lock is removed when the last task executing a protected function leaves the object.

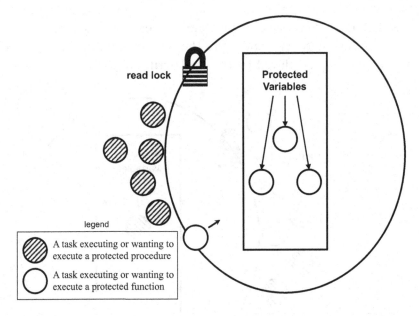

read lock

Protected
Variables

legend

A task executing or wanting to
execute a protected procedure

A task executing or wanting to
execute a protected function

Figure 4.2 The read lock

The two locks provide mutually exclusive read/write access and mutually exclusive read access to the data within the protected object. As tasks may be delayed by these locks, it is important to keep the code in the bodies of protected procedures and functions (the *critical sections*) as short as possible.

Locks do not provide any synchronization. It is possible, therefore, that a group of reader tasks executing protected functions can starve writer tasks wanting to execute protected procedures. One can imagine from Figure 4.2 the possibility of newly arriving reader tasks replacing departing reader tasks, delaying those tasks that need the read/write access provided by the protected procedures.

4.3 Synchronization

In Chapter 1 we introduced synchronization with the example of two cooks preparing a recipe of scalloped potatoes. Horace has to peel a potato before Mildred can slice it. A shared bowl allows them to work at different paces. If Mildred is delayed, Horace could continue working, placing the peeled potatoes into the bowl — at least until the bowl could hold no more. If Horace has to take a break, Mildred could continue slicing — at least until she exhausts the supply of peeled potatoes in the bowl. We could extend the example with additional people peeling and slicing potatoes, all sharing a common bowl. This need to coordinate the asynchronous production and consumption of information or objects is common in concurrent programs — it is known as the **producer-consumer pattern**. Let us see how to implement it in Ada.

We'll use a FIFO queue to buffer the objects between the producers and consumers. Producer tasks will add items to the queue and consumer tasks will remove them. Since the queue is shared by different tasks, we must ensure that any update of the queue is made with mutually exclusive access. Encapsulating the queue within a protected object provides the necessary exclusive access. While protected functions and procedures provide the required mutual exclusion, they do not provide any form of ordering needed to ensure that the tasks' actions are synchronized. Synchronization for our buffer requires that a consumer task must wait if the buffer is empty and a producer task must wait if there is no room in the queue for another item. We use the protected entry to achieve the necessary synchronization.

4.4 The protected entry

The protected entry is the third operation available for accessing the data encapsulated within a protected object. A protected entry call is like a protected procedure call. The protected entry uses the read/write lock in the same way a protected procedure does and the body of a protected entry has mutually exclusive read/write access to the data encapsulated within the object. The object-locking behavior demonstrated for protected procedures in Figures 4.1 and 4.2 applies equally to protected entries.

Synchronization requires the enforcement of an order in which the tasks execute protected operations. To achieve this order, each protected entry includes a Boolean expression called a **barrier**. A barrier that evaluates to True is said to be *open* and a barrier that evaluates to False is said to be *closed*. A task calling a protected entry with a closed barrier will be blocked until that barrier becomes open. The Boolean expression of a barrier should test the state of the protected object. Barriers should not test variables outside of the protected object. The barriers are evaluated when an entry is first called. They are reevaluated when something happens that could possibly change the barrier. Only protected procedures and entries may change the state of the protected object; a protected function may only query the state. Thus barriers are evaluated when an entry is first called and reevaluated upon the completion of an entry or procedure body by some task.

Before looking at the details of the barrier mechanism, let's look at a full example. The program below illustrates the use of protected entries to implement a producer-consumer pattern. It has five producer tasks and one consumer task that communicate through a buffer encapsulated within a shared protected object.

```ada
with Ada. Integer_Text_IO ;        use Ada. Integer_Text_IO ;
with Ada. Text_IO ;               use Ada. Text_IO ;
with Ada. Numerics. Float_Random ;  use Ada. Numerics ;
with Bounded_Queue ;
procedure Producer_Consumer_Demo is

    Number_Of_Producers : constant := 5;
    Producer_Iterations : constant := 8;


    ------------------------------------------------------------

    package Integer_Queue is new
            Bounded_Queue ( Element_Type => Positive );


    ------------------------------------------------------------

    protected type Bounded_Buffer ( Max_Size : Positive ) is
        procedure Clear ;
        -- delete all of the items in the buffer
        entry Put ( Item : in Positive );
        -- add a value to the buffer
        entry Take ( Item : out Positive );
        -- remove a value from the buffer
    private
        Buffer : Integer_Queue. Queue_Type ( Max_Size );
    end Bounded_Buffer ;

    protected body Bounded_Buffer is
        procedure Clear is
        begin
            Integer_Queue. Clear ( Buffer );
        end Clear ;

        entry Put ( Item : in Positive )
                when not Integer_Queue. Full ( Buffer ) is
        begin
            Integer_Queue. Enqueue ( Queue => Buffer ,
                                     Item  => Item );
        end Put ;

        entry Take ( Item : out Positive )
```

```ada
          when not Integer_Queue.Empty (Buffer) is
      begin
         Integer_Queue.Dequeue (Queue => Buffer,
                                 Item  => Item);
      end Take;
end Bounded_Buffer;

-- The buffer object.  Holds a maximum of 3 entries.
The_Buffer : Bounded_Buffer (Max_Size => 3);


----------------------------------------------------

protected ID_Generator is
   procedure Get (ID : out Positive);
   -- Returns a unique positive ID number
private
   Next_ID : Positive := 1;
end ID_Generator;

protected body ID_Generator is
   procedure Get (ID : out Positive) is
   begin
      ID := Next_ID;
      Next_ID := Next_ID + 1;
   end Get;
end ID_Generator;


----------------------------------------------------------

protected Random_Duration is
   procedure Get (Item : out Duration);
   -- Returns a random duration value
   -- between 0.0 and 1.0 seconds
private
   First_Call   : Boolean := True;
   My_Generator : Ada.Numerics.Float_Random.Generator;
end Random_Duration;

protected body Random_Duration is
   procedure Get (Item : out Duration) is
   begin
      if First_Call then
         -- On the first call, reset the generator
         Ada.Numerics.Float_Random.Reset (My_Generator);
         First_Call := False;
      end if;
      -- Get a random value and convert it to a duration
      Item := Duration (Float_Random.Random (My_Generator));
   end Get;
end Random_Duration;


----------------------------------------------------------
```

```
task type Producer;

task body Producer is
    My_ID     : Positive;
    My_Delay : Duration;
begin
    -- Get a unique ID for this task
    ID_Generator.Get (ID => My_ID);
    -- Put my ID into the bounded buffer 8 times
    for Count in 1 .. Producer_Iterations loop
        -- Put my ID into the buffer
        The_Buffer.Put (My_ID);
        -- Simulate the time to do the work
        -- to actually produce something
        Random_Duration.Get (My_Delay);
        delay My_Delay;
    end loop;
end Producer;


-- A number of producer tasks
type Producer_Array is array (1 .. Number_Of_Producers)
                        of Producer;
Producers : Producer_Array;

-----------------------------------------------------------------
Value           : Positive;
Consumer_Delay : Duration;
begin
    -- Consume everything in the bounded buffer
    for Count in 1 .. Number_Of_Producers * Producer_Iterations
    loop
        The_Buffer.Take (Value);
        Put (Item => Value, Width => 2);
        New_Line;
        -- Simulate the time to do the work
        -- to actually consume something
        Random_Duration.Get (Consumer_Delay);
        delay Consumer_Delay / Number_Of_Producers;
    end loop;
end Producer_Consumer_Demo;
```

Let's begin with the protected type Bounded_Buffer. We use this type to declare the protected object The_Buffer. As with task types, we can include a discriminant with the declaration of a protected type. In this program, the discriminant specifies the capacity of the buffer. Protected type Bounded_Buffer has three operations. The protected procedure Clear may be called to empty the buffer. The protected entry Put appends a positive integer to the buffer and the protected entry Take removes and returns the first number from the buffer. The data encapsulated within this protected type is a FIFO queue of positive integers instantiated from the generic bounded queue package from Chapter 2. We use the value of the protected type's discriminant to specify the capacity of the FIFO queue.

The body of the protected type Bounded_Buffer includes the definition of a barrier for each of our two entries. Recall that the barrier must be open (True) for the call to the entry to take place. The barrier for entry Put states that the encapsulated FIFO queue Buffer must not be full. The barrier for entry Take states that the encapsulated FIFO queue Buffer must not be empty. These two barriers ensure that a calling task does not take a value from an empty buffer or attempt to add a value to a full buffer. The bodies of the protected procedure and the two protected entries call the appropriate FIFO queue operations to accomplish their jobs.

Now let's move down to the producer tasks. We define the task type Producer and use it to declare the array of five tasks, Producers. The body of task type Producer begins with a call to the protected object ID_Generator's procedure Get to obtain a unique identification number. ID_Generator encapsulates a counter used to provide these numbers. The producer task then puts eight copies of its identification number into The_Buffer. After placing each number into the buffer, the task blocks itself for a random time. The amount of time is obtained from the random number generator encapsulated in the shared protected object Random_Duration.

The one consumer task in this example executes the main subprogram. It takes numbers out of The_Buffer and displays them. Like the producer tasks, the consumer task obtains a random delay time from the shared protected object Random_Duration which it uses in a delay statement before taking the next number out of The_Buffer.

In Chapter 1 we introduced the scenario as a means for understanding concurrent algorithms. Let's look at a scenario that illustrates the behavior of the protected entries in program Producer_Consumer_Demo.

1. Producers(1) obtains its ID number
2. Producers(2) obtains its ID number
3. The consumer task calls entry Take, the barrier is closed (because Buffer is empty) so the consumer task is blocked
4. Producers(1) calls entry Put, the barrier is open so its number is enqueued into Buffer
5. Take's barrier is now open, the consumer task is unblocked and removes the number from Buffer
6. Producers(3) obtains its ID number
7. Producers(2) calls entry Put, the barrier is open so its number is enqueued into Buffer
8. Producers(4) obtains its ID number

9. `Producers(1)` gets a random delay value

10. `Producers(1)` executes the delay statement and is blocked

11. `Producers(4)` calls entry `Put`, the barrier is open so its number is enqueued into `Buffer`

12. `Producers(3)` calls entry `Put`, the barrier is open so its number is enqueued into `Buffer`

13. `Producers(5)` obtains its ID number

14. `Producers(5)` calls entry `Put`, the barrier is closed (because `Buffer` is full) so the task is blocked

15. The consumer task's delay time has expired

16. The consumer task calls entry `Take`, the barrier is open so a number is removed from the `Buffer`

17. `Put`'s barrier is now open, `Producers(5)` is unblocked and enqueues its number into `Buffer`

18. And so on ...

Steps 3 and 5 illustrate how entry `Take`'s barrier blocks consumers until there is something in `Buffer`. Steps 14 and 17 show how entry `Put`'s barrier blocks producers when `Buffer` is full. Mutual exclusion of shared data and task synchronization are completely handled by the protected objects. We need not include any special code within the tasks to obtain these necessary protections.

4.5 Restrictions

A *critical section* is a group of instructions that must not be executed concurrently by multiple tasks. The bodies of protected operations are critical sections. Other tasks are forced to wait while one task is executing a protected operation. It is therefore important to keep the code in protected operations as short as possible.

It is also important that a task is not blocked while executing a protected operation.[1] It is a bounded error[2] to execute a *potentially blocking* operation from within a protected operation. Potentially blocking operations include

- Delay statements
- Calls to protected object entries
- Creation or activation of a task
- Calls to subprograms whose body contains a potentially blocking operation

---

[1] Reasons for this restriction include a very efficient implementation of mutual exclusion and decreasing the potential of deadlock scenarios.

[2] A bounded error need not be detected either prior to or during run time.

- Others to be described in Chapter 5

Most input/output operations are potentially blocking. You should never call a Get or Put procedure within a protected operation. While calling a protected entry is potentially blocking, calling a protected function or a protected procedure is not potentially blocking.

While we are discussing restrictions, we'll remind you again that the Boolean expressions used in barriers should limit their testing to variables within the protected object. This limitation facilitates the reevaluation of the barrier. Barriers should not test variables outside of the protected object. The barriers are only reevaluated when some task completes the execution of the body of a protected procedure or entry. A task changing some variable global to the protected object does not trigger a reevaluation of the barriers.

4.6 Entry queues

Each protected entry has a queue associated with it. When a task calls an entry whose barrier is closed, it is added to that entry's queue. Figure 4.3 illustrates the two entry queues in our protected object The_Buffer from the program Producer_Consumer_Demo. Currently, the consumer task is executing the protected entry Take. The read/write lock is active, delaying tasks Producer(1) and Producer(3). The entry queue for Take is empty and its barrier, indicated by the hinged gate on the right side of the queue, is open. Three producer tasks are blocked and waiting in the entry queue for Put. As the Buffer is currently full, the barrier for Put is closed.

When the consumer task completes the removal of a number from the buffer and exits the protected object, all barriers are reevaluated. Entry Put's barrier is opened and depending on whether or not the consumer removed the last item in the queue, entry Take's barrier either remains open or is closed. As there are producer tasks waiting in the queue, the task at the head of the queue is selected, removed from the queue, and allowed to put its value into the buffer.

Our simple example demonstrates the order that Ada imposes on the selection of the task that executes next within the protected object. Queued entry calls have precedence over other operations on the protected object. Figure 4.3 shows producer tasks (1) and (3) outside of the protective shell of the read/write lock. Producer tasks (2), (4) and (5) are within the shell. When each of these latter three tasks *began* the execution of entry Put, the read/write lock was not active. Each activated the lock and checked the barrier condition. As the barrier was closed, the task was blocked and placed on Put's entry queue. Upon joining the entry queue, the newly blocked task released the read/write lock. These three tasks will not be delayed again by

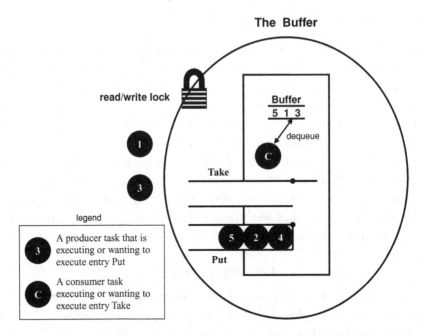

Figure 4.3 Entry queues for the protected bounded buffer

a read lock or a read/write lock before they execute the body of entry Put. These tasks, as Ben-Ari (2009) states, "have already passed the outer shell and are considered part of the 'club' and have preference over calls that have not yet commenced."

When a task completes the execution of a protected procedure or protected entry and leaves the protected object, all barriers are reevaluated. If one or more barriers are open, one of the entry queues is serviced — the task at the head of that queue is removed and begins execution of the entry body. The read/write lock remains active during the switch from the task that exited the protected object to the task now executing within it. Figure 4.4 shows The_Buffer just after the consumer task completed its removal of the number from Buffer in Figure 4.3. After Producer task (4) completes the body of entry Put and leaves the protected object, the two barriers are reevaluated. Since Buffer is again full, the barrier for entry Put will close.

After evaluating all the barriers, it is possible to have more than one entry queue with waiting tasks and open barriers. Ada does not specify which of these queues is serviced. You should assume that the selection is arbitrary. However, the Real-Time Systems Annex (Appendix D of the ARM) provides the pragma Queuing_Policy which we may use to specify a deterministic selection. We'll discuss this pragma in Chapter 8.

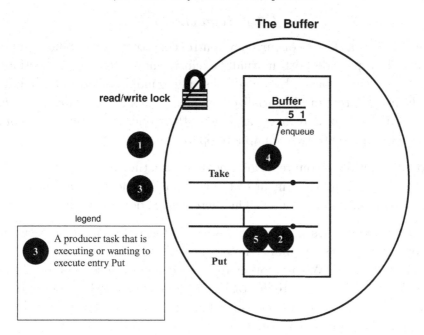

Figure 4.4 Tasks in the entry queues have precedence over those delayed behind the lock

The bodies of protected operations may use the 'Count attribute to query the current length of an entry queue. The 'Count attribute may also be used in barriers. We'll look at some examples using this attribute in the next section. While the 'Count attribute would seem a useful operation, one must use it with care in programs that use abort statements or timed entry calls (Chapter 5). A queue with five entries becomes a queue of four entries after one task in the queue is aborted.

4.7 Some useful concurrent patterns

The concurrent programming literature is filled with many patterns for communication between and synchronization of processes. The protected object provides a simple efficient mechanism for implementing many of these patterns. We have already showed you how the bounded buffer pattern can easily be implemented by a protected object. In this section we look at a number of additional patterns and their implementations. The implementations given here are based on those of Burns and Wellings (1998). These same authors provide an updated set of concurrency utilities based on Ada's object-oriented features (Burns and Wellings, 2007).

4.7.1 Semaphores

A semaphore is a classic concurrency control construct. It combines a counter and a lock to provide both mutually exclusive access to critical sections of code and synchronization between tasks. The semaphore's counter is initialized during its creation. If initialized to one, it is called a *binary semaphore* and if it is initialized to a value greater than one, it is called a *counting semaphore*. There are two semaphore operations.

Wait Wait until the counter is greater than zero, then decrement the counter. The test and decrement of the counter is done as an atomic action.

Signal Increment the counter. The increment is done as an atomic action.

Each semaphore has an associated queue of tasks. When a task performs a wait operation on a semaphore whose counter is zero, the task is added to the semaphore's queue. When another task increments the semaphore through a signal operation and there are tasks on the queue, a task is removed from the queue and it resumes execution. The first thing that the task does on resumption is to decrement the counter.

We associate a different semaphore with each shared resource. This association is done informally; there is no formal syntax to connect the resource and the semaphore. To ensure mutually exclusive access to a shared resource, every task that accesses the resource must call wait before accessing the resource and call signal after completing its use of the resource. The following code fragment illustrates the use of a binary semaphore to provide mutually exclusive access to the global variable `Population` in the first version of our museum visitor counting program.

```
-- The shared variable
Population : Natural := 0;
-- A binary semaphore which we have associated with Population
Sem : Semaphore (Initial_Value => 1);
```

```
-------------------------------------------------------------------
-- Use of the semaphore to protect the shared variable Populati
Sem.Wait;      -- Wait until the resource (Population) is availabl
Population := Population + 1;    -- Critical Section
Sem.Signal;   -- Signal that the resource is now available
```

The `Wait` operation provides the pre-protocol and the `Signal` operation provides the post-protocol for ensuring mutually exclusive access to the shared resource. Each task that accesses the shared resource must include the calls to `Wait` and `Signal` before and after the access. Contrast this approach to that of the protected object in which each shared resource is encapsulated in an object. The pre- and post-protocols are associated with the data rather than repeated within every task that accesses the data.

Semaphores may also be used to provide synchronization. Two semaphores are required to achieve the necessary synchronization for the bounded buffer in our producer-consumer pattern. A third semaphore is needed to ensure mutually exclusive access to the buffer.

The need for multiple semaphores to implement most simple synchronization patterns, having to include semaphore operations within *each* task accessing a shared resource, and the the need to manually match up signal/wait operations make the semaphore an error-prone construct. It is indeed a low-level mechanism which some people liken to the "assembly language" of concurrent programming.

In Ada, the semaphore may be used to overcome the restriction that a protected operation may not execute a potentially blocking operation. Let's look at an example of creating and using a semaphore in Ada. It is common for multiple tasks to write to the console. We require mutually exclusive access to the console to prevent the interleaving of characters in messages produced by various tasks. Normally we would achieve mutually exclusive access by encapsulating the resource (calls to `Text_IO.Put`) within a protected object. However, because input/output operations in package `Text_IO` are potentially blocking, it is not possible to do so. The semaphore provides a workable alternative. So that we need not enclose every call to `Text_IO.Put` between Wait and Signal, we will encapsulate the semaphore and code to call `Text_IO.Put` within a package. Here is a specification and body for a very simple such package.

```
package Protected_Output is

    -- This package provides task safe output procedures.
    -- The execution of a procedure in this package has
    -- mutually exclusive access to the console

    procedure Put (Item : in String);

    procedure Put_Line (Item : in String);

end Protected_Output;


with Ada.Text_IO;
package body Protected_Output is

    protected type Semaphore (Initial_Value : Natural) is
        procedure Signal;
```

```
      entry Wait;
   private
      Count : Natural := Initial_Value;
   end Semaphore;

   protected body Semaphore is
      procedure Signal is
      begin
         Count := Count + 1;
      end Signal;

      entry Wait when Count > 0 is
      begin
         Count := Count - 1;
      end Wait;
   end Semaphore;

   My_Semaphore : Semaphore (Initial_Value => 1);

   ---------------------------------------------------------
   procedure Put (Item : in String) is
   begin
      My_Semaphore.Wait;
      Ada.Text_IO.Put (Item);
      My_Semaphore.Signal;
   end Put;

   procedure Put_Line (Item : in String) is
   begin
      My_Semaphore.Wait;
      Ada.Text_IO.Put_Line (Item);
      My_Semaphore.Signal;
   end Put_Line;

end Protected_Output;
```

Let's first look at the definition of the semaphore in the package body. The semaphore type is a protected object encapsulating a counter which is initialized to the value of the discriminant, Initial_Value. We initialize My_Semaphore to one, indicating that the resource (the console) is currently available. The protected procedure Signal implements the semaphore signal operation and the protected entry Wait with its barrier implements the semaphore wait operation. The entry queue serves as the semaphore's queue of waiting tasks.

The body of each output operation defined in the specification encloses a call to the appropriate output operation in package Ada.Text_IO between a semaphore wait and a semaphore signal operation. Should the console be in use when a task calls the semaphore wait operation, it will wait its turn in the entry queue until the task ahead of it has signaled its completion of console use.

4.7.2 Barriers

A barrier provides a type of synchronization. Do not confuse this synchronization pattern with the term barrier associated with Ada's protected entries. The barrier pattern is used to block several tasks until a set number of tasks have arrived. It is like a horse race that begins only when all of the horses have arrived at the starting gate. At that point, all of the tasks are released. Here is a specification and body for a package that implements barriers.

```ada
package Barriers is

    protected type Barrier (Group_Size : Positive) is
        -- wait until Group_Size tasks are waiting at this entry
        entry Wait;
    private
        Gate_Open : Boolean := False;
    end Barrier;

end Barriers;
```

```ada
package body Barriers is

    protected body Barrier is
        entry Wait
                when Wait'Count = Group_Size or Gate_Open is
        begin
            if Wait'Count > 0 then
                -- The first task released opens the gate
                -- for the rest. Tasks released before the
                -- last task keep the gate open.
                Gate_Open := True;
            else
                -- The last task released closes the gate
                Gate_Open := False;
            end if;
        end Wait;
    end Barrier;

end Barriers;
```

Wait's entry barrier opens when the value of the Wait'Count (the number of tasks in the entry queue) is equal to the number of tasks set by Group_Size. When the barrier opens, the first task on the entry queue is selected and executes the body of `Wait`. At this point, the number of tasks in `Wait`'s entry queue is below the `Group_Size`. To allow these remaining tasks in the group to execute entry `Wait`, the first task sets the protected Boolean variable `Gate_Open` to True. Thus even though `Wait'Count` is less than `Group_Size`, the entry barrier remains open. The last task selected from the queue resets the protected Boolean variable `Gate_Open` to False. "The last person leaving turns off the lights" is an analogy frequently given to this programming paradigm.

Because tasks in entry queues have precedence over those delayed behind the protected object's lock, we are guaranteed that the tasks queued on `Wait`'s entry barrier execute the body of `Wait` before any other tasks even test the barrier condition. Any tasks delayed behind the lock will be queued for the next release. A program that demonstrates the barrier synchronization pattern is available on our web site.

4.7.3 Broadcasts

We use the broadcast pattern to send a message to a group of tasks waiting for it. Like a radio broadcast, only the tasks that are "tuned in" and waiting for the message receive it. Tasks that tune in later miss the message and must wait for the next message to be sent. We'll use a generic package to implement our broadcast pattern. We can instantiate it for any message type we desire. Here is the specification.

```
generic
   type Message_Type is private;
package Broadcasts is

   protected type Broadcast is
      procedure Send (Message : in Message_Type);
      -- Send a message to all waiting tasks
      entry Tune_In (Message : out Message_Type);
      -- Wait for a message
   private
      The_Message  : Message_Type;
      Have_Message : Boolean := False;
   end Broadcast;

end Broadcasts;
```

Tasks call the entry `Tune_In` to wait for a message. A task calls the procedure `Send` to broadcast a message to the waiting group. Here is an instantiation of a package for broadcasting temperatures.

```
type Degrees is delta 0.1 range -100.0 .. 100.0;
package Broadcast_Temperature is new
            Broadcasts (Message_Type => Degrees);
```

And here is the body of the generic broadcast package.

```
package body Broadcasts is

  protected body Broadcast is

    procedure Send (Message : in Message_Type) is
    begin
        -- Do something only if tasks are waiting
        if Tune_In 'Count > 0 then
            The_Message  := Message;
            Have_Message := True;
        end if;
    end Send;

    entry Tune_In (Message : out Message_Type)
          when Have_Message is
    begin
        Message := The_Message;
        if Tune_In 'Count = 0 then
            Have_Message := False;
        end if;
    end Tune_In;

  end Broadcast;

end Broadcasts;
```

The protected procedure **Send** first checks to see if any listeners are waiting in the queue for entry **Tune_In**. If no tasks are waiting, **Send** does nothing with its message. Otherwise, it stores its message in the protected variable **The_Message** and opens the entry barrier by setting the Boolean variable **Have_Message** to True. Once the barrier is open, all of the waiting tasks take a copy of the message. The last task in the queue closes the barrier to prevent any non-queued tasks from accessing the message. A program that demonstrates the broadcast synchronization pattern is available on our web site.

4.8 Requeue and private operations

Assigning limited resources is a basic problem in concurrent programming as well as in life. For example, suppose a school has a supply of 100 special pencils for their ancient mark sense exam scoring machine. When a teacher gives an exam to their class, they request a number of pencils from the principal. When the exam is finished, the teacher returns the pencils. Should the principal not have enough pencils to satisfy all requests, some teachers may have to wait until another teacher returns pencils. Because pencils wear out and are stolen, the teachers may not return as many pencils as they requested. New pencils are occasionally added to the inventory.

We can use a protected object to model the principal. As teachers may have to wait until the principal has sufficient pencils for their needs, we use an entry for pencil requests. There should be no waiting to return pencils, so we use a procedure for that operation. Here is our first attempt at defining the protected object.

```
package Resource_Allocation_1st_Attempt is

    protected type Manager (Initial_Inventory : Positive) is
        entry Take (Number_Required : in Positive);
        -- Make a request for resources.  The caller is blocked
        -- until the amount requested is available
        procedure Replace (Number_Returned : in Positive);
        -- Return resources so some other task may use them.
    private
        Inventory : Natural := Initial_Inventory;
    end Manager;

end Resource_Allocation_1st_Attempt;
```

The body of the package would seem to be trivial — just decrement the inventory when resources are taken and increment the inventory when resources are returned. And, of course, we will need to add a barrier to our entry to block any task requesting more resources than are currently in memory. Here is that package body.

```
package body Resource_Allocation_1st_Attempt is

    protected body Manager is

        entry Take (Number_Required : in Positive)
                    when Number_Required >= Inventory is
        begin
            Inventory := Inventory - Number_Required;
        end Take;

        procedure Replace (Number_Returned : in Positive) is
        begin
            Inventory := Inventory + Number_Returned;
        end Replace;

    end Manager;

end Resource_Allocation_1st_Attempt;
```

Unfortunately, this package body does not compile. The Ada compiler balks at the condition we used in our barrier. Here is the errant line and the error message.

```
entry Take (Number_Required : in Positive)
        when Number_Required <= Inventory is
```

ERROR "Number_Required" is undefined

We may not use parameters in our barrier expressions. This restriction makes sense when you recall that this barrier must be evaluated after resources are returned as well as when requests are made. We may only determine the value of an entry parameter within the entry body.[3] Returning to our school analogy, we cannot block a teacher at the principal's door with a barrier that tests the number of pencils the teacher needs. We must let the teacher into the office to find out how large their request is. Everything is fine if the principal has enough pencils to satisfy that request. However, there is a problem if the principal does not have a sufficient inventory of pencils. Our solution is to move the teacher into a private waiting room adjacent to the principal's office where they will wait until another teacher returns some pencils. At that point the principal can let the teacher waiting in the private room back into the office to see if their request may now be filled. If it can, we are done. If it can't, we'll return the teacher to the private waiting room. Here is the specification of a resource controller based on this new model.

```
package Resource_Allocation is

    protected type Manager (Initial_Inventory : Positive) is
        entry Take (Number_Required : in Positive);
        -- Make a request for resources.  The caller is blocked
        -- until the amount requested is available
        procedure Replace (Number_Returned : in Positive);
        -- Return resources so some other task may use them.
    private
        Inventory          : Natural := Initial_Inventory;
        Tasks_Waiting      : Natural;
        Resource_Released  : Boolean := False;
        entry Wait (Number_Required : in Positive);
    end Manager;

end Resource_Allocation;
```

---

[3] There are two additional reasons for prohibiting the use of a parameter in a barrier expression. First, it is costly to implement. Second, it would allow a programmer to define their own entry queueing policy which would make the analyses discussed in Chapter 7 far more complex.

The specification of the protected type includes three more items in the private part. Entry `Wait` corresponds to the private waiting room in our school analogy. We'll use the variables `Tasks_Waiting` and `Resource_Released` to process all of the tasks in the private waiting room whenever resources are returned.

The only remaining problem is how we move the unsatisfied requester to the private waiting room. Making an entry call from an entry body is not allowed as it is a potentially blocking operation. The solution is Ada's requeue statement. The **requeue statement** redirects an entry call to a new entry queue. It may also redirect the call to the same entry queue. There is one restriction with the requeue statement — the entry to which we requeue a task must either have no parameters or have the same signature (parameter profile) as the entry from which it is being moved. Here is the body of our resource controller that makes use of the requeue statement.

```
package body Resource_Allocation is

    protected body Manager is

        entry Take (Number_Required : in Positive)
                when Inventory > 0 is
        begin
            if Number_Required <= Inventory then
                Inventory := Inventory - Number_Required;
            else
                requeue Wait;
            end if;
        end Take;

        procedure Replace (Number_Returned : in Positive) is
        begin
            Inventory := Inventory + Number_Returned;
            Tasks_Waiting := Wait'Count;
            if Tasks_Waiting > 0 then
                Resource_Released := True;
            end if;
        end Replace;

        entry Wait (Number_Required : in Positive)
                when Resource_Released is
        begin
            -- Decrement number of tasks waiting
            Tasks_Waiting := Tasks_Waiting - 1;
            -- Am I the last task to be checked?
            if Tasks_Waiting = 0 then
                -- Close the barrier
                Resource_Released := False;
            end if;
            -- Are there enough resources for my request
```

```
   if Number_Required <= Inventory then
        Inventory := Inventory - Number_Required;
   else    -- Get back in line and wait for more resources
        requeue Wait;
   end if;
  end Wait;

 end Manager;

end Resource_Allocation;
```

The body of entry **Take** is straightforward. If there are enough resources in the inventory, we allocate them. Otherwise, we requeue the caller on the private entry **Wait**. Procedure **Replace** is a little more complicated than our first attempt. After incrementing the inventory, we check to see how many tasks are waiting at the private entry **Wait**. If there are one or more tasks in that entry's queue, we set the Boolean variable **Resource_Released** to True. This change will open the barrier of the private entry **Wait**. The logic of entry **Wait** is similar to what we used in our implementations of barriers and broadcasts. But the "last one out turn off the lights" pattern is different. Because we might requeue a task back onto entry **Wait**, we cannot use the **Wait'Count** to test whether or not to close the barrier. Instead, we use the variable **Tasks_Waiting** in this role. This variable is initialized to **Wait'Count** by a task returning a resource. It is decremented by each task as they check to see whether the recently released resources are sufficient to satisfy their needs. A program that demonstrates the resource allocation pattern is available on our web site.

One final note on this implementation of a resource controller. It assumes that the entry queues are FIFO queues. In Chapters 7 and 8 we'll introduce the notion of priority and how we can request that entry queues be priority queues rather than FIFO queues. Burns and Wellings (1998; 2007) discuss solutions for resource allocation with priority entry queues.

4.9 Pragmas Atomic and Volatile

In this chapter we have shown how tasks can cooperate through shared resources. Shared resources allow tasks to communicate and synchronize. We emphasized the need to protect variables that are shared by multiple tasks. The museum example clearly demonstrated the consequences of failing to provide mutually exclusive access to a shared variable. We introduced the protected object and described how its locks ensure mutually exclusive access to its data and its entry barriers provide the means for synchronization. In this section, we look at the special circumstances in which we can do without the protected object and allow multiple tasks to access a simple shared variable directly.

If the following three conditions are met, it is safe for multiple tasks to access an "unprotected" shared variable.

1. Each task either reads the variable or writes the variable, but not both.
2. Each read and write is done as an indivisible action.
3. There are no temporary copies of the variable.

The first condition eliminates the problem that we saw in the original museum software. To update the shared variable **Population**, the turnstile tasks had to both read and write the shared variable. The problems arose when a second task's reading and writing were interleaved with the first task's. The second condition ensures that a read or write operation has no interference from simultaneous write operations. To meet this condition, the processor must be able to read or write the variable in a single indivisible machine cycle. The third condition is broken when the compiler, in an attempt to optimize our code, creates temporary copies of the variable in a register. All of the tasks must access the same memory location, not some temporary copy.

The burden of satisfying the first condition is the responsibility of the program designer. Ada provides two pragmas to direct the compiler to meet the other two. Pragma **Atomic** will either ensure that the compiler satisfies the last two conditions or produce a syntax error to inform us that it cannot ensure those conditions. Here is an incomplete program which demonstrates the use of pragma **Atomic**. The shared global variable **Value** is written to by three tasks (one being the main task) while eight tasks read variable **Value**.

```
procedure Atomic_Demo is

    Value : Natural := 0;
    pragma Atomic (Value);

    task type Writer;
    task body Writer is
        My_Value : Natural := 0;
    begin
        loop
            -- Create My_Value
            -- My_Value := ...
            --Write My_Value to the shared global
            Value := My_Value;
            delay 0.1;
        end loop;
    end Writer;
```

```
task type Reader;
task body Reader is
    My_Value : Natural;
begin
    loop
        -- Read the shared global
        My_Value := Value;
        -- Do something with My_Value
        -- ...
        delay 0.2;
    end loop;
end Reader;

type Writer_Array is array (1 .. 2) of Writer;
type Reader_Array is array (1 .. 8) of Reader;

The_Writers : Writer_Array;
The_Readers : Reader_Array;

begin
    Value := 25;
end Atomic_Demo;
```

It is unlikely that an array can be read or written in a single machine cycle. However, the pragma `Atomic_Components` may be used to ensure that the reading and writing of a single array component satisfies the last two conditions for shared access.

In our discussion of assigning package variables to memory-mapped device registers in Chapter 2, we introduced the pragma `Volatile`. This pragma ensures that reads and writes to the named variable go directly to memory rather than to a possible copy that the compiler optimizes into registers. The related pragma `Volatile_Components` ensures that the compiler does not create copies of individual components of the named array variable.

4.10 Interrupts

The device driver we wrote for the analog to digital converter (page 94) used a loop with a delay statement to repeatedly check the done bit. This **polling loop** uses valuable processor time waiting for the device to complete the conversion of an analog voltage. The interrupt provides an alternative to the polling loop. An **interrupt** is an asynchronous event indicating a need for attention. Humans constantly process "interrupts." Suppose we are reading a book and the telephone rings. We insert a bookmark, set down our book, and take the call. When we are finished with the call, we return to reading our book. Imagine a phone system that used polling instead of interrupts. Such a system would require us to periodically pick up the phone and say "hello" to see if anyone was connected to us. If we don't check the phone frequently enough, we might miss a call. On the other hand, checking it too frequently wastes our valuable time.

Interrupts are commonly generated by hardware devices such as our analog to digital converter. When a device generates an interrupt, the processor saves its current state and begins execution of a sequence of instructions called an **interrupt handler**. Interrupts may also be generated by software through the execution of an interrupt instruction. Like hardware interrupts, the generation of a software interrupt causes the processor to save its current state and begin execution of an interrupt hander. After the execution of the interrupt handler is complete, the processor returns to the state that was saved at the point that the interrupt was generated.

Sometimes we must handle multiple interrupts. Suppose we are reading a book and the telephone rings at the same time there is a knock on our door. Can we process both interruptions? Which interrupt do we deal with first? Can we be interrupted while processing an interrupt? To manage such cases, interrupts are generally assigned priorities. These priorities are often set by the hardware.

Section C.3 of the Ada Reference Manual (Taft *et al.*, 2006) describes a model for interrupts in Ada programs. Here are the key definitions of this model.

- An *interrupt* represents a class of events that are detected by the hardware or the system software.
- Interrupts are said to *occur*.
- An *occurrence* of an interrupt is separable into generation and delivery.
- The *generation* of an interrupt is the event in the underlying hardware or system that makes the interrupt available to the program.
- *Delivery* is the action that invokes part of the program in response to the interrupt occurrence.
- Between generation and delivery, the interrupt occurrence is *pending*.
- Some or all interrupts may be *blocked*. When an interrupt is blocked, all occurrences of that interrupt are prevented from being delivered.
- Certain interrupts are *reserved*. The set of interrupts that are reserved is implementation-defined. A reserved interrupt is either an interrupt for which user-defined handlers are not supported, or one which already has an attached handler by some other implementation-defined means.

- Program units can be connected to non-reserved interrupts. While connected, the program unit is said to be *attached* to that interrupt. The execution of that program unit, the *interrupt handler*, is invoked upon delivery of the interrupt occurrence.
  Beginning with Ada 95, the preferred program unit for an interrupt handler is a *parameterless protected procedure*.
- While a handler is attached to an interrupt, it is called once for each delivered occurrence of that interrupt. While the handler executes, the corresponding interrupt is blocked.
- While an interrupt is blocked, all occurrences of that interrupt are prevented from being delivered. Whether such occurrences remain pending or are lost is implementation-defined.
- Each interrupt has a default handler which determines the system's response to an occurrence of that interrupt when no user-defined handler is attached.

Ada's support for interrupts includes two pragmas and the packages `Ada.Interrupts` and `Ada.Interrupts.Names`. We use the analog to digital converter described in Chapter 2 to illustrate interrupt handling. Here is the specification for the device.

```ada
with Common_Units;   -- See Chapter 2
package ADC_Intrpt is
-- Specification of a make-believe analog to digital converter

    type      Channel_Number is range 0 .. 31;
    subtype Input_Volts     is Common_Units. Volts
                               range 0.0 ..  5.0;
    type      Gain_Choice     is (One, Two, Four);

    Over_Range : exception;

    procedure Read (Channel : in   Channel_Number;
                    Gain    : in   Gain_Choice;
                    Value   : out Input_Volts);
    -- Returns the voltage on the given channel
    -- Potentially blocking (waits on an entry)
    -- Raises Over_Range if the amplified voltage
    --                        exceeds 5 volts

private
    for Channel_Number ' Size use 5;
    for Gain_Choice use (One  => 2#001#, Two => 2#010#,
                         Four => 2#100#);
    for Gain_Choice ' Size use 3;
end ADC_Intrpt;
```

The only change from the specification in Chapter 2 is the comment that the caller may be blocked by an entry barrier instead of by a delay statement. Here is the body of our interrupt-based analog to digital converter.

```ada
with System . Storage_Elements ;   use System . Storage_Elements ;
with Ada . Interrupts . Names ;
package body ADC_Intrpt is

    use Common_Units ;   -- For operators on Volts

    -- Addresses of the ADC's two registers (memory mapped I/O)
    CSR_Address  : constant System . Address :=
                            To_Address (16#60008010#);
    Data_Address : constant System . Address :=
                            To_Address (16#60008012#);

    type CSR_Rec is   -- For the control and status register
        record
            Start       : Boolean ;
            Done        : Boolean ;
            Int_Enable  : Boolean ;
            Overflow    : Boolean ;
            Gain        : Gain_Choice ;
            Channel     : Channel_Number ;
        end record ;
    for CSR_Rec use
        record
            Start       at 0 range 0 .. 0;
            Done        at 0 range 1 .. 1;
            Int_Enable  at 0 range 2 .. 2;
            Overflow    at 0 range 3 .. 3;
            Gain        at 0 range 8 .. 10;
            Channel     at 0 range 11 .. 15;
        end record ;

    for CSR_Rec'Size use 16;
    for CSR_Rec'Bit_Order use System . Low_Order_First ;

    type Data_Type is range 0 .. 4095; -- for the data register
    for Data_Type'Size use 16;

    -- The two device registers
    Control_Status_Register : CSR_Rec ;
    for Control_Status_Register 'Address use CSR_Address ;
    for Control_Status_Register 'Size use 16;
    pragma Volatile (Control_Status_Register );

    Data_Register : Data_Type ;
    for Data_Register 'Address use Data_Address ;
    for Data_Register 'Size use 16;
```

```ada
pragma Volatile (Data_Register);


-------------------------------------------------------------
-- The interrupt handler is in this protected object
-------------------------------------------------------------
protected ADC_Interrupt is
   entry Read (Channel : in  Channel_Number;
               Gain    : in  Gain_Choice;
               Value   : out Input_Volts);
private
   Busy                : Boolean := False;
   Conversion_Complete : Boolean := False;
   procedure Handler;   -- The actual interrupt handler
   pragma Attach_Handler (Handler,
                     Ada.Interrupts.Names.SIGINT);
   pragma Interrupt_Priority;
   entry Wait_For_Completion (Channel : in  Channel_Number;
                              Gain    : in  Gain_Choice;
                              Value   : out Input_Volts);
end ADC_Interrupt;

protected body ADC_Interrupt is
   entry Read (Channel : in  Channel_Number;
               Gain    : in  Gain_Choice;
               Value   : out Input_Volts) when not Busy is
      Shadow : CSR_Rec;
   begin
      -- Set up for the conversion
      Shadow := (Start      => True, Done     => False,
                 Int_Enable => True, Overflow => False,
                 Gain       => Gain, Channel  => Channel);
      -- Start the conversion (by setting the start bit)
      Control_Status_Register := Shadow;
      -- Don't let anyone else execute this entry
      Busy := True;
      requeue Wait_For_Completion; -- Wait for interrupt
   end Read;
   ----------------------------------------------------
   procedure Handler is
   begin
      Conversion_Complete := True;
   end Handler;
   ----------------------------------------------------
   entry Wait_For_Completion (Channel : in  Channel_Number;
                              Gain    : in  Gain_Choice;
                              Value   : out Input_Volts)
                             when Conversion_Complete is
   begin
      -- Set up for the next conversion
      Busy := False;
```

```
      Conversion_Complete := False;
      -- Check for possible overflow
      if Control_Status_Register . Overflow then
         raise Over_Range;
      end if;
      -- Convert whole number data to a fixed point voltage
      Value := 5 * Volts (Data_Register) / 4095;
   end Wait_For_Completion;
end ADC_Interrupt;
```

```
procedure Read (Channel : in   Channel_Number;
                Gain    : in   Gain_Choice;
                Value   : out  Input_Volts) is
begin
   ADC_Interrupt . Read (Channel, Gain, Value);
end Read;
```

```
end ADC_Intrpt;
```

The implementation of our interrupt-based analog to digital converter is based on the protected object **ADC_Interrupt**. The public portion of the specification of this protected object has a single entry, **Read**. This entry is called by procedure **Read** defined in the package specification. The private portion of the protected object includes two Boolean variables used for synchronization, the parameterless procedure **Handler**, and the entry **Wait_For_Completion** with the same parameter profile as the public entry **Read**.

The pragma **Attach_Handler** designates procedure **Handler** as an interrupt handler. This pragma also associates the interrupt handler with a particular interrupt. Package **Ada.Interrupts.Names** provides the names of the available interrupts. The pragma **Interrupt_Priority** sets the priority of the protected object to that required for interrupts. An understanding of priorities is not important to our discussion of interrupt handlers. We'll look at priorities in detail in Chapters 7 and 8.

Let's trace a call to procedure **Read**. This procedure calls the entry **Read** in the protected object. The value of **Busy** is initially False so the entry's barrier is open and we execute the body. We set up and start the analog to digital conversion just as we did in the polling version — we write the setup values to the control and status register. The only difference is that we set the **Int_Enable** bit to True. Now when the conversion is complete, the device will generate an interrupt. After starting the device, the calling task sets the Boolean variable **Busy** to True, which closes entry **Read**'s barrier.

At this point we must wait until the hardware completes the conversion and generates the interrupt. In the polling version we temporarily blocked execution of the calling task with a delay statement. In the interrupt version we block execution of the calling task by moving it to an entry queue whose barrier is closed. We use the requeue statement to accomplish this transfer. In our example, requeue moves the task from the **Read** entry to the **Wait_For_Completion** entry. As the value of **Conversion_Complete** is False, the barrier is closed and our calling task is blocked. Once we are blocked, the read/write lock is removed. Should another task attempt to start a new voltage conversion while the original task is waiting, it will be blocked in **Read**'s closed entry queue.

When the analog to digital hardware completes the conversion and generates the interrupt, the processor saves its current state and invokes the interrupt handler — the protected procedure **Handler**. This procedure sets the Boolean variable **Conversion_Complete** to True. Once the interrupt handler completes its execution, the processor returns to its previous state. But now the entry barrier on which our task is blocked has opened so it can execute the entry body. First we set both synchronization variables to False for the next conversion. Then we check the status bit to see if the voltage exceeded the range of the converter. Finally, we obtain the data and convert it to the required voltage range. Once our task leaves the protected object, another task can begin the voltage reading process anew. You'll notice that we do not use the parameters **Channel** or **Gain** in the body of entry **Wait_For_Completion**. We had to include these parameters to create the same parameter profile as entry **Read**. The requeue statement requires that the entry to which we requeue either has no parameters or has a parameter profile identical to that of the entry from which we are transferring.

Our sample code illustrates the *static association* of an interrupt handler. Package **Ada.Interrupts** provides procedures for attaching, exchanging, and detaching interrupt handlers while our program is executing. It also includes functions to query whether a particular interrupt is reserved, whether it is currently attached to some handler, and to what handler it is attached. To use these operations for the *dynamic association* of interrupt handlers, you must include the pragma **Interrupt_Handler** rather than the pragma **Attach_Handler** for each protected procedure you might use as an interrupt handler.

Summary

- Communication is the exchange of data or control signals between processes.

- Shared variables provide a means for processes to communicate with each other.
- Mutual exclusion is a mechanism that prevents two processes from simultaneously using the same resource.
- Synchronization ensures that cooperating processes complete the steps of a job in the correct order.
- Ada's protected objects provide a safe and efficient mechanism for multiple tasks to share data.
- Protected objects encapsulate shared data and provide protected functions, protected procedures, and protected entries to access that data.
- Protected functions provide mutually exclusive read access to the shared data. Many tasks can simultaneously read the data.
- Protected procedures provide mutually exclusive read/write access to the shared data. Only a single task at a time can update the shared data.
- Like protected procedures, protected entries provide mutually exclusive read/write access to the shared data. In addition, each entry has a barrier which we use to synchronize the tasks' access to the shared data.
- Each protected entry has a queue for tasks waiting on a closed barrier.
- It is an error to execute a potentially blocking operation from within a protected operation.
- We use protected objects to implement most concurrent patterns such as the bounded buffer, the semaphore, the barrier, the broadcast and resource allocators.
- The requeue statement redirects an entry call to a new entry queue.
- An interrupt is an asynchronous event indicating a need for attention.
- When an interrupt occurs, the processor saves its current state and executes a sequence of instructions called an interrupt handler.
- Interrupt handlers are written as parameterless protected procedures.

Exercises

4.1 Define the terms *communication, mutual exclusion,* and *synchronization.*

4.2 The scenario given to demonstrate the problem in the first version of our museum visitor counting program showed an example where the count was less than the actual number of visitors within the museum. Describe how this can give rise to the Constraint_Error seen occasionally with this program.

4.3 Write a scenario for the first version of our museum visitor counting program that demonstrates how the count becomes greater than the actual number of visitors in the museum.

4.4 The protected object **The_Buffer** in program **Producer_Consumer_Demo** has two entries, **Put** and **Take**.

    1. Is it possible to have the barriers for these two entries closed simultaneously? If so, give a scenario that results in this state.

    2. If we had multiple consumers as well as multiple producers, is it possible to have tasks waiting in both entry queues simultaneously?

4.5 Given the following code fragment:

```
subtype Word_String is String (1 .. 16);

protected type Word_Holder is
   procedure Set (Word : in Word_String);
   procedure Clear;
   entry Get (Word : out Word_String);
   entry First (Letter : out Character);
private
   The_Word : Word_String;
   Valid    : Boolean := False;
end Word_Holder;

protected body Word_Holder is

   procedure Set (Word : in Word_String) is
   begin
      The_Word := Word;
      Valid    := True;
   end Set;

   procedure Clear is
   begin
      Valid := False;
   end Clear
   ;
   entry Get (Word : out Word_String) when valid is
   begin
      Word := The_Word;
   end Get;

   entry First (Letter : out Character) when valid is
   begin
      Letter := The_Word (1);
   end First;
end Word_Holder;
```

Suppose that the value of **Valid** is false so that the barriers on entries **Get** and **First** are closed. Further suppose that three tasks are waiting in the entry queue for **Get** and two tasks are waiting in the entry queue for **First**. Now a task calls procedure **Set** which opens both barriers. From which entry queue is the next task allowed to access the protected data selected?

4.6 Design a protected object that stores a shared integer. Use a discriminant to assign the initial value to the integer. Include a protected operation that obtains the value of the integer and a protected operation that updates the integer.

4.7 Modify the protected object you designed in the previous question to handle the following two additions.

1. A reader task should always read a fresh value. That is, after one task has read the value, the next task must wait until a new value has been written to the integer variable before reading it. Assume that the initial value is fresh.

2. Each value must be used before a new value can be assigned to the integer variable. A task wanting to change the value must wait until some task has read the current value. This condition applies to the initial value.

4.8 Write a package that implements the concurrent blackboard pattern. The two primary operations on a blackboard are writing a message and reading a message. We can also erase the blackboard. A task wanting to read a message on the blackboard must wait until there is a message.

4.9 The package body for the analog to digital converter on page 94 is not safe for use with multiple tasks. While one task is delayed waiting to complete a conversion of the voltage on one channel, a second task may attempt to begin a conversion on a second channel. Add a protected object to this body that ensures that only one task at a time can perform a conversion. Remember that the body of a protected operation (function, procedure, or entry) may not include any code that is potentially blocking.

4.10 Our solution for resource allocation could possibly starve a task waiting for a large number of resources. Explain how this starvation could occur.

4.11 Rewrite our protected object for resource allocation so that a task will not be starved waiting for a large number of resources. Here is one possible solution (explained in terms of our teacher/pencil analogy). The principal only allows one teacher to wait in the private waiting room. When a teacher returns some pencils, the teacher waiting in the private room is allowed back into the principal's office to see if there are enough pencils for their need. While there is a teacher in the private waiting room, all other teachers who want pencils must wait outside the main (public) door to the principal's office.

4.12 We stated that our resource allocation package does not work when the entry queues are priority queues rather than FIFO queues. Explain why it fails with priority-based entry queues.

4.13 The following package specification defines an event pattern.

```
package Events is
    type State_Type is (On, Off);

    protected type Event (Initial_Value : State_Type) is
        procedure Turn_On;
        procedure Turn_Off;
        entry Wait (Desired_State : in State_Type);
    private
        State : State_Type := Initial_Value;
        entry Wait_For_On;
        entry Wait_For_Off;
    end Event;
end Events;
```

The two protected procedures change the state of the event. The public entry `Wait` allows a task to wait until the state of the event is `On` or until the state of the event is `Off`. The parameter `Desired_State` determines which *Wait_For* entry is entered. Complete the body of this package.

4.14 The requeue statement may include the option **with abort**. Read section 9.5.4 of the Ada Reference Manual and determine the effects of this option. You may also find section 9.8 useful in answering this question.

4.15 Define the terms *interrupt, interrupt generation, interrupt delivery, pending interrupt,* and *interrupt handler*.

5

Communication and synchronization based on direct interaction

In Chapter 4 we showed how protected objects can provide an indirect means for tasks to communicate and synchronize. Protected functions and procedures provide safe access to shared data while protected entries provide the means for tasks to synchronize their activities. In this chapter we look at direct communication between tasks through Ada's rendezvous.

5.1 The rendezvous

Rendezvous is a sixteenth century French word which literally translates to "present yourself." To rendezvous is to come together at a prearranged meeting place. In Ada, the rendezvous is a mechanism for controlled direct interaction between two tasks. The rendezvous provides a second way to synchronize tasks and transfer data between them.

Ada's rendezvous is based on a *client-server* model. One task, called the server, declares one or more services that it can offer to other tasks, the clients. These services are defined as *entries* in the server task's specification. Task entries are similar to protected entries. In fact, we may requeue a protected entry call onto a task entry and vice versa. A client task requests a rendezvous with a server by making **entry calls** just as if the server was a protected object. Server tasks indicate a willingness to accept a rendezvous on an entry by executing an **accept** statement. The accept statement may include code to be executed during the rendezvous.

For the rendezvous to take place, both the client and the server must have issued their requests. Should the client make an entry call before the server executes an accept statement, the client is blocked. If the server executes an accept statement before the client makes an entry call, the server is blocked. When both requests have been made, the tasks begin their rendezvous. When the rendezvous occurs, the two tasks are synchronized — we know that the server is available to provide its service and that the client is at the point in its execution that it requires that service. During the rendezvous:

1. The values of any *in* and *in out* entry parameters are passed from the client task to the server task.
2. The client task is blocked.
3. The server task executes any code within the accept statement.
4. The values of any *out* and *in out* entry parameters are transferred from the server task to the client task.
5. Both the server task and the client task continue their independent and concurrent execution.

The parameters passed during the rendezvous provide direct communication between the client and the server. The client is blocked while the server executes the optional rendezvous code — the sequence of statements included within the accept statement. To minimize blocking, the rendezvous code should be kept as short as possible.

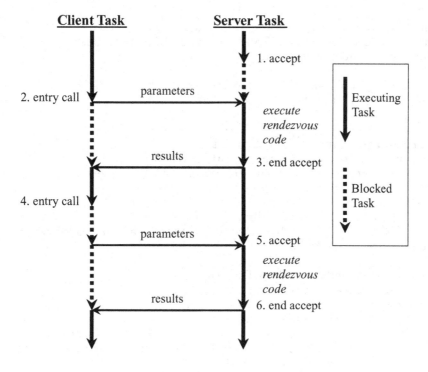

Figure 5.1 Statement sequencing in rendezvous

Figure 5.1 illustrates the behavior of the rendezvous. Time flows down in this figure. At the start, both tasks are executing. At time 1, the server task executes an accept statement. Since no client task has made an entry call, the server task is blocked. At time 2, the client task makes an entry call. As the server is waiting for this call, the rendezvous begins immediately with the passing of parameters from the client. The client is blocked while the server executes the code within its accept statement. When control reaches the end of the accept statement at time 3, the rendezvous ends and any results are returned to the client. Both the client and the server continue to execute concurrently. At time 4, the client makes a second entry call to the server. But as the server is not executing an accept statement, the client is blocked. At time 5, the server executes an accept statement. There is a client waiting so the rendezvous begins immediately with the passing of parameters from the client. The client is again blocked while the server executes the code within its accept statement. When control reaches the end of the accept statement at time 6, the rendezvous ends and any results are returned to the client. Both the client and the server continue to execute concurrently.

Let's look at some sample Ada code.

```ada
with  Ada.Text_IO;                    use  Ada.Text_IO;
with  Ada.Numerics.Float_Random;  use  Ada.Numerics;
procedure  Rendezvous_Demo  is

   Number_Of_Clients      :  constant := 5;
   Number_Of_Iterations  :  constant := 4;


   -----------------------------------------------------------------
   protected  Random_Duration  is
      procedure  Get (Item  :  out  Duration);
      -- Returns a random duration value between
      -- 0.0 and 1.0 seconds
   private
      First_Call     :  Boolean := True;
      My_Generator  :  Ada.Numerics.Float_Random.Generator;
   end  Random_Duration;

   protected  body  Random_Duration  is
      procedure  Get (Item  :  out  Duration)  is
      begin
         if  First_Call  then
            -- On the first call, reset the generator
            Ada.Numerics.Float_Random.Reset (My_Generator);
            First_Call := False;
         end  if;
         -- Get a random float value and
         -- convert it to a duration
         Item := Duration (Float_Random.Random (My_Generator));
      end  Get;
   end  Random_Duration;
```

```ada
-------------------------------------------------------------------
task Counter is
   entry Increment (Client : in  Positive;
                    Value  : out Natural);
end Counter;

task body Counter is
   Count    : Natural := 0;
   My_Delay : Duration;
begin
   loop    -- Each iteration, rendezvous with two clients
      Random_Duration.Get (My_Delay);
      delay My_Delay;
      accept Increment (Client : in Positive;
                        Value  : out Natural) do
         Put_Line ("Counter is in #1 rendezvous with task"
                      & Positive'Image (Client));
         Count := Count + 1;
         Value := Count;
      end Increment;
      Random_Duration.Get (My_Delay);
      delay My_Delay;
      accept Increment (Client : in Positive;
                        Value  : out Natural) do
         Put_Line ("Counter is in #2 rendezvous with task"
                      & Positive'Image (Client));
         Count := Count + 1;
         Value := Count;
      end Increment;
   end loop;
end Counter;


-------------------------------------------------------------------
task type Client is
   entry Assign_ID (Assigned_ID : in Positive);
end  Client;

task body Client is
   My_ID    : Positive;
   My_Delay : Duration;
   Current  : Natural;
begin
   accept Assign_ID (Assigned_ID : in Positive) do
      My_ID := Assigned_ID;
   end Assign_ID;
   for Count in 1 .. Number_Of_Iterations loop
      Random_Duration.Get (My_Delay);
      delay My_Delay;
      Counter.Increment (Client => My_ID,
                         Value  => Current);
```

```
            Put_Line ("Client" & Positive 'Image (My_ID) &
                 " got a value of" &
                 Natural 'Image (Current));
        end loop;
    end Client;

    type Client_Array is array (1 .. Number_Of_Clients)
                     of Client;
    Clients : Client_Array;

begin
    -- Rendezvous will all the tasks in array Clients
    for Index in Client_Array 'Range loop
        -- Rendezvous with a client,
        -- give it the same ID as its index
        Clients (Index). Assign_ID (Assigned_ID => Index);
    end loop;
end Rendezvous_Demo;
```

Program **Rendezvous_Demo** contains the singleton task **Counter** and task type **Client**. Task **Counter** includes the declaration of the entry **Increment** and task type **Client** includes the declaration of the entry **Assign_ID**. **Clients** is an array of five **Client** tasks.

The main subprogram executes a for loop that makes an entry call to each task in the array **Clients**. The first statement in the body for task type **Client** is an accept statement. When both the entry call and the accept have been made, the rendezvous between the main task and one of the five tasks making up array **Clients** begins. During this rendezvous, the ID from the main task is copied to the local variable **My_ID**. When the assignment statement inside the accept statement is completed, both the main task and the task **Clients(ID)** continue to execute concurrently. In these five rendezvous, the five tasks making up the array **Clients** act as servers for the main task.

After the main task makes its five rendezvous, each of the client tasks has an ID equal to the index of its position in the array **Clients**. In Chapter 4, we used task discriminants to assign IDs to tasks (see, for example, the four door monitoring tasks in the museum program on page 130). Discriminants cannot be used with arrays of tasks so the rendezvous is a common approach for assigning IDs to tasks making up an array.

After receiving their IDs, each of the five client tasks executes a loop in which they delay for a random duration and then call task **Counter**'s entry **Increment**. When the rendezvous is complete, the client displays its ID and the value of the count it got back from **Counter**.

Task **Counter** contains a loop in which it participates in two different rendezvous. While we could obtain the same results with one accept statement instead of two in our loop, we wanted to demonstrate that there can be multiple accept statements for every entry declared in a task's specification. With five client tasks calling the one server task's entry, there is sure to be some competition between the clients for the server's attention. As with protected entries, each task entry includes a queue in which entry calls wait their turn. Note that this queue is associated with the entry, not each accept statement. When tasks are waiting on an entry queue, the execution of any accept statement in the task removes the first client task from the entry queue for the rendezvous.

The basic rendezvous follows a *wait forever* model. Once a client has made an entry call, it must wait until the server accepts the call. There is no limit on the amount of time the client will wait for the server to rendezvous. Similarly, once a server has executed an accept statement, it must wait until some client issues an entry call. Again, there is no limit on the amount of time the server will wait for a client to rendezvous. In the next sections, we'll look at methods for giving servers and clients more control over the indefinite wait for their rendezvous partner.

5.2 The selective accept statement

The selective accept statement gives the server member of the rendezvous pair more control in the acceptance of entry calls. As this statement has many options, it is worthwhile looking at its definition in Ada's variant of BNF.[1]

selective_accept ::= **select**
        [guard]
        select_alternative
    {**or**
        [guard]
        select_alternative }
    [**else**
        sequence_of_statements]
    end select;

The select statement provides one or more alternatives. Like an if statement, when the select statement is executed only one of the alternatives is

---

[1] Backus-Naur Form. Section 1.1.4 of the ARM describes this BNF variant. The symbol ::= is read "is defined as." Bold text and punctuation are literals. Square brackets, [ ], enclose optional expressions. Curly brackets, { }, enclose expressions that may occur zero or more times. Vertical bars, |, separate alternatives.

executed. Here are the definitions of the two new terms given in the definition of the selective_accept.

select_alternative ::= accept_alternative
                      | delay_alternative
                      | terminate_alternative

accept_alternative ::= accept_statement
                      [sequence_of_statements]

guard   ::= **when** condition =>

The delay alternative, terminate alternative, and else part are mutually
exclusive — only one of them can be included in a given select statement.
We will examine all these alternatives in the next sections.

5.2.1 The accept alternative

We use the accept alternative with its optional sequence of statements to
wait for a rendezvous on one of several entries. Here is an example of its use.
The following task is part of an application that controls the preparation of
hot drinks in a beverage vending machine. Other tasks in this application
include one that takes orders, accepts money, and makes change, one that
plays music to attract customers, and one that controls the animated signage
on the front of the machine.

```
task  Make_Beverage  is
    entry  Coffee (Sugar  :  in  Boolean;
                   Cream  :  in  Boolean);
    entry  Tea (Sugar  :  in  Boolean;
                Milk   :  in  Boolean;
                Lemon  :  in  Boolean);
    entry  Cocoa;
end  Make_Beverage;

task  body  Make_Beverage  is
    With_Sugar  :  Boolean;
    With_Cream  :  Boolean;
    With_Milk   :  Boolean;
    With_Lemon  :  Boolean;
begin
    loop
        select
            accept  Coffee (Sugar  :  in  Boolean;
                            Cream  :  in  Boolean)  do
```

```
            With_Sugar := Sugar;
            With_Cream := Cream;
          end Coffee;
          Run_Coffee_System (With_Sugar, With_Cream);
          Sanitize_Coffee_System;
      or
          accept Tea (Sugar : in Boolean;
                       Milk  : in Boolean;
                       Lemon : in Boolean) do
            With_Sugar := Sugar;
            With_Milk  := Milk;
            With_Lemon := Lemon;
          end Tea;
          Run_Tea_System (With_Sugar, With_Milk, With_Lemon);
          Sanitize_Tea_System;
      or
          accept Cocoa;
          Run_Cocoa_System;
          Sanitize_Cocoa_System;
        end select;
        Sanitize_Dispenser_System;
    end loop;
  end Make_Beverage;
```

Task Make_Beverage has three entries. The select statement in the task body has three accept alternatives. When the select statement is executed, all the entry queues are evaluated. There are three possibilities.

- If all the entry queues are empty, the server task is blocked. The server task will wake up as soon as some client calls one of the three entries. The server task then makes the rendezvous with the appropriate accept statement.
- If all of the entry queues save one are empty when the server task executes the select statement, the server task will immediately rendezvous with the first task in that non-empty entry queue.
- If there are tasks waiting in more than one entry queue when the server task executes the select statement, the server task will immediately rendezvous with a task from one of the entry queues. Which entry queue is selected is not specified by the language. You should assume that the selection is arbitrary. The Real-Time Systems Annex (Appendix D of the ARM) provides pragma Queuing_Policy which we may use to specify a deterministic selection. We'll discuss this pragma in Chapter 8.

The entry Cocoa has no parameters. For parameterless entries, we usually omit the accept statement's optional sequence of statements executed during the rendezvous. Compare the accept statement for Cocoa with those for

Coffee and **Tea**. The rendezvous code for **Coffee** and **Tea** is short — it copies the parameters to local variables. The client task is not blocked during the actual brewing or cleaning of the system. These jobs are done after each rendezvous is complete.

5.2.2 Guarded alternatives

The BNF definition of the selective accept shows that each selective accept can have a guard associated with it. A guard serves the same function as the protected entry's barrier. A **guard** is a Boolean expression that is evaluated when the select statement is executed. If the expression is False, the alternative is said to be closed. A closed select alternative is not eligible for selection during this execution of the select statement. If the expression is True, the alternative is said to be open and is eligible for selection during this execution of the select statement. An alternative without a guard is always open. The exception **Program_Error** is raised if all alternatives are closed.

It is important to note that all of the guards in a select statement are evaluated when the select statement first begins its execution — they are *not* reevaluated if the task is blocked by the select statement.

Let's look at an example. The following task controls an electric motor. We can set the motor's direction, start the motor, and stop the motor. To start the motor, we first energize a set of low-current draw windings. After the motor begins turning, we switch over to the running windings. The motor could be damaged if we change its direction while it is running. To ensure that the motor is not damaged, we include a guard on the select alternative that sets the motor's direction. When the motor is running, the guard is False and the accept for **Set_Direction** is not eligible for selection.

```
type Direction_Type is (Clockwise, Counter_Clockwise);
type Winding_State is (Off, On);

task Motor is
   entry Start;
   entry Stop;
   entry Set_Direction (Direction : in Direction_Type);
end Motor;

task body Motor is
   Running : Boolean := False;
begin
   loop
      select
         accept Start;
         Set_Start_Windings (To => On);
```

```
            Running := True;
            delay 30.0;
            Set_Start_Windings (To => Off);
            Set_Run_Windings   (To => On);
        or
            accept Stop;
            Set_Run_Windings (To => Off);
            Running := False;
        or
            when not Running =>
            accept Set_Direction (Direction : Direction_Type) do
                Set_Winding_Polarity (Direction);
            end Set_Direction;
        end select;
    end loop;
end Motor;
```

As with barriers, we recommend that guards do not use global variables which may be changed by other tasks.

5.2.3 *The terminate alternative*

The terminate alternative provides a means for ending the execution of a task when it is no longer required. The terminate alternative is selected when two conditions are true:

- The task's master (see Section 3.3.2) is completed.
- Each task that depends on the master considered is either already terminated or similarly blocked at a select statement with an open terminate alternative.

Here is the select statement for our coffee vending machine example with the addition of a terminate alternative.

```
        select
            accept Coffee (Sugar : in Boolean;
                           Cream : in Boolean) do
                With_Sugar := Sugar;
                With_Cream := Cream;
            end Coffee;
            Run_Coffee_System (With_Sugar, With_Cream);
            Sanitize_Coffee_System;
        or
            accept Tea (Sugar : in Boolean;
                        Milk  : in Boolean;
                        Lemon : in Boolean) do
                With_Sugar := Sugar;
                With_Milk  := Milk;
```

```
          With_Lemon := Lemon;
        end Tea;
        Run_Tea_System (With_Sugar, With_Milk, With_Lemon);
        Sanitize_Tea_System;
    or
        accept Cocoa;
        Run_Cocoa_System;
        Sanitize_Cocoa_System;
    or
        terminate;
    end select;
```

With the terminate alternative, task **Make_Beverage** will terminate when
any task that could rendezvous with it is either finished or also waiting on
a select statement with an open terminate alternative.

5.2.4 The delay alternative

The delay alternative provides a means to limit the amount of time that a
server waits for a client to rendezvous. You can use either of two different
delay statements to express this time. Here are the BNF definitions for the
delay alternative.

delay_alternative   ::= delay_statement
                                [sequence_of_statements]

delay_statement   ::= delay_relative_statement | delay_until_statement

delay_relative_statement ::= **delay** *delay*_expression;

delay_until_statement   ::= **delay until** *delay*_expression;

The expected type for the *delay*_expression in a delay_relative_statement
is the predefined type Duration. We have already used the relative delay
statement in many examples. The expected type for the *delay*_expression in
a delay_until_statement is a time type, either the type **Time** from package
Ada.Calendar (described in section 9.6 of the ARM) or the type **Time** from
the package **Ada.Real_Time** (described in section D.8 of the ARM). The
clock in package **Ada.Calendar** is often referred to as a "wall clock." Its
value is adjusted for leap years and may jump forward or backward as a result of daylight savings time changes and leap seconds. The high-resolution
clock in package **Ada.Real_Time** keeps monotonic time — time that never de-
creases. A call to that clock returns the amount of time that has passed since
some implementation-defined epoch unaffected by the events that change

wall clock time. We will discuss package `Ada.Real_Time` in more detail in Chapter 8.

Relative delays

As an example of a delay alternative with a relative delay, let's look at a task that controls the temperature of a house. Here is its specification:

```
task Thermostat is
   entry Enable (Set_Point : in Degrees);
   entry Disable;
end Thermostat;
```

Entry `Enable` turns on the heating system and sets the desired temperature. Entry `Disable` turns off the heating system. When it is enabled, the thermostat turns the furnace on when the temperature is half a degree below the desired temperature and turns the furnace off when the temperature is half a degree above the desired temperature. When the furnace is off, the thermostat checks the temperature every 0.5 seconds. While the furnace is running, it checks the temperature every 1.5 seconds. Here is the body of the thermostat task:

```
task body Thermostat is
   Current    : Degrees; -- Current house temperature
   Target     : Degrees; -- Desired house temperature
   Furnace_On : Boolean := False; -- Flag for guards
begin
   accept Enable (Set_Point : in Degrees) do
      Target := Set_Point;
   end Enable;
   loop
      select
         accept Enable (Set_Point : in Degrees) do
            Target := Set_Point;
         end Enable;
      or
         accept Disable;
         Turn_Furnace_Off;
         Furnace_On := False;
         accept Enable (Set_Point : in Degrees) do
            Target := Set_Point;
         end Enable;
      or
         when Furnace_On =>
            delay 1.50;
      or
         when not Furnace_On =>
            delay 0.50;
      end select;
```

```
         Get_Temperature (Current);
         if Furnace_On and Current >= Target + 0.5 then
            Turn_Furnace_Off;
            Furnace_On := False;
         elsif not Furnace_On and Current <= Target - 0.5 then
            Turn_Furnace_On;
            Furnace_On := True;
         end if;
      end loop;
   end Thermostat;
```

Initially, the heating system is off. The **accept Enable** statement before the loop turns on the system. The select statement in the loop has four alternatives. We may call **Enable** to change the desired temperature or **Disable** to turn the system off. After **Disable** is called, the furnace is turned off and the thermostat task is blocked until **Enable** is called. Note that the accept statement for this **Enable** is a simple accept statement, not a select alternative. The other two alternatives are guarded delay statements. At a given time, only one of these alternatives will be open. If neither **Enable** nor **Disable** is called before the open delay expires, that delay alternative is selected. Control continues to the code that checks the current temperature and, if necessary, makes appropriate calls to the furnace.

Absolute delays

Now let's look at an example of a delay alternative with an absolute delay. The following task body controls a commercial-size tea kettle. So that the water is hot when the staff arrives in the morning, we have included a delay alternative that will turn the heater on at 5:00 AM every morning. Another delay alternative turns the heater off when the café closes at 11:00 PM. Two entries allow us to turn the heater on and off manually. For this application, the clock in **Ada.Calendar** is appropriate.

```
   task body Kettle is
      Year     : Ada.Calendar.Year_Number;
      Month    : Ada.Calendar.Month_Number;
      Day      : Ada.Calendar.Day_Number;
      Seconds  : Ada.Calendar.Day_Duration;
      On_Time  : Ada.Calendar.Time;
      Off_Time : Ada.Calendar.Time;
   begin
      -- Read the clock for current date/time
      On_Time := Ada.Calendar.Clock;
      -- Split the time value into Year, Month, Day, and Seconds
      Ada.Calendar.Split (On_Time, Year, Month, Day, Seconds);
      -- Set the turn on time to midnight (the start of today)
      On_Time := Ada.Calendar.Time_Of (Year, Month, Day, 0.0);
```

```
-- Set the turn on time to 5:00 AM (5 hrs after midnight)
On_Time := On_Time + Duration (5 * 60 * 60);
-- Set the turn off time to 11:00 PM (18 hrs after on time)
Off_Time := On_Time + Duration (18 * 60 * 60);
loop
   select
      accept Turn_On;            -- manual turn on
      Turn_On_Heat;
   or
      accept Turn_Off;           -- manual turn off
      Turn_Off_Heat;
   or
      delay until On_Time;   -- automated turn on
      Turn_On_Heat;
      -- Turn on again in 24 hours
      On_Time := On_Time + Duration (24 * 60 * 60);
   or
      delay until Off_Time;  -- automated turn off
      Turn_Off_Heat;
      -- Turn off again in 24 hours
      Off_Time := Off_Time + Duration (24 * 60 * 60);
   end select;
   end loop;
end Kettle;
```

Function `Ada.Calendar.Clock` returns the current time. We split the time value into the components `Year`, `Month`, `Day`, and `Seconds`. Then we recombine these components with a value of zero for `Seconds` to obtain the time of midnight of the current day. Finally, we add five hours to midnight to obtain our 5:00 AM start time. Our closing time is then calculated to be 18 hours after the opening time. Each time one of the two delay alternatives expires, we carry out the operation and reset the time for 24 hours later.

5.2.5 The else part

The optional else part of the select statement and its sequence of statements is executed if no other alternative can be selected *immediately*. Such is the case if no client has issued a entry call for the server or the guards have closed any entry whose queue is not empty. Use this option with caution as removing the possibility of not blocking the task on some entry can lead to busy waiting (polling) logic that may starve other tasks. Here is an example.

```
task body Monitor_Temperature is
   My_Delay : Duration := 5.0;
   Current  : Degrees;
begin
```

```
loop
   select
      accept Change_Rate (Value : in Duration) do
         My_Delay := Value;
      end Change_Rate;
   else
      null;
   end select;
   Get_Temperature (Current);
   Display_Temperature (Current);
   delay My_Delay;
end loop;
end Monitor_Temperature;
```

Task `Monitor_Temperature` periodically obtains a temperature and displays it. At the beginning of each iteration, the task checks to see if it should change the temperature sampling rate. Usually, no change is requested and the task executes the empty else part, samples and displays the temperature, and delays until the next cycle. As there is a delay statement after the select statement, the use of the else part does not create a busy waiting loop that could starve other tasks. An alternative solution would be to use a delay alternative in place of the else part. However, with this alternative, a request change will result in a shortening of the cycle for that one period. Moving the delay out of the select statement ensures that the delay is never terminated by an entry call.

5.3 Entry call options

In the last section we looked at options that the server (the called task) has available when handling entry calls. The server may wait indefinitely, wait for a specific amount of time, wait until all of its clients have terminated, or not wait at all. The client tasks also have options when making entry calls. The calls can be to task entries or to protected entries. We'll look at the options for entry calls in this section.

5.3.1 Timed entry calls

A timed entry call allows a client to specify how long they are willing to wait for the protected object or server to accept the call. Here is an example of a timed entry call to the `Disable` entry of the `Thermostat` task on page 177.

```
select
   Thermostat.Disable;   -- Attempt to rendezvous
```

```
    Put_Line ("Disabled the thermostat");
or
    delay 5.0; -- Wait for 5 seconds for rendezvous
    Put_Line ("Gave up waiting for rendezvous");
end select;
```

After disabling the furnace once, a second entry call to **Disable** is blocked since task **Thermostat** is waiting to accept an entry call to **Enable**. Using the timed entry call, our client can abandon the attempt to rendezvous with the thermostat task.

When the time specified in a timed entry call expires, the task is removed from the entry queue in which it was waiting. Removal from the queue can cause problems for a server or protected object that uses the **'Count** attribute to determine how many client tasks are waiting in a queue. See Section 4.7 and Exercise 4.14 for some examples that may be complicated by the use of timed entry calls or abort statements.

5.3.2 Conditional entry calls

Conditional entry calls may be used to call protected entries or to perform a rendezvous. A conditional entry call is equivalent to a timed entry call with an immediate expiration time. Here is an example of a conditional entry call to the **Disable** entry of the **Thermostat** task.

```
select
    Thermostat.Disable;   -- Attempt to rendezvous
    Put_Line ("Disabled the thermostat");
else
    Put_Line ("Could not rendezvous right away");
end select;
```

5.4 State machines

The state machine is an important model in the design of real-time and embedded systems. We assume that the reader is familiar with the basics of state machine diagrams and their usefulness in the design of applications. For a detailed description of state diagrams in software design see Blaha and Rumbaugh (2004) or Douglass (1998). A state diagram describes the behavior of an object. Each state represents a stage in the behavior pattern of an object. A transition is a change from one state to another. It is triggered by an event that is either internal or external to the object. In Chapter 3 we used simple state diagrams to illustrate the behavior of the Ada task.

We typically draw a state diagram for each object in our design that has non-trivial behavior.

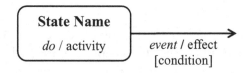

Figure 5.2 State machine diagram notation

A state diagram is built from the two primary elements shown in Figure 5.2: rounded boxes representing states and arrows indicating transitions from one state to another. The rounded rectangle includes the name of the state and a *do option* that indicates an activity that continues while the object is in this state. Do activities include continuous operations such as flashing a light and sequential activities that terminate by themselves after an interval of time, such as closing an airlock door. A do activity may be interrupted by an event that is received during its execution. For example, a closing door may encounter an obstacle, causing it to cease moving. The arrow is annotated with the name of the event that causes the transition out of a state. A transition may include an optional effect and an optional guard condition. An *effect* is an action that happens instantaneously such as displaying a message, incrementing a counter, or setting a bit. Like the guard on a select alternative, the *guard condition* on a state transition closes the transition when the condition is False. When a transition is closed, the event does not cause a change of state.

There are a number of techniques for implementing state machines in Ada. Since a state is an abstraction of an object's attributes, we can represent it as a collection of values. We change the state by changing these values. When the state of the object is controlled by a single task, this collection of values can be as simple as a record. When multiple tasks generate state-changing events, we can encapsulate the data within a protected object. Both of these approaches work well for passive objects. A **passive object** is one whose state changes only in response to events generated by other objects. A passive object does not change its state by itself. An **active object** is one that can change its state by itself. An active object requires its own thread of control to change itself. So active objects are often implemented as tasks. Usually, we can determine whether an object is active or passive from its state diagram. Indications that an object is active include do activities and transitions based on time. In the next sections we'll look at some techniques for implementing the state machines for passive and active objects.

5.4.1 Implementing state machines for passive objects

Figure 5.3 is a state diagram for the headlights in a car. The black circle with an unlabeled transition to the *Off* state indicates that *Off* is the initial state for this diagram. In the *On* state, the headlights are illuminated at the normal brightness level. In the *High* state, the high beam filament is powered to give additional light. The driver controls the headlights with two switches on the dashboard. These switches may be polled by a task that periodically checks all dashboard controls or may generate an interrupt when a switch is changed. In either case, some external object generates the events shown in the figure. The *switch off* event is also generated by the main task when the car is turned off.

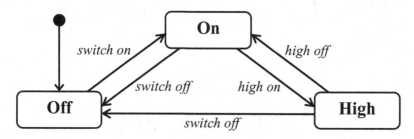

Figure 5.3 State diagram for car headlights

As is usual for state diagrams, each state in Figure 5.3 is affected by only a few of the possible events. For example, while in the state *Off*, the event *high on* does not change the state of the headlights; they remain off.

Here is a package specification for the headlights object.

```
package Headlights is

    type State_Type is (Off, On, High);
    type Event_Type is (Switch_On, Switch_Off, High_On, High_Off);

    procedure Signal_Event (Event : Event_Type);
    -- Signal an event that may possibly
    -- change the state of the headlights

    function Current_State return State_Type;
    -- Return the current state of the headlights

end Headlights;
```

Nested case statements

We will show you two of the many techniques for implementing a passive object state machine. The most common technique uses nested case statements. Since multiple tasks generate headlight events, we'll encapsulate these case statements within a protected object. Here is the body that uses this approach.

```
with Lights;   -- Package with light control/status registers
package body Headlights_V1 is

   protected Control is
      procedure Signal_Event (Event : Event_Type);
      function Current_State return State_Type;
   private
      State : State_Type := Off;
   end Control;

   protected body Control is
      procedure Signal_Event (Event : Event_Type) is
      begin
         case State is
            when Off =>
               case Event is
                  when Switch_On =>
                     State := On;
                     Lights.Set_Headlights_On;
                  when Switch_Off | High_On | High_Off =>
                     null;
               end case;
            when On =>
               case Event is
                  when Switch_Off =>
                     State := Off;
                     Lights.Set_Headlights_Off;
                  when High_On =>
                     State := High;
                     Lights.Set_High_Beams_On;
                  when Switch_On | High_Off =>
                     null;
               end case;
            when High =>
               case Event is
                  when Switch_Off =>
                     State := Off;
                     Lights.Set_Headlights_Off;
                     Lights.Set_High_Beams_Off;
                  when High_Off =>
                     State := On;
                     Lights.Set_High_Beams_Off;
```

```
              when Switch_On | High_On =>
                  null;
              end case;
          end case;
      end Signal_Event;

      function Current_State return State_Type is
      begin
          return State;
      end Current_State;
  end Control;

  -- External Operations -----------------------------------
  procedure Signal_Event (Event : Event_Type) is
  begin
      Control.Signal_Event (Event);
  end Signal_Event;

  function Current_State return State_Type is
  begin
      return Control.Current_State;
  end Current_State;

end Headlights_V1;
```

The bodies for the two operations defined in the package specification make calls to operations in the protected object `Control`. The outer case statement in the protected procedure `Signal_Event` selects the alternative for the current state. Within each of those alternatives, a case statement based on the event may change the state or not. When the state does change, calls are made to appropriate procedures to change the powering of the headlight filaments. These are the effects of the state change.

With the nested case statement approach, the amount of code necessary is proportional to the product of the number of states and the number of events. This approach can become unwieldy when the number of states or the number of events is large.

State transition tables

Another technique for implementing passive state machines is based on the state transition table. Given the current state and an event, the state transition table can tell us the next state. Table 5.1 is a state transition table for our headlight state diagram. The first row shows the states we can transition to from the *Off* state, the second row shows the states we can transition to from the *On* state, and the third row shows the states we can transition to from the *High* state.

	switch on	switch off	high on	high off
Off	On	Off	Off	Off
On	On	Off	High	On
High	High	Off	High	On

Table 5.1 *A state transition table for the state machine of Figure 5.3*

If we are in the *Off* state and the event *switch on* occurs, we can look at the first column and determine that the next state is *On*. If we are in the *Off* state and the event *high on* occurs, we can look at the third column and determine that the next state is *Off* — there is no change of state.

We can put the data from a state transition table into a two-dimensional array with the state as the row index and the event as the column index. To find the next state, we simply look up the value in the row for the current state and the column for the event.

There is one additional problem to solve for this implementation. With each transition, there is often an effect that requires that we execute some code. For example, when our headlights transition from the *Off* state to the *On* state, we must change the bit in the control/status register of the car's lighting system that energizes the main bulb filaments. We implement this by storing a pointer to an appropriate effect procedure with each entry in our two-dimensional array. We first declare a pointer type that designates a procedure with no parameters. Then we define a pointer to each of our five effect procedures using the attribute 'Access with each procedure name. Here is the package body that uses a state transition table approach.

```
with Lights;    -- Package with light control/status registers
package body Headlights_V2 is

    procedure Both_Off is
    begin
        Lights.Set_Headlights_Off;
        Lights.Set_High_Beams_Off;
    end Both_Off;

    type Effect_Ptr is access procedure;

    L_Off : constant Effect_Ptr := Lights.Set_Headlights_Off'Acce
    L_On  : constant Effect_Ptr := Lights.Set_Headlights_On'Acces
    H_Off : constant Effect_Ptr := Lights.Set_High_Beams_Off'Acce
    H_On  : constant Effect_Ptr := Lights.Set_High_Beams_On'Acce
    B_Off : constant Effect_Ptr := Both_Off'Access;
```

```ada
type Table_Entry is
   record
      Next_State : State_Type;
      Effect     : Effect_Ptr;
   end record;
type Transition_Array is array (State_Type, Event_Type)
                          of Table_Entry;

Transition_Table : constant Transition_Array :=
   (((On,    L_On), (Off, null),  (Off,    null), (Off,  null)),
    ((On,   null), (Off, L_Off), (High, H_On), (On,   null)),
    ((High, null), (Off, B_Off), (High, null), (On,   H_Off)));

protected Control is
   procedure Signal_Event (Event : Event_Type);
   function Current_State return State_Type;
private
   State : State_Type := Off;
end Control;

protected body Control is
   procedure Signal_Event (Event : Event_Type) is
   begin
      -- Carry out any effect for the state change
      if Transition_Table (State, Event).Effect /= null then
         Transition_Table (State, Event).Effect.all;
      end if;
      -- Determine the next state from the table
      State := Transition_Table (State, Event).Next_State;
   end Signal_Event;

   function Current_State return State_Type is
   begin
      return State;
   end Current_State;
end Control;

-- External Operations -----------------------------------
procedure Signal_Event (Event : Event_Type) is
begin
   Control.Signal_Event (Event);
end Signal_Event;

function Current_State return State_Type is
begin
   return Control.Current_State;
end Current_State;

end Headlights_V2;
```

The array `Transition_Table` is defined as a constant. The value of this constant is set by a two-dimensional array aggregate. The elements of this array aggregate are record aggregates.

5.4.2 Implementing state machines for active objects

Figure 5.4 is a state diagram for a large electric induction motor. To start this motor, we apply power to a set of low-current draw start windings. After one minute, the motor is turning fast enough that we can switch over to the normal run windings. While the motor is running, we monitor its temperature. Should the temperature exceed some maximum value, we turn the motor off.

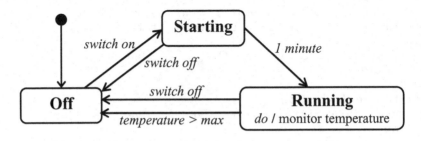

Figure 5.4 State diagram for a large induction motor

Two features of this state diagram indicate that the motor controller is an active object. First, the transition between *Starting* and *Running* is based on time. Second, while in the *Running* state the *do activity* requires that the motor continually check its temperature. Here is our specification for this motor.

```
package Induction_Motor is

    type State_Type is (Off, Starting, Running);

    -- External motor events
    procedure Switch_On;
    procedure Switch_Off;

    function Current_State return State_Type;

end Induction_Motor;
```

Our implementation of this active motor object uses a task that responds to external events and generates its own events. The code within the motor control task is similar to our nested case statement solution for passive objects. We use a case statement based on the three possible states of the motor. In each case alternative we use a select statement. Each select statement includes an alternative for each possible entry.

We keep the state of the motor in a protected object that is shared by the motor control task and any external task that calls function Current_State. Here is the package body.

```
with Induction_Motor.Operations;  use Induction_Motor.Operations;
package body Induction_Motor is

   protected Motor is  -- For the shared state
      procedure Set_State (To : in State_Type);
      function Current_State return State_Type;
   private
      State : State_Type := Off;
   end Motor;

   protected body Motor is
      procedure Set_State (To : in State_Type) is
      begin
         State := To;
      end Set_State;
      function Current_State return State_Type is
      begin
         return State;
      end Current_State;
   end Motor;

   ----------------------------------------------------------

   task Control is
      entry Switch_On;
      entry Switch_Off;
   end Control;

   task body Control is
   begin
      loop
         case Motor.Current_State is
            when Off =>
               select
                  accept Switch_Off;
               or
                  accept Switch_On;
                  Motor.Set_State (To => Starting);
                  Operations.Set_Start_Windings (To => On);
               end select;
            when Starting =>
               select
                  accept Switch_Off;
                  Motor.Set_State (To => Off);
                  Operations.Set_Start_Windings (To => Off);
```

```
              or
                  accept Switch_On;
              or
                  delay 60.0;  -- for motor to get up to speed
                  Motor.Set_State (To => Running);
                  Operations.Set_Start_Windings (To => Off);
                  Operations.Set_Run_Windings   (To => On);
              end select;
          when Running =>
              select
                  accept Switch_Off;
                  Motor.Set_State (To => Off);
                  Operations.Set_Run_Windings (To => Off);
              or
                  accept Switch_On;
              or
                  delay 1.0;  -- Check temperature once a second
                  if Operations.Current_Temperature > Max then
                      Motor.Set_State (To => Off);
                      Operations.Set_Run_Windings (To => Off);
                  end if;
              end select;
        end case;
    end loop;
end Control;

-- External Operations ------------------------------------
procedure Switch_On is
begin
    Control.Switch_On;
end Switch_On;

procedure Switch_Off is
begin
    Control.Switch_Off;
end Switch_Off;

function Current_State return State_Type is
begin
    return Motor.Current_State;
end Current_State;

end Induction_Motor;
```

The child package `Operations` contains the low-level operations (setting the windings bits and reading the temperature) called by task `Control`. The external procedures `Switch_On` and `Switch_Off` rendezvous with task `Control` on entries of the same names. The external function `Current_State` calls the protected function of the same name in the shared object `Motor`.

It is important that every select statement has an accept alternative for each of the task's entries. If we, for example, left out the accept alternative for `Switch_Off` in the case alternative for state `Off`, a task calling `Switch_Off` when the motor is in the *off* state would be blocked indefinitely.

Summary

- The rendezvous is a mechanism for direct communication between two tasks.
- The rendezvous uses a client-server model.
- A rendezvous does not take place until both the client and the server request it. The client requests a rendezvous by executing an entry call. The server requests a rendezvous by executing an accept statement.
- The client and server synchronize when a rendezvous takes place.
- The entry parameters provide two-way direct communication between the client and the server.
- The client is blocked while the server executes the optional rendezvous code — the sequence of statements within the accept statement. The rendezvous code should be as short as possible to minimize blocking.
- The selective accept statement allows a server to wait for one of several different entries. Only one alternative is serviced during the execution of the select statement.
- We use guards to control individual alternatives in a selective accept statement. Closed alternatives are not considered during the execution of the selective accept statement.
- The delay alternative of the selective accept statement allows a server to give up waiting for a rendezvous after some period of time.
- The terminate alternative is used to shut down a server task when all of its potential clients are finished.
- The optional else clause of the selective accept statement is executed when none of the alternatives are ready. Use it with care to avoid busy wait loops.
- The delay alternative, terminate alternative, and else part are mutually exclusive — only one of them can be included in a given select statement.
- The timed entry call allows a task to limit how long it will wait to start a protected entry or rendezvous.
- The conditional entry call is similar to a timed entry call with no wait time.

- State machines are important models for objects in real-time embedded applications. Objects may be active (change state by themselves) or passive (only change state in response to some external event).

Exercises

5.1 Modify program Museum (page 130). Replace the four separate task variables, North_Door, South_Door, East_Door, and West_Door, with an array of tasks indexed by compass direction. Replace the discriminant of task type Entrance_Monitor with an entry that is called to give the task its identity (door). Add the code to the main program to rendezvous with each task in the array and give them an identity equal to their location in the array.

5.2 The body of the server task Counter in program Rendezvous_Demo (page 168) contains an infinite loop. Why is this loop necessary? What would happen if we removed the loop from this task body?

5.3 True or false. When a select statement is executed, only one of the alternatives is executed.

5.4 Suppose that when the select statement in task Make_Beverage (page 172) is executed, there are two tasks waiting to rendezvous on entry Coffee, three tasks waiting to rendezvous on entry Tea, and one task waiting to rendezvous on entry Cocoa. Which beverage will be prepared?

5.5 Download program Coffee_Vending from the book website. This program makes random rendezvous with task Make_Beverage (page 172). Compile and run the program. Delete the terminate alternative from task Make_Beverage, then compile and run the program again. What is different between the two executions? Explain the difference.

5.6 In this exercise you will extend the task Make_Beverage (page 172) to handle the restocking of materials in the vending machine. The machine holds enough supplies to make 500 cups of each drink. Here is a new extended task specification.

```
type Beverage_Type is (Coffee, Tea, Cocoa);

task Make_Beverage is
    entry Coffee (Sugar : in Boolean;
                  Cream : in Boolean);
    entry Tea (Sugar : in Boolean;
               Milk  : in Boolean;
               Lemon : in Boolean);
    entry Cocoa;
    entry Refill (Beverage : in Beverage_Type);
end Make_Beverage;
```

1. Entry **Refill** restocks the supply of the given drink. Extend the code of the original task body to handle this new entry.
2. Add guards so that when the machine is out of stock of a particular drink the appropriate select alternative is closed.
3. Finally, add appropriate calls in the task to the following procedure that controls three out-of-stock lights on the front of the vending machine.

```
type Light_State is (Off, On);

procedure Switch_Light (Which : in Beverage_Type;
                        To    : in Light_State);
```

5.7 After adding the guards described in the previous question to task **Make_Beverage**, the order-taking task seems to hang when the customer selects a beverage that is out of stock. When the guarded alternative is closed, the order-taking task is blocked until the vending machine is restocked. This is a serious problem as no other orders can be taken while the order-taking task is waiting.

1. Write a timed entry call for the order-taking task that displays "Out of stock, please make another selection" if it is unable to rendezvous with the **Make_Beverage** task within two seconds.
2. Using a timed entry call works fine as long as there is only a single task calling the beverage entries. Explain why this solution would fail if the vending machine were to have multiple order-taking tasks.
3. Devise a solution that works for multiple order-taking tasks.

5.8 Write a program that calls the function **Ada.Calendar.Clock** to obtain the current time. Your program should then display this time in the format

Day/Month/Year Hour:Minute:Seconds

where Hour ranges from 0 to 23.

5.9 All of the state machine examples in this chapter have been singletons with the state machine object encapsulated in a package body. In this exercise you will develop a state machine class and declare multiple state machine objects. The following simple state machine describes the behavior of a turnstile in the museum described in Chapter 4. There is a turnstile at each of the four entrances to the museum.

Write a package called **Turnstiles** that implements a state machine type. The specification of **Turnstiles** should contain the types for the states and events. It should also contain the specification for the protected type **Turnstile_Control** that implements the state machine.

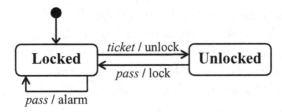

Type `Turnstile_Control` should include the discriminant `ID` of type `Natural`.

Write the body for package `Turnstiles`. This body will contain the body for protected type `Turnstile_Control`. It should also contain the three procedures `Alarm`, `Lock`, and `Unlock` that carry out the three effects for each state transition. Each procedure should simply display an appropriate message that includes the identification number of the turnstile and the effect (turnstile jumper detected, locking, or unlocking).

Finally, write a program that tests all possible combinations of states and events. Use at least two variables of type `Turnstile_Control`.

5.10 Suppose that entry `Switch_On` in our induction motor control task (page 189) is called when a start button is pressed by an operator. A particularly impatient operator pushes the start button to switch on the motor. After 30 seconds have passed, the operator notices that the motor is running slowly so he pushes the start button again. After another 30 seconds, the motor is still being powered by the start windings. So the operator presses the start button a third time. The operator continues to press the start button every 30 seconds. The motor never switches from the start windings to the run windings.

1. Explain why the switch from start windings to run windings was never made.

2. Make the necessary changes and additions to fix the problem. You may assume that the motor will never be started during a daylight savings time change.

6

Distributed systems with Ada

Distribution is an important issue in software engineering, providing scalable systems across networks. Distribution supports a variety of new services from banking systems to social networks to video-on-demand. It is also used in embedded systems like cars and planes built with numerous interconnected computation-intensive blocks. When one processor is not enough, distribution is a natural complement to concurrency. In this chapter, we provide some of the elements to build a distributed system using Ada.[1]

6.1 What are distributed systems?

Formally speaking, a **distributed system** is a federation of interconnected computers that collaborate to fulfill a task. As an example, one can cite web-based applications or constellations of satellites. Distributed systems rely on mechanisms to let information circulate from one node to another. In this section, we review key elements of distributed systems and discuss their strengths and limits.

6.1.1 Why distribute systems?

Before entering into the details of distribution and middleware, it is important to clarify the reasons why someone would want to build a distributed system. Distributing an application across several nodes requires an understanding of (1) the network (topology, technology, etc.), (2) its maintenance lifecycle (potential down time), and (3) its cost (performance and money). In addition, we need to be able to evaluate the value it adds to our application.

---

[1] We focus only on the communication aspects of distributed systems: programming language artifacts and library support. Distributed algorithms are not discussed.

From an historic point of view (Vinoski, 2004), distribution was introduced in the early 1960s in large mainframe computer systems used for airline ticketing and banking. The objective was to share information quickly across a large geographic area without the need for traditional paper mail. To support these operations, the first *middleware* was developed to allow communication over regular phone lines in a point-to-point topology.

The use of a dedicated network topology, with many-to-many connection, provided a way to avoid single points of failure. The United States's DARPA[2] commissioned several teams to build a decentralized network capable of providing an acceptable level of service when a portion of the network fails. In 1969, the first four nodes of ARPANET[3] were deployed in California and Utah. From this pioneering work, ARPANET evolved into the internet, a network used by universities in the 1980s. With the introduction of HTML in the 1990s, internet usage rapidly spread to a wider audience.

Several applications such as electronic mail and bulletin boards used this network to allow people to communicate and exchange data. Computers could now share information in order to provide more computational power for large applications.

Distributed systems are now mature and are present in a large variety of systems. The smart electronic systems of today's cars are built from interconnected microcontrollers. Nearly every company and many homes now have networks to connect all of their resources. Web 2.0 provides social networking, cloud computing, and the infrastructure required for computation-intensive simulations needed to build the next generation of automobiles, aircraft, and energy systems. Distribution fulfills many needs including:

- **Information exchange** Information is exchanged in order to share knowledge or to build a bigger knowledge set. For instance, the list of seats available for a concert allows attendees to make a better purchasing decision.
- **Information availability** A piece of information may be made available to multiple recipients. Distributed systems allow us to transmit it quickly.
- **Information redundancy** Information can be duplicated among multiple sites. This redundancy provides a backup in case one of the copies is not available.
- **Sharing CPU resources** For large applications, one may need more than one processor. Distributed systems can provide load-balancing features, or build a virtual processor by aggregating several nodes.

[2] Defense Advanced Research Projects Agency.
[3] Advanced Research Projects Agency Network.

In addition to satisfying these needs, middleware must also provide support services such as **security** to guarantee data integrity, **safety** to ensure the system is resilient to faults, and **performance** or even **real-time** guarantees for systems with stringent timing requirements. Services are also needed to solve **heterogeneity** across nodes, to provide **naming** in order to access entities through a logical name rather than a cryptic numeric ID, and to define **protocols** that provide a standard organization of the data being exchanged.

Middleware was introduced to provide a framework for building distributed systems. A middleware provides a collection of supporting routines to help in the development of distributed systems. There is a large variety of middleware designed to cope with the even larger variety of application needs.

6.1.2 Family of middleware

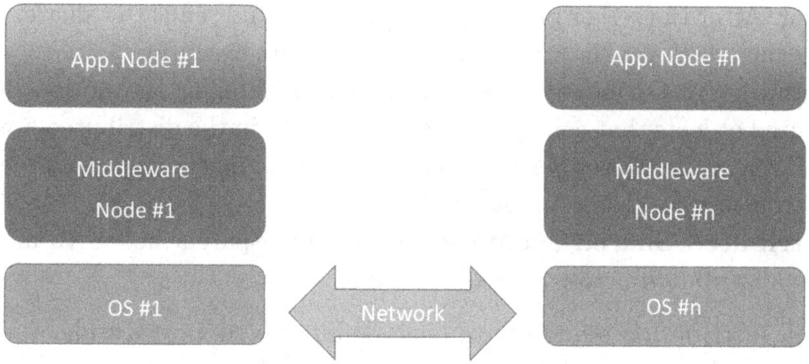

Figure 6.1 Overview of a middleware

A **middleware** is a set of software components that sits between the application and the operating system (see Figure 6.1). It provides an abstract view of the operating system and transport mechanisms to provide a uniform framework. A middleware supports one or more distribution models.

A *distribution model* is defined by the various *distribution mechanisms* it makes available to applications. Remote Procedure Calls (RPC), Distributed Objects, and Message Passing are the most commonly used distribution mechanisms. See Figure 6.2.

- **Message Passing** is notionally equivalent to sending a message from a publisher to a consumer. Messages contain data defined by the application.

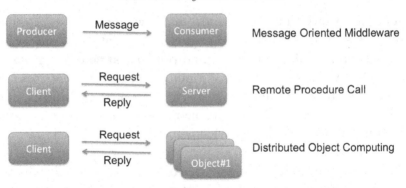

Figure 6.2 Distribution models

- **Remote Procedure Call** (RPC) is a distributed analog of Ada's procedure call. Calling a remote procedure ultimately results in a set of messages on the network and interaction with a remote server that processes the messages. The client becomes blocked after sending the request to the server. After the server processes the messages and sends the answer back, the caller retrieves the results and continues its execution.
- **Distributed Objects** extend the RPC by defining the notion of distributed objects that can be placed on any node in the distributed application. When the object has been located on a particular node, interactions are equivalent to those in an RPC.
- **Distributed Shared Memory** provides transparent access to memory areas distributed across nodes.

Other distribution models have been defined to support a wider range of semantics. "Web-services" are close to Distributed Objects over the internet. "Distributed Components" provide a stricter consistency check of interfaces. "Service-Oriented Architecture" and "Cloud Computing" address scalability and reliability issues to meet requirements for large internet-based applications like social networks. For more details about distribution, please refer to Coulouris *et al.* (2005).

To support these mechanisms, middleware are defined as an API[4] or as an extension to a programming language. Middleware is a proxy between application code and operating system primitives that implement the distribution model. In a message-based middleware, an API is defined to support the full message life cycle (creation, sending, receiving, and analyzing) and the quality of services (policies for retransmission, buffering, etc). In an RPC or Distributed Object Computing middleware, stubs and skeletons are

---

[4] Application Program Interface.

defined to support transparent request building and sending. The stub is reponsible for client-side management of requests; the skeleton performs the dual role on the server side. In addition, middleware may define different qualities of service policies to exchange requests.

6.1.3 Misconceptions of distributed systems

We commonly think that distributing a system across a network helps solve many problems of modern computing (e.g. scalability and gaining access to more computation power). Actually, distribution may hinder our application.

Building a distributed system requires an understanding of many heterogeneous concerns including protocols, operating system issues, concurrency issues, and system engineering. Debugging a distributed system can be extremely challenging. The occurrence of transient errors that are hard to reproduce when logging or debugging tools are activated is particularly frustrating. Such errors are often called "Heisenbugs," named after the Heisenberg uncertainty principle.

Peter Deutsch, a Sun Fellow, published what are now known as the "Eight Fallacies of Distributed Computing." They remind the developer that building a distributed system is always a complex task that should not be underestimated:

The Eight Fallacies of Distributed Computing
Peter Deutsch
Essentially everyone, when they first build a distributed application, makes the following eight assumptions. All prove to be false in the long run and all cause big trouble and painful learning experiences.
1. *The network is reliable*
2. *Latency is zero*
3. *Bandwidth is infinite*
4. *The network is secure*
5. *Topology doesn't change*
6. *There is one administrator*
7. *Transport cost is zero*
8. *The network is homogeneous*

Middleware may help address these issues by providing an analytical framework to evaluate and use resources. Middleware also helps us to configure and deploy applications. In the following sections, we introduce the key elements of middleware.

6.2 Middleware, architectures, and concepts

Middleware is software between your application and the underlying operating system and hardware. Being "in-between" adds some fuzziness to the concept. Where exactly does middleware stand?

There are different families of middleware ranging from generic ones for all-purpose application to ones specialized for video streaming, banking systems, etc. In this chapter, we restrict our focus to generic middleware.

Middlewares share common assets. To illustrate them, let us consider a simple interaction between two nodes. We will use the following convention: the "client" is a node requesting a service, provided by a "server." A "node" is a software process.

Let us suppose we want to build a system to manage students' registration to courses. A student is a "client" of this system, requiring a service from a "server." This client can perform activities like registering to a course, or getting its score to a course.

To support this interaction, depicted in Figure 6.3, we need to coordinate several elementary services. Each service provides one small step to support this interaction,[5] and provide an answer to one simple question: "What do I need to enable interaction?" To do so a middleware needs to address many issues.

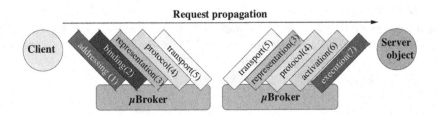

Figure 6.3 Interaction using a middleware

---

[5] This list of services has been fully defined in the POLYORB middleware (Hugues *et al.*, 2003) that we present later in this chapter.

- **Naming** The client needs to "find" the server. The naming service manages a directory that stores mapping from logical name (e.g. "Student Management System") to its actual location (e.g. network address + node-specific identifier).

- **Binding** Once the server has been located, the student's client needs to be "bound" to the server in a way that enables communication. The binding service handles resource allocation, such as opening a communication channel.

- **Protocol/transport** Now that both the client and the server are connected, they need to agree on an exchange mechanism. One usually splits it into two parts: protocol and transport. Protocol defines the organization and semantics of a set of messages: meta-data and a payload; it also defines how to combine these to form valid interactions. A typical case is an RPC made of a request and a reply message. The transport mechanism defines how it is transferred. In most cases, the Internet Protocol TCP/IP is used, but embedded systems may use other transport mechanisms based on dedicated buses.

- **Marshalling** The payload is the user's data. We need to agree on a representation mechanism for a serialized version of the user data we want to send. The marshalling scheme defines the corresponding value for each type. So, for example, in one scheme, 20_{16} represents the space character while in another scheme it represents the integer 32.

    This common representation also helps resolve heterogeneous representation of data by different processors: all data exchanged shall use this unique description.

- **Activation** Prior to engaging in any interaction with the client, the server needs to declare its willingness to do so. It first needs to activate some elements to accept it. Basically, the server has to register some software element with the middleware to make it accessible to the client through the naming service.

- **Execution** The client may now engage interaction with the server. But to do so, the server needs to allocate some execution resource, provided by the execution service. Execution resources may be memory to handle the incoming request, threads to process it, etc.

One can show these services are the root of all distribution middleware, for all distribution models. In the following two sections, we illustrate how these services are coordinated to support two well-known models: Ada's Distributed Systems Annex, and CORBA.

6.3 DSA, the Distributed Systems Annex

The Ada standard defines a set of annexes to address various issues: the standard library, connections with other languages, etc. The 1995 revision of Ada defined the Distributed Systems Annex (Annex E). In this section, we introduce this annex, illustrate its behavior, and discuss one implementation based on POLYORB.

6.3.1 Introduction to the Distributed Systems Annex

The Distributed Systems Annex (DSA) defines a set of compilation pragmas to map an ordinary monolithic application onto a distributed one. This is a major strength of the annex: we write the code for a system the same way whether it is going to be executed distributed across several interconnected nodes or as a program running on a single processor. Annex E was designed to minimize the number of modifications of the source needed to convert a monolithic program into a distributed one.

As defined by the Ada Reference Manual, a distributed system is the interconnection of several *processing nodes* and zero or more *storage nodes*. A distributed program is made of several *partitions*. A **partition** is an aggregate of library units,[6] communicating using shared data or RPCs. The DSA distinguishes between active partitions, housing threads of control, and passive partitions, which are storage nodes.

The application programmer controls which library units are assigned to a partition. In the spirit of the DSA, partitioning is a post-compilation process: the programmer categorizes each unit making up the program. This information is processed during the building process to build the full application. Four pragmas are used to categorize library units:

1. **Pure** To categorize stateless packages.
2. **Remote subprograms** A remote subprogram is an extension of a subprogram call to the distributed case. Such subprograms are declared in units categorized as *Remote Call Interface.*
3. **Distributed Objects** Access types can designate remote objects. A remote call is performed transparently when a primitive dispatching operation is invoked on an object. Such types are declared in units categorized as *Remote Types.*
4. **Shared objects** Shared objects provide a shared memory space for active partitions. Entryless protected objects allow safe concurrent access and

---

[6] See Section 2.5.

update of shared objects such as a database. Such types are declared in units as *Shared Passive*.

To support these mechanisms, the DSA defines a set of coding guidelines. In order to enable distribution and to ensure that the application is fast and reliable, these guidelines restrict some constructs. For instance, the notion of remote rendezvous does not exist — tasks cannot be invoked directly from one partition to another.

6.3.2 Categorization pragmas

A pragma is a compiler directive. Pragmas are used by the compiler to configure the application. We have already described a number of pragmas including **Atomic**, **Inline**, **Pack**, **Storage_Size**, and **Volatile**. In this section, we introduce the configuration pragmas that are used to distribute a program.

pragma Pure

Pragma **Pure** indicates that a package does not contain any state information (e.g. variables). Packages designated as pure are useful to define entities (types, constants, subprograms) shared by several packages. Because it has no state, a pure package can be safely replicated on several partitions.

```
package Pure_Package is

   pragma Pure; -- Package defined as "pure", i.e. stateless

   type A_Type is new Integer;

end Pure_Package;
```

pragma Remote_Call_Interface

Library units categorized by the pragma **Remote_Call_Interface** (RCI) can include subprograms that may be called and executed remotely. RCI units are servers for remote calls.

A subprogram call that invokes such a subprogram is an RPC operation. It is a statically bound call because the compiler can compute the identity of the subprogram being called.

We can also define dynamically bound calls using access types:

- *Remote Access-to-Subprogram* (RAS) is the dereference of an access-to-subprogram.

- *Remote Access-to-Class-Wide* (RACW) is a dispatching call whose dispatching argument is an access-to-class-wide type. They can be defined in RCI packages.

RAS and RACW types define logical names to refer to remote entities. Internally, such a name is composed of an identifier of the remote partition for a particular protocol, and a local identifier for representing the subprogram or the object.

The Ada Reference Manual indicates that an implementation may allow multiple copies of an RCI unit, provided that internal states are propagated to all replicas. As the propagation of internal states requires significant overhead at run-time, RCI units are rarely replicated.

In the following, we will show how to implement the example we presented in Section 6.2 using the DSA, using the different mechanisms to support interactions: first using Remote Access-to-Suprogram, then Remote Access-to-Class-Wide.

The example below[7] illustrates statically bound RCIs. It defines a "student management system." A server provides basic services for accessing and managing a student's account with operations for checking scores, managing course registrations, etc. Our example is built from three packages:

- The `Types` package defines some types, shared by both the client (`RCIClient`) and the server (`RCIStudent`).
- The `RCIStudent` package defines the server side of the application: the server managing student information. It uses the pragma `Remote_Call_Interface` to indicate that these subprograms may be called remotely. All other declarations are ordinary Ada code having nothing to do with the distribution.
- The `RCIClient` procedure defines the client side of the application: a client requesting scores for the student "joe," for the Ada lectures.

```
package Types is
   --  This package defines some types to be used by the
   --  "Student" example.

   pragma Pure;

   type Student_Type is new String (1 .. 10);
   type Password_Type is new String;
end Types;
```

---

[7] See the "RCIClient example" on our website for the full code of this example.

```
with Types; use Types;
package RCIStudent is
    --   This package defines subprograms that can be accessed
    --   remotely by clients , thanks to the pragma:
    pragma Remote_Call_Interface;

    function Get_Score (Student   : in Student_Type;
                        Password : in Password_Type;
                        Course    : in String)
                        return Integer;

    procedure Register_To_Course (Student   : in Student_Type;
                                  Password : in Password_Type;
                                  Course    : in String);

    --   ...
end RCIStudent;
```

```
with Types; use Types;
with RCIStudent;
with Ada. Text_IO; use Ada. Text_IO;

procedure RCIClient is
    Score : Integer;
    S     : Student_Type := "John Doe   ";
    P     : Password_Type := "xxxx";
begin
    --   Possibly a remote call
    Score := RCIStudent. Get_Score (S, P, "Ada");
    Put_Line ("Here is my score" & Integer 'Image (Score));
end RCIClient;
```

In the next example,[8] we use a three-tier architecture. In addition to the client and the student management server, we add a third tier with the computations to be performed. This addition allows us to separate the application across two servers: one for displaying the data and another for performing the computations. This architecture is typical in many web-based applications. The user code registers itself to the middle tier (the student management server) using an access-to-subprogram during the elaboration[9] of the package Compute_Score. The access-to-subprogram is defined in the package RASStudent. As the operations in both of these packages may be called remotely, each is categorized as Remote_Call_Interface.

---

[8] See the "RASClient example" on our website for full code of these examples.

[9] Recall from Chapter 3 that the elaboration of a package body consists of the elaboration of any declarations followed by the execution of the optional package body initialization sequence. We use the initialization code to register procedure Compute.

```ada
with Types; use Types;
package RASStudent is
   pragma Remote_Call_Interface;

   type Compute_Score is access
        function (Student  : in Student_Type;
                  Password : in Password_Type)
                  return Integer;

   procedure Register (Compute_Function : in Compute_Score);

   function Get_Compute_Function return Compute_Score;

   -- [...] Other services
end RASStudent;
```

```ada
with Types; use Types;
package Compute_Score is
   pragma Remote_Call_Interface;

   function Compute (Student  : in Student_Type;
                     Password : in Password_Type)
                     return Integer;

   -- [...] Other services
end Compute_Score;
```

```ada
with RASStudent;
with Types;  use Types;
package body Compute_Score is

   function Compute (Student  : in Student_Type;
                     Password : in Password_Type)
                     return Integer is
      The_Score : Integer := 0;
   begin
      --   ...
      return The_Score;
   end Compute;

begin
   --  Register a dynamically bound remote subprogram (Compute)
   --  through a statically bound remote subprogram (Register)
   --  during the elaboration of this package
   RASStudent.Register (Compute'Access);
end Compute_Score;
```

Now, let us suppose we want the Registrar of the University to send messages to students when their registration has been validated.[10] We wish to send messages using whatever mechanism a student prefers (mobile phones, electronic mail, etc.). We can define a generic terminal using polymorphic (tagged) types to handle all possible mechanisms. Each student can register their own "terminal" to the server. In the code below, `Terminal_Type` is the root type of the distributed terminal hierarchy.

```ada
with Types; use Types;
package Terminal is
   pragma Pure;

   type Terminal_Type is abstract tagged limited private;
   --  Terminal_Type is an abstract tagged type, meaning it
   --  is an interface that will be later implemented by other
   --  types that specialize it.

   procedure Notify (MyTerm  : access Terminal_Type;
                     Student : in Student_Type;
                     Score   : in Integer) is abstract;
   --  Notify is an abstract procedure attached to the
   --  Terminal_Type. Each specialization of Terminal_Type
   --  shall either be abstract itself, or provide an
   --  implementation of this procedure

private
   type Terminal_Type is abstract tagged limited null record;
end Terminal;
```

The RCI unit `RACWStudent` defines `Terminal_Access`, a remote access to a class-wide type. `Terminal_Access` is a reference to a distributed object so it is declared as a general access type.

```ada
with Types;    use Types;
with Terminal; use Terminal;
package RACWStudent is
   pragma Remote_Call_Interface;

   type Terminal_Access is access all Terminal_Type'Class;

   procedure Register (MyTerminal : in Terminal_Access;
                       Student    : in Student_Type;
                       Password   : in Password_Type);
   --  ..

   function Compute_Score (Student  : in Student_Type;
                           Password : in Password_Type)
                           return Integer;
end RACWStudent;
```

[10] See the "RACWClient example" on our website for the full code of this example.

In the next section, we will see how to derive and extend `Terminal_Type`, how to create a distributed object and how to use a reference to it using remote types.

pragma Remote_Types

Library units categorized with the pragma `Remote_Types` (RT) define distributed objects and remote methods attached to them. RCI and RT units can both define a remote access type (RACW). It is important to note that the subprogram itself is not distributed, only the access type is. The code of the unit is replicated on each partition that uses it.

If we want to implement the notification feature proposed in the previous section, we must create a specialized `Terminal_Type` for each user. This extension of our tagged type can be done in a remote types unit as in `A_Terminal` below. Any object of type `Email_Terminal_Type` becomes a distributed object and any reference to such an object becomes a *fat pointer* — a reference to a distributed object (see the declaration of `Terminal_Access` in the previous section). A typical pointer is just a numerical value referring to a memory area; a fat pointer has more information to refer to both the partition and the memory area on this partition.

From that point, the server implementation in `RACWStudent` can call back the student notification function. Note that we have to be cautious when manipulating references to objects. Since there is no global address space, we cannot exchange references to objects that are dynamically allocated, but only to statically allocated objects, as shown in `Student_Terminal`. This restriction ensures we can easily compute the fat pointer associated to this variable.

```
with Types;      use Types;
with Terminal; use Terminal;
package A_Terminal is
   pragma Remote_Types;

   type Email_Terminal is new Terminal_Type with null record;
   --   Email_Terminal is a specialization of Terminal_Type

   overriding
   procedure Notify (MyTerm  : access Email_Terminal;
                     Student : in Student_Type;
                     Score   : in Integer);
end A_Terminal;
```

```
with A_Terminal;
package Student_Terminal is

    The_Terminal : aliased A_Terminal.Email_Terminal;

end Student_Terminal;
```

```
with Types;  use Types;
with RACWStudent;
with Terminal;
with Student_Terminal;
with Ada.Text_IO;  use Ada.Text_IO;

procedure Student1 is
    My_Id      : Student_Type := "John Doe    ";
    Password : Password_Type := "secret";
    My_Score : Integer;
begin
    RACWStudent.Register
       (Student_Terminal.The_Terminal'Access, My_Id, Password);
    My_Score := RACWStudent.Compute_Score (My_Id, Password);
    Put_Line ("My score is" & Integer'Image (My_Score));
    --   ..
end Student1;
```

Here is the body of package RACWStudent whose specification was given
earlier.

```
with Types; use Types;
package body RACWStudent is

    type Student_Record is record
       Term : Terminal_Access;
       Student : Student_Type;
    end record;

    Student_Table : array (1 .. 10) of Student_Record
       := (others => (null, "              "));

    procedure Register (MyTerminal : in Terminal_Access;
                        Student    : in Student_Type;
                        Password   : in Password_Type) is
    begin
       for J in Student_Table'Range loop
          if Student_Table (J).Term = null then
             Student_Table (J) := (MyTerminal, Student);
             return;
          end if;
       end loop;
```

```
      raise Constraint_Error;
      --  If we reach this point, it means that there is
      --  no free slot in the table
end Register;

function Find_Terminal (Student : in Student_Type)
                               return Terminal_Access is
begin
      for J in Student_Table 'Range loop
         if Student_Table (J). Student = Student then
            return Student_Table (J). Term;
         end if;
      end loop;

      return null;
end Find_Terminal;

function Compute_Score  (Student  : in Student_Type;
                         Password : in Password_Type)
                          return Integer is
      Score : Integer := 0;
      Term  : Terminal_Access := Find_Terminal (Student);
      --  Find Student terminal

begin
      --  Compute score
      --  Score := ...

      if Term /= null then
         --  Notify on student terminal
         Notify (Term, Student, Score);
      end if;

      return Score;
end Compute_Score;

end RACWStudent;
```

pragma Shared_Passive

Units categorized with the pragma **Shared_Passive** (SP) define entities to be mapped onto a shared address space such as a file, memory or database. When two partitions intend to access such a shared area, the middleware uses the most appropriate mechanism (filesystem, database APIs, etc.). Entryless protected objects can be used to provide atomic access to shared data, allowing for limited transactional support.

In the code below, we define two kinds of shared objects: **Unprotected_Scores** requires that the different partitions updating this data synchronize to avoid conflicting operations on shared objects; **Protected_Scores** provides a way to get an atomic operation on shared objects. Note that only entryless protected objects are allowed in a shared passive unit.[11] Synchronization must be done with protected procedures.

```ada
package SharedObjects is
   pragma Shared_Passive;

   Max_Student : constant Integer := 42;

   type Score_Array is array (1 .. Max_Student) of Integer;

   Unprotected_Scores : Score_Array;
   --  The user needs to provide protection
   --  against concurrent access

   protected Protected_Scores is
      procedure Set (Index : in  Integer;
                     Score : in  Integer);
      procedure Get (Index : in  Integer;
                     Score : out Integer);
   private
      The_Scores : Score_Array;
   end Protected_Scores;

end SharedObjects;
```

Categorization and dependencies

Categorization pragmas impose a hierarchy of dependency rules:

- Pure packages can depend on (can *with*) only other pure packages.
- Shared_Passive ones can depend either on other Shared_Passive packages, or Pure packages.
- Remote_Types can depend on other Remote_Types, Shared_Passive, or Pure packages.
- Remote_Call_Interface can depend on any other categorized packages.

Conclusion

Ada's Distributed Systems Annex provides support for the distribution of an Ada program. It supports the common distribution models: Remote Procedure Calls, Distributed Objects, and Shared Memory. We use categorization pragmas to add distribution features to an Ada program. We can add

---

[11] The rationale for forbidding entries in shared protected objects is to avoid distributed locks and queues. The potential blocking of callers would require some high run-time cost mechanism to maintain the queue associated with the entry. Additional problems could arise from the disconnection of the blocked task from the network.

these pragmas to any valid monolithic Ada program. We can then compile this program as usual to build an executable to run on a single CPU. Or we may use a special compilation chain to build a distributed system. In the next section we will illustrate a mechanism for building the distributed version.

6.4 PolyORB: compilation chain and run-time for the DSA

In the previous section, we focused on how to describe distribution features as part of an Ada program. In this section, we present how the Ada run-time helps supporting distribution features of the Distributed Systems Annex. Let us first review how an Ada program is compiled and executed.

A complete Ada program is formed by a set of compilation units (its packages) that are checked for compliance with the Ada standard. During the compilation process, an Ada compiler checks many naming and legality rules (typing rules, syntactic rules, etc.). This process results in an Abstract Syntax tree that is fully decorated with cross-reference information.

When this process is completed, the compiler enters into an expansion phase where each high-level Ada construct is turned into much simpler ones. For instance, Ada task creations are mapped onto lower-level calls to the Ada run-time (see Section 9.1 for more details).

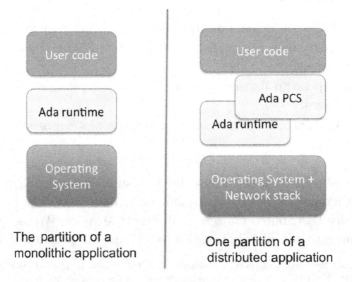

Figure 6.4 Ada user code and the Ada run-time

The Ada run-time provides a software library to support language constructs. It is a wrapper onto lower-level services provided by the host operating system (see left side of Figure 6.4).

When building distributed systems, the compiler uses a different expansion scheme, adding calls to the Ada Partition Communication Subsystem (PCS). The Ada PCS is responsible for routing subprogram calls from one partition to another.

There exists only one validated PCS for Ada, implemented by the POLYORB middleware. It is the successor of GLADE (Pautet and Tardieu, 2000), an early implementation of a PCS. Both POLYORB and GLADE work in conjunction with the GNAT compilation chain. They were developed by joint work between AdaCore and Telecom ParisTech CS laboratory.

POLYORB (Duff *et al.*, 2010) is an Ada middleware that is generic and highly configurable. It is part of AdaCore's offering of Ada products. We can, for example, set how tasks are used to process requests, how to use memory, the level of debug information, etc. Generic middleware is an extension of the concept of a generic package (see Section 2.5.3). After many years of distributed systems design and middleware implementations, people noticed that middleware implementations have similar design, thus they may be built around canonical elements using a functionality-oriented approach; these elements are then adapted to conform to a specific distribution model during a *personalization* process.

POLYORB uses this idea of personalization to build a "schizophrenic middleware," that is, a middleware that can have multiple personalities. In this section, we present the Distributed Systems Annex personality. We'll introduce the CORBA personality later.

The Ada standard document mandates only the semantic requirements an Ada program must fulfill to be compiled and used as a distributed system. It leaves many aspects unspecified.

From the previous examples, and the discussion on middleware services in Section 6.2, you may wonder for instance: how do we map Ada entities onto partitions? What is the protocol used? How can one partition know about the others? The Ada standard leaves all of these details implementation-defined. It is details such as these that are covered by internals of the POLYORB middleware.

Since the developer has little to add to distribute an application onto partitions, the PCS must be tightly coupled to the Ada compiler in order to generate intermediate code to turn a subprogram call into a remote interaction. Yet, one important issue remains: how do we specify where to put each partition? POLYORB defines a configuration language that defines the various partitions, as well as additional parameters. Here is an example. It is the configuration file for the "RCIStudent" example we discussed in Section 6.3.2.

```
configuration RCIStudent_1 is
    pragma Name_Server (Embedded);
    --  Naming server is part of the application

    --  A server partition that executes the server package
    Server_Partition : partition := (rcistudent);

    --  A client partition that executes the client main procedure
    Client_Partition : partition;
    procedure RCIClient is in Client_Partition;

    --  The partitions' executables should be put in ./bin
    for Partition'Directory use "rci_student_bin";
end RCIStudent_1;
```

This configuration file defines two partitions, one that hosts the RCI from the `RCIStudent` package and one that hosts the client code (`RCIClient` procedure). From these two definitions, the compilation chain knows enough to deduce which units form each partition.

- For `Server_Partition`, we list the library units hosted in the partition. Actual code is deduced from the packages that are depended upon, and the fact that some packages are categorized as `Remote_Call_Interfaces` or `Remote_Types`. It is just a container for "server-side" code, i.e. code that can be called by clients.
- For `Client_Partition`, we list the main entrypoint of the program.
- Finally, the `Name_Server` pragma indicates how the naming service, managing reference of all objects, is deployed: in this case, it is embedded in the application.

The POLYORB utility `po_gnatdist` uses this configuration file to produce an executable file for each partition. For each partition, it computes the list of files to be compiled and creates the additional run-time code required to marshal/unmarshal requests and configure the communication channels and other services. Some configurable services are discussed in the next section.

From this high-level description, one may wonder "what goes where?" The compilation chain will process the Ada code, and interpret the configuration pragmas to allocate source code to either the "client" or "server" role. There are some general guidelines to this mapping.

1. First, the definition of a "client" role (sending requests) and a "server" role is on a per-invocation basis. Hence, a partition can be client of one partition, and server for another.

2. For each kind of invocation, we have the following rules:

   - The specification of `Pure`, `Remote_Types`, `Remote_Call_Interface`, and `Shared_Passive` packages are replicated on each partition that requires them.

   - The body of `Shared_Passive`, `Remote_Types`, and `Remote_Call_Interfaces` are replicated on each "server" partition that supports them, for instance as specified in the configuration file used by `po_gnatdist`.

     Note: as mentioned before, RCI units are rarely replicated since it is hard to propagate any modification of its internal state to all replicas.

3. Depending on the "role" for a particular invocation, the compilation chain will duplicate code required to produce requests (stubs) on the client side, and the skeletons that process them.

The DSA mandates that a semantically correct program shall be mapped transparently to a distributed application. Hence, all these allocations are performed transparently to the end user, after semantic checks performed by both GNAT compilation chain and `po_gnatdist`. This mechanism saves a lot of time to the developer.

6.5 Advanced DSA concepts

In this section, we discuss some of the more advanced concepts in the Distributed Systems Annex of Ada.

6.5.1 Exceptions

The Distributed Systems Annex mandates that calls are executed at most once: they are made exactly one time or they fail with an exception. When a communication error occurs, the exception `System.RPC.Communication_Error` is raised. However, it provides limited information on the actual cause of error: network disconnection, marshalling error, server not ready, etc.

Any exception raised in a remote method or subprogram call is propagated back to the caller. Exception semantics are preserved in the normal Ada way.

6.5.2 pragma Asynchronous

To be equivalent to the monolithic case, all remote calls are, by default, blocking. This behavior is illustrated in Figure 6.5. The caller waits until the remote call is complete and the response has been received. The middle-ware performs all actions to configure both the caller and the callee, open communication channels, and allocate resources to process the request: tasks and memory buffers.

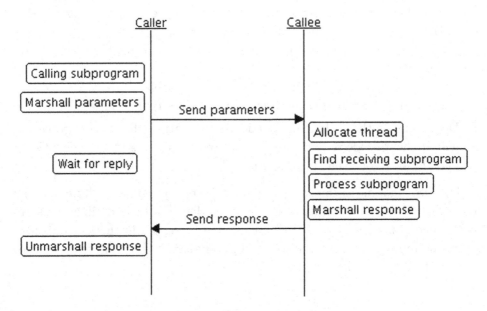

Figure 6.5 Sequence of actions for *synchronous* calls

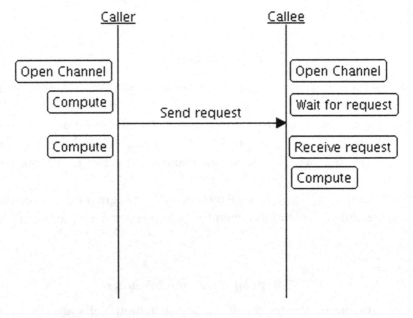

Figure 6.6 Sequence of actions for *asynchronous* calls

When a remote subprogram is labeled with the **pragma Asynchronous**, remote calls to these subprograms will be executed asynchronously. The caller of an asynchronous procedure does not wait for the completion of the remote call, it continues its execution. Figure 6.6 illustrates the behavior of an asynchronous call.

As the caller does not wait, an asynchronous call cannot return any information. Hence, the remote procedure can have only **in** mode parameters. Another consequence of asynchronous execution is that any exception raised during the execution of the remote procedure is lost.

Pragma **Asynchronous** can be applied directly to a regular subprogram or to a remote access-to-subprogram (RAS) type. Here is an example that illustrates both of these options.

```
package AsynchronousRCI is
    pragma Remote_Call_Interface;

    procedure Asynch_Example (X : in Integer);
    pragma Asynchronous (Asynch_Example);

    procedure Synch_Example (X : in Integer);

    type AsynchRAS is access procedure (X : in Integer);
    pragma Asynchronous (AsynchRAS);
end AsynchronousRCI;
```

Any direct call to procedure **Asynch_Example** will be executed asynchronously. An indirect call to *any* remote procedure designated by an access value of type **AsynchRAS** will also be executed asynchronously.

We can also apply pragma **Asynchronous** to remote access-to-class-wide (RACW) types as well. In this case, the invocation of any operation with a dispatching **in** mode parameter is always performed asynchronously. Invocation of operations with **out** or **in out** parameter modes are, as you would expect, performed synchronously. The following package defines potentially asynchronous dispatching calls for the class hierarchy rooted at **Object**.

```
package AsynchronousRT is
    pragma Remote_Types;

    type Object is tagged limited private;

    type AsynchRACW is access all Object'Class;
    pragma Asynchronous (AsynchRACW);

    procedure Asynch_Operation (X : in      Object);
    procedure Synch_Operation  (X : in out Object);
    function Create return AsynchRACW;
```

```
private
    type Object is tagged limited null record;
end AsynchronousRT;
```

An asynchronous RAS can be both asynchronous and synchronous. The mode depends on the designated subprogram. For instance, in the program AsynchronousMain below, remote call (1) is asynchronous (the referenced subprogram is marked as asynchronous) whereas remote call (2) is synchronous (for similar reasons — the referenced subprogram is synchronous).

Calls (3) and (4) illustrate calls to methods of an object designated by an asynchronous RACW. These examples show both the standard procedure call syntax and the object.method syntax that we may use with tagged objects. The two calls (3) to Asynch_Operation are performed asynchronously as the method's only parameter is mode **in**. As the procedure has an **in out** mode parameter, the two calls (4) to Synch_Operation are performed synchronously.

```
with AsynchronousRCI, AsynchronousRT;
procedure AsynchronousMain is
    -- Access (pointer) variables
    RAS   : AsynchronousRCI.AsynchRAS;  -- to a procedure
    RACW  : AsynchronousRT.AsynchRACW;  -- to an object
begin
    -- Asynchronous Dynamically Bound Remote Call (1)
    RAS := AsynchronousRCI.Asynch_Example'Access;
    RAS.all (0);
    -- Synchronous Dynamically Bound Remote Call (2)
    RAS := AsynchronousRCI.Synch_Example'Access;
    RAS.all (0);

    RACW := AsynchronousRT.Create;
    -- Asynchronous Dynamically Bound Remote Calls (3)
    AsynchronousRT.Asynch_Operation (RACW.all);
    RACW.all.Asynch_Operation;    -- Object.Method syntax
    -- Synchronous Dynamically Bound Remote Calls (4)
    AsynchronousRT.Synch_Operation (RACW.all);
    RACW.all.Synch_Operation;    -- Object.Method syntax
end AsynchronousMain;
```

The behavior we have illustrated follows the conventional message-passing paradigm defined in object-oriented language. A dispatching call to an object can be seen as sending a message to it.

Note that pragma **Asynchronous** can be dangerous. Its use breaks the assumption that the distributed system behaves exactly like the monolithic one (assuming that (1) the monolithic one runs on a multi processor system, and (2) there is no error in the communication channel). Asynchronous calls are not available in monolithic programs. This difference has two impacts:

1. It makes debugging distributed programs more difficult. We can't simply debug our program by running it on a single CPU.
2. It can introduce race conditions on the server side.

6.5.3 pragma All_Calls_Remote

A pragma `All_Calls_Remote` in an RCI unit forces remote procedure calls to be routed through the partition communication subsystem even for a local call. This eases the debugging of an application in a non-distributed situation that is very close to the distributed one, because the communication subsystem (including marshalling and unmarshalling procedures) can be exercised on a single node.

6.5.4 Starting and terminating a distributed application

One of the most complex issues in running a distributed application is how to actually start it. We need to coordinate multiple nodes, and start the application. Later, the application may eventually finish, and we need to stop all nodes gracefully. The Distributed Systems Annex includes some features to address these issues.

Elaboration and consistency

We introduced elaboration in Chapter 2. Elaboration performs the steps to "initialize" all entities (constants, variables, tasks, packages, etc.) in an ordered fashion. The DSA extends elaboration to distributed applications. The DSA's underlying Partition Communication Subsystem (PCS) and associated compilation tool-chain will order the elaboration of all packages, and its own run-time, so that the user code can make remote calls even when executing statements (such as function calls) in the declarative part.

Yet, this is not enough to ensure that the system may run. A distributed system is made up of a collection of partitions, possibly geographically scattered all over the world. We need to make sure the system is consistent — that all functions come from the same set of compilation sources. The DSA defines some attributes that check the internal consistency of an application.

Ada defines the **Version** attribute, attached to compilation units. If P is a compilation unit, then P'**Version** yields a value of the predefined type String that identifies the version of the compilation unit that contains the declaration of the program unit. The version of a compilation unit changes when the unit changes "significantly." Since this is a rather vague concept, it is left implementation-defined. This attribute is checked at elaboration time to ensure that all partitions are based on the same set of compilation units. The exception **Program_Error** will be raised in one or both partitions.

Naming of partitions

There is no need for a naming service to be visible at the user level — all partitions are connected transparently by the PCS. However, it might be useful for an application to display information about its partitions.

The **Partition_Id** attribute returns a universal integer. It applies to library-level declaration, and identifies the partition in which the entity was elaborated. If this entity is an RCI unit, the value corresponds to the partition where the body was elaborated.

Abortion

From a developer point of view, calls to local or remote subprograms are equivalent. Therefore, the DSA places no restrictions on the abortion of remote subprograms. The remote subprogram is canceled. The actual way to cancel a remote call is implementation-defined.

Termination

In the monolithic case, Ada defines a full list of rules to determine when to finish a task, and how to handle a full hierarchy of tasks (see Section 3.2.4).

The DSA extends these rules to the distributed case. A partition terminates when its environment task terminates; a set of partitions terminates when no messages are to be delivered. These conditions can be checked in several ways, each involving sending PCS-private messages among the nodes. Determining when a program reaches the terminated state is known as a "consensus problem" (Pease *et al.*, 1980). In the general case, it is known to be NP-hard. POLYORB includes several algorithms we may use to specify how we want to finish the application.

6.5.5 Some final comments on the DSA

Ada's Distributed Systems Annex provides a set of mechanisms to transform a monolithic Ada program into a distributed one. It has several limitations. It is restricted to Ada, it does not address the definition of the protocol layer, it does not allow for interoperability with other languages, and it leaves many elements as implementation-defined (compilation chain, deployment, etc.).

It would be useful to have a server using Ada for highly critical computations while allowing clients that display some information to be written in Java. In the next section, we present CORBA, the Common Object Request Broker Architecture, and show how it addresses DSA's limitations to provide interoperability among languages and transport mechanisms.

6.6 CORBA, the Common Object Request Broker Architecture

In this section, we introduce some concepts of the Common Object Request Broker Architecture (CORBA). CORBA is the Object Management Group's (OMG)[12] answer for building scalable information systems. It defines a full set of technology standards to support the construction of such systems.

OMG is a not-for-profit consortium made up of hundreds of organizations across the computing industry. Its goal is to develop integration technology standards to support the development of computer-based systems. Its main standards are UML and CORBA. UML (Unified Modeling Language) is a standard for modeling computer-based systems prior to implementation. We used a UML class diagram in Chapter 2 to illustrate the relationships between different kinds of commercial ovens. CORBA is a set of technology standards to support the construction of applications that are based on distributed, interacting objects.

The object-oriented paradigm is the heart of OMG technologies. Object orientation allows us to structure a design as a set of classes and relationships between them. OMG uses object concepts to provide standards that are independent of any particular programming language. The motivation behind this independence is to allow us to design complex applications without thinking about implementation details. Of course, eventually we must use a particular language or set of languages to implement the application.

CORBA provides a complete framework that defines both a run-time infrastructure (including the APIs and the protocol layer) and a development process. The API is defined using the CORBA Interface Definition Language (IDL). The mappings defined by OMG allow us to use this API with each programming language.

In the following sections, we'll briefly introduce CORBA. A detailed reference on CORBA can be found in McHale (2007). The complete CORBA standard is freely available (OMG, 2004).

---

[12] http://www.omg.org

6.6.1 CORBA concepts

A CORBA-based application is a collection of nodes. Each node can act either as a *client* that requests a service or a *server* that provides the service. One node can be both a client and a server depending on the context.

Application services are *objects* defined through an interface written in the Interface Definition Language (IDL). The IDL specification defines the publicly visible facets of an object — the list of services and attributes it offers. This IDL specification is processed by an *IDL compiler* to produce **stubs** for the client and **skeletons** for the server. Stubs are the client-side glue code responsible for building requests to a server. Skeletons are the server-side glue code responsible for handling requests from a client. Figure 6.7 shows the relationships between the client, stub, skeleton, and server object. The stub and skeleton hide the details of the actual network communication through the Object Request Broker (ORB).

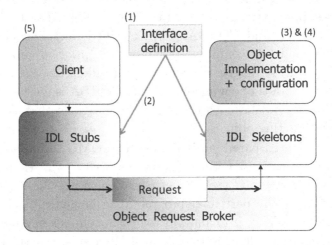

Figure 6.7 Overview of CORBA

Clients and objects are implemented in a target language (Ada, C, C++, Python, etc.) following the rules of the IDL-to-*x* mapping specification. These rules detail how to map each construct of the IDL to language *x*. Once implemented, application objects are bound to CORBA **servants**. A servant encapsulates all the machinery to make the object visible through the ORB. The ORB handles all the details of routing a request from a client to a server.

In the following sections, we illustrate the development of a CORBA application. We use the same student management example we used to illustrate the Distributed Systems Annex of Ada. The steps we use to build our CORBA application are:

1. Use the Interface Definition Language (IDL) to define an interface to our server object that manages student information.
2. Use an IDL-to-Ada compiler to create Ada packages for the stub used by clients and the skeleton that *defines* the servant.
3. Implement the server object (the servant) in Ada.
4. Write the Ada code to set up the node that hosts the servant.
5. Implement the client in Ada. Clients call subprograms defined in the stub package to obtain services from the server object.

CORBA is a very powerful middleware with many features and options,[13] and requires some investment to master them all. In the following, we design our examples to give you a sufficient understanding to build your own CORBA applications.

6.6.2 CORBA IDL

Like the DSA, CORBA middleware hides the details of the network connecting the distributed components of our application. Unlike the DSA, CORBA was designed to be independent of programming language. Using CORBA, we can write our application's mission-critical code running on one computer in Ada and write the user interface running on other computers in Java.

To obtain such interoperability, we need to define contracts between clients and servers in a neutral language: the Interface Definition Language. This language borrows many features from the C language family.

An IDL specification is made of a set of one or more **modules**. Modules define a namespace hierarchy similar to the hierarchy provided by Ada's child packages. Modules may contain declarations of types, interfaces, and other modules. The **interfaces** define the visible facets of a remote object that provides services to clients. Modules are optional, but highly recommended to define libraries of reusable components. Like all C family languages, IDL is case-sensitive. Let us suppose we wish to implement the "Student Management" system using CORBA.

IDL for the "Student Management" service
```
module CORBAStudents {

    // Definition of two unbounded string types
```

---

[13] Its full specifications are more than three times as large as the Ada Reference Manual.

```
typedef string student_type;
typedef string password_type;

exception invalid_student {string name;};

interface Student_Management {
  // Interface definition of the Student_Management object

  short Get_Score
    (in student_type student,
     in password_type password,
     in string course) raises (invalid_student);

  void Register_To_Course
    (in student_type student,
     in password_type password,
     in string course) raises (invalid_student);
  };
};
```

The above listing defines the interface of the CORBA version of the "student management" system we developed earlier for the DSA. Lines beginning with // indicate comments. The first non-comment lines in this listing define the types that our client and server share. A **typedef** defines a new name for an existing type. In this case we declare the names **student_type** and **password_type** to be new names for the CORBA type **string**. In our DSA example, these types were defined in the definition package **Types**.

The interface **Student_Management** defines the two services that our server provides. As in Ada, the parameters of an operation have a specified direction, which can be *in* (meaning that the parameter is passed from the client to the server), *out* (the parameter is passed from the server back to the client), or *inout* (the parameter is passed in both directions). Operations can have a return value (like an Ada function) or not (like an Ada procedure). In the above listing, the operation **Get_Score** has three *in* parameters and returns a **short** value. The word **void** indicates that operation **Register_To_Course** does not return a value.

As in Ada, an operation can raise an exception. CORBA uses the term "throw" instead of raise. CORBA has predefined exception types, called system exceptions, that may be thrown when using services provided by the CORBA run-time (e.g. communication errors, invalid parameters, etc.). A CORBA programmer can also define his own exceptions. IDL exceptions include a string with information. Here, we use this feature to return the offending name when a student name is invalid. Programmer-defined exceptions that may be raised by an operation must be included in that operation's declaration. The caller of such operations should be ready to process these exceptions.

Parameters to an operation (and the return value) can be one of the built-in CORBA types, such as **string, boolean,** and **long,** or a programmer-defined type that is declared in an IDL file. Of course, we can always use typedef to create synonyms that are more meaningful in our application than the built-in type names (e.g. **student_type** is a more descriptive name in our application than **string**).

Programmer-defined types allow us to define the following additional types in our IDL modules and interfaces:

- An **enum** is conceptually similar to a collection of constant integer declarations. For example:

    ```
    typedef enum  { red , green , blue } color ;
    typedef enum  { Dublin , London , Paris , Rome } city ;
    ```

    Internally, CORBA uses integer values to represent different enum values. Except for the specific link to integer constants, enum is equivalent to Ada's enumeration types.

- A **fixed type** holds fixed-point numeric values, whereas the float and double types hold floating-point numeric values (see Section 2.3.1, page 36).

    ```
    typedef fixed <18,2> Money ;
    ```

- A **sequence**. This is a collection type. It is like a one-dimensional array. IDL defines unbounded and bounded sequences.

    ```
    // Unbounded sequence of short
    typedef sequence<short> U_sequence ;

    // Bounded sequence of short , of size 10
    typedef sequence<short ,10> B_sequence ;
    ```

- An **array**. The dimensions of an IDL array are specified in the IDL file, so an array is of fixed size. The sequence type is more flexible and so is more commonly used.

    ```
    // An array of 5 long values indexed from 0 to 4
    typedef long simple_array [5];
    ```

- A **struct**. This is similar to an Ada record. The following typedef defines the struct type **array_struct** with two members (fields) — the array elements and **length**.

    ```
    typedef struct  {
      long elements [10];
      unsigned short length ;
    } array_struct ;
    ```

- A **union**. This type can hold one of several values at run-time, for example:

```
typedef union switch(short) {
  case 1: boolean  boolVal;
  case 2: long     longVal;
  case 3: string   stringVal;
} Foo;
```

An instance of `Foo` could hold a boolean, a long, or a string. The case label (called a discriminant) indicates which value is currently active. An IDL union is equivalent to an Ada record with a variant part. To learn about variant parts, consult one of the general Ada references listed at the beginning of Chapter 2.

Like Ada packages, IDL modules define a set of namespaces. IDL provides the **import** keyword which is similar to Ada's "with" mechanism. **Import** allows us to access definitions from other modules. Names are fully qualified using the syntax $< module\_name >::< module\_name\_2 >::< entity >$, where *entity* is defined in *module_name_2*, which is nested within *module_name*.

6.6.3 IDL-to-Ada mapping

The IDL defines the interface of objects that are remotely accessible through the ORB. Clients use this interface to interact with them. To do so, an IDL compiler will generate the glue code to enable interaction. This mapping follows the rule of the IDL-to-Ada mapping defined as part of the CORBA specifications (OMG, 2001). The IDL compiler translates an IDL module into an Ada package hierarchy. This hierarchy includes:

- A root package with the same name as the IDL module.
  The specification of this package defines the Ada types and exceptions equivalent to the CORBA types and exceptions defined in the IDL module. These types and exceptions are shared by the client code and server object. This package plays the same role as package **Types** in our DSA example. The application programmer uses these types with no concern of the code within the package body generated by the IDL compiler.
- A child package for each interface defined in the IDL module.
  The child package specification contains the Ada definition of the object that provides the service defined by the IDL interface. The operations defined in this package are called by the client to request a service from

the object. As with the parent package, the application programmer needs not be concerned with the code inside the child package body.

The application programmer must write the code to implement the object defined in a child package. We make use of Ada's inheritance mechanism to provide this implementation in a grandchild package.

For each element of the IDL specification, the IDL compiler will apply specific rules to map IDL constructs onto semantically equivalent Ada constructs. The mapping rules are summarized in Table 6.1. The package CORBA, supplied with the IDL-to-Ada compiler, contains the Ada type equivalents to CORBA's built-in types.

IDL	Ada
short	CORBA.Short
long	CORBA.Long
long long	CORBA.Long_Long
float	CORBA.Float
double	CORBA.Double
long double	CORBA.Long_Double
char, wchar	CORBA.Char, CORBA.WChar
string, wstring	CORBA.String, CORBA.WString
boolean	Standard.Boolean
octet	CORBA.Object
any	CORBA.Any
void	*Nothing*
struct	record type
enum	enumerated type
union	discriminanted type
fixed	Ada fixed point
array	array
sequence	instance of CORBA.Sequences
const	constant
exception	Ada exception + accessors
module	package
interface	package + a tagged type
attribute	Ada methods
operation	Ada methods

Table 6.1 *IDL-to-Ada mapping rules*

Let us now study the Ada packages generated by the IDL compiler[14] for the CORBAStudents module given on page 223. Here is the root package generated by the IDL compiler.

---

[14] These Ada packages were generated using the **iac** IDL compiler, part of the POLYORB middleware.

```
with CORBA;
with Ada.Exceptions;

package CORBAStudents is

    Repository_Id : constant String :=
      "IDL:CORBAStudents:1.0";

    type student_type is new CORBA.String;

    student_type_Repository_Id : constant String :=
      "IDL:CORBAStudents/student_type:1.0";

    type password_type is new CORBA.String;

    password_type_Repository_Id : constant String :=
      "IDL:CORBAStudents/password_type:1.0";

    invalid_student : exception;

    type invalid_student_Members is
      new CORBA.Idl_Exception_Members with record
          name : CORBA.String;
      end record;

    invalid_student_Repository_Id : constant String :=
      "IDL:CORBAStudents/invalid_student:1.0";

    procedure Get_Members
      (From : Ada.Exceptions.Exception_Occurrence;
       To : out CORBAStudents.invalid_student_Members );

end CORBAStudents;
```

Let us look at each of the elements in this root package specification.

- The types **student_type** and **password_type** were constructed from the IDL type definitions using the IDL-to-Ada mapping rules. Both our client code and server code will make use of these two types.
- A number of **Repository_Id** constants provide information on the current package and trace it and its types back to the IDL specifications. Like the DSA's version attribute, these IDs hold information on the version of the interface.
- The Ada exception **invalid_student** is a mapping of the IDL exception. IDL allows us to attach information to an exception. To implement this feature in Ada, the IDL mapping prescribes the generation of a "Members" type and a conversion procedure that allows us to retrieve this information.

The body of the root package does not contain anything of direct interest to the application programmer so we do not show it here.

Now let's look at the specification of the child package CORBAStudents. Student_Management. This package defines the server object specified by the interface CORBAStudents::Student_Management given on page 224. You can see the entire specification on our web site.

```
with CORBA.Object;

package CORBAStudents.Student_Management is

    type Ref is new CORBA.Object.Ref with null record;

    Repository_Id : constant String :=
      "IDL:CORBAStudents/Student_Management:1.0";

    function Get_Score
      (Self : Ref;
       student  : CORBAStudents.student_type;
       password : CORBAStudents.password_type;
       course : CORBA.String)
      return CORBA.Short;

    procedure Register_To_Course
      (Self : Ref;
       student  : CORBAStudents.student_type;
       password : CORBAStudents.password_type;
       course : CORBA.String);

    --   ...

    function Is_A
      (Self : Ref;
       Logical_Type_Id : String)
      return CORBA.Boolean;

private
    --   ...
end CORBAStudents.Student_Management;
```

Elements to observe in this child package include:

- This package also defines a Repository_Id constant.
- IDL and CORBA are object-based. Therefore, the basic unit of processing is the object. Each interface is supported by one object. CORBA.Object.Ref is the root type of all remotely accessible objects. The type Ref extends this root type and adds the two new primitive operations, Get_Score and Register_To_Course, defined in the IDL specification. Both

of these operations include the parameter **Self**, a reference to the server object.

- It would appear that the IDL compiler failed to fill in the parameter modes for the subprograms. This omission is not an error. When a parameter mode is not given, the Ada compiler uses the default mode *in*.

- CORBA mandates the definition of an **Is_A** function for each server object type to test membership. This function returns true if the parameter is of the correct type as deduced from its repository ID.

You can see the complete package on our web site. Again, the body of this IDL compiler-generated package does not contain anything of direct interest to the application programmer so we do not show it here.

All of this Ada code is generated from the IDL specification. In the next three sections, we look at the code the programmer must write to complete the distributed application. From the description we made in Section 6.6.1, we must first implement the servant object that will hold the application logic, then define the server that will host it, and finally the client that will interact with the server.

6.6.4 Implementing the servant

We have completed the first two of our five steps to create a CORBA-based distributed application: the creation of an IDL specification of the server object and the compilation of that specification to create a root package for our CORBA module, **CORBAStudents**, and a child package for the interface, **CORBAStudents::Student_Management**. In this section we will construct the servant that encapsulates our server object.

The IDL-to-Ada mapping rules mandate that the implementation code for a server object is in a child package of the interface package named **Impl**. So the complete package name is in the form **<Module_Name>.<Interface_Name>.Impl**. This naming convention ensures that the implementation code can be used by the code automatically generated for the skeleton. The IDL compiler produces a dummy version of this package for the application programmer to fill in. Here is the dummy version the IDL compiler produced for our example.

```
with PortableServer;
with CORBA;

package CORBAStudents. Student_Management. Impl is

    type Object is
        new PortableServer. Servant_Base with private;
```

```
function Get_Score
  (Self : not null access Object;
   student : CORBAStudents.student_type;
   password : CORBAStudents.password_type;
   course : CORBA.String)
  return CORBA.Short;

procedure Register_To_Course
  (Self : not null access Object;
   student : CORBAStudents.student_type;
   password : CORBAStudents.password_type;
   course : CORBA.String);

private
  type Object is new PortableServer.Servant_Base with record
    --  Insert components to hold the state of
    --  the implementation object.
    null;
  end record;

end CORBAStudents.Student_Management.Impl;
```

Package Impl defines an implementation type whose mandatory name is Object. Type Object is an extension (subclass) of the CORBA type PortableServer.Servant_Base. The package declares the two subprograms Get_Score and Register_To_Course, versions of the operations originally defined in our IDL specification. Each of these subprograms has a formal parameter named Self that is a pointer to our server object. As you might imagine, the notation not null prevents us from calling these subprograms with a null value for Self.

To complete this dummy package, the application programmer must:

1. Complete the full definition of type Object in the private section. We must add all of the components necessary to hold the state of our server object.
2. Complete the package body. We must write the code for the operations defined in the package specification.

You can find the completed Impl package specification and body on our web site.

6.6.5 Setting up the server node

Our next task is to write the program that contains the server object and runs on the server node. We need to configure this program so it will accept remote calls. Here is the server program for our example application. It

contains a great deal of CORBA-specific operations that we shall examine
next. You may use this program as a template for creating your own server
programs.

```ada
with Ada.Text_IO;   use Ada.Text_IO;

with CORBA.Impl;
with CORBA.Object;
with CORBA.ORB;

with PortableServer.POA.Helper;
with PortableServer.POAManager;

with CORBAStudents.Student_Management.Impl;

with PolyORB.Setup.No_Tasking_Server;
pragma Warnings (Off, PolyORB.Setup.No_Tasking_Server);
--  Configure server with basic services, without tasking

procedure Server is

    procedure Configure_Servants is
        Root_POA : PortableServer.POA.Local_Ref;
        Ref : CORBA.Object.Ref;
        Obj : constant CORBA.Impl.Object_Ptr
            := new CORBAStudents.Student_Management.Impl.Object;

    begin
        --  Retrieve Root POA
        Root_POA := PortableServer.POA.Helper.To_Local_Ref
            (CORBA.ORB.Resolve_Initial_References
                (CORBA.ORB.To_CORBA_String ("RootPOA")));

        PortableServer.POAManager.Activate
            (PortableServer.POA.Get_The_POAManager (Root_POA));

        --  Set up new object
        Ref := PortableServer.POA.Servant_To_Reference
            (Root_POA, PortableServer.Servant (Obj));

        --  Output IOR
        Put_Line (CORBA.To_Standard_String
                    (CORBA.Object.Object_To_String (Ref)));

    end Configure_Servants;

begin
    --  Perform CORBA configuration and initialisation
    CORBA.ORB.Init (CORBA.ORB.To_CORBA_String ("ORB"),
                    CORBA.ORB.Command_Line_Arguments);
```

```
    --   Configure  application-specific  servant
    Configure_Servants;

    --  Launch  the  server
    CORBA.ORB.Run;
end  Server;
```

The context clause of our server program indicates that this program depends on many packages. The package CORBAStudents.Student_Manager. Impl is the implementation of the server object developed in the previous section. The three packages rooted at CORBA are obviously CORBA-related. The two packages rooted at PortableServer are also CORBA packages.

The package rooted at PolyORB contains the code to set up and configure the server with basic services. We have used the open-source CORBA provided by PolyORB in our examples. Other vendors[15] would supply equivalent packages to set up the server. Pragma Warnings is an implementation-defined pragma. The GNAT compiler issues a warning when a package is with'ed but not directly used. Program Server makes no direct use of the resources in package PolyORB. However, this package must be elaborated to set up the server. The pragma disables the warning that package PolyORB is not used by program Server.

When we execute procedure Server from the command line, we can include some optional command line arguments to configure the server's object request broker (ORB). These optional arguments are retrieved using the CORBA.ORB.Command_Line_Arguments function.

The call to procedure CORBA.ORB.Init initializes the ORB, including tasking policies, protocol stacks, and other internal objects. The two parameters passed to this procedure are the name we wish to assign to this ORB (we used the name "ORB") and the optional ORB configuration parameters from the command line. One important internal object initialized by CORBA.ORB.Init is the "RootPOA."[16] This object is responsible for managing the servant's lifecycle.

Once the call to CORBA.ORB.Init has configured the ORB, we call the Configure_Servants procedure to configure our application. It builds one instance of a CORBA.Impl.Object: it sets up our server object so it can handle the remote requests later. The elaboration of the constant Obj allocates the actual server object whose type we defined earlier in the private part of package CORBAStudents.Student_Manager.Impl.

---

[15] Objective Interface Systems and PrismTech are two vendors of commercial CORBA products with Ada support.

[16] POA stands for Portable Object Adapter. We'll look more at the POA in Section 6.7.3.

After the elaboration of the procedure's declarations, there are five steps needed to prepare our server for processing requests from clients on other nodes.

- Call the function `CORBA.ORB.Resolve_Initial_References` to *lookup the RootPOA object* that was created earlier to dispatch requests to our object. This function provides a reduced name service, local to a node, that retrieves objects configured on and accessible from the current node.
- *Activate the RootPOA* (that we just looked up) with a call to procedure `PortableServer.POAManager.Activate`. The activation is performed through the RootPOA's attached POAManager object. Once activated, our RootPOA can process incoming requests.
- *Create a reference to our servant* that is accessible from other nodes. To accomplish this task, we call function `Servant_To_Reference` passing our RootPOA and the local reference to our server object. This function returns a remote reference called an Interoperable Object Reference (IOR) that clients running on other nodes use to access our server object.
- *Display the IOR.* The function `CORBA.Object.Object_To_String` converts the IOR stored in the variable `Ref` to a unique string. We'll make use of the value displayed on the console in the next section when we start up our client.
- Finally, we call the procedure `CORBA.ORB.Run` which launches the server. The ORB is now up and running. It can now direct requests from other nodes to our server object.

6.6.6 Setting up the client node

The client program follows a path similar to that of the server. Here is the client program for our example application. You may use this program as a template for creating your own client programs.

```
with  Ada.Command_Line;
with  Ada.Text_IO;
with  CORBA.ORB;

with  CORBAStudents.Student_Management;

with  PolyORB.Setup.Client;
pragma Warnings (Off, PolyORB.Setup.Client);
--   Configure client with basic services

procedure Client is
   use Ada.Command_Line;
   use Ada.Text_IO;
```

```
use CORBAStudents. Student_Management;
use CORBAStudents;
use CORBA;

A_Student : CORBAStudents. Student_Management. Ref;

begin
    CORBA.ORB. Initialize ("ORB");
    if Argument_Count /= 1 then
        Put_Line ("usage : client <IOR_string_from_server>");
        return;
    end if;

    -- Getting the CORBA.Object

    CORBA.ORB. String_To_Object
        (CORBA. To_CORBA_String (Ada. Command_Line. Argument (1)),
                                 A_Student);

    -- Checking if it worked

    if CORBAStudents. Student_Management. Is_Nil (A_Student) then
        Put_Line ("main : cannot invoke on a nil reference");
        return;
    end if;

    Register_To_Course
        (A_Student , To_CORBA_String ("John Doe"),
        To_CORBA_String ("xxx"), To_CORBA_String ("Ada"));
end Client;
```

Our client program first initializes the ORB. Next it must set up a reference to the remote object we created on the server. We have taken a very simple approach to setting up this reference. When we start up the client program, we include the string value of the IOR displayed on the console by the server program given in the previous section.[17]

We make use of the operations in package **Ada.Command_Line** to process the command line that started the execution of program **Client**. If the user did not include an IOR string on the command line, the program displays an error message and terminates.

Next we call the procedure **CORBA.ORB.String_To_Object** to convert the IOR string into an actual IOR stored in variable **A_Student**, and initialize all internal structures to enable interaction. Given the complexity of the IOR string, there is a high likelihood that we may make an error when typing the command line. The call to the Boolean function *Is_Nil* returns True if

---

[17] The server hosting one instance of a **Student_Management** servant displayed the IOR string
'IOR:010000002900000049444c3[..]'.

the call just made to `String_To_Object` fails. In this case we also terminate the client program.

Finally, the client can do its job. In our example client, that job is to register one student on one course. We simply make the remote call to procedure `Register_To_Course` using the remote reference stored in variable `A_Student`. All of the messages necessary to make this remote procedure call are managed by CORBA.

From the perspective of the application programmer, once the initialization part of the code has been performed, the client behaves exactly like a monolithic application. From the server side, the deployment phase (setting up servants, and publishing their references) allows one to control on which node elements are set. This is explicitly part of the CORBA model of computation.

We used a string copied from the server to supply the IOR of the server object to our client. This simple method of making the service known to the client is inconvenient and error prone. In the next section we discuss how to use a naming service to locate the remote object.

Compared to the DSA, we note there is no explicit mechanism by which one can allocate functions to partitions. All is done implicitly through Ada "with" mechanisms and an API:

- Clients have a dependency on stubs generated by the IDL compiler, and use it to interact with the servers.
- Servers depend on the implementation code to set up servants on each partition.
- Then, the CORBA naming mechanisms are used to bind clients and servers. This is discussed in the next section.

6.7 Advanced CORBA concepts

In the previous section we focused on the basic concepts of CORBA. In this section, we'll introduce some additional useful features and discuss some of the concepts that underlie CORBA.

6.7.1 CORBA naming service

As we saw in the previous sections, the use of an IOR string to identify a service requires some effort on the end user's part. They need to write down the IOR string displayed when they start up the server program and type it on the command line when they start up each client that uses the service. Having multiple services further complicates this process. To solve this problem, CORBA defines the *Naming Service* — like a telephone white pages, where we can store or retrieve object references associated with a logical name.

As will all CORBA resources, the functionality of the Naming Service is defined through the operations of its IDL interfaces. There are operations we can use to create/modify/delete a naming context hierarchy. There are operations to bind (that is, advertise) an IOR in the Naming Service with a specified name. And there are other operations to resolve (that is, look up) an IOR associated with a specified name. Here is a portion of the CORBA module for the Naming Service.

```
module CosNaming {
  // ...

  typedef string Istring;

  struct NameComponent {
    Istring id;
    Istring kind;
  };
  typedef sequence<NameComponent> Name;

  interface NamingContext {
    exception InvalidName{};

    void bind(in Name n, in Object obj)
      raises(InvalidName /* ,... */ );
    void rebind(in Name n, in Object obj)
      raises(InvalidName /* ,... */ );
  };

};
```

The Naming Service defines a full hierarchy: each level is called a "naming context." It is per construction a CORBA object, defined by the CosNaming::NamingContext interface. Furthermore, the IDL-to-Ada mapping indicates that the corresponding Ada type is called **Ref**, and is found in the CosNaming.NamingContext package. Since CORBA objects can be accessed remotely, the Naming Service can itself be distributed across several nodes. Still, one needs to be able to "find" the root of the Naming Service.

As we did for the RootPOA, we rely on the initial reference to find the root of the Naming Service. This reference is stored as part of the configuration of the ORB, passed at start-up time. CORBA defines a

command-line based mechanism to register an initial reference using the
-ORBInitRef NamingService=<IOR>. Once this initial "bootstrap" problem has been solved, the Naming Service can be used.

```
RNS   : constant NamingContext.Ref :=
To_Ref (CORBA.ORB. Resolve_Initial_References
(CORBA.ORB. To_CORBA_String ("NamingService")));
```

It is common for an implementation of the Naming Service to provide
some command-line utilities and/or a GUI tool that can be used to do
administrative tasks on the Naming Service, such as create/modify/delete a
naming context hierarchy. Such administrative functionality is implemented
by invoking corresponding IDL operations on the Naming Service. Hence,
instead of manipulating IOR, we can rewrite our client and server, and use
the following mechanisms to store and retrieve a reference to a student by
its name in the Naming Service.

```
--  Attach a name to an object
declare
   A_Student : CORBA.Object.Ref;  -- initialized by user
   A_Student_Name : CosNaming.Name;
begin
   Append (A_Student_Name,
           NameComponent'(id => To_CORBA_String ("john_doe"),
                          kind => To_CORBA_String ("")));
   bind (RNS, A_Student_Name, A_Student);
end;
```

```
-- Retrieve an object from its name
declare
   A_Student_Name : CosNaming.Name;
   A_Student : CORBA.Object.Ref;
begin
   Append (A_Student_Name,
           NameComponent'(id => To_CORBA_String ("john_doe"),
                          kind => To_CORBA_String ("")));
   A_Student := resolve (RNS, A_Student_Name);
end;
```

6.7.2 Asynchronous requests

As a default, all CORBA requests are processed synchronously. The oneway
IDL keyword allows for "at-most-one" semantics, meaning that the request
will be issued only once, and eventually be processed by the receiver. Note
there is no synchronization mechanism in place to ensure the request is
actually processed. In most cases, CORBA ORB will use an asynchronous
communication mode when issuing a request. See the following example:

```
interface async_i {
  oneway void async_request (in string S);
};
```

Since the request is now asynchronous, it cannot have return values. Hence, the IDL legality rules forbid return values, out and inout parameters, or exceptions.

6.7.3 How does CORBA work?

In this section we examine some of the details of the underlying mechanisms CORBA uses to implement distributed systems. While they may not be directly applicable to writing distributed Ada programs, a better understanding of such details gives us a better idea of the power and flexibility of CORBA.

GIOP and CDR marshalling

CORBA fully defines its infrastructure. This includes the network transport layer and associated protocol. GIOP is the "Generic Inter-ORB Protocol." It is an abstract protocol that defines how to build messages. These messages are then sent through a particular transport mechanism. IIOP is the "Internet Inter-ORB Protocol," an instance of GIOP on top of TCP/IP. Other variants exist for other buses such as CAN.[18]

GIOP defines eight different types of messages that can be transmitted between client and server applications. A knowledge of the different message types can be useful when debugging a CORBA application using a low-level packet sniffer.

The GIOP message types are:

- *Request* and *Reply* messages: these message types are used to send requests from a client to a server and to send replies back from the server to a client.

  A request holds some meta data that indicates how the request should be processed (also called "Quality of Service" or QoS), e.g. information on code sets for strings, priority, etc.; an identifier of the remote servant; the name of the method to invoke and its arguments. All these pieces of information are used by the Portable Object Adapter to process the request.

- *LocateRequest* and *LocateReply* messages: a LocateRequest message is like a ping message that asks: is the object there? The reply is sent back in a LocateReply message.

---

[18] The Controller Area Network is a bus commonly used to connect computing components in automobiles.

- *Fragment* messages: if a Request or Reply message is very large then the CORBA run-time system may decide to transmit it in several pieces rather than as one monolithic message. In such cases, the first piece is sent as a normal Request or Reply message, but a flag in the header of the message indicates that there are more pieces to follow. The remaining pieces are transmitted as Fragment messages.

- *CancelRequest* messages: a CORBA client may specify a timeout value when making a remote call, or the CORBA run-time system in the client may also (but is not obliged to) send a CancelRequest message to the server, to let the server know that the client will ignore a Reply message if one is later sent.

  The CORBA run-time system in the server can use the CancelRequest message as a hint to discard the previously received Request. However the server can ignore this hint and, in fact, will ignore it if the server has already started dispatching the previously received Request message. Such hints are usually ignored because the CORBA run-time system in the server cannot cancel partially executed application-level code in the body of an operation.

- *CloseConnection* messages: CORBA allows idle socket connections to be closed. If a connection from a client to a server is closed then a new connection can be opened transparently if, later on, the client makes more calls to the server.

- *MessageError* messages: they are sent when a CORBA node receives a message that is not in the correct format.

GIOP messages are defined by a complete description of the packet structure, and the method used to "encode" data onto streams. We call marshalling the act of placing native types (e.g. an Ada integer) into a binary buffer. Conversely, extracting types from a binary buffer is called unmarshalling.

The CORBA marshalling scheme is called Common Data Representation (CDR). CDR has two main objectives: handling heterogeneity between processors (endianess, memory alignment, etc) and efficiency. Here are the main rules of CDR:

- CDR can use either big-endian or little-endian. The marshalled data use the endianess of the sender. The sender's endianess is included in the GIOP header.

- For each basic data type, CDR defines how many bytes are used, and the associated memory alignment requirements:

- Char, octet, and boolean use 1 byte, and have no alignment requirements.
- Short and unsigned short use 2 bytes, and must be aligned on a 2-byte boundary.
- Long, unsigned long, and float use 4 bytes, and must be aligned on a 4-byte boundary.
- Long long, unsigned long long, and double use 8 bytes, and must be aligned on an 8-byte boundary.
- Long double use 16 bytes, and must be aligned on an 8-byte boundary.

The alignment rules of CDR were chosen to match alignments of CPUs, allowing for another level of optimization: instead of processing data, one may just copy them.

- For compound types, CDR defines a recursive scheme based on basic type marshalling rules:

  - An enum is marshalled as an unsigned long.
  - A string is marshalled as the length of the string (an unsigned long), followed by each character of the string, and is followed with a terminating null character.
  - A struct is marshalled by marshalling each field.
  - An exception is marshalled as the exception's repository id, which is a string, followed by each of its members.
  - A union is marshalled as its discriminant followed by the active branch (if any).
  - A sequence is marshalled as the number of elements it contains (represented as an unsigned long) followed by each element.
  - An array is marshalled by marshalling every element in the array.
  - An object reference is marshalled by marshalling an IOR, which is a struct shown in Figure 6.8.

This list is far from being complete, yet it is representative of how CDR works. Let us note that memory alignment rules imply that a GIOP message may contain padding bytes, which is wasted memory (and thus bandwidth). Fortunately, padding bytes usually account for a small percentage of a GIOP message.

The Interoperable Object Reference (IOR)

We use an IOR to exchange the "contact details" required to reach the server node. In our student management application, we manually transferred the IOR displayed by our server to our client. The IOR encapsulates all relevant information in a compact form. Interoperability means that all CORBA implementations are able to process it. CORBA defines a limited set of mandatory elements for an IOR and allows for the inclusion of extensions, either standard ones or vendor-specific ones. However, an implementation may ignore extensions.

Figure 6.8 lists the content of an IOR. The IOR is a struct with many components. The type_id field of the IOR struct contains the object's repository id. It defines the type of the object (see the listing on page 228).

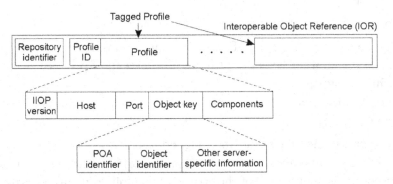

Figure 6.8 Components of an IOR

Following the Repository_Id is a sequence of TaggedProfiles. Each profile lists contact information for the node, the "tag" being there to specify how to interpret it (just like Ada tagged types). For instance, the tag value TAG_INTERNET_IOR denotes the use of the IIOP protocol; other values can be defined for future usage. This sequence allows one to define multiple access mechanisms (such as IIOP, DIOP, or SOAP) to reach an object.

Each profile contains the information needed to reach the servant itself in the hierarchy of the POAs: POA identifier, Object identifier, and other information. The Portable Object Adapter is the subject of the next section.

An IOR is defined as a stringified component. CORBA implementations usually provide tools to parse an IOR. The server hosting one instance of a `Student_Management` servant displays the following IOR:

```
'IOR:010000002900000049444c3[..]'
```

Using the `po_catref` tool provided with POLYORB, we extracted the following information:

```
Type Id: IDL:CORBAStudents/Student_Management:1.0

Found:  2 profiles in IOR

Profile number: 1
```

```
IIOP Version: 1.2
Address: 127.0.0.1:56196
Object_Id: /000000011Tf813dc581180cf8f
Tagged components:  1
   Component #1:
      Tag:  1
      Type: TAG_Code_Sets
         SNCS-C: 0x00010001; ISO 8859-1:1987; Latin Alphabet No. 1
         SNCS-W: 0x00010100; ISO/IEC 10646-1:1993; UCS-2, Level 1
            SCCS-W: 0x00010101; ISO/IEC 10646-1:1993; UCS-2, Level 2
            SCCS-W: 0x00010102; ISO/IEC 10646-1:1993; UCS-2, Level 3

Profile number: 2
   DIOP Version: 1.0
   Address: 127.0.0.1:49727
   Tagged components:  0
```

The two different GIOP profiles in this IOR indicate that the servant can be reached using either the IIOP or the DIOP (a variant of IIOP over UDP sockets) protocol. The IOR also displays information on the GIOP version (version 1.2 for the IIOP), the Object_Id of the servant managed by the POA, and some information related to code set manipulations (how to interpret strings).

The Portable Object Adapter (POA)

When discussing the implementation of the CORBA Student Management example, we made a distinction between a CORBA object and a servant. A CORBA object is the natural element of the "Distributed Object Computing" paradigm. It is the element on which to reason when running the application: a client requests a service from an instance of a particular object, this instance processes the request, and returns a value. A servant is part of the machinery behind CORBA.

A servant is a placeholder to bridge the gap between the run-time infrastructure of CORBA and the implementation code. A servant is associated with an Object Adapter (OA). This Object Adapter "adapts" the concepts of a CORBA object to the abilities and requirements of the host language. In cooperation with the ORB, an OA handles low-level issues such as:

- Reading incoming data, unmarshalling the request's parameters, and dispatching to the corresponding operation on a servant.
- Providing an API to map the object reference to a servant, and vice versa.
- Dynamic creation of servants and management of servant lifecycles.
- Allocating tasks to process the request.

The CORBA Portable Object Adapter (POA) is the second generation of object adapters defined by the CORBA specification. It defines a collection of servants, organized as a tree. Each node in this tree can host servants and can have child OAs. Each OA in the hierarchy can be configured through service policies. The tree hierarchy may be used as a way to organize a namespace of servants or as a way to segregate between different levels of policies.

The CORBA standard mandates that the name "RootPOA" be used for the root OA in the hierarchy. From that point, the application developer can build a hierarchy of POAs as a tree (see Figure 6.9): the two children of "RootPOA" are "POA A" and "POA B," and "POA C" is a child of "POA B." Each POA can be configured with its own policy to handle requests.

A POA handles a collection of servants. CORBA provides the developer with several options for how the servants are handled by a POA.

- The application developer can register the servant in the *Active Object Map* prior to allowing invocations. Upon reception of a request, the POA will look up the reference provided in the request in this map to find the actual servant on which to dispatch. This is the option chosen in all our examples (see RootPOA or POA A).

- To avoid preallocating resources for all servants, the developer can configure a *Servant Activator* to build servants "on demand" for his POA (see POA B). The Servant Activator defines an interface to be implemented. It allows the developer to perform proper action to create a servant from a given reference.

- The *Servant Locator* complements the activator with the ability to build your own "cache" of servants (see POA C). It defines a set of mechanisms to be implemented by the developer to build this cache, e.g. to retrieve servant information from a database, and then later save it, etc.

- The developer can register a *Default Servant* that will handle all requests to be served by the POA (see POA A). This allows us to have a unique servant instance to handle calls to services to be provided by a family of references, e.g. services to be performed by an object representing accounts of all students on a campus, or when no matching servant is found in the Active Object Map.

- Finally, the `Adapter Activator` allows one to create a child POA on demand (see POA B).

Each POA is associated with a *POA Manager*. The manager's role is to allow or disallow request processing by a POA. When the manager stops request processing, incoming requests can be stored in a queue or discarded. A single POA Manager can control multiple POAs.

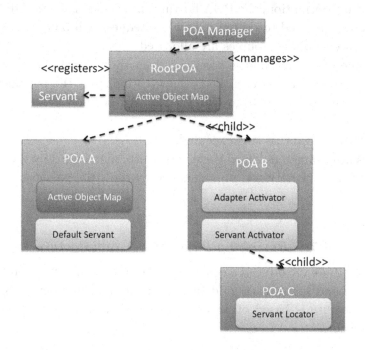

Figure 6.9 Hierarchy of POAs

6.7.4 Details of a CORBA remote invocation

We have detailed both how to implement a client and a server using CORBA, and the internals of the CORBA model. We now show they combine together to support remote interactions. Let us suppose both the client and the server are configured as explained in Sections 6.6.5 and 6.6.6 and let us suppose the client initiates a remote call using one of the available methods.

On the client side, calling this method wil invoke code that is part of the stub. This code is in charge of formatting the request: arguments are marshalled and a GIOP request message is built from the information on the remote object (known QoS parameters, identifier of the servant, name of the method, and marshalled arguments).

This request is sent through the network. Upon reception of a request on the server side, the GIOP protocol stack and the Portable Object Adapter collaborate to process the request:

- First, the servant identifier and QoS parameters are extracted from the request by the GIOP protocol stack.
- Using this information, the POA hosting the servant is retrieved; the QoS parameters are used to configure how the request will be processed; tasks are allocated, other resources are allocated.
- The name of the method is retrieved from the request. From the name of the method, the skeleton knows how to interpret the arguments. Arguments are extracted from the request. We are now ready to call the servant code.
- Finally, the servant code is executed.
- Any result parameters follow the reverse path: marshalled by the skeleton, send through the network, unmarshalled by the stub, passed back to user code.

6.7.5 Revisiting the CORBA architecture

In Section 6.2, we introduced a generic middleware architecture, and claimed it is generic and serves as a guideline to understand middleware internals. This architecture is based on several services. Let us review how CORBA fits this scheme.

- **Naming** is the mechanism by which we can "find" a remote entity. This is supported by CORBA IOR or CORBA Naming Service.
- **Binding** performs all the internal steps required to enable interaction. This is performed, on the client side, when calling `CORBA.ORB.String_To_Object`, or other functions that retrieve a CORBA object from a reference like the `resolve` function of the CORBA Naming Service.
- **Protocol/Transport** is defined as part of the GIOP protocol, and its associated IIOP variant that maps GIOP concepts on top of TCP/IP.
- **Marshalling** mechanisms are supported by the CDR marshalling scheme.
- **Activation** is supported, on the server side, by the Portable Object Adapter, which turns a servant into a remotely accessible entity.
- **Execution** service is provided, on the server side, by the POA. It ensures execution resources are available when demultiplexing a request: it first retrieves the corresponding servant, then allocates a task to process it.

6.7.6 Some final comments on CORBA

CORBA provides a large set of APIs and mechanisms to support distributed systems. In this chapter, we covered a limited subset of mechanisms.

CORBA defines a range of services for transactional support, messaging, security, and even real-time systems (RT-CORBA). Because of this ever-increasing complexity, the OMG defines the CORBA Component Model (CCM), a paradigm that provides a clear separation between user code and deployment/configuration of the application through XML-based descriptors; and associated modeling tools to generate them.

CORBA is now widely used as the middleware for distributed applications in many different domains. Its interoperability and performance satisfy the requirements of many applications. Since there is no "one size fits all" middleware, CORBA coexists with many other middleware technologies including SOAP, XML-RPC, and Enterprise Java Beans. CORBA concepts are present in various forms in most other middleware. We might then say that CORBA is the root of many middleware technologies.

6.8 CORBA versus the DSA

In this chapter, we have introduced concepts of distributed systems, and presented the Distributed Systems Annex of Ada and the Common Object Request Broker Architecture. Let's compare these two middlewares.

The DSA allows a seamless migration from a monolithic program to a distributed program. We simply add the necessary configuration pragmas to our packages to indicate the distribution. The ability to run the same program on a single node or distributed over several nodes is extremely useful for debugging a distributed program. The DSA does not specify the steps necessary to build a distributed program from a collection of units. Nor does the DSA specify the Partition Communication System (PCS) responsible for routing subprogram calls. Currently the only PCS is that supplied in POLYORB for the GNAT compiler.

The object is the basis for distribution in CORBA. As CORBA is programming language neutral, these objects are defined in the independent interface definition language, IDL. We compile the IDL modules to create the stubs and skeletons that act as glue code between our application and the CORBA code that sends all of the messages between nodes. Unlike the DSA approach, we must include calls to CORBA APIs in our servers and clients to register the server objects and initialize the CORBA run-time system. Some of these API calls are specific to a particular CORBA vendor. Being language neutral, CORBA infrastructure can be used to allow interoperability between programming languages.

In Section 6.2 we described a number of services that middleware need to provide to enable interactions between clients and servers. Let's compare the DSA and CORBA in terms of these services.

- **Naming** The naming service is implicit in DSA, based on the identifier names in the program. These names must be included in the POLY-ORB/DSA deployment configuration file. The DSA relies on explicit object reference exchange, and can be dynamic. CORBA defines a hierarchical naming service through IDL interfaces. The application programmer must make specific API calls to register or locate services.
- **Binding** It is transparent in both cases, through variables of object references.
- **Protocol/Transport/Marshalling** The DSA does not mandate any transport, protocol, or marshalling mechanism. It is implementation-defined. CORBA mandates each one to ensure interoperability.
- **Activation/Execution** They are implicit in DSA, whereas CORBA provides full control on execution resources through the POA.

One may note an important difference in the process of building a distributed application: DSA uses an explicit configuration file to define the deployment of client or server capabilities onto specific partitions using a PCS-specific configuration file. CORBA relies on dependencies across packages to set up a file. This implicit mechanism requires some glue code to be manually written. This can be an error-prone and complex process for large applications.

Despite their differences, CORBA and DSA share many elements. That the POLYORB middleware implements both DSA and CORBA is strong evidence for this claim. POLYORB "borrows" many mechanisms from CORBA to implement the DSA. POLYORB's ability to handle both the DSA and CORBA has earned it the name "schizophrenic middleware." Pautet *et al.* (1999) discuss these two complementary technologies in some detail.

The choice of a middleware technology is the result of a careful analysis of requirements: fixed or dynamic topology, interoperability, legacy code. All these elements must be clearly evaluated as they deeply affect the entire architecture of your application.

Summary

- Distribution allows us to map one application onto several processing nodes interconnected through a network.

- The ISO Ada standard document defines the Distributed Systems Annex (DSA) in its Annex E.
- The DSA allows a seamless migration from a monolithic to a distributed configuration — it preserves Ada semantics (tasking, exceptions, protected objects, types, and subprograms).
- The DSA relies on configuration pragmas to indicate distributable features. Here is the list of standard pragmas:
  - The `Remote_Call_Interface` categorization allows: subprograms to be called and executed remotely, statically bound remote calls (remote subprograms), and dynamically bound remote calls (remote access types). It forbids variables and non-remote access types and prevents the specification from depending on (withing) normal units.
  - The `Remote_Types` categorization supports the definition of distributed objects. It allows dynamically bound remote calls (via remote access types) and non-remote access types (with marshalling subprograms). Units with this categorization cannot have a specification that depends on any normal unit.
  - The `Shared_Passive` categorization allows direct access to data from different partitions. It provides support for shared (distributed) memory. It supports memory protection by means of entryless protected objects. Units with this categorization cannot have a specification that depends on any normal unit.
- Even in the presence of categorization pragmas, one can still build a monolithic application, using the traditional compilation chain. To build a distributed system, you need to use an alternative compilation chain.
- If no asynchronous calls are used and there are no network errors, and if we assume there is no fault in the communication stack, then a monolithic and a distributed application built with the DSA behave identically, from a functional point of view. Actual interleaving of tasks may change.
- The DSA allows for interoperability between heterogeneous processors, using specific marshallers. However, it does not mandate interoperability with other languages or other protocols.
- The Distributed Systems Annex of Ada is implemented by the GNAT compiler; its PCS is based on the POLYORB middleware.
- The DSA compilation chain handles the allocation of source code to each partition transparently, based on (1) the Ada configuration pragmas and (2) a PCS-specific configuration file. This allocation is done transparently.
- CORBA defines the notion of "object," a remotely accessible entity. This object can be reached through an "Object Request Broker" (ORB).

- CORBA clients request services hosted by server nodes. A node can be simultaneously a client of one service and a server for another.
- CORBA defines the notion of contracts between clients and servers. They are written using the IDL, a C-like interface definition language.
- An IDL compiler is used to generate stubs and skeletons. They are in charge of building and processing requests. There is a dedicated mapping from IDL to most programming languages.
- On the server side, CORBA objects are built from a servant, a placeholder for user code, connected to a Portable Object Adapter (POA).
- On the client side, CORBA objects are proxies to the remote object. They are built from references. CORBA defines IOR and a Naming Service that allows units to look up references from a logical name.
- An IOR is a stringified representation of a CORBA object reference.
- All CORBA services (POA, Naming Service, etc.) are defined as a set of CORBA objects, with IDL specifications.
- The user must explicitly write glue code to set up client and server using CORBA services and the POA.

Exercises

6.1 Have you ever encountered a Heisenbug? How did you fix it?

6.2 Explain why each of the eight fallacies is actually a fallacy.

6.3 How do you compare rendezvous and synchronous RPC? The use of protected objects and message passing?

6.4 Discuss portability issues of an Ada-based middleware compared to other languages like C or Java.

6.5 What are stubs in an RPC implementation?

6.6 Name different occurrences of a naming service you've ever used.

6.7 What are some of the error conditions we need to guard against in a distributed environment that we do not need to worry about in a local programming environment?

6.8 Why are pointers (references) not usually passed as parameters to a Remote Procedure Call?

6.9 Compare the power of expression of CORBA and DSA, and balance it with the ease of control of some of their internals.

6.10 In Section 6.4, we indicate where each element of the user code is located after compilation. Review the example in 6.3.2 and indicate the location of each package for the RCI and RACW variants of this example.

7

Real-time systems and scheduling concepts

Real-time systems are defined as those "systems in which the correctness of the system depends not only on the logical result of computation, but also on the time at which the results are produced" (Stankovic, 1988). When we design a real-time system, we must ensure that it meets three properties:

- **Correctness of functionality.** We expect that our system will produce the correct output for every set of input data. Meeting this property is an expectation of all types of software including information technology and web applications. Traditional verification techniques such as testing and formal proof may be used to demonstrate functional correctness.

- **Correctness of timing behavior.** As we stated in Chapter 1, the requirements of a real-time system include timing properties that must be met by the implementation. Deadlines may be assigned to particular system functions, and then to the tasks that implement these functions. Correct timing behavior is verified by checking that task execution times never exceed the required deadlines. This analysis of the timing behavior is called "schedulability analysis."

- **Reliability.** Software reliability is the probability of failure-free software operation for a specified period of time in a specified environment (Lyu, 1995). Real-time systems are often safety or mission critical — a failure may result in loss of life or property. Therefore, reliability is usually an important property of a real-time system.

In this chapter we examine methods for checking the correctness of timing behavior. Our goal is to *compute* the timing behavior of the system *before* execution time. Computing the timing behavior of a real-time system is a complex job. Many real-time systems are built with operating systems providing multitasking facilities. Multitasking facilities increase efficiency of the overall systems since they make it possible to perform efficient I/O operations and to run applications on multiprocessor architectures. Multitasking facilities also ease the design of complex systems running on single processors. Each function of the system can be mapped to one or more tasks. Our example of the pressure cooker in Section 1.3.2 demonstrated the simplicity of a multitasking design over a sequential one. Unfortunately, multitasking makes the timing behavior analysis more difficult to do. We must take the scheduling of different tasks into account in order to check that all specified temporal constraints are met.

If the system is small enough, a timing analysis can be performed by hand. But if the system is complex, containing a large number of tasks with varying deadlines, the analysis requires the use of models and tools such as formal methods (Heitmeyer and Mandrioli, 1996), queuing systems theory (Kleinrock, 1975a, 1975b), or real-time scheduling theory (Briand and Roy, 1999; Burns and Wellings, 2009; Cottet *et al.*, 2002; George *et al.*, 1996; Klein *et al.*, 1994).

The foundations of real-time scheduling theory came out in the 1970s (Liu and Layland, 1973) and led to extensive research. Real-time scheduling theory provides two different methods for verifying timing constraints:

- **Analytical methods** (also called feasibility tests). These methods provide a means for the designer to analyze (compute) the system's timing behavior without computing potential scenarios of task interleavings. Feasibility tests usually lead to a proof that time constraints are met.
- **Simulations** based on algorithms that determine a set of task interleavings constrained by some timing requirements. Usually, simulations do not lead to a proof that the timing constraints are met. But with some task types and some schedulers, real-time scheduling theory allows verification by exhaustive simulations. By **exhaustive simulations**, we mean simulations that inspect *all* possible states of the real-time system to be verified. Exhaustive simulations involve running simulations during a time interval called hyper-period, which is repeated during the entire lifetime of the system. If we can prove that all deadlines are met during this time interval, we prove that deadlines are met at any time during execution time.

This chapter introduces you to the foundations of real-time scheduling theory. We show how this theory can help you model and analyze a real-time system. Aside from a few brief examples to aid in the understanding of terminology, our discussions in this chapter are independent of any programming language. In Chapter 8, we will show you how to implement real-time applications in Ada which are compliant with the real-time scheduling theory assumptions we discuss in this chapter.

In the next section we define the terms that describe tasks in the context of real-time scheduling theory. Then in the remaining sections we will describe two widely used real-time schedulers and show how to verify timing constraints with each. At first we will make some unrealistic assumptions to simplify the analysis. Once you are comfortable with the underlying principles, we will remove these assumptions and extend the theory to realistic systems. In this book, we focus only on real-time scheduling theory related to monoprocessor systems. You should notice that real-time scheduling theoretical results may be quite different for multiprocessors or distributed systems. For further reading, a comprehensive presentation of real-time scheduling theory is provided by Briand and Roy (1999), Burns and Wellings (2009), Cottet *et al.* (2002), George *et al.* (1996) and Klein *et al.* (1994).

7.1 Task characteristics

We may view a task as a set of statements and a set of data. Task statements run sequentially. Task data includes values stored in memory and registers. A task's **context** is the minimal set of data that must be saved in order to suspend the execution of the task at one point and resume its execution later. Such suspensions may be the result of an interrupt (described in Chapter 4) or a context switch carried out by the task scheduler (described in this chapter). The context usually includes the processor registers and memory management unit (MMU) registers that manage the memory used by the task.

A task's context also includes the state of the task. We discussed the possible states of an Ada task in Chapter 3. The three task states relevant to real-time scheduling are *ready*, *blocked*, and *running*. These task states and the transitions between them are shown in Figure 3.2 on page 112.

A task that is in the *running* state holds all the resources, including the processor, that are required to run its set of statements. A running task stays on the processor (remains in the running state) until

1. It has completed the execution of its set of statements or
2. It becomes blocked or
3. The scheduler chooses to run a different task.

When the scheduler chooses to stop the running task to run another one, the change is called a **preemption**. One task must always be running on the processor. When a task leaves the processor, we must replace it with another.[1] The process of replacing the currently running task with another is called a **context switch**. To perform a context switch, we must save the context of the currently running task and restore the context of the replacement task. The context is stored in a data structure called the *task control block* associated with each task. The task control block is created when the task is created (see Section 3.2.1). As the saving and restoring of data during a context switch requires a certain amount of time, we like to minimize the number of context switches.

A *blocked* task is a task that is waiting for one or more resources other than the processor. An input/output operation, an access to a protected entry with a closed barrier, or an attempt to rendezvous with a task that is not executing an accept statement are examples of statements that lead to a blocked task. Since a blocked task requires resources beyond the processor, a blocked task is ignored by a scheduler when it selects the next task to run on the processor.

Finally, a task may hold all the resources it needs except for the processor. Such a task is called a *ready* task. A scheduler always chooses the next task to run from among the set of *ready* tasks of the system.

7.1.1 Task types

We can classify tasks into different types based on behavior properties. A **critical task** is a task for which missing a timing constraint results in the failure of the application. Using the terminology from Chapter 1, an application with one or more critical tasks is a hard real-time application. Missing a timing constraint in a hard real-time application leads to serious damage to the system and the services it provides.

An **urgent task** is a task which has a short deadline to meet. An urgent task may also be a critical task if missing that short deadline results in the failure of the application. If missing the short deadline has no disastrous consequences, that urgent task is not a critical task. As it is possible to have a critical task with a long deadline, not all critical tasks are urgent tasks.

We may also classify a task as an independent task or a dependent task. An **independent task** runs independently of the other tasks in the application. It does not communicate with other tasks either directly via a rendezvous or indirectly via shared data. An independent task can run at any time, provided that the processor is available and that the scheduler chooses to

---

[1] Should none of the application tasks be ready to run, some operating systems run a default task called the *idle task* or shut down the processor to reduce energy consumption.

run it. Independent tasks do not interfere with the execution of other tasks in the application. The concurrent pressure cooker example in Section 1.3.2 consisted of two independent tasks — one task maintains the temperature of the cooker while the other maintains the pressure. These two tasks do not communicate with each other.

In contrast, a **dependent task** may have to wait for an event before being run. This event is usually generated by the execution of another task. For example, suppose some value in memory is shared by two tasks. If one of those tasks is currently using that shared memory, the other task must wait to access it. In this example, the second task must wait for the event of the shared memory becoming available. The four entrance monitoring tasks in our museum application (page 130) all share the protected object `Population` and are therefore dependent tasks. Another form of task dependence, called a **precedence constraint**, occurs when two tasks must synchronize their execution. The bounded buffer producer-consumer pattern described in Chapters 1 and 4 is a classic example of a precedence constraint. A consumer task cannot proceed unless there is a value in the buffer. Similarly, a producer task cannot proceed unless there is space in the buffer for a new value. The barrier, broadcast, and resource allocation patterns described in Chapter 4 and the rendezvous discussed in Chapter 5 are also examples of precedence constraints.

It is common for a task to perform the same job multiple times. Many of the task examples in previous chapters included loops which repeatedly carried out an activity. The time that a task first requests the processor is called the **activation time** or **release time**. Each request for the processor to begin work on another iteration marks another release time. We classify tasks on the basis of their release times.

If a fixed duration exists between two successive activation/release times of a task, the task is called a **periodic task**. The two tasks in the pressure cooker example of Chapter 1 are periodic tasks. In both cases, the time between successive task releases is a constant. As you will see later in this chapter, the characterization of periodic tasks plays an important part in the use of real-time scheduling theory to compute an accurate model of processor demand. We can construct models from periodic tasks to analyze the timing of critical and urgent application functions.

Tasks that are activated by events outside of our system are rarely periodic. Consider, for example, the tasks that monitor the turnstiles at the entrances of the museum described in Chapter 4. Each task waits until someone passes through its turnstile. As the time between turnstile events is unlikely a constant, these tasks are not periodic tasks. Tasks that are not periodic are divided into two types.

A **sporadic task** is one for which we can specify a *minimum amount of time* between releases. Perhaps the mechanical nature of the turnstile limits the rate of entry to one person every two seconds. Of course, the time between turnstile events is usually much longer. Our scheduling theory can provide a worst case evaluation of the processor demand by sporadic tasks. It is likely that in order to meet such a worst case, our processor will usually be under-loaded. Sporadic tasks are well suited for the modeling of event-driven functions that are critical to an application. To check deadlines of sporadic tasks, we can apply feasibility tests that are devoted to periodic tasks. There are also some feasibility tests that are specifically designed for sporadic tasks (Baker and Cirinei, 2006). We do not address sporadic tasks any more in this chapter.

An **aperiodic task** is one for which we have no limit on the time between activations. Like sporadic tasks, aperiodic tasks are event-driven. Since we can say nothing about the minimum time between event arrivals, we cannot determine whether or not the task can meet its deadline for processing an event before the next event arrives. Therefore we cannot use aperiodic tasks to model critical functions in an application.

7.1.2 Scalar properties of periodic tasks

Periodic tasks are the foundation of real-time scheduling theory. Each periodic task is defined by a set of parameters. The four most frequently used periodic task parameters are (Cottet *et al.*, 2002):

- S_i, the first release time of task i. This is the first time that the task requests the processor.

- C_i, the worst case execution time (WCET) of the task i, also called the task's **capacity**. Although the actual amount of time a task requires for a particular iteration can vary, we always use the WCET in our scheduling analyses to ensure that deadlines are met even in the worst cases. The capacity of a task is usually determined by running the task alone on the processor and making measurements of its execution time or by static analysis of the sequential code of the task (Wilhelm *et al.*, 2008).

- P_i, the **period** of task i. P_i is a fixed delay between two successive activations of the task. Each P_i units of time, the task is supposed to run on the processor and use C_i units of processor time.

- D_i, the timing constraint the task i has to meet. This constraint is called a **deadline**. If the task is released at time t, we expect that it has run its capacity before or at time $t + D_i$. D_i is a relative timing constraint.

Figure 7.1 illustrates three of these periodic task parameters. The arrow indicates the flow of time from left to right. The vertical bar labeled S_i marks the time of the first release of task i. The other four vertical bars show four successive releases of the task. The amount of time between releases of task i is constant and labeled P_i. In this example, the period is 10 units of time. The black rectangles indicate the times for which task i is in the running state (has the processor). In this example, the capacity of task i, C_i, is two time units — shown as two black squares in the figure. The task runs immediately after its first release at time S_i. The gap between the black squares during the first period indicates that task i was preempted by the scheduler and then resumed and completed its execution before the second release. The task did not run immediately after its second release but did complete the execution of its capacity in time for the third release. The task also completes the execution of its capacity in the third and fourth periods shown in the figure.

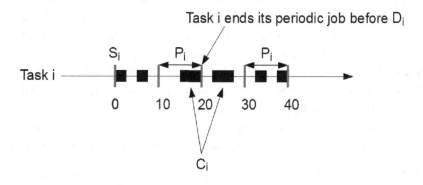

Figure 7.1 Parameters of a periodic task

7.2 Real-time schedulers

A **scheduler** is responsible for selecting the *running* task for each unit of time from among the set of *ready* tasks. There are various ways to make this choice. The literature is filled with descriptions of different schedulers. Each scheduler provides a solution to the needs of some specific real-time system requirements. We can classify schedulers based on those needs (Panwalkar and Iskander, 1976). A scheduler may be based on fixed priorities or based on dynamic priorities. Scheduling may be done off-line or on-line. Finally, schedulers may be preemptive or not. In this section, we look at each of these possibilities.

All real-time schedulers use the notion of priority in making scheduling decisions. A **priority** is a task attribute (usually an integer) that allows the scheduler to choose the next task to run. As you might expect, when there are multiple tasks ready to run, the scheduler will pick the task with the highest priority. When task priorities are assigned at design time and do not change at execution time, we call them *fixed priorities*. A **fixed priority scheduler** is a scheduler that handles tasks whose priorities are determined prior to the execution of the application and do not change during execution. A **dynamic priority scheduler** is one that makes use of priorities that may change at execution time.

Depending on the nature of our application, we use different criteria to assign fixed priorities to tasks. These criteria include:

- **Urgency:** tasks that have shortest timing constraints will have the highest priority level.

  Rate Monotonic and *Deadline Monotonic* are two methods for assigning fixed priorities to tasks based on urgency. With Rate Monotonic, a task's priority is inversely proportional to its period. The task with the shortest period has the highest priority. Deadline Monotonic assigns the highest priority level to the task with the shortest deadline.
- **Criticality:** the most critical task has the highest priority level.
- **Shared resources:** in Section 7.3, we explain how a task's priority may change while it is using shared resources.
- **Precedence:** when task a must be run before task b, a simple way to enforce this execution order is to assign a higher priority to a than to b.

Priority assignment also depends on the properties of the system on which the application is run. Different operating systems provide different numbers of priority levels. In some operating systems, the higher the priority number, the higher the priority level, while in other operating systems, the lower the priority number, the higher the priority level. For example, VxWorks provides 256 different priority levels (numbered 0 to 255) with 0 as the highest priority level. Linux provides 100 priority levels (numbered 0 to 99) with 99 as the highest priority level. The number of processors in a system may also have an impact on the assignment of fixed priorities.

An **on-line scheduler** is a scheduler that makes scheduling decisions while the application is executing. An **off-line scheduler** works out a complete schedule at design time. This schedule is then hardcoded into the application so no operating system is required. The **cyclic executive** is an example of an off-line scheduler. The cyclic executive uses a single thread of control which cycles through a repeated set of activities at a set rate. Each activity is a portion of a task's capacity. Here, for example, is an algorithm for a cyclic executive which schedules three "tasks":

loop
    Do the first part of task #1
    Do the first part of task #2
    Do the second part of task #1
    Do all of task #3
    Do the last part of task #1
    Do the last part of task #2
end loop

The sequential control algorithms for cooking chutneys developed in Chapter 1 are really cyclic executives for scheduling two tasks — one that controls the temperature and one that controls the pressure. Off-line scheduling is well suited for highly critical systems since it leads to a very deterministic task scheduling. The space shuttle's flight control software is a hard real-time control system that uses a cyclic executive to schedule activities (Carlow, 1984). Of course, off-line scheduling is not flexible. If we need to modify the system later by adding an additional task or changing the timing constraints, the overall scheduling must be completely redesigned and analyzed again.

A **preemptive scheduler** is a scheduler which is allowed to stop the running task in order to run a higher priority task that has just changed its state from blocked to ready. A task running under a **non-preemptive scheduler** does not relinquish the processor until it executes some blocking operation such as a delay, an entry call, or an input/output operation. Usually, a preemptive scheduler allows the tasks to meet more deadlines than a non-preemptive scheduler. However, non-preemptive schedulers have two advantages over preemptive schedulers:

1. Non-preemptive schedulers ease the sharing of resources. There is no need for mutual exclusion if instructions for the task accessing the shared resource are not interleaved with the execution of instructions by other tasks.

2. The scheduling overhead is lower in non-preemptive systems since fewer context switches occur.

Each of the types of schedulers we have described has properties which designers must consider when deciding which type of scheduler to use with their application. The trade-offs they must take into account include:

- **Predictability.** Usually, static priority schedulers are more deterministic than dynamic priority schedulers and are therefore more suitable for very critical systems.
- **Efficiency.** In the best case, we look for schedulers that have a low overhead (induce few context switches) and which are optimal. An *optimal scheduler* is a scheduler which is always able to compute a valid schedule if one exists. A *valid schedule* is one in which all task deadlines are met. Efficiency of a scheduler may also include the ability to build feasibility tests that are not complicated. The tests should be easy to implement and scalable (can be applied on architectures with a large number of tasks and processors). Optimal schedulers are usually dynamic priority schedulers.
- **Suitability** for the operating system. The selected scheduler should be easy to implement and run under the operating system used for the application. The most efficient schedulers are usually more complex, and therefore more difficult to implement.

In the next two sections, we present two widely used on-line schedulers. The first scheduler is a fixed priority scheduler. We mostly focus on task sets with priorities assigned according to Rate Monotonic. The second one is a dynamic priority scheduler called Earliest Deadline First. We will look at both preemptive and non-preemptive versions of these two schedulers.

7.2.1 Fixed priority scheduling

Properties and assumptions

Fixed priority schedulers are particularly well suited for static, hard real-time systems. A **static real-time system** is one in which the number of tasks does not change during execution time. The timing of static real-time systems can be fully analyzed at design time (in case of periodic tasks) — a property that is important for engineers developing systems with critical functions.

One of the most widely used real-time scheduling methods based on fixed priority schedulers is called Rate Monotonic. The term **Rate Monotonic** may refer to one or more of three different aspects of real-time scheduling:

- A scheduling algorithm
- An analysis method
- A priority assignment rule

The context in which the term Rate Monotonic is used usually makes it clear to which of these aspects it refers. The primary use of Rate Monotonic is the analysis and scheduling of periodic tasks. However, extensions exist for analyzing systems containing both periodic and aperiodic tasks (Sprunt *et al.*, 1989). Rate Monotonic is known to be the optimal priority assignment rule for fixed priority scheduling.

Fixed priority scheduling is very easy to implement with real-time operating systems. It is implemented in a large number of them including VxWorks (Wind River, 1997) and RTEMS (OAR, 2004).

To begin our explanation of fixed priority scheduling and Rate Monotonic priority assignment we make the following assumptions:

1. All tasks are independent.
2. $\forall i : D_i = P_i$ A task's deadline is the same as its period. That is, a task must finish its current job before its next release time.
3. $\forall i : S_i = 0$ All tasks are released at the same time.

In this book, periodic tasks that meet these three assumptions are called **synchronous periodic tasks**. The first assumption, that all tasks are independent, is not a very realistic one for actual real-time systems. We will relax this assumption in Section 7.3. The second assumption, that a task's deadline is equal to its period, is sometimes called *deadlines on requests*. The third assumption, that all tasks have an equal first release time defines a point in time called the *critical instant*. Having a critical instant leads to a worst case on processor demand: all tasks request the processor at the same time. If deadlines are met when a critical instant occurs, then subsequent task deadlines will also be met. Many feasibility tests are built with the assumption that this critical instant exists.

How it works

This type of scheduling can be seen as a two-step process. The first step is the priority assignment step and the second one, the election step.

The priority assignment step is an off-line process: priorities are assigned to tasks at design time. Priorities can be assigned on the basis of urgency: a task's priority can be inversely proportional to its period (with Rate Monotonic priority assignment rule) or to its deadline (with Deadline Monotonic priority assignment rule). In these cases, the task with the shortest period (or deadline) has the highest priority.

But engineers may also assign priorities according to other rules. For example, they may consider:

- Critically of tasks: the highest critical task will have the highest priority.
- Task precedence relationships: if task i must be scheduled before task j, task i will have the highest priority.
- Other problem or domain specific criteria.

The election step is an on-line statement. During execution time, the scheduler ensures that the running task has the highest priority level among all the ready tasks of the application.

Let's look at an example. Suppose we have two synchronous periodic tasks, T_1 and T_2. Task T_1 has a period of 10 units of time and a capacity of 6 units of time. Task T_2 has a period of 30 units of time and a capacity of 9 units of time. We assume Rate Monotonic priority assignment. The following table summarizes the task attributes and shows the Rate Monotonic priority assignments.

Task	Period	Capacity	Deadline	Priority
T_1	$P_1 = 10$	$C_1 = 6$	$D_1 = 10$	High
T_2	$P_2 = 30$	$C_2 = 9$	$D_2 = 30$	Low

Figure 7.2 shows the scheduling of these two tasks with a preemptive scheduler. Since T_1 is the higher-priority task, each time T_1 is released, T_2 is preempted and T_1 is immediately run. You can check that for each task release, both tasks have enough time to run all their capacity before their deadline (their next release time).

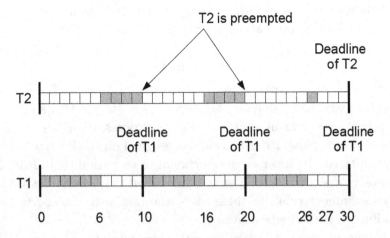

Figure 7.2 Example of scheduling with preemptive fixed priority scheduler and Rate Monotonic priority assignments

Figure 7.3 shows the scheduling of the same task set but with a non-preemptive scheduler. In contrast to Figure 7.2, the scheduling of Figure 7.3 shows a missed deadline of task T_1. This example shows that a non-preemptive scheduler is usually less efficient than the corresponding preemptive scheduler.

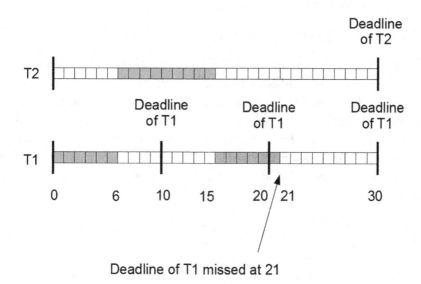

Figure 7.3 Example of scheduling with non-preemptive fixed priority scheduler and Rate Monotonic priority assignments

Checking deadlines

Fixed priority schedulers are important for practitioners because they have a deterministic behavior which leads to simple and efficient ways to check deadlines. At the beginning of this chapter we briefly described two methods for verifying that we can meet all deadlines in a real-time system: exhaustive simulations and feasibility tests.

Exhaustive simulations involve running simulations during the hyper-period. The **hyper-period** is a duration containing a scheduling sequence which is repeated during the entire lifetime of the system. If we can prove that all deadlines are met during the hyper-period, we prove that deadlines are met at any time during execution time. In the context of a synchronous period task set, the hyper-period is the interval:

$$[0, LCM((P_i)_{i=1..n})]$$ (7.1)

with $LCM(\forall i : P_i)$, the least common multiple[2] of all period values of the task set. In the case of Figures 7.2 and 7.3, the hyper-period is the interval $[0, 30]$.

The determination of the hyper-period is a little more complex when the periodic tasks have different first release times. In this case, the hyper-period is given by the interval:

$$[0, LCM((P_i)_{i=1..n}) + 2 \cdot max(\forall i : S_i)] \qquad (7.2)$$

At the end of this section, we will show an exhaustive simulation of three tasks in an application embedded within a car.

The second approach to check deadlines is to apply a feasibility test. There are a number of different feasibility tests for fixed priority schedulers. A very simple feasibility test for fixed priority scheduling is the processor utilization factor test. The **processor utilization factor** expresses the fraction of the time that the processor is busy executing our set of tasks. With a set of synchronous periodic tasks, it is computed as follows:

$$U = \sum_{i=1}^{n} \frac{C_i}{P_i} \qquad (7.3)$$

with n being the number of tasks in our application.

We are guaranteed that all task deadlines are met when this processor utilization factor is less than or equal to the bound computed by

$$B = n \cdot (2^{\frac{1}{n}} - 1)$$

(Liu and Layland, 1973). When n is large, this bound tends to $B = 0.69$. This test is valid only when priorities have been assigned according to Rate Monotonic and the tasks are run with a preemptive scheduler.

This feasibility test is a *sufficient but not necessary* schedulability test which means that:

1. When $U \leq B$, all task deadlines will be met.
2. When $U > B$, the result is not definitive. It is still possible that all our task deadlines may be met. But it is also possible that one or more task deadlines will be missed. In other words, when $U > B$ the feasibility test cannot prove whether or not task deadlines will be met.

A harmonic set of periodic tasks is a case that illustrates the second property. A **harmonic set** of periodic tasks is one in which the period of

---

[2] The LCM is the smallest non-zero number that is a multiple of two or more numbers.

each task is an exact multiple of every task that has a shorter period. For example, a set of four tasks with periods 10, 20, 40, and 120 form a harmonic set. Harmonic sets never miss deadlines when $U \leq 1$.

The processor utilization factor test is a pessimistic test. In contrast to exhaustive simulations, which compute the exact scheduling of the system, the processor utilization factor test is not always able to provide an exact result. Furthermore, it is limited to simple task sets as in our example of synchronous periodic tasks.

Another feasibility test, based on worst case response time, provides a more accurate test of schedulability. The **worst case response time feasibility test** consists of computing for each task its worst case response time. We can then compare that with its deadline. A task's worst case response time, noted r_i, is the delay between task release time and task completion time.

Equation (7.4), conceived by Joseph and Pandya (1986), expresses the worst-case response time for a set of synchronous periodic tasks with a pre-emptive fixed priority scheduler.

$$\begin{cases} \forall i : r_i \leq D_i \\ with \; r_i = C_i + \sum_{\forall j \in hp(i)} \left\lceil \frac{r_i}{P_j} \right\rceil \cdot C_j \end{cases} \qquad (7.4)$$

$hp(i)$ is the set of tasks which have a higher priority level than task i and $\lceil x \rceil$ returns the smallest integer not smaller than x.[3]

In the context of synchronous periodic tasks, this feasibility test is a *sufficient and a necessary* condition to check task deadlines. In contrast to the processor utilization factor test, equation (7.4) can be easily extended to take into account different delays such as those due to shared resource access, the execution environment, message exchanging, and others. Note that this test does not require that task priority assignment follow Rate Monotonic.[4] The test makes no assumptions on how priorities are assigned. However, the analysis of an application is easier if all tasks have *different* priority levels.

To see how equation (7.4) is derived, let us assume that task priority levels are assigned according to Rate Monotonic. The worst case response time of task i shown by this equation is the sum of two terms:

1. The execution time of task i: C_i.

2. The time that task i has to wait while higher-priority tasks execute.

---

[3] This operator is called the ceiling operator.
[4] Highest priority levels are assigned to the tasks with shortest periods.

Figure 7.4 helps show us how to calculate the second term of the sum. Assume a task j that has a higher priority level than task i. With Rate Monotonic, if task j has a priority level greater than i, it means that the period of j is smaller than the period of i. Then, during the response time of task i (duration from 0 to r_i, see Figure 7.4), task j is released

$$\left\lceil \frac{r_i}{P_j} \right\rceil$$

times. Then, the waiting time of task i due to task j is:

$$\left\lceil \frac{r_i}{P_j} \right\rceil \cdot C_j$$

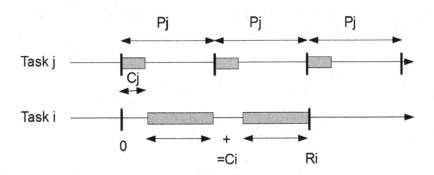

Figure 7.4 Task i worst case response time

Since several tasks may have a higher priority level than task i, the set $hp(i)$ may contain several tasks and the actual waiting time delay of task i due to higher priority tasks is:

$$\sum_{\forall j \in hp(i)} \left\lceil \frac{r_i}{P_j} \right\rceil \cdot C_j$$

Now let's see how to solve equation (7.4) to determine the worst case response time, r_i, of each task, i, in a program. Because r_i appears on both sides of this equation, it is difficult to solve. One technique we can use to solve equation (7.4) is to repeatedly use an approximate value of r_i to calculate a better approximation of r_i. Newton's method, which we used to calculate square roots on page 29, uses this approach. From equation (7.4), we derive the following recurrence equation:

$$w_i^{n+1} = C_i + \sum_{j \in hp(i)} \left\lceil \frac{w_i^n}{P_j} \right\rceil \cdot C_j \tag{7.5}$$

Each evaluation of recurrence equation (7.5) uses an approximation of the worst case response time for task i, w_i^n, to compute a better approximation, w_i^{n+1}. We use the following algorithm to compute the final value:

- We compute the first element of the recurrence equation (7.5) by $w_i^0 = C_i$.
- Then, we compute w_i^1, w_i^2, w_i^3, ..., w_i^k until:

  - Either $w_i^k > P_i$. In this case, the recurrence equation will never converge. Therefore, no task response time can be computed for task i. We can conclude that task i's deadline will be missed.
  - Or $w_i^k = w_i^{k-1}$. In this case, w_i^k is the actual worst case response time for task i. We can then compare w_i^k with the task deadline. When convergence exists, it also means that $w_i^k < P_i$.

Let us look at an example of worst case task response time analysis with a task set composed of three synchronous periodic tasks T_1, T_2, and T_3 defined by the following parameters:

Task	Period	Capacity	Deadline	Priority
T_1	$P_1 = 7$	$C_1 = 3$	$D_1 = 7$	High
T_2	$P_2 = 12$	$C_2 = 2$	$D_2 = 12$	Medium
T_3	$P_3 = 20$	$C_3 = 5$	$D_3 = 20$	Low

We compute each worst case response time individually:

1. The highest priority task T_1 never has to wait for the processor at its release times. Its response time is equal to its capacity: $r_1 = C_1 = 3$. Note that the set $hp(T_1)$ is empty.
2. The task T_2 is the middle priority task. Sometimes it has to wait for the execution of task T_1: the set $hp(T_2)$ contains T_1. We apply equation (7.5) to compute the following first elements of the recurrence equation:

- $w_2^0 = C_2 = 2$
- $w_2^1 = C_2 + \left\lceil \frac{w_2^0}{P_1} \right\rceil \cdot C_1 = 2 + \left\lceil \frac{2}{7} \right\rceil \cdot 3 = 5$
- $w_2^2 = C_2 + \left\lceil \frac{w_2^1}{P_1} \right\rceil \cdot C_1 = 2 + \left\lceil \frac{5}{7} \right\rceil \cdot 3 = 5$

We stop at w_2^2 since $w_2^2 = w_2^1$. The actual worst case response time of T_2 is then equal to $r_2 = 5$.

3. The task T_3 is the lowest-priority task. It is delayed by both T_1 and T_2: the set $hp(T_3)$ contains both T_1 and T_2, which leads to the following elements of the recurrence equation:

- $w_3^0 = C_3 = 5$
- $w_3^1 = C_3 + \left\lceil \frac{w_3^0}{P_1} \right\rceil \cdot C_1 + \left\lceil \frac{w_3^0}{P_2} \right\rceil \cdot C_2 = 5 + \left\lceil \frac{5}{7} \right\rceil \cdot 3 + \left\lceil \frac{5}{12} \right\rceil \cdot 2 = 10$
- $w_3^2 = C_3 + \left\lceil \frac{w_3^1}{P_1} \right\rceil \cdot C_1 + \left\lceil \frac{w_3^1}{P_2} \right\rceil \cdot C_2 = 5 + \left\lceil \frac{10}{7} \right\rceil \cdot 3 + \left\lceil \frac{10}{12} \right\rceil \cdot 2 = 13$
- $w_3^3 = C_3 + \left\lceil \frac{w_3^2}{P_1} \right\rceil \cdot C_1 + \left\lceil \frac{w_3^2}{P_2} \right\rceil \cdot C_2 = 5 + \left\lceil \frac{13}{7} \right\rceil \cdot 3 + \left\lceil \frac{13}{12} \right\rceil \cdot 2 = 15$
- $w_3^4 = C_3 + \left\lceil \frac{w_3^3}{P_1} \right\rceil \cdot C_1 + \left\lceil \frac{w_3^3}{P_2} \right\rceil \cdot C_2 = 5 + \left\lceil \frac{15}{7} \right\rceil \cdot 3 + \left\lceil \frac{15}{12} \right\rceil \cdot 2 = 18$
- $w_3^5 = C_3 + \left\lceil \frac{w_3^4}{P_1} \right\rceil \cdot C_1 + \left\lceil \frac{w_3^4}{P_2} \right\rceil \cdot C_2 = 5 + \left\lceil \frac{18}{7} \right\rceil \cdot 3 + \left\lceil \frac{18}{12} \right\rceil \cdot 2 = 18$

This time we stop at w_3^5 since $w_3^5 = w_3^4$. The actual worst case response time of T_3 is then equal to $r_3 = 18$.

Since $\forall i : r_i \leq D_i$, we have shown that this set of tasks is schedulable.

An example: analysis of a car with embedded software

In this section we look at an example to help clarify the analytic techniques discussed in the previous sections. Suppose we have a car with an embedded processor. This processor runs a real-time application which is composed of the following three synchronous periodic tasks:

1. $T_{display}$,   a task which displays the car's speed.
2. T_{speed},   a task which reads the car's speed sensor.
3. T_{engine},   a task which performs an engine monitoring algorithm.

We extracted the necessary timing requirements from the customer's specification and determined that the deadlines are equal to the task periods. For the execution environment, we use the VxWorks operating system. This operating system provides 256 levels of priority, ranging from 0 to 255. The highest priority level is 0.

The scheduling analysis has to check that the customer's requirements can be met according to the functional parts of the system and the execution environment chosen for this application. After the implementation of the functional parts of each task, we made some measurements by running each task alone several times. These measurements have allowed us to compute an approximation of their WCET. The following table summarizes the requirements and the capacity test results. Priorities are assigned by Rate Monotonic.

Task	Period (milliseconds)	Capacity (milliseconds)	Deadline (milliseconds)	Priority
$T_{display}$	$P_{display} = 100$	$C_{display} = 20$	$D_{display} = 100$	0
T_{engine}	$P_{engine} = 500$	$C_{engine} = 150$	$D_{engine} = 500$	2
T_{speed}	$P_{speed} = 250$	$C_{speed} = 50$	$D_{speed} = 250$	1

With these parameters, we can perform analyses with the three different methods presented in the previous section.

Analysis with the processor utilization test The processor utilization factor is computed as:

$$U = \sum_{i=1}^{n} \frac{C_i}{P_i} = 20/100 + 150/500 + 50/250 = 0.7$$

and the bound as:

$$Bound = n \cdot (2^{\frac{1}{n}} - 1) = 3 \cdot (2^{\frac{1}{3}} - 1) = 0.779$$

Since $U \leq Bound$, we can be sure that all task deadlines will be met.

Analysis with worst case task response times We use equation (7.5) to calculate the worst case response time for the three tasks in our system. Task $T_{display}$ is the highest priority task. This task is never delayed by another task. Its worst case response time is equal to its capacity, 20 milliseconds.

Task T_{speed} is the middle priority task. It is delayed by the one higher priority task, $T_{display}$. Its worst case response time is computed by:

- $w^0_{speed} = C_{speed} = 50$

- $w^1_{speed} = C_{speed} + \left\lceil \frac{w^0_{speed}}{P_{display}} \right\rceil \cdot C_{display} = 50 + \left\lceil \frac{50}{100} \right\rceil \cdot 20 = 70$

- $w^2_{speed} = C_{speed} + \left\lceil \frac{w^1_{speed}}{P_{display}} \right\rceil \cdot C_{display} = 50 + \left\lceil \frac{70}{100} \right\rceil \cdot 20 = 70$

We stopped iterating at w^2_{speed} since $w^2_{speed} = w^1_{speed}$. The worst case response time for task T_{speed} is 70 milliseconds.

Task T_{engine} has the lowest priority level of the three tasks. It is delayed by both of the other tasks in the application. Its worst case response time is computed by:

- $w_{engine}^0 = C_{engine} = 150$

- $w_{engine}^1 = C_{engine} + \left\lceil \frac{w_{engine}^0}{P_{display}} \right\rceil \cdot C_{display} + \left\lceil \frac{w_{engine}^0}{P_{speed}} \right\rceil \cdot C_{speed} = 150 + \left\lceil \frac{150}{100} \right\rceil \cdot 20 + \left\lceil \frac{150}{250} \right\rceil \cdot 50 = 150 + 40 + 50 = 240$

- $w_{engine}^2 = C_{engine} + \left\lceil \frac{w_{engine}^1}{P_{display}} \right\rceil \cdot C_{display} + \left\lceil \frac{w_{engine}^1}{P_{speed}} \right\rceil \cdot C_{speed} = 150 + \left\lceil \frac{240}{100} \right\rceil \cdot 20 + \left\lceil \frac{240}{250} \right\rceil \cdot 50 = 150 + 60 + 50 = 260$

- $w_{engine}^3 = C_{engine} + \left\lceil \frac{w_{engine}^2}{P_{display}} \right\rceil \cdot C_{display} + \left\lceil \frac{w_{engine}^2}{P_{speed}} \right\rceil \cdot C_{speed} = 150 + \left\lceil \frac{260}{100} \right\rceil \cdot 20 + \left\lceil \frac{260}{250} \right\rceil \cdot 50 = 150 + 60 + 100 = 310$

- $w_{engine}^4 = C_{engine} + \left\lceil \frac{w_{engine}^3}{P_{display}} \right\rceil \cdot C_{display} + \left\lceil \frac{w_{engine}^3}{P_{speed}} \right\rceil \cdot C_{speed} = 150 + \left\lceil \frac{310}{100} \right\rceil \cdot 20 + \left\lceil \frac{310}{250} \right\rceil \cdot 50 = 150 + 80 + 100 = 330$

- $w_{engine}^5 = C_{engine} + \left\lceil \frac{w_{engine}^4}{P_{display}} \right\rceil \cdot C_{display} + \left\lceil \frac{w_{engine}^4}{P_{speed}} \right\rceil \cdot C_{speed} = 150 + \left\lceil \frac{330}{100} \right\rceil \cdot 20 + \left\lceil \frac{330}{250} \right\rceil \cdot 50 = 150 + 80 + 100 = 330$

We stopped iterating at w_{engine}^5 since $w_{engine}^5 = w_{engine}^4$ and its worst case response time is 330 milliseconds.

The worst case response times of this task set are: $r_{engine} = 330$ milliseconds, $r_{display} = 20$ milliseconds, and $r_{speed} = 70$ milliseconds. All worst case response times are shorter than the corresponding deadlines.

Analysis by exhaustive scheduling simulation: scheduling simulation during the hyper-period We can also check the deadlines of our car application by determining the scheduling during a hyper-period. We use the interval computed from $[0, LCM(P_i)]$ for the hyper-period. With our set of tasks, the interval is $[0, 500]$.

We start by drawing a time line of the length of the hyper-period for each of our three tasks. On each time line we mark the release times of each task with vertical bars. Figure 7.5 shows the hyper-period marked with six release times for $T_{display}$, two release times for T_{engine}, and three release times for T_{speed}.

Now we fill in the execution times of each of the tasks. Since $T_{display}$ has the highest priority, it always runs when it is ready. We can fill in its 20 millisecond capacity beginning at each release. The top line of Figure 7.6 shows the results.

Moving on to the second highest priority task, T_{speed}, we fill in its 50 millisecond executions. It begins its first execution after $T_{display}$ has relinquished the processor. At its second execution, there is no need to wait as

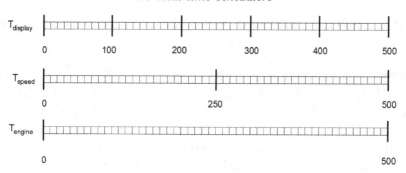

Figure 7.5 Template for analysis with exhaustive simulations

$T_{display}$ is not executing at this point in time. The middle line of Figure 7.6 shows the results. The worst case response time for T_{speed} is 70 milliseconds.

Lastly we fill in the 150 millisecond capacity of the lowest priority task, T_{engine}. We may only fill in the squares for this task when the other two tasks are not executing. The bottom line of Figure 7.6 shows the results. T_{engine} does not start running until the other two tasks have completed their first release. Then it is preempted twice by $T_{display}$ and once by T_{speed}. Despite these interruptions, task T_{engine} is able to complete its capacity 330 milliseconds after its release.

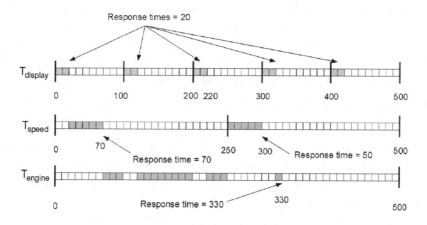

Figure 7.6 Analysis with exhaustive simulations

As all deadlines were met within the hyper-period, we are guaranteed that all deadlines beyond that interval will also be met. Note that the worst case task response times determined by Figure 7.6 are exactly the same as the ones computed with equation (7.5).

7.2.2 Earliest Deadline First, a dynamic priority scheduler

Properties and assumptions

We present now an example of dynamic priority scheduler: Earliest Deadline First (EDF). Earliest Deadline First is a scheduler based on task priorities that change during the execution of the application. EDF is then a dynamic priority scheduler. It works in a manner similar to the way many students determine an order for completing their class assignments. The assignment whose due date is closest is usually given the highest priority while an assignment due in the distant future is given the lowest priority. Assignment priorities change as time passes, assignments are completed, and more assignments are received. Assignments may be periodic (prepare for the weekly quiz) or aperiodic (on Tuesday, the instructor gives an assignment to complete exercises 7.1 through 7.4 for Thursday's class).

EDF can handle:

- **Dynamic real-time systems**   A dynamic real-time system is one in which the number of tasks may change during execution time. The runtime creation and destruction of tasks makes it impossible to fully analyze the schedulability of the application at design time.

- **Synchronous periodic tasks**   With synchronous periodic tasks, EDF is known to be optimal: if EDF is not able to find a scheduling sequence in which all task deadlines are met, no other scheduler will be able to find it. The processor utilization for EDF-scheduled synchronous periodic tasks can reach 100 percent with no missed deadlines.

- **Aperiodic tasks**   Tasks whose release times are not fixed.

EDF has some drawbacks. It is more difficult to implement within an operating system than fixed priority schedulers. But the biggest drawback of EDF is its behavior when the processor becomes overloaded, a condition that can occur in dynamic systems. When overloading occurs, it is difficult to predict which tasks will miss their deadlines. With fixed priority scheduling, we know that the lowest priority tasks will miss their deadlines when the processor is overloaded. For this reason, EDF is not suitable for critical real-time systems. However, EDF is very useful for *off-line* scheduling of applications with high levels of criticality. We can compute a scheduling sequence at design time and embed it into the application which can then be executed without a scheduler in the operating system but with a cyclic executive (see page 258).

How it works

At each unit of time during the execution of the application, EDF performs two steps:

1. First, the scheduler computes a dynamic priority for each task. Dynamic priorities are deadlines that the scheduler will try to meet. The dynamic priority of task i at time t is noted $D_i(t)$ and is computed as follows:

   - If i is an aperiodic task, then $D_i(t) = S_i + D_i$.
   - If i is a periodic task, then $D_i(t) = k_i + D_i$, where k_i is the last task i release time prior to t.

2. Second, after all task dynamic priorities are updated, EDF runs the ready task with the smallest dynamic priority — the task with the closest deadline.

Let's look at an example. Here is a set of three synchronous periodic tasks.

Task	Period	Capacity	Deadline
T_1	$P_1 = 8$	$C_1 = 4$	$D_1 = 8$
T_2	$P_2 = 12$	$C_2 = 3$	$D_2 = 12$
T_3	$P_3 = 4$	$C_3 = 1$	$D_3 = 4$

It is not necessary to compute the dynamic priorities of the tasks at each time unit. The priority changes occur only at a task release time — when some k_i changes. Therefore, for our set of tasks, we need only to calculate the dynamic priorities at times 0, 4, 8, 12, 16 and 20. Table 7.1 shows the dynamic priorities that EDF computes during the scheduling of the task set.

t	$D_1(t)$ $(k_1 + D_1)$	$D_2(t)$ $(k_2 + D_2)$	$D_3(t)$ $(k_3 + D_3)$
0..3	$0 + 8 = 8$	$0 + 12 = 12$	$0 + 4 = 4$
4..7	$0 + 8 = 8$	$0 + 12 = 12$	$4 + 4 = 8$
8..11	$8 + 8 = 16$	$0 + 12 = 12$	$8 + 4 = 12$
12..15	$8 + 8 = 16$	$12 + 12 = 24$	$12 + 4 = 16$
16..19	$16 + 8 = 24$	$12 + 12 = 24$	$16 + 4 = 20$
20..23	$16 + 8 = 24$	$12 + 12 = 24$	$20 + 4 = 24$

Table 7.1 *Dynamic priorities handled by Earliest Deadline First*

Figure 7.7 shows the scheduling of our three synchronous periodic tasks with EDF and a preemptive scheduler. We used the dynamic priorities calculated in Table 7.1 to fill in this timing diagram.

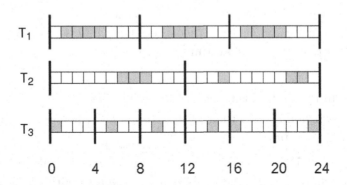

Figure 7.7 Scheduling with a preemptive EDF scheduler

At the critical instant, task T_3 has the greatest dynamic priority. After this task completes its capacity, the second greatest priority task, T_1, executes its 4 units of capacity. At time 4, T_3 is released again and then, its dynamic priority is re-computed: its dynamic priority is 8. Then, T_3 has the greatest dynamic priority and runs again during its capacity.

At time 6, only one task is ready to run: task T_2. Task T_2 runs during 2 units of time and at time 8, T_1 and T_3 are released again with new dynamic priorities of 16 and 12. At this time T_2 and T_3 have the same priority level and the scheduler can choose any of them for the next unit of time. Running task T_2 at time 8 avoids requiring the scheduler doing a context switch.

The remainder of the schedule illustrated in Figure 7.7 is derived in the same manner. We have seen that at some times, EDF leads to the scheduling of tasks with the same dynamic priority. This is also the case at the end of the hyper-period: at $t = 20$, all three tasks of our example have the same dynamic priority. At this time, we could run either T_2 or T_3 or T_1. Each such choice between equal priority tasks leads to different scheduling sequences. The actual choice is implementation-defined: it depends on how the scheduler is actually implemented inside the operating system. This lack of predictability is one of the reasons EDF is less suitable for critical real-time applications.

Figure 7.8 shows the same task set, but scheduled with a non-preemptive EDF scheduler. This scheduling sequence changes at time 16 where task T_2 cannot be preempted by task T_3 due to the non-preemptive scheduler.

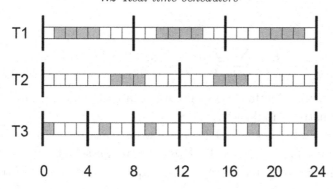

Figure 7.8 Scheduling with a non-preemptive EDF scheduler

Checking deadlines

Even if EDF is less predictable than fixed priority schedulers, a designer can use methods similar to those for fixed priority schedulers to check task deadlines at design time. The deadlines of a set of synchronous periodic tasks can be checked by exhaustive simulations, by processor utilization factor feasibility tests, or by worst case response time feasibility tests.

To perform exhaustive simulations with EDF, we must compute a scheduling sequence during the hyper-period. To determine the hyper-period with EDF, we use the same equations as with fixed priority scheduling/Rate Monotonic — equation (7.1) or (7.2) depending on the first release time of the tasks. For our sample set of tasks, the hyper-period is 24 time units. Figure 7.7 shows that each of our three tasks run their full capacity for each release time in the hyper-period. Therefore, this task set is schedulable with EDF. Rate Monotonic priority assignment and fixed priority scheduling fail to schedule this particular set of tasks (see Exercises 7.15 and 7.16).

Deadlines can also be checked with processor utilization factor tests. Equation (7.6) presents an example of such a test. This test is a sufficient and necessary condition and demonstrates the optimality of EDF. We can meet all task deadlines even if the bound on the processor utilization factor reaches 100 percent. This is another illustration which shows that EDF efficiency is better than fixed priority scheduling/Rate Monotonic efficiency.

$$\begin{cases} U \leq 1 \\ with\ U = \sum_{i=1}^{n} \frac{C_i}{P_i} \end{cases} \qquad (7.6)$$

For our example set of tasks, the processor utilization factor is computed as:

$$U = \sum_{i=1}^{n} \frac{C_i}{P_i} = 4/8 + 3/12 + 1/4 = 1$$

A processor utilization factor not greater than 1.0 confirms our earlier analysis by exhaustive simulation.

Finally, feasibility tests based on the worst case response time were proposed by Spuri (1996). Since EDF is a dynamic scheduler, worst case response time feasibility tests are more complex and are outside the scope of this chapter. You can read more about feasibility tests for EDF and fixed priority scheduling in George and Spuri (1996).

7.2.3 EDF versus fixed priority scheduling

In the previous sections, we presented a fixed and a dynamic priority scheduler.

- Fixed priority scheduling is well suited for critical and static real-time embedded systems. EDF is better suited to less critical systems.
- From an implementation point of view, fixed priority scheduling is simple to implement in a real-time operating system. Most real-time operating systems include such a scheduler. EDF is more difficult to implement so it is rarely implemented in real-time operating systems.
- Fixed priority scheduling with Rate Monotonic priority assignment is used to easily schedule periodic tasks. EDF can easily schedule both periodic and aperiodic tasks.
- Fixed priority scheduling is more predictable than EDF, especially in the case of over-loading. Even in the absences of over-loading the random choice made when two EDF tasks have the same dynamic priority introduces a lack of predictability.
- Fixed priority scheduling with Rate Monotonic priority assignment efficiency (69%) is lower than EDF efficiency (100%).

Table 7.2 summarizes these two schedulers. Of course, the real picture is a bit more complicated than this summary.

Both EDF and fixed priority scheduling have been adapted in different contexts to increase their usability, their flexibility, or their efficiency. For example, we previously stated that fixed priority scheduling with Rate Monotonic priority assignment has a limited efficiency: the processor utilization factor should not be greater than 69% to be sure that all task

	Fixed priority scheduling	EDF
Applications	critical, static	dynamic, less critical
RTOS [a] implementation	easy	more difficult
Tasks	periodic (Rate Monotonic)	aperiodic and periodic
Efficiency	up to 69% (Rate Monotonic only)	up to 100%
Predictability	high	less than fixed priority if $U > 1$

Table 7.2 *A simple comparison of fixed priority scheduling and EDF*

[a] Real-Time Operating System.

deadlines are met. In fact, in some systems, task deadlines can be met even when this bound is exceeded. This is the case of a harmonic task set for which a processor utilization factor reaching 1 is possible with no missed deadlines.

The behavior of EDF is non-deterministic during a transient processor over-load. However, an adaption of EDF, called *D-over*, has been developed to take care of processor over-loads (Koren and Shasha, 1992).

Another adaption is related to the scheduling of aperiodic tasks with fixed priority scheduling and Rate Monotonic priority assignment. Several approaches have been proposed to handle aperiodic tasks with fixed priority scheduling (Sprunt *et al.*, 1989). The polling server is one of these approaches. Basically, a polling server is a periodic task defined by a period and a capacity. When aperiodic tasks are released in the system, they are stored in a queue. At each periodic release time of the polling server, it runs aperiodic tasks which are waiting for the processor in the queue. The polling server runs aperiodic tasks for the duration of its capacity. If the aperiodic task queue is empty at the polling server's release times, the server does nothing. It waits for its next periodic release time. This mechanism allows the processor to run aperiodic tasks as soon as possible but without delaying periodic tasks that are critical. A polling server can be included in a feasibility test, such as the processor utilization factor test, as a normal periodic task. The system is checked assuming the worst case aperiodic task arrivals — when the polling server runs aperiodic tasks during *all its capacity* at *all its release times*.

For further reading, Buttazzo (2003) presents a more detailed comparison of Rate Monotonic and EDF.

7.3 Dependent tasks

In the previous sections, we made an unrealistic assumption: all tasks in the application are independent. Most real applications contain dependent tasks.

When two tasks share a resource, this data is usually accessed through a synchronization construct such as a protected object or semaphore (see Chapter 4). Both provide a pre-protocol to assert a desire to access the shared resource and a post-protocol to indicate that the shared resource is available. These protocols are encapsulated within a protected type. The programmer using semaphores must explicitly invoke the protocols to protect shared data. We will use the semaphore in our discussions in this section so that the protocols are completely visible. The same principles apply to protected objects. A task wanting to access shared data has to wait when the semaphore is locked by another task. This shared resource waiting time may increase the worst case response time of the waiting task.

Precedence constraints are a second type of dependency. These constraints are raised when tasks exchange messages as in a rendezvous (see Chapter 5). A task receiving a message may have to wait until its message actually arrives. Similarly, a task wanting to send a message may have to wait for the receiver task to accept the message. These waiting times may also change the worst case response times of tasks.

The basic analysis methods presented in the previous sections do not deal with these additional waiting times. The next two sections describe what we need to add to the basic analysis methods to handle the delays resulting from shared resources and precedence constraints.

7.3.1 Shared resource problems

Figure 7.9 shows a set of three tasks, two of which share a resource. This resource is protected by a semaphore called *mutex*. In the figure, $P(mutex)$ depicts the semaphore locking and $V(mutex)$ the semaphore unlocking. P and V come from the original Dutch words chosen by Dijkstra. In Chapter 4, we used the names *Wait* and *Signal* for these operations.

Tasks T_1 and T_3 share the resource. These tasks are scheduled with a preemptive fixed priority scheduler. Task T_3 is the highest priority task and T_1 is the lowest priority task. T_2 is a medium priority level task that does not use the shared resource protected by the semaphore *mutex*.

Figure 7.9 shows the scheduling sequence of this task set. This scheduling leads to a priority inversion. A **priority inversion** is a scheduling sequence

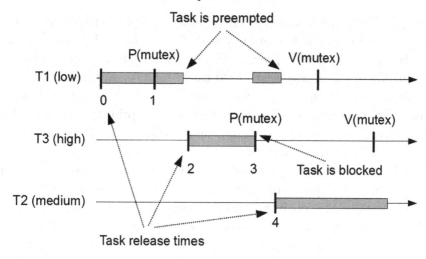

Figure 7.9 A priority inversion

in which a lower priority task blocks a higher priority task. In this figure, a priority inversion occurs between task T_3 and task T_2 as follows:

1. At time 0, task T_1 is released. T_1 locks the semaphore at time 1.
2. Task T_3 is released at time 2 and immediately preempts the lower priority task, T_1. T_1's preemption occurs before it has released the semaphore.
3. T_3 becomes blocked when it requests the semaphore at time 3.
4. Task T_1 resumes its execution, continuing its use of the shared resource protected by semaphore *mutex*.
5. At time 4, T_1 is preempted as T_2 is released. Task T_1's second preemption occurs before it has released the semaphore.
6. At this point the medium priority task T_2 blocks the high priority task T_3 through the low priority task T_1 — this is a priority inversion.

Task T_2 delays task T_3 even though these two tasks are independent of each other. The problem results from the medium priority task preempting a low priority task that has locked a resource that a high priority task requires. We must accept the fact that while it is using the shared resource, low priority task T_1 blocks high priority task T_3. We saw the consequences of unprotected resource sharing in Chapter 4. But this is not the case between T_2 and T_3 — they do not share a resource.

We need to determine how long a task can be blocked while waiting to access a shared resource. We represent the worst case shared waiting time of task i by B_i. This delay must be taken into account by feasibility tests such as equation (7.4).

The problem is made worse when we introduce additional tasks with priority levels between our low priority task T_1 and our high priority task T_3. These tasks can effectively prevent the low priority task from releasing the resource. The high priority task could easily miss its deadline.

While we cannot eliminate priority inversion, it is possible to *limit* the amount of time a task will be blocked by a lower priority task that shares the resource. If we know the maximum value of B_i, we can determine whether or not task i will meet its deadlines.

Priority inheritance protocols provide the means to put an upper bound on B_i. These protocols increase the priority of the low priority task to a value above the medium priority tasks. Then the low priority task can finish its use of the shared resource and release it to the high priority task. Various priority inheritance protocols have been proposed for both fixed priority schedulers and dynamic priority schedulers. They include the Priority Ceiling Protocol – PCP (Sha *et al.*, 1990), the Priority Inheritance Protocol – PIP (Sha *et al.*, 1990), and the Stack Based Resource Control – SRP (Baker, 1991). In the next section we will look at PIP and PCP.

7.3.2 Shared resource protocols

PIP is the simplest inheritance protocol. With PIP, a task which blocks a high priority task due to a shared resource sees its priority increased to the priority level of the blocked task. With such a mechanism, B_i can be computed as the sum of the critical section durations of the tasks which have a priority lower than the priority of task i.

Figure 7.10 presents a new scheduling sequence of the task set of Figure 7.9 but with PIP. At time 3, when the high priority task T_3 attempts to lock the semaphore *mutex*, the low priority task T_1 sees its priority level increased up to the priority level of the high priority task T_3. This priority change prevents the medium priority task T_2 from preempting T_1 when T_2 is released at time 4. T_1 signals that it is finished with the shared resource at time 5 allowing the high priority task T_3 to access it before the medium priority task T_2 ever ran. Of course, when T_1 is finished with the shared resource, its priority level returns to its initial value.

Our example shows that PIP is a very simple protocol. However, it has a major drawback: PIP cannot be used with more than one shared resource as it leads to deadlock. So while PIP provides a simple model to explain priority inheritance, it is not used in practice. Instead, PCP is widely used in real-time operating systems to prevent unbounded priority inversions and task deadlocks.

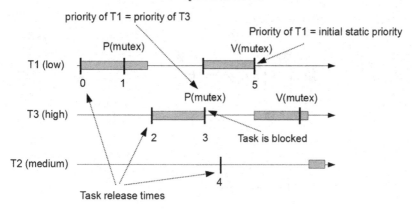

Figure 7.10 A scheduling sequence with PIP

There are several versions of PCP. We will look at one called Immediate Ceiling Priority Protocol – ICPP. ICPP works as follows:

- Each task has a static and a dynamic priority. The static priority is assigned according to rules such as Rate Monotonic or Deadline Monotonic.

- Each shared resource has a priority. This priority is called a *ceiling priority* and its value is equal to the maximum static priority of all the tasks which use the shared resource.

- The scheduler always selects the ready task with the highest dynamic priority. The dynamic priority is equal to the maximum of the task's static priority and the ceiling priorities of any resources the task has locked.

Figure 7.11 shows our task set scheduled with ICPP. The ceiling priority of the resource protected by the semaphore is equal to the static priority assigned to our high priority task T_3. When task T_1 first locks the semaphore at time 1, its dynamic priority is increased to the ceiling priority of the shared resource. As T_1 is now running with the highest priority, it very quickly completes its access to the shared resource and releases it at time 2. At that point, the priority of task T_1 returns to its low static value and the scheduler runs T_3.

With ICPP, the priority inheritance is applied sooner than with PIP. This allows the task T_1 to quickly leave the critical section. With ICPP, B_i can be computed more accurately than with PIP. B_i is the largest critical section of the tasks sharing the same set of resources.

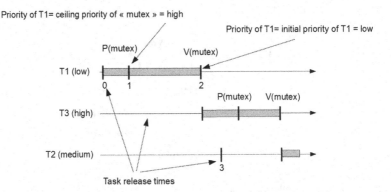

Figure 7.11 A scheduling sequence with ICPP

7.3.3 Feasibility tests extended with shared resources

With known values of B_i, we can perform deadline verifications with two of the feasibility tests presented in Section 7.2.1: tests on processor utilization factor and tests on worst case response time.

The processor utilization factor test (Klein *et al.*, 1994) extended with shared resource blocking time, with a preemptive fixed priority scheduler and Rate Monotonic priority assignment, is:

$$\forall\, i, 1 \leq i \leq n : \sum_{k=1}^{i-1} \frac{C_k}{P_k} + \frac{C_i + B_i}{P_i} \leq i \cdot (2^{\frac{1}{i}} - 1) \qquad (7.7)$$

The same feasibility test with a preemptive EDF scheduler instead is:

$$\forall\, i, 1 \leq i \leq n : \sum_{k=1}^{i-1} \frac{C_k}{P_k} + \frac{C_i + B_i}{P_i} \leq 1 \qquad (7.8)$$

Tests 7.7 and 7.8 assume that tasks are ordered according to their priority level in a decreasing manner: task $i - 1$ has a lower priority level than task i.

Furthermore, worst case response times r_i, that take into account blocking time B_i with a preemptive fixed priority scheduler, can be computed as follows (Klein *et al.*, 1994):

$$r_i = C_i + B_i + \sum_{j \in hp(i)} \left\lceil \frac{r_i}{P_j} \right\rceil \cdot C_j \qquad (7.9)$$

with $hp(i)$ the set of tasks which have a lower priority level than task i. Equation (7.9) can be solved by the recurrence equation:

$$w_i^{n+1} = C_i + B_i + \sum_{j \in hp(i)} \left\lceil \frac{w_i^n}{P_j} \right\rceil \cdot C_j$$

7.3.4 Precedence constraints

There are various kinds of precedence constraints. In this section we focus on a precedence constraint that delays the release of a task until the completion of another task. For example, a task i waiting to receive a message won't be released until after the execution of a task j which sends the message. To compute a worst case response time of tasks i and j, we can apply a feasibility test based on equation (7.4) adapted to take into account this precedence relationship (Audsley *et al.*, 1993; Tindell and Clark, 1994). This feasibility test introduces a new parameter called jitter (noted J_i). The **jitter** J_i of task i is an upper bound on the delay that task i may suffer between the time it is supposed to be released and the time it is actually released.

Tindell and Clark (1994) initially used the jitter parameter to model various latencies within an operating system. Modeling these latencies allows the designer to include them in feasibility tests to ensure that the analysis is consistent with the real-time application behavior.

Let's look at a simple example before we directly address the delays due to precedence constraints. Suppose a periodic task i has a period of 15 ms. It should be released at $t = 15, 30, 45, ...$ However, measurements indicate that the first release of this task is at 21 ms!

What is responsible for this 6 ms delay in the release of task i? In most operating systems, periodic tasks are released by a timer. The timer is usually an interrupt handler that is triggered by a clock device. On each interrupt, the timer updates the system clock, checks task statuses, and re-schedules them. The timer can be seen as a periodic task that is defined by a period and a capacity:

- The period defines the accuracy of the system clock. For example, in the case of a Linux system with an Intel architecture, the clock period is about 10 ms.[5]

- As any program, the interrupt handler has a worst case execution time.

---

[5] Some processors, such as Intel Pentium, have registers to store the system clock. These registers allow users to read the system clock with a higher resolution (e.g. nanosecond with Pentium processors). However, it does not mean that the system is able to wake up tasks with the same accuracy: timer periods are usually longer in order to reduce system overhead.

Let us assume $P_{timer} = 10$ ms and $C_{timer} = 1$ ms. Figure 7.12 shows the 1 ms execution times of the timer task when the system clock interrupts at 0, 10, and 20 ms. This figure also shows why our periodic task that was supposed to be released at $t = 15$ was delayed 6 ms. At $t = 10$, the timer task checks the status of all tasks waiting on the timer. Task i is not ready to be released at this time. The next timer interrupt does not occur until $t = 20$. At this time, the timer detects that task i must be released. Since the timer capacity is 1 ms, task i will actually be released at $t = 21$ ms.

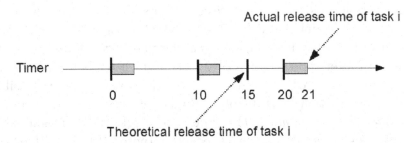

Figure 7.12 Task release time jitter

Therefore, the nature of the operating system timer guarantees that

- Tasks will be not released before the theoretical release time.
- But tasks may be released after the theoretical release time.

To compute the worst case response time of task i that takes into account this timer lateness, the jitter of task i is set to $J_i = 6$ ms and the task worst case response times are computed as follows:

$$\begin{cases} r_i \leq D_i \\ r_i = w_i + J_i \end{cases} \tag{7.10}$$

with

$$w_i = C_i + \sum_{\forall j \in hp(i)} \left\lceil \frac{w_i + J_j}{P_j} \right\rceil \cdot C_j$$

Equation (7.10) can be used to model any lateness in a real-time system. In particular, we can use this equation to compute the worst case response time of tasks that have precedence constraints: if a task i must be released after the completion time of task j, the worst case response time of i can be computed with $J_i = r_j$.

This approach is called the *holistic analysis approach* and can be used to compute end to end worst case response times (Tindell and Clark, 1994).

In the context of the holistic analysis, tasks are organized into sequences of tasks. A sequence of tasks is composed of several tasks that have to run sequentially — a precedence constraint exists between each pair of successive tasks in the sequence. Often, we also assume that tasks are assigned to different processors. In this case, the deadline we want to check is not a deadline that is local to a given scheduler. Instead, we expect to check that the lateness defined by the release time of the first task in the sequence and the completion time of the last task in the sequence is not greater than some global deadline.

$$
\begin{aligned}
&10 \quad \forall i : J_i := 0, r_i := 0, r_i' := 0; \\
&20 \quad \forall i : \text{Compute\_worst\_case\_response\_time } (r_i); \\
&30 \quad \text{while}(\exists i : r_i \neq r_i') \ \{ \\
&40 \qquad \forall i : J_i := max(J_i, \forall j \text{ with } j \prec i : r_j); \\
&50 \qquad \forall i : r_i' := r_i; \\
&60 \qquad \forall i : \text{Compute\_worst\_case\_response\_time } (r_i); \\
&\quad \}
\end{aligned}
$$

Figure 7.13 Holistic analysis

To check this global deadline with an end to end worst case response time, the task scheduling of several processors may be investigated simultaneously. Figure 7.13 presents an algorithm for this analysis. In line 40, we update the jitter of tasks i with worst case response times of tasks j that have to be run before tasks i. The worst case response time is then computed with these modified jitters in line 60. Lines 40 to 60 are run up to convergence of worst case response times. In Figure 7.13, the symbol $\prec$ expresses that a precedence constraint exists between two tasks: $j \prec i$ means that task i cannot be released before the completion time of task j.

Summary

- A task is defined by a set of parameters which specify its temporal behavior.
- Tasks can be classified as critical, urgent, independent or dependent, and periodic or aperiodic.
- Critical functions of real-time systems are modeled by periodic tasks. Non-critical functions are modeled by aperiodic tasks.

- Real-time schedulers usually provide algebraic analysis methods which allow the designer to check task temporal constraints without computing the scheduling sequences. These algebraic analysis methods are called feasibility tests.
- Most of the schedulers implemented in real-time operating systems are fixed priority schedulers.
- Fixed priority scheduling is well suited for critical and static real-time embedded applications. Rate Monotonic is an optimal rule to assign priorities in the context of fixed priority schedulers.
- Earliest Deadline First is a dynamic scheduler. It is optimal and less suitable for critical real-time embedded applications.
- Two types of task dependencies must be taken into account: shared resources and precedence constraints of tasks.

Exercises

7.1 Define the terms *context, preemption*, and *context switch*.

7.2 When is a task

1. Both critical and urgent?
2. Critical but not urgent?
3. Urgent but not critical?

7.3 What distinguishes a dependent task from an independent task?

7.4 Describe two forms of task dependency.

7.5 Define the terms *activation time, release time, periodic task, sporadic task*, and *aperiodic task*.

7.6 What distinguishes a fixed priority scheduler from a dynamic priority scheduler?

7.7 How are task priorities assigned differently when using Deadline Monotonic than when using Rate Monotonic?

7.8 Explain why there is no need to use protected objects or semaphores to provide mutually exclusive access to resources shared by tasks scheduled by a *cyclic executive*.

7.9 What distinguishes a preemptive scheduler from a non-preemptive scheduler?

7.10 Define the terms *optimal scheduler* and *valid schedule*.

7.11 What distinguishes a static real-time system from a dynamic real-time system?

7.12 What properties must a set of tasks possess in order to be a set of *synchronous periodic tasks*?

7.13 Define the terms *deadlines on request* and *critical instant*.

7.14 What does the *processor utilization factor* express?

7.15 Practice with scheduling and analysis with fixed priority scheduling and Rate Monotonic priority assignment. Given the following set of synchronous periodic tasks:

Task	Initial release	Period	Capacity	Deadline
T_1	$S_1 = 0$	$P_1 = 8$	$C_1 = 4$	$D_1 = 8$
T_2	$S_2 = 0$	$P_2 = 12$	$C_2 = 3$	$D_2 = 12$
T_3	$S_3 = 0$	$P_3 = 4$	$C_3 = 1$	$D_3 = 4$

1. Calculate the processor utilization factor and the utilization bound.
2. What do these calculations tell us about our ability to schedule this task set with fixed priority scheduling and Rate Monotonic priority assignment?

7.16 Using the task set from the previous exercise:

1. What is the hyper-period?
2. Using preemptive fixed priority scheduling with Rate Monotonic priority assignment, draw a scheduling sequence (as in Figure 7.2) of this task set to demonstrate that a deadline is missed.

7.17 Practice with scheduling and analysis with fixed priority scheduling and Rate Monotonic priority assignment. Given the following set of synchronous periodic tasks:

Task	Initial release	Period	Capacity	Deadline
T_1	$S_1 = 0$	$P_1 = 29$	$C_1 = 7$	$D_1 = 29$
T_2	$S_2 = 0$	$P_2 = 5$	$C_2 = 1$	$D_2 = 5$
T_3	$S_3 = 0$	$P_3 = 10$	$C_3 = 2$	$D_3 = 10$

1. We schedule this task set according to a preemptive fixed priority scheduling and a Rate Monotonic priority assignment. Apply the processor utilization factor test. Do the tasks meet their deadlines?
2. Draw the scheduling sequence of this task set (as in Figure 7.2) during the first 30 units of time.
3. Re-draw the scheduling sequence of this task set during the first 30 units of time with a **non**-preemptive fixed priority scheduler and with Rate Monotonic. Compare the results with the drawing you made for the previous question.

7.18 Practice with scheduling and analysis with Rate Monotonic and fixed priority scheduling. Given the following *harmonic* set of synchronous periodic tasks:

Task	Initial release	Period	Capacity	Deadline
T_1	$S_1 = 0$	$P_1 = 30$	$C_1 = 6$	$D_1 = 30$
T_2	$S_2 = 0$	$P_2 = 5$	$C_2 = 3$	$D_2 = 5$
T_3	$S_3 = 0$	$P_3 = 10$	$C_3 = 2$	$D_3 = 10$

1. Why is this task set harmonic?
2. We schedule this task set according to a preemptive fixed priority scheduler and Rate Monotonic. Apply the processor utilization factor test. Do the tasks meet their deadlines?
3. Draw the scheduling sequence of this task set (as in Figure 7.2) during the first 30 units of time.
4. Compute the worst case response time of each task with the Joseph and Pandia method (equations (7.4) and (7.5)). You should find worst case response times that are consistent with the response times in the picture you drew for the first part of this exercise.

7.19 Practice with scheduling and analysis with Earliest Deadline First. Given the following set of synchronous periodic tasks:

Task	Initial release	Period	Capacity	Deadline
T_1	$S_1 = 0$	$P_1 = 10$	$C_1 = 6$	$D_1 = 10$
T_2	$S_2 = 0$	$P_2 = 30$	$C_2 = 9$	$D_2 = 30$

1. We schedule this task set according to a preemptive Earliest Deadline First scheduler. Apply the processor utilization factor test. Do the tasks meet their deadlines?
2. Compute the hyper-period of this task set. How many idle units of time should we have during this hyper-period?
3. Draw the scheduling sequence (as in Figure 7.7) of this task set during the hyper-period. (Hint: fill in a table of dynamic priorities like Table 7.1.) Is the number of idle units of time consistent with your answer to part 2?
4. Now assume a **non**-preemptive Earliest Deadline First scheduler. Re-draw the scheduling sequence of this task set during the hyper-period and compare this scheduling with the scheduling sequence of

part 3. Compare the behaviors of the preemptive and non-preemptive schedulers for this task set.

7.20 Practice with scheduling and analysis with Earliest Deadline First. Given the following set of synchronous periodic tasks:

Task	Initial release	Period	Capacity	Deadline
T_1	$S_1 = 0$	$P_1 = 12$	$C_1 = 5$	$D_1 = 12$
T_2	$S_2 = 0$	$P_2 = 6$	$C_2 = 2$	$D_2 = 6$
T_3	$S_3 = 0$	$P_3 = 24$	$C_3 = 5$	$D_3 = 24$

1. We schedule this task set according to a preemptive Earliest Deadline First scheduler. Apply the processor utilization factor test. Do the tasks meet their deadlines?

2. Compute the hyper-period of this task set. How many idle units of time should we have during this hyper-period?

3. Draw the scheduling sequence (as in Figure 7.7) of this task set during the hyper-period. (Hint: fill in a table of dynamic priorities like Table 7.1.) Is the number of idle units of time consistent with your answer to part 2?

4. Now assume a **non**-preemptive Earliest Deadline First scheduler. Re-draw the scheduling sequence of this task set during the hyper-period and compare this scheduling with the scheduling sequence of part 3. Compare the behaviors of the preemptive and non-preemptive schedulers for this task set.

5. Now assume that some aperiodic tasks are released: tasks TA_1 and TA_2. TA_1 has a capacity of 1 unit of time, is released at time 7, and has to meet a deadline at time 9. TA_2 has a capacity of 3 units of time, is released at time 12, and has to meet a deadline at time 21. We assume that the deadlines of aperiodic tasks defined above are the dynamic priorities that the EDF must handle to schedule the task set (e.g. $D_i(t)$). Draw the scheduling sequence of this new task set for the first 30 units of time. Can we meet all the deadlines under the preemptive EDF scheduler?

7.21 Practice with fixed priority scheduling and Rate Monotonic with aperiodic tasks. Given the following set of synchronous periodic tasks:

Task	Initial release	Period	Capacity	Deadline
T_1	$S_1 = 0$	$P_1 = 15$	$C_1 = 4$	$D_1 = 15$
T_2	$S_2 = 0$	$P_2 = 7$	$C_2 = 1$	$D_2 = 7$

These periodic tasks are scheduled with a preemptive fixed priority scheduling and Rate Monotonic. We expect to schedule aperiodic tasks together with the periodic task set. To analyze the schedule, we define a polling server with a period of 5 units of time and a capacity of 1 unit of time.

1. Check the schedulability of this set of **three** periodic tasks.
2. Now consider the arrival of two aperiodic tasks: tasks TA_1 and TA_2. TA_1 has a capacity of 1 unit of time, is released at time 7, and has to meet a deadline at time 9. TA_2 has a capacity of 3 units of time, is released at time 12, and has to meet a deadline at time 21. Draw the scheduling sequence of this new task set.

7.22 In this exercise, you will investigate the schedulability of a set of tasks that share a block of memory. Given the following set of periodic tasks:

Task	Initial release	Period	Capacity	Deadline
T_1	$S_1 = 0$	$P_1 = 6$	$C_1 = 2$	$D_1 = 6$
T_2	$S_2 = 0$	$P_2 = 8$	$C_2 = 2$	$D_2 = 8$
T_3	$S_3 = 0$	$P_3 = 12$	$C_3 = 5$	$D_3 = 12$

These three tasks are scheduled with a preemptive fixed priority scheduler and Rate Monotonic. T_1 and T_3 make use of a block of memory. This block of memory is protected by a semaphore to enforce a critical section.

T_1 requires the block of memory during the second half of its capacity while T_3 needs the block of memory during all its capacity.

1. First, we assume that no inheritance protocol is activated with the semaphore. Draw the scheduling of this task set during its hyper-period. In the scheduling sequence, find when the semaphore is allocated and released by tasks T_1 and T_3. Can you see on the graph at which time a priority inversion occurs?
2. Now we assume that the PIP protocol is active during semaphore allocations and releases. Draw the scheduling sequence of this task set during its hyper-period. In the scheduling sequence, find when

the semaphore is allocated and released. Also check that no priority inversion occurs.

3. Compute worst case blocking times B_1, B_2, and B_3.

7.23 In the previous exercise, you investigated the use of PIP to put an upper bound on the length of time a high priority task has to wait for a shared resource. Because PIP is difficult to implement, PCP protocols are more commonly used. In this exercise, we study the ICPP, a kind of PCP. Given the following set of periodic tasks:

Task	Initial release	Period	Capacity	Deadline
T_1	$S_1 = 0$	$P_1 = 31$	$C_1 = 8$	$D_1 = 31$
T_2	$S_2 = 2$	$P_2 = 30$	$C_2 = 8$	$D_2 = 30$

We schedule this task set with a preemptive fixed priority scheduler and Rate Monotonic.

T_1 and T_2 require access to two shared resources called R_1 and R_2 that are controlled by the two semaphores *mutex1* and *mutex2*.

- T_1 needs R_1 from the 2nd to the 8th units of time of its capacity.
- T_1 needs R_2 from the 4th to the 8th units of time of its capacity.
- T_2 needs R_1 from the 6th to the 8th units of time of its capacity.
- T_2 needs R_2 from the 2nd to the 8th units of time of its capacity.

1. First, we assume that PIP is activated with the semaphores. Draw the scheduling sequence of this task set during the first 30 units of time. In the scheduling sequence, find when the semaphores are allocated and released by the tasks T_1 and T_2. Describe what you see in the scheduling sequence.

2. Second, we assume that ICPP is activated for these semaphores. Draw the scheduling sequence of this task set during the first 30 units of time. On the scheduling sequence, find when the semaphores are allocated and released by the tasks T_1 and T_2. Compare the scheduling sequences of questions 1 and 2.

7.24 This exercise summarizes the different topics presented in this chapter. You will investigate performances of an application responsible for displaying data to the driver of a car. The application is composed of 5 tasks:

- Task $SENSOR\_1$ reads a speed sensor every 10 ms.
- Task $SENSOR\_2$ reads the temperature inside the car every 10 ms.
- Task $SENSOR\_3$ reads the GPS location of the car every 40 ms.

- Task $DISPLAY\_1$ computes every 12 ms a summary of the data produced by $SENSOR\_1$, $SENSOR\_2$, and $SENSOR\_3$ and displays the results on a first screen.
- When the driver requests it, task $DISPLAY\_2$ displays, on a second screen, the road map centered around the current location of the car. This screen is refreshed every 6 ms.

We have implemented this set of tasks, and, after some measurements, we have noticed that:

- Execution time of tasks $SENSOR\_2$ and $DISPLAY\_1$ is bounded by 2 ms.
- Task $SENSOR\_3$ needs a processor time ranging from 2 to 4 ms.
- Execution times of tasks $SENSOR\_1$ and $DISPLAY\_2$ never exceeded 1 ms.

We also assume that all tasks have the same first release time. The engineers would like to check that all tasks finish their current work before being released to do the next one. They have selected an operating system that provides 32 priority levels ranging from 0 to 31. Priority level 31 is the highest priority. The scheduler is a preemptive fixed priority scheduler. This system does not allow us to assign the same priority level to several tasks.

1. The engineers would like you to help them with the priority assignment of each task.

   - Explain the common criteria that people use to assign priorities to tasks.
   - Assign a priority for each task of this system. Explain your choice.

2. From your priority assignment, and without drawing the scheduling sequence, compute the worst case response time for tasks $SENSOR\_1$, $SENSOR\_2$, and $SENSOR\_3$.

3. In practice, tasks $SENSOR\_1$, $SENSOR\_2$, and $SENSOR\_3$ share a block of memory through the semaphore *mutex*. $SENSOR\_1$ and $SENSOR\_2$ need the *mutex* during all their capacity. $SENSOR\_3$ needs the *mutex* during the two first units of time of its capacity. The *mutex* uses ICPP.

   Explain why the worst case response times of part 2 are incorrect with the use of this *mutex*.

4. Draw the scheduling sequence of this system up to time 25. Show when each shared resource is allocated or/and released.

5. In order to decrease the response time of the system, we run the task set on an architecture with two processors, a and b. The task parameters are now defined by:

Task	Processor	Capacity	Period
DISPLAY_1	b	4	6
SENSOR_3	b	2	20
DISPLAY_2	a	2	3
SENSOR_1	a	2	5
SENSOR_2	a	2	5

These tasks stay scheduled with a preemptive fixed priority scheduler. Priorities are assigned according to Rate Monotonic. We will not take the shared resources into account for this question. **You may assume that all tasks are independent.** Show that at least one task cannot meet its deadline.

6. In the previous question, the engineers assigned tasks to processors randomly. Each task may be run on either processor a or on processor b. However, running a given task on a or on b changes the task worst case execution time: processor b is twice as fast as processor a.

Assign each task to processor a or b in order to meet all task deadlines. Explain how you made this assignment and how you have checked deadlines. **You may again assume that all tasks are independent.**

8

Real-time programming with Ada

In Chapter 7, we presented an overview of real-time scheduling theory. Those discussions were independent of any programming language. This chapter explains how to write real-time applications in Ada that are compliant with that scheduling theory. A compliant Ada program can be analyzed thereby increasing the application's reliability.

Ada practitioners have two international standards available for producing compliant Ada programs: Ada 2005 and POSIX 1003.1b. In order to apply real-time scheduling theory with these standards, we need some means to:

1. Implement periodic tasks. This implementation requires a way to represent time, a way to enforce periodic task release times, and a way to assign priorities to both tasks and shared resources.
2. Activate priority inheritance protocols for the shared resources.
3. And of course, select and apply a scheduler such as those presented in Chapter 7 (e.g. fixed priority scheduler or Earliest Deadline First).

The Ada 2005 and POSIX 1003.1b standards provide the means to create compliant programs through pragmas and specific packages. Real-time specific pragmas and packages for Ada 2005 are defined in Annex D of the Ada Reference Manual. The Ada binding POSIX 1003.5 provides the packages that allow us to create compliant real-time Ada programs using the POSIX standard.

The first six sections of this chapter discuss and use the packages and pragmas of Annex D. Section 8.1 shows how to express timing constraints of tasks with an Ada package called `Ada.Real_Time`. Section 8.2 explains how to implement periodic tasks. Periodic task release times are enforced with the `delay until` statement introduced in Chapter 5. We also show how to assign priorities to tasks and to protected objects with the priority pragma. Section 8.3 uses the concepts of the first two sections to implement the car application introduced and analyzed in Chapter 7. Section 8.4 explains how to deal with priority inversion. Section 8.5 is devoted to Ada's scheduling model and explains how we can select a particular scheduler for a given application. Finally, Section 8.6 focuses on Ravenscar, a set of restrictions of Ada features that allows us to easily check real-time scheduling theory compliance at compile time.

The remainder of this chapter is devoted to POSIX 1003.1b. Section 8.7 presents the POSIX 1003.1b scheduling model and the POSIX application programming interface (API) for Ada. The POSIX 1003.1b Ada API provides a simple means for implementing Ada applications that run under an operating system which does not provide an Ada 2005 standard compliant run-time. We will talk more about run-time systems in Chapter 9. In Section 8.8, we'll revisit the car application and implement it with POSIX processes rather than Ada tasks.

Finally, in Section 8.9 we'll compare the Ada tasking and POSIX approaches for developing real-time applications. For a more comprehensive treatment of both the POSIX C and the Ada 2005 application programming interfaces see Gallmeister (1995), Burns and Wellings (2007), and Burns and Wellings (2009).

8.1 Expressing time

To implement periodic tasks with Ada, we need some means to express the timing parameters of these tasks. The package `Ada.Real_Time` provides the necessary resources. `Ada.Real_Time` is similar to `Ada.Calendar` but is more suited for real-time applications. `Ada.Real_Time` provides a documented, monotonic, high-resolution clock. Monotonic time does not jump forward or backward as wall clock time does for leap seconds or changes due to daylight savings time. Here is the specification of this package.

```
package Ada.Real_Time is

    type Time is private;
    Time_First :  constant  Time;
    Time_Last   :  constant  Time;
    Time_Unit   :  constant := implementation−defined−real−number;

    type Time_Span is private;
    Time_Span_First :  constant  Time_Span;
    Time_Span_Last   :  constant  Time_Span;
    Time_Span_Unit   :  constant  Time_Span;
    Tick :  constant  Time_Span;
```

```
function  To_Duration   (TS  :  Time_Span)  return  Duration;
function  To_Time_Span  (D   :  Duration )  return  Time_Span;

function  Clock  return  Time;

function  "+"  (Left  :  Time;  Right  :  Time_Span)  return  Time;
function  "+"  (Left  :  Time_Span;  Right  :  Time)  return  Time;
function  "-"  (Left  :  Time;  Right  :  Time_Span)  return  Time;
function  "-"  (Left  :  Time;  Right  :  Time)  return  Time_Span;
function  "<"  (Left,  Right  :  Time)  return  Boolean;
function  "<="(Left,  Right  :  Time)  return  Boolean;
function  ">"  (Left,  Right  :  Time)  return  Boolean;
function  ">="(Left,  Right  :  Time)  return  Boolean;

function  "+"  (Left,  Right  :  Time_Span)  return  Time_Span;
function  "-"  (Left,  Right  :  Time_Span)  return  Time_Span;
function  "-"  (Right  :  Time_Span)  return  Time_Span;
function  "*"  (Left  :  Time_Span;  Right  :  Integer)
   return  Time_Span;
function  "*"  (Left  :  Integer;  Right  :  Time_Span)
   return  Time_Span;
function  "/"  (Left,  Right  :  Time_Span)  return  Integer;
function  "/"  (Left  :  Time_Span;  Right  :  Integer)
   return  Time_Span;
   ...

function  Nanoseconds   (NS  :  Integer)  return  Time_Span;
function  Microseconds  (US  :  Integer)  return  Time_Span;
function  Milliseconds  (MS  :  Integer)  return  Time_Span;
function  Seconds       (S   :  Integer)  return  Time_Span;
function  Minutes       (M   :  Integer)  return  Time_Span;
   ...

private
   ...  -- not specified by the language
end  Ada.Real_Time;
```

Package **Ada.Real_Time** defines the two time related types: **Time** and **Time_Span**. Let's look at the definitions of these two types provided in section D.8 of the Ada Reference Manual.

1. Type **Time** implements an absolute time. Time begins at an arbitrary starting point called the **epoch** that is the same for all values of **Time**. As the exact starting point is not important for the analysis of real-time applications, Ada does not define the epoch. It might be the time of system initialization or some time standard (e.g. 1 January 1970 00:00:00 UT). The range of type **Time** shall be sufficient to represent real ranges up

to 50 years from the start of our program's execution. Package Ada.Real_Time provides several constants of type Time.

- Time_First and Time_Last are the smallest and largest values of the Time type, respectively.
- Time_Unit is the smallest amount of real-time representable by the Time type. It is implementation-defined and shall be less than or equal to 20 microseconds.

2. Type Time_Span represents the length of a duration of time. Package Ada.Real_Time provides several constants of type Time_Span.

- Time_Span_First and Time_Span_Last are the smallest and largest values of the Time_Span type, respectively. Time_Span_First shall be no greater than −3600 seconds, and Time_Span_Last shall be no less than 3600 seconds.
- Tick is a constant of Time_Span that represents the average length duration in which the clock value does not change. Tick shall be no greater than 1 ms.
- Time_Span_Unit is the difference between two successive values of the Time type. It is also the smallest positive value of type Time_Span.

In addition to these types and constants, package Ada.Real_Time provides various subprograms for obtaining and manipulating time-related values. Function Clock is called to determine the "current time." It returns the amount of time that has passed since the epoch. The functions To_Duration, To_Time_Span, Nanoseconds, Microseconds, Milliseconds, Seconds, and Minutes allow us to convert timing values to and from Time, Time_Span, Duration, and Integer variables. As we will show in Section 8.2, we use these functions to assign periods to our tasks.

Finally, package Ada.Real_Time provides a variety of arithmetic and relational operators that allow us to write expressions containing values of Time_Span, Time, and Integer types.

Besides defining types and subprograms, package Ada.Real_Time explicitly states the timing performances that Ada run-time system implementers must document. As the clock hardware on various platforms differs, such documentation is critical to analyzing the timing requirements of our application on a particular target. Section D.8 of the Ada Reference Manual requires that an implementation shall document:

1. The values of Time_First, Time_Last, Time_Span_First, Time_Span_Last, Time_Span_Unit, and Tick.

2. The properties of the underlying time base used for the clock and for type Time. These properties include the range of values supported and any relevant aspects of the underlying hardware or operating system facilities used.

3. The upper bound on the real-time duration of a clock tick.

4. The upper bound on the drift rate of Clock with respect to real-time.

5. The upper bound on the size of a clock jump. A clock jump is the difference between two successive distinct values of the clock (as observed by calling the Clock function).

6. The upper bound on the execution time of a call to the Clock function.

7. and more ...

Some of these documentation requirements allow us to perform schedulability verifications, a feature available for very few programming languages. These documentation requirements help practitioners to write Ada applications that are compliant with real-time scheduling theory. This is the case for the second item, which is mandatory to evaluate worst case response time of tasks.

8.2 Implementing periodic tasks

Now, let us see how to implement periodic tasks with Ada. The scheduling models discussed in Chapter 7 require that the periodic release times of our periodic tasks be deterministic. The *release time* is the time at which a task begins to work on its activity. A periodic task is released periodically. The scheduling models also require that each task be assigned a priority. In this section, we look at implementing both of these requirements in Ada.

8.2.1 Implementing periodic release times

Periodic release times can be implemented with the **delay** statement. In Section 5.2.4, we showed that the **delay** statement makes it possible to block a task for a relative duration of time (e.g. delay seven seconds) or until an absolute time (e.g. delay until 15:07).

A task can be blocked for a relative delay with the **delay expr** statement, where **expr** is the relative delay. This statement blocks a task for *at least* **expr** seconds of time. The task will not be released *before* this amount of time but it can be released *after* this amount of time.

A task can also be blocked for an absolute delay with the **delay until expr** statement, where **expr** is the time at which the task can be released.

The `delay until` statement blocks a task *at least* up to the time `expr` is reached. A task will not be released *before* time `expr` but can be released *after* this time.

The Ada Reference Manual does not require any bound on the lateness of a task's release time. But again, the Ada Reference Manual provides the information needed to make verifications with real-time scheduling theory. It requires the documentation of metrics on the implementation of `delay` and `delay until` statements. One of the required metrics is the upper bound on the lateness of a `delay` statement. We can then use this upper bound as a jitter parameter (see page 283) in our calculation of worst case response times. Documentation of metrics is related to the implementation of Ada run-time, which is discussed in Section 9.3.1.

Let's look at an example of a simple periodic task.

```ada
with Ada.Real_Time;   use Ada.Real_Time;
with Text_IO;         use Text_IO;
procedure A_Periodic_Task_Demo is

    -- The following procedure contains a "job" that
    -- we want to execute periodically
    procedure Run_Job_Of_The_Task is
    begin
        Put_Line("Periodic task is released and executes its job");
    end Run_Job_Of_The_Task;


    task A_Periodic_Task;   -- Define a task

    -- The body of our periodic task
    task body A_Periodic_Task is
        Next_Time : Ada.Real_Time.Time := Clock;
        Period    : constant Time_Span := Milliseconds (250);
    begin
        loop
            -- The task is released : it runs its job
            Run_Job_Of_The_Task;

            -- Determine the next release time
            Next_Time := Next_Time + Period;

            -- Wait for the next release time
            delay until Next_Time;
        end loop;
    end A_Periodic_Task;

begin
    null;
end A_Periodic_Task_Demo;
```

In Chapter 7, we characterized a synchronous periodic task with a period
and a capacity. The period of this task is 250 ms. At each release time the
task runs the procedure `Run_Job_Of_The_Task`. The capacity of this example
is the worst case execution time (WCET) of the procedure `Run_Job_Of_The_`
`Task`.

Periodic release times of the task in this example are implemented with
the `delay until` statement. We prefer the absolute delay to the relative
delay because the latter suffers from cumulative drift. Figure 8.1 illustrates
the concepts of cumulative and local drift.

Figure 8.1a shows the release times (heavy vertical bars) of a periodic
task that uses the relative `delay 0.250;` statement to periodically release
it. The first release is at time 0. The second release is at $250 + \delta_1$ ms where
δ_1 is the release time jitter. The third release is $250 + \delta_2$ ms *after the second
release* — at $500 + \delta_1 + \delta_2$ ms. The fourth release is at $750 + \delta_1 + \delta_2 + \delta_3$
ms. You can see that each successive release is further from the regular 250
ms intervals. The drift is a result of the *accumulation* of jitters.

Figure 8.1b shows the release times (heavy vertical bars) of a periodic task
that uses the absolute `delay until Next_Time;` statement to periodically
release it. The first release is at time 0. The second release is at $250 + \delta_1$ ms.
The third release is at $500 + \delta_2$ ms. The fourth release is at $750 + \delta_3$ ms.
While the jitter causes some local drift from the regular 250 ms intervals,
the jitter does not accumulate over the lifetime of the periodic task.

8.2.2 *The Ada priority model*

Another important property of a periodic task is its priority level. Ada's
priority model is based on two values. Each task has a base priority and an
active priority.

The task's **base priority** is the priority that is assigned to the task prior
to the execution of the application. The task's **active priority** is the priority that is actually handled by the operating system (or the Ada run-time
system) to schedule the set of ready tasks. A base priority is a fixed priority
while the active priority is a dynamic one. Different ways exist to assign
fixed/base priorities to tasks. In Chapter 7, we described one of the most
famous fixed priority assignment rules — Rate Monotonic. In that chapter
we also discussed shared resource protocols such as ICPP that allow a task's
priority to change as a result of priority inheritance. Active priorities represent those changing priority levels. At any time, the active priority of a

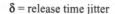

δ = release time jitter

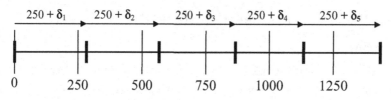

a) Cumulative drift of relative delay

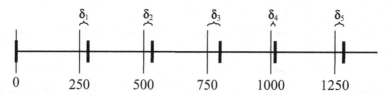

b) Local drift of absolute delay

Figure 8.1 A comparison of the drift in release times for using relative and absolute delays

task is the maximum of its base priority and all the priorities the task is inheriting at that instant. Priority inheritance may occur:

- During the execution of protected operations, if ICCP is activated. The task inherits the priority of the protected object. See section D.3 of the Ada Reference Manual. We will look at ICCP in Section 8.4.
- During a rendezvous. A task which accepts an entry call inherits the priority of the task making the entry call. See sections 9.5.3 and D.1 of the Ada Reference Manual.
- During task activation. During activation, a task inherits the active priority of its parent. See section 9.2 of the Ada Reference Manual.

Ada types related to priority are defined in the **System** package. Here are the relevant parts of this package for a particular target:

```
package System is
   ...
   --   Priority-related  Declarations  (Reference  Manual  D.1)

   Max_Priority             : constant Positive :=  30;
   Max_Interrupt_Priority   : constant Positive :=  31;

   subtype Any_Priority      is Integer      range  0 ..  31;
   subtype Priority          is Any_Priority range  0 ..  30;
```

```
    subtype Interrupt_Priority is Any_Priority range 31 .. 31;

    Default_Priority : constant Priority := 15;
        ...
end System;
```

Priority levels can be assigned to both tasks and interrupt handlers. System.Interrupt_Priority defines priority levels for interrupt handlers. The range of System.Interrupt_Priority shall include at least one value. We assigned an interrupt priority to our interrupt handler in our analog to digital device driver (page 158). System.Priority defines priority levels that are available for tasks. System.Priority must provide at least 30 priority levels but the actual number of available priority levels depends on the operating system or run-time system. Having more levels is better for real-time scheduling analysis. Most of the feasibility tests presented in Chapter 7 are easier to use when each task has a unique priority level.

Two pragmas are available to assign priority levels to interrupt handlers and base priority levels to tasks.

The pragma dedicated to interrupt handlers is:

```
pragma Interrupt_Priority [( expression )];
```

The expression in this pragma is optional. When not given, the priority value assigned to the interrupt handler is Interrupt_Priority'Last. We do not discuss interrupt handlers further in this chapter. You can review Chapter 4 for further details.

The second pragma, the Priority pragma, is used to assign base priorities to tasks and ceiling priorities to protected objects.

```
pragma Priority ( expression );
```

Here expression represents the priority level to be assigned. We can place pragma Priority immediately within a task definition, a protected object or protected type definition, or the declarative part of a subprogram body. The value of the priority expression must be in the range of System.Priority. A priority pragma can also be assigned to the main procedure. If you do not use this pragma to assign a priority to a task, it is assigned a priority equal to the priority of the task that created it. Finally, if no priorities are assigned, each task is assigned the default priority value defined by the constant System.Default_Priority.

Here is an example that assigns priority level 10 to the periodic task within our example program on page 299. Notice that we must use the long form of the task declaration that we previously used only when our task had entries.

```
task A_Periodic_Task is
   pragma Priority (10);
end A_Periodic_Task;
```

8.3 Ada implementation of the car application

Let's use what we have learned to implement the car application introduced
and analyzed in Chapter 7 (see page 268). This application has three tasks.
Rather than write three different tasks, we will make use of Ada's generic
facilities. While we cannot define a generic task, we can define a generic
package that includes a task type. Then, we can instantiate three separate
instances for our three tasks. Here is the specification of our generic package:

```
with System;
generic
   with procedure Run; -- The "job" of the periodic task
package Generic_Periodic_Task is

   -- Two discriminants characterize this periodic task
   task type Periodic_Task
              (Task_Priority            : System.Priority;
               Period_In_Milliseconds : Natural) is
       pragma Priority (Task_Priority);
   end Periodic_Task;

end Generic_Periodic_Task;
```

This generic package has a single formal parameter, **Run**, that is a parameterless procedure. We will supply an actual procedure that our periodic task
will call each time it is released.

The task type **Periodic_Task** has two discriminants: **Task_Priority** and
Period_In_Milliseconds. Notice that the priority pragma associated with
this task type uses the value of the first discriminant to set the priority
of the task. When we create an actual task from this type, we will specify
its priority through the first discriminant and its period through the second
discriminant. We use the discriminant **Period_In_Milliseconds** in the delay
logic of the task body which is in the package body below.

```
with Ada.Real_Time; use Ada.Real_Time;
package body Generic_Periodic_Task is

   task body Periodic_Task is
      Next_Time : Ada.Real_Time.Time := Clock;
      Period    : constant Time_Span :=
                   Milliseconds (Period_In_Milliseconds);
```

```
   begin
      loop
         Run; -- Call the procedure with the code for this job
         -- wait until the next period
         Next_Time := Next_Time + Period;
         delay until Next_Time;
      end loop;
   end Periodic_Task;

end Generic_Periodic_Task;
```

Now let's see how to use this generic periodic task package to implement the car application. Here are the relevant characteristics with priority levels determined by Rate Monotonic assignment for each of the three tasks:

Task	Period (ms)	Priority
$T_{display}$	$P_{display} = 100$	12
T_{engine}	$P_{engine} = 500$	10
T_{speed}	$P_{speed} = 250$	11

We will create one instance of our generic task type for each of our three tasks using the priorities and periods from this table. Here is the complete program:

```
with Generic_Periodic_Task;
with Text_IO; use Text_IO;
procedure Car_System is

   -- The following three parameterless procedures are stubs for
   -- the actual code that runs in the car

   procedure Display_Speed is
   begin
      Put_Line ("Tdisplay displays the speed of the car");
   end Display_Speed;

   procedure Read_Speed is
   begin
      Put_Line ("Tspeed reads speed sensor");
   end Read_Speed;

   procedure Monitor_Engine is
   begin
      Put_Line ("Tengine performs engine monitoring algorithm");
   end Monitor_Engine;
```

```
-- Instantiate a periodic task package from the generic package
-- for each of our three run procedures

package P1 is new Generic_Periodic_Task (Run => Display_Speed);
package P2 is new Generic_Periodic_Task (Run => Read_Speed);
package P3 is new Generic_Periodic_Task (Run => Monitor_Engine);

-- Our three tasks
Tdisplay : P1.Periodic_Task (Task_Priority => 12,
                             Period_In_Milliseconds => 100);

Tspeed   : P2.Periodic_Task (Task_Priority => 11,
                             Period_In_Milliseconds => 250);

Tengine  : P3.Periodic_Task (Task_Priority => 10,
                             Period_In_Milliseconds => 500);

pragma Priority (20);   -- Priority of main subprogram

begin
   Put_Line ("Tasks will start after the main subprogram completes!");
end Car_System;
```

We defined stubs for the three jobs each of our tasks must perform. Each stub simply displays a message. Following the definition of these stubs, we instantiate three different packages, one for each of our tasks. We pass the appropriate "job" to run for each of our tasks. Next are the declarations of our three tasks. We include the values of the priority and period discriminants in the declarations that create the three tasks.

We also choose to assign priority level 20 to the environment task, the task that executes the main procedure of this program. This higher priority level ensures that the three tasks will not start running before the main procedure has finished its initialization. This approach makes our program compliant with the critical instant assumption (see page 261). The pragma Partition_Elaboration_Policy (see section 5.7 of the Ada Reference Manual) can also be used to defer task activations to implement a critical instant.

8.4 Handling shared resources

As we discussed in Chapter 4, protected objects are the preferred construct for encapsulating resources shared among tasks. In Chapter 7, we showed that in order to perform a schedulability analysis, specific locking protocols are needed with shared objects. In Section 7.3.2, we discussed priority inheritance protocols. These protocols require us to assign priorities to both tasks and shared resources. We discussed the use of pragma `Priority` for tasks in the last section. The same pragma can be used to assign a priority to a protected object. We simply place the pragma in the declaration of our protected type or protected object. Below is the declaration of the protected bounded buffer type used in the producer-consumer demonstration program on page 136. We have used the priority pragma to assign a priority of 15 to all objects of this type.

```
protected type Bounded_Buffer (Max_Size : Positive) is

    pragma Priority (15);

    procedure Clear;
    -- delete all of the items in the buffer
    entry Put (Item : in Positive);
    -- add a value to the buffer
    entry Take (Item : out Positive);
    -- remove a value from the buffer
private
    Buffer : Integer_Queue.Queue_Type (Max_Size);
end Bounded_Buffer;
```

8.4.1 Locking policies

Each protected object also has a **locking policy**. Protected object priorities are properties which are related to the protected object locking policy. The locking policy specifies how the protected object can be accessed and the relationships between task priorities and protected object priorities. If a protected object declaration does not contain a priority pragma, then a default priority is specified by the assigned locking policy.

We specify a given locking policy with the following pragma:

```
pragma Locking_Policy (policy-to-activate);
```

where **policy-to-activate** is the protected object locking policy. Ada compiler and run-time implementers are allowed to define any locking policies but must implement at least the Immediate Ceiling Priority Protocol (ICPP) described in Section 7.3.2. ICPP is identified by the policy name `Ceiling_Locking`. To activate ICPP during protected object access, we must add the following pragma to the application:

```
pragma Locking_Policy (Ceiling_Locking);
```

The Ada Reference Manual describes exactly how `Ceiling_Locking` works:

- Each protected object priority level is called a **ceiling priority**. If no ceiling priority has been assigned to a protected object, then it has a default priority of `System.Priority'Last`.

- The ceiling priority of a protected object must be equal to the *maximum* active priority of all the tasks which may call the protected object. The exception `Program_Error` is raised when a task attempts to access a protected object whose ceiling priority is less than the task's active priority.

- When a task gains access to a protected object and if its active priority is lower than the ceiling priority, the task inherits the ceiling priority of the protected object — the task's active priority is increased to reach the ceiling priority. Thus the active priority of a task at a given time is equal to the maximum of its base priority and the ceiling priorities of any protected objects the task has locked.

You should notice that this specification of `Ceiling_Locking` is similar to the description we gave in Section 7.3.2 for ICPP.

8.4.2 Queuing policies

Section D.4 of the Real-Time Systems Annex defines a second important pragma for protected objects.

pragma Queuing_Policy(policy_identifier);

Two language-defined policy identifiers exist: `FIFO_Queuing` and `Priority_Queuing`. A compiler vendor may supply additional policies. `FIFO_Queuing` is the default when no `Queuing_Policy` pragma is specified. Each queuing policy governs:

- The order in which tasks are queued for entry service.
- The order in which *different* entry queues are considered for servicing.

`FIFO_Queuing` orders entry callers according to the time the entry calls are made. All of our examples of entry queues in Chapters 4 and 5 were based on `FIFO_Queuing`. With `Priority_Queuing`, entry callers are ordered in the queues according to their active priority.

In Chapter 4 we said that when two or more open entry queues in a protected object have waiting tasks, the language does not specify which entry queue is selected; the selection is arbitrary. This non-deterministic behavior is defined by the default `FIFO_Queuing` policy. The `Priority_Queuing` policy provides a deterministic selection — the entry queue with the highest priority task is selected. Should more than one entry queue contain tasks with the highest priority, the selection is based on the *textual position* of the entry declaration. Each entry has priority over the entries declared after it.

In Chapter 5 we said that when there are tasks waiting on more than one alternative of a selective accept statement, the language does not specify which accept alternative is selected for a rendezvous; the selection is arbitrary. Again, this non-deterministic behavior is defined by the default FIFO_Queuing policy. The Priority_Queuing policy provides a deterministic select statement — the accept alternative whose entry queue contains the highest priority task is selected. Should there be more than one open accept alternative with tasks of equal priority waiting, the selection is based on the *textual position* of the accept alternative within the selective accept statement. Each accept alternative has priority over the accept alternatives that follow it. If we were to use Priority_Queuing in our beverage vending machine software, task Make_Beverage on page 172 would rendezvous with a task requesting coffee before those with equal priority requesting tea or cocoa.

8.5 The Ada scheduling model

In the previous sections, we explained how to implement and parameterize tasks and protected objects so our application is compliant with real-time scheduling theory. In this section we look at the model that Ada uses to schedule our tasks. We see now how such applications are scheduled by an Ada compliant run-time.

8.5.1 Conceptual design of an Ada scheduler

Figure 8.2 illustrates how tasks are organized by the Ada run-time system. Each processor has several ready queues. Each queue is devoted to a single priority level and stores ready tasks that have the same active priority level. Each queue has a tail and a head. In the example shown in Figure 8.2, the queue associated with active priority 8 contains two tasks that are ready, the queue of active priority 7 contains four ready tasks, and the queue of active priority Priority'First contains one ready task.

Each queue has an associated dispatching policy. The dispatching policy specifies when tasks are inserted and deleted from the ready queue and how the ready tasks are ordered in the queue. The dispatching policy defines the rules for selecting which ready task the processor must run and how task preemption is handled. Recall that preemption is where the scheduler chooses to stop the running task and replace it with another ready task.

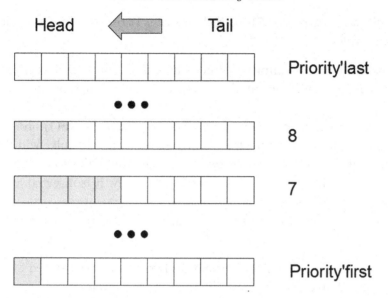

Figure 8.2 Ada's scheduling model

With the Ada scheduling model, preemption may only occur at specific instants called **task dispatching times.** Each dispatching policy specifies what operations can be or must be done at these task dispatching times.

The scheduling model of Ada can be seen as a two-level scheduling. At any time, the scheduler:

1. Selects the highest priority queue that is not empty.
2. Using the queue's dispatching policy, selects the next task to run from that queue.

8.5.2 Task dispatching policies

Dispatching is the process of giving the processor to a ready task. As dispatching is dependent on the states of the various tasks in the application, you may find it useful to review the basic states a task goes through during its execution, shown in Figure 3.2 on page 112. Ada provides several different dispatching policies. A dispatching policy is specified by the Task_Dispatching_Policy pragma. The most important dispatching policy is FIFO_Within_Priorities and is specified by including the following pragma in the application:

pragma Task_Dispatching_Policy (FIFO_Within_Priorities);

The dispatching policy `FIFO_Within_Priorities` specifies the following scheduling rules:

- The scheduler is preemptive. When there is a ready task with an active priority higher than the running task, the scheduler will preempt the running task.
- The tasks in the ready queue are in *first in first out* (FIFO) order. When the running task blocks itself or is preempted, the scheduler will dispatch the task at the head of the ready queue with the highest active priority.
- When a task changes state from blocked to ready, it is inserted at the tail of the ready queue for its active priority.
- Should the active priority of a task in one of the ready queues change, that task is moved to the tail of the queue for its new active priority.

The dispatching policy `FIFO_Within_Priorities` is well suited for critical applications. If all the tasks have different priority levels, we can easily apply the fixed priority scheduling feasibility tests described in Section 7.2.1. Because of the widespread use of the fixed priority scheduling feasibility tests, this policy is perhaps the most commonly used dispatching policy for real-time systems. However, `FIFO_Within_Priorities` may not be suitable for all applications. Ada provides other dispatching policies that can be useful for less critical applications. The Ada 2005 standard defines three additional dispatching policies:

- `Round_Robin_Within_Priorities` is a preemptive dispatching policy that allows us to assign a time quantum to each priority level. The scheduler preempts a running task when it has exhausted its quantum of time and inserts it at the tail of the ready queue. The ready queues are FIFO. When the running task blocks itself or is preempted, the scheduler will dispatch the task at the head of the ready queue with the highest priority. Round robin scheduling is popular in time sharing environments.
- `Non_Preemptive_FIFO_Within_Priorities` is a scheduling policy without preemption. The running task must voluntarily relinquish the processor by executing some blocking statement such as a delay statement, an accept statement, a select statement, or an entry call. The ready queues are FIFO. When the running task blocks itself, the scheduler will dispatch the task at the head of the ready queue with the highest priority.
- `EDF_Across_Priorities` is a preemptive dispatching policy that implements the Earliest Deadline First scheduler described in Section 7.2.2. The tasks in the ready queues are ordered by their deadlines. The task at the head of each queue has the shortest deadline. The package `Ada.Dispatching.EDF` provides operations for setting and querying task

deadlines. It also provides the procedure `Delay_Until_And_Set_Deadline` for the implementation of periodic tasks that reset their deadlines at the beginning of each iteration. As we mentioned in Section 7.2.3, EDF is less predictable than fixed priority scheduling during overload conditions. However, it can effectively utilize 100% of the processor compared to only about 69% for fixed priority scheduling with Rate Monotonic priority assignment.

We can specify different dispatching policies for different priority queues. This approach allows an application to run its tasks according to several policies at the same time. We use pragma `Priority_Specific_Dispatching` in place of pragma `Task_Dispatching_Policy` to assign a scheduling policy to each priority level. Here is an example that divides our ready queues into three different groups, each with its own scheduling policy.

```
pragma  Priority_Specific_Dispatching
        (FIFO_Within_Priorities, 3, 31);
pragma  Priority_Specific_Dispatching
        (EDF_Across_Priorities, 2, 2);
pragma  Priority_Specific_Dispatching
        (Round_Robin_Within_Priorities, 0, 1);
```

With this set of pragmas, we assign FIFO preemptive fixed priority scheduling to the highest levels of priority — from level 3 to 31. These priority levels are devoted to high critical tasks. The other priority levels are devoted to EDF (priority level 2) and round robin schedulers (priority levels 0 and 1). Figure 8.3 illustrates the assignment of scheduling policies to priority queues specified by these three pragmas.

In this design, priority levels ranging from 0 to 2 are intended for tasks that are less critical. Since they are hosted by the lowest priority levels, they can not disturb high priority/critical tasks and worst case response times of these high priority/critical tasks can always be computed with the methods described in Section 7.2.1. These mechanisms provide a natural and easy means to run both critical and non-critical tasks together.

Of course, for high critical applications, the picture must be simpler so we can use the highly predictable fixed priority scheduling approach to schedule *all* of our tasks. For such applications we use the following two pragmas that specify our scheduler satisfy the conditions for fixed priority scheduling and ICPP:

```
pragma  Task_Dispatching_Policy (FIFO_Within_Priorities);
pragma  Locking_Policy (Ceiling_Locking);
```

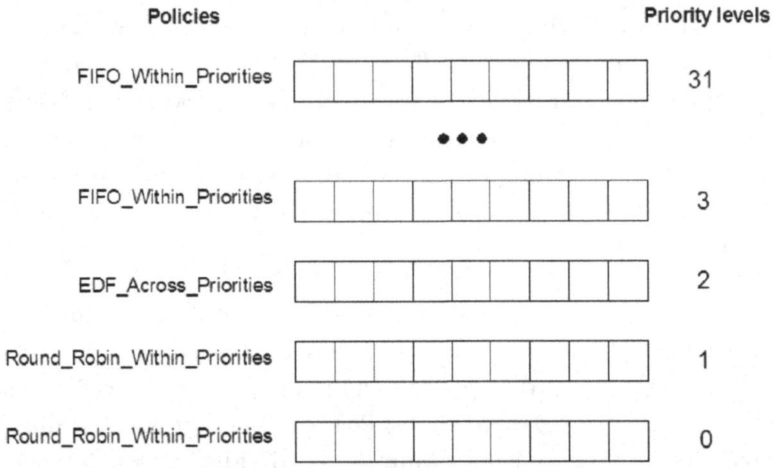

Policies   **Priority levels**

FIFO_Within_Priorities   [ ][ ][ ][ ][ ][ ][ ][ ]   31

● ● ●

FIFO_Within_Priorities   [ ][ ][ ][ ][ ][ ][ ][ ]   3

EDF_Across_Priorities   [ ][ ][ ][ ][ ][ ][ ][ ]   2

Round_Robin_Within_Priorities   [ ][ ][ ][ ][ ][ ][ ][ ]   1

Round_Robin_Within_Priorities   [ ][ ][ ][ ][ ][ ][ ][ ]   0

Figure 8.3 Example of an application using several different dispatching policies

8.6 Ravenscar

The richness of the Ada language provides numerous features that may not be compliant with the analysis methods available in *current* real-time scheduling theory. For example, in the previous sections, we have shown that Ada allows a program to assign a different dispatching protocol to each priority level. Use of such features may lead to the development of an application that cannot be analyzed with the feasibility tests such as the worst case response time feasibility test for fixed priority scheduling presented in Chapter 7.

We must ensure that our application meets all the assumptions of the feasibility tests we use. To meet these requirements, we must be sure not to use an Ada feature that violates some feasibility test assumption. Fortunately, Ada provides a mechanism which performs this check automatically: the Ravenscar profile.

Ravenscar is a profile which defines a subset of the Ada language that is compliant with fixed priority scheduling feasibility tests.[1] A **profile** is a set of restrictions a program must meet. Restrictions are expressed with pragmas that are checked at compile time and enforced at execution time. We use the following pragma to activate *all* of the restrictions in the Ravenscar profile:

pragma profile(Ravenscar);

---

[1] The Ravenscar profile is described in section D.13.1 of the Ada Reference Manual.

This one pragma is equivalent to the following collection of pragmas:

```
pragma Task_Dispatching_Policy (FIFO_Within_Priorities);
pragma Locking_Policy (Ceiling_Locking);
pragma Detect_Blocking;
pragma Restrictions (
    No_Abort_Statements,
    No_Dynamic_Attachment,
    No_Dynamic_Priorities,
    No_Implicit_Heap_Allocations,
    No_Local_Protected_Objects,
    No_Local_Timing_Events,
    No_Protected_Type_Allocators,
    No_Relative_Delay,
    No_Requeue_Statements,
    No_Select_Statements,
    No_Specific_Termination_Handlers,
    No_Task_Allocators,
    No_Task_Hierarchy,
    No_Task_Termination,
    Simple_Barriers,
    Max_Entry_Queue_Length => 1,
    Max_Protected_Entries => 1,
    Max_Task_Entries => 0,
    No_Dependence => Ada.Asynchronous_Task_Control,
    No_Dependence => Ada.Calendar,
    No_Dependence => Ada.Execution_Time.Group_Budget,
    No_Dependence => Ada.Execution_Time.Timers,
    No_Dependence => Ada.Task_Attributes);
```

Together, these restrictions help make it possible to perform a static analysis of an Ada program. Some of these restrictions are directly related to the scheduling analysis with fixed priority scheduling feasibility tests presented in Chapter 7. In particular:

1. Restrictions enforced by the pragmas Task_Dispatching_Policy (FIFO_Within_Priorities) and No_Dynamic_Priorities require that all tasks are scheduled by preemptive, fixed priority scheduling.
2. Restrictions enforced by the pragma Locking_Policy (Ceiling_Locking) ensure that protected objects are shared between tasks according to the ICPP protocol. This pragma makes it possible to give an upper bound on the time each task waits to access protected objects.
3. Restrictions enforced by No_Task_Hierarchy and No_Task_Allocators forbid dynamic task allocations and allow task declarations only at the library level. These constraints help to produce a critical instant, an instant in which all tasks are started at the same time. The critical instant is a major assumption of most of the feasibility tests (see Section 7.3).

4. Restriction No_Relative_Delay disables the use of the relative delay statement to implement periodic release times. As we showed in Figure 8.1, the use of the relative delay to implement periodic task releases yields a cumulative drift away from the desired intervals.

5. Finally, the Ravenscar profile includes a number of restrictions that forbid non-deterministic temporal behaviors. These restrictions are necessary for determining the capacity (WCET) of each task. This is the case of the restrictions No_Task_Allocators, No_Protected_Type_Allocators, and No_Implicit_Heap_Allocation that forbid dynamic memory allocation, and also the restrictions No_Requeue_Statements and No_Select_Statement that prevent the use of overly complex (and non-deterministic) synchronization mechanisms.

These pragmas do not cover *all* fixed priority scheduling feasibility test assumptions. The Ravenscar profile does not specify how priorities are assigned to each task. The use of equation (7.3) to calculate the processor utilization factor requires that priorities must be assigned according to Rate Monotonic. However, such priority assignment is not required to use equation (7.4) to calculate worst case response times. Furthermore, both equations (7.3) and (7.4) assume periodic tasks, a property also not addressed by the Ravenscar profile.

These feasibility tests also require that we know the number of tasks in the application. Again, this information is not specified by the Ravenscar profile. We can, however, include the additional restriction Max_Tasks in our program to bound the number of tasks.

So while the Ravenscar profile does not provide checks for all the necessary restrictions, it is an excellent first step to ensure that a program is compliant with real-time scheduling theory assumptions. We still need to follow good software engineering principles that complement the tools provided by Ada.

Besides its schedulability analysis support, the Ravenscar profile also provides very significant size and speed improvements, both of which are important to real-time and embedded applications (Dobing, 1999; Shen and Baker, 1999).

8.7 POSIX 1003.1b and its Ada binding

In the previous sections of this chapter, we described how to use features in Ada's Real-Time Systems Annex to implement applications that are compliant with real-time scheduling theory. Since annexes are optional, some

Ada compilers and run-times may not provide support for this annex. Fortunately, another standard is available for Ada practitioners — POSIX.

POSIX is a standardized application programming interface (API) to an operating system similar to Unix (Vahalia, 1996). POSIX helps programmers port their Unix programs from one Unix operating system to another. Many programmers assume that only C programs may use the POSIX API. However, POSIX also defines a standard API for Ada programs. The POSIX standard is published by ISO and IEEE. Table 8.1 lists the chapters in the standard relevant to this discussion. Each chapter covers a family of Unix operating system facilities. Chapter 1003.1 and chapter 1003.2 are the most well known chapters. Chapter 1003.1 defines an operating system API that provides the usual Unix services such as **fork** and **exec**. Chapter 1003.2 defines programs or commands that Unix shells should provide.

Chapter	Content
POSIX 1003.1	System Application Program Interface
POSIX 1003.2	Shell and utilities
POSIX 1003.1b	Real-time extensions
POSIX 1003.1c	Threads
POSIX 1003.5	Ada POSIX binding

Table 8.1 *Some chapters of the POSIX 1003 standard*

In this book, we are most concerned with chapters 1003.1b, 1003.1c and 1003.5. Chapters 1003.1b and 1003.1c standardize concurrency and real-time features for C programs and chapter 1003.5 provides the Ada binding for the other chapters (including 1003.1b and 1003.1c).

Each chapter provides a set of services. A service may be mandatory or optional. Some of the services provided in chapter 1003.1b are:

- _POSIX_PRIORITY_SCHEDULING provides fixed priority scheduling resources.
- _POSIX_REALTIME_SIGNALS is related to Unix signals which cannot be lost.
- _POSIX_ASYNCHRONOUS_IO provides subprograms to perform asynchronous input and output.
- _POSIX_TIMERS provides watchdog timer services. We'll use these timers to implement periodic task releases.
- _POSIX_SEMAPHORES contains several usual synchronization tools.

Implementations of chapter 1003.1b are available for most real-time operating systems including Lynx/OS^{TM}, VxWorks^{TM}, Solaris^{TM}, and QNX^{TM}. Unfortunately, most of the services in chapter 1003.1b are designated as optional — a major weakness of this POSIX chapter. However, POSIX is a flexible standard and POSIX programs (both C and Ada) are able to discover at run-time if the services they need are provided by the underlying operating system. In addition, POSIX compliant programs are able to adapt themselves to the underlying operating system capabilities. For example, when a POSIX program starts, it can check how many priority levels the operating system provides and could then change its priority level assignments (see Section 8.7.2). Still, the large number of services not designated as mandatory may encourage the development of programs that are not portable.

There is a major difference between the Ada standard with its Ravenscar profile and the POSIX 1003 standard with its real-time extensions. Ada checks at compile time whether the application is compatible with services and resources of the underlying operating system. POSIX gives hints to the application so that it might adapt itself to the features and resources that are actually available. Another important difference for Ada programmers is related to the concurrency abstraction. POSIX relies on system processes rather than on Ada tasks. Rather than declaring tasks, the POSIX Ada programmer must use the more primitive `fork` mechanism to create the processes for their program.

8.7.1 Scheduling model

POSIX uses preemptive fixed priority scheduling that is quite similar to Ada's. Figure 8.4 illustrates the POSIX scheduling model. It is composed of several queues that store ready processes with each queue devoted to a given priority level. This model is identical to that of Ada depicted in Figure 8.2. A POSIX compliant system must provide at least 32 priority levels. At any time, the running process is chosen from among the processes of the highest non-empty priority level queue.

POSIX dispatching is also similar to Ada's. When a given priority queue is selected, the choice of the process to run is performed according to a policy. In a POSIX compliant operating system, we usually at least find the following three policies:

1. `SCHED_FIFO`. This policy is quite similar to the `FIFO_Within_Priorities` scheduling policy of Ada. But instead of dispatching Ada tasks we dispatch Unix processes. With this policy, ready processes in a given priority level get the processor according to their order in the FIFO queue. The process at the head of the queue runs first and keeps the processor until it executes some statement that blocks it, explicitly releases the processor, or finishes.

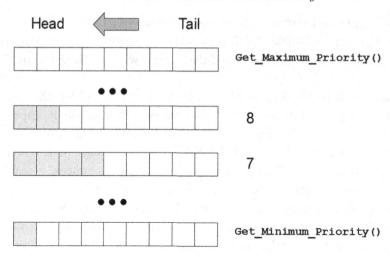

Figure 8.4 POSIX 1003.1b scheduling model

2. SCHED_RR. This policy provides a round-robin mechanism inside a priority level. It can be seen as a SCHED_FIFO policy but with a time quantum and some extra rules on queue management. A time quantum is a maximum duration that a process can run on the processor before being preempted by another process of the same queue. When the quantum is exhausted, the preempted process is moved from the head to the tail of the queue and the new process at the head of the queue is dispatched.

3. SCHED_OTHER. The behavior of this policy is not defined in the POSIX standard. It is implementation-defined. Sometimes, this policy provides a time-sharing scheduler. This policy is used by Linux for all processes with a priority level of 0. These processes are put in a SCHED_OTHER queue. With Linux, the process in the SCHED_OTHER queue that has waited longest for the processor is dispatched first.

Different operating systems can implement the POSIX scheduling policy differently. For example, some operating systems allow each individual process to specify the policy under which it is scheduled, while others do not.

In VxWorks 5.3, the quantum can be initialized by programmers with the kernelTimeSlice operation. By default, the quantum is equal to zero and all VxWorks tasks are SCHED_FIFO tasks. If a programmer changes the quantum with kernelTimeSlice, then all tasks in the application become SCHED_RR tasks. In contrast to VxWorks, Solaris allows us to specify a given policy for each Solaris process (Mauro and Dougall, 2001).

As we mentioned earlier, Linux also implements POSIX 1003. Priority level 0 is devoted to SCHED_OTHER processes. Processes which have a priority level between 1 and 99 can be scheduled either with SCHED_FIFO or SCHED_RR.

Due to all these implementation differences, an Ada POSIX compliant application is generally not as portable as an Ada compliant application. The portability issue is exacerbated when the operating system also implements POSIX 1003.1c — the POSIX chapter related to threads. Processes and threads are distinguished by their address spaces — each process has its own address space while threads share an address space. Depending on the operating system, POSIX threads may be implemented either as kernel threads or as user-level threads (Anderson *et al.*, 1992; Mauro and Dougall, 2001). This may also change the scheduling of the application.

Programmers must carefully check how POSIX (process or thread) scheduling is actually implemented in order to analyze the schedulability of their applications.

8.7.2 *POSIX Application Programming Interface*

Using the Ada binding POSIX 1003.5, Ada programmers can write and run POSIX 1003 applications. In this section we will look at two package specifications that are a small part of Florist, a POSIX 1003.5 implementation written by Baker and Oh (1997) for the GNAT compiler (see Chapter 9).

Implementing periodic POSIX processes

Package POSIX.Timers provides the Ada bindings for the POSIX 1003 service _POSIX_TIMERS. Here is a portion of that package.

```ada
with POSIX. Signals;
package POSIX.Timers is

   type Clock_ID is private;
   type Timer_ID is private;

   Clock_Realtime : constant Clock_ID;

   procedure Set_Initial
     (State   : in out Timer_State;
      Initial : in     POSIX.Timespec);

   procedure Set_Interval
     (State    : in out Timer_State;
      Interval : in     POSIX.Timespec);
```

```ada
function Get_Interval
   (State : in Timer_State)
    return POSIX.Timespec;

procedure Set_Time
   (Clock : in Clock_ID;
    Value : in POSIX.Timespec);
function Get_Time
   (Clock : in Clock_ID := Clock_Realtime)
    return POSIX.Timespec;

function Create_Timer
   (Clock : in Clock_ID;
    Event : in POSIX.Signals.Signal_Event)
    return Timer_ID;
procedure Arm_Timer
   (Timer     : in Timer_ID;
    Options   : in Timer_Options;
    New_State : in Timer_State);
    ...
private
    ...
end POSIX.Timers;
```

Like package `Ada.Real_Time`, package `POSIX.Timers` provides subprograms to handle time. This POSIX package allows Ada programmers to activate timers. Timers are used to implement periodic releases by waking up a process after a delay (Harbour *et al.*, 1997). Let's look at an example. The following program demonstrates how to use a timer to implement a periodic process with a period of one second.

```ada
with POSIX;          use POSIX;
with POSIX.Signals;  use POSIX.Signals;
with POSIX.Timers;   use POSIX.Timers;
with Text_IO;        use Text_IO;
procedure Posix_Timer_Example is

   -- The job carried out by the periodic process
   procedure Run_Periodic_Job_Of_The_Process is
   begin
      Put_Line("Periodic task is released and executes its job");
   end Run_Periodic_Job_Of_The_Process;

   Info       : POSIX.Signals.Signal_Info;
   Waited_Set : POSIX.Signals.Signal_Set;
   Event      : POSIX.Signals.Signal_Event;
   Timerid    : POSIX.Timers.Timer_Id;
   Timerdata  : POSIX.Timers.Timer_State;
   Options    : POSIX.Timers.Timer_Options;
```

```
Nanosecond_Period   :  Nanoseconds  :=  0;
Second_Period       :  Seconds      :=  1;
Period              :  POSIX.Timespec;
```

begin

```
    -- Set up signal management

    POSIX.Signals.Set_Signal
        (Event => Event,
         Sig   => POSIX.Signals.SIGUSR1);
    POSIX.Signals.Set_Notification
        (Event  => Event,
         Notify => POSIX.Signals.Signal_Notification);
    POSIX.Signals.Delete_All_Signals (Waited_Set);
    POSIX.Signals.Add_Signal
        (Set => Waited_Set,
         Sig => POSIX.Signals.SIGUSR1);

    -- Create and initialize the timer to the period of the proces

    Timerid := POSIX.Timers.Create_Timer
                    (Clock => POSIX.Timers.Clock_Realtime,
                     Event => Event);

    Period := POSIX.To_Timespec (S  => Second_Period,
                                 NS => Nanosecond_Period);
    POSIX.Timers.Set_Initial
        (State   => Timerdata,
         Initial => Period);
    POSIX.Timers.Set_Interval
        (State    => Timerdata,
         Interval => Period);
    POSIX.Timers.Arm_Timer
        (Timer     => Timerid,
         Options   => Options,
         New_State => Timerdata);

    -- The periodic process
    loop
        -- Block until the signal is received
        Info := POSIX.Signals.Await_Signal (Waited_Set);
        -- Carry out the job of the periodic process
        Run_Periodic_Job_Of_The_Process;
    end loop;

end Posix_Timer_Example;
```

The first part of this program issues calls to various procedures in package
POSIX.Signals to set up the POSIX signal SIGUSR1 we have decided to
use for our timer. Then the program calls the function Create_Timer to

define a POSIX timer. The calls to `Set_Initial` and `Set_Interval` set up the timer so it will periodically raise the Unix signal `SIGUSR1`. We raise this signal once per second. POSIX timer delays can be expressed in seconds and nanoseconds. Of course, the actual precision will depend on the underlying operating system's clock. The POSIX timer is then activated by the call to procedure `ARM_Timer`.

The loop at the end of this example program implements our periodic process. The process calls function `Await_Signal` which blocks it until the timer sends a `SIGUSR1` signal to the process. The process then runs its job and starts the loop again.

Compare this example to program `A_Periodic_Task_Demo` on page 299 which uses only Ada constructs to execute a periodic job. POSIX requires a large number of variables and API calls to accomplish the same thing.

POSIX scheduling

Now let's look at how we can control scheduling policies in POSIX compliant Ada programs. Our second Florist package, `POSIX.Process_Scheduling`, allows programmers to customize the scheduling of their processes. Here is a portion of that package.

```
with POSIX. Process_Identification ;
package POSIX. Process_Scheduling is

    subtype Scheduling_Priority    is Integer;
    type    Scheduling_Parameters is private;

    function Get_Priority (Parameters : in Scheduling_Parameters)
       return Scheduling_Priority ;
    procedure Set_Priority
       (Parameters : in out Scheduling_Parameters;
        Priority   : in     Scheduling_Priority );

    type Scheduling_Policy is new Integer ;

    Sched_FIFO  : constant Scheduling_Policy := ...;
    Sched_RR    : constant Scheduling_Policy := ...;
    Sched_Other : constant Scheduling_Policy := ...;

    procedure Set_Scheduling_Parameters
       (Process    : in POSIX_Process_Identification . Process_ID ;
        Parameters : in Scheduling_Parameters );
    function Get_Scheduling_Parameters
       (Process : in POSIX_Process_Identification . Process_ID )
       return Scheduling_Parameters ;
```

```
procedure Set_Scheduling_Policy
   (Process      : in POSIX_Process_Identification . Process_ID ;
    New_Policy : in Scheduling_Policy ;
    Parameters : in Scheduling_Parameters );
function Get_Scheduling_Policy
   (Process : in POSIX_Process_Identification . Process_ID )
   return Scheduling_Policy ;

function Get_Maximum_Priority (Policy : in Scheduling_Policy )
   return Scheduling_Priority ;
function Get_Minimum_Priority (Policy : in Scheduling_Policy )
   return Scheduling_Priority ;
function Get_Round_Robin_Interval
   (Process : in POSIX_Process_Identification . Process_ID )
   return POSIX . Timespec ;
   ...
private
   ...
end POSIX . Process_Scheduling ;
```

This package contains subprograms to handle priority and policy. Functions **Get_Priority**, **Get_Scheduling_Parameters**, and **Get_Scheduling_Policy** read the current priority and scheduling policy of a given process. Processes are identified by unique numbers whose type is defined in the package POSIX.Process_Identification. In the same way, procedures **Set_Priority**, **Set_Scheduling_Parameters**, and **Set_Scheduling_Policy** change the priority and scheduling policy of a process.

Package POSIX.Process_Scheduling also defines subprograms that permit an application to adapt itself to the underlying operating system. Functions **Get_Maximum_Priority**, **Get_Minimum_Priority**, and **Get_Round_Robin_Interval** may be called to obtain the maximum priority level, the minimum priority level, and the quantum that will be applied to SCHED_RR processes.

The following program demonstrates how the operations in package Posix.Process_Scheduling can be used to query and change process scheduling characteristics. It first displays the priority level and the policy of the current process. Then it changes the process so that it is scheduled under the SCHED_FIFO policy with a priority level of 10.

```
with Ada . Text_IO ;                     use Ada . Text_IO ;
with Ada . Integer_Text_IO ;            use Ada . Integer_Text_IO ;
with POSIX . Process_Identification ;   use POSIX . Process_Identificatio
with POSIX . Process_Scheduling ;       use POSIX . Process_Scheduling ;
procedure Posix_Scheduling_Example is

   procedure Display_Policy (Policy : in Scheduling_Policy ) is
   begin
      if Policy = SCHED_RR then
```

```
        Put  ("/SCHED_RR" );
    elsif  Policy = SCHED_OTHER then
        Put("/SCHED_OTHER" );
    elsif  Policy = SCHED_FIFO then
        Put("/SCHED_FIFO" );
    else
        Put("/unknown policy" );
    end if;
end Display_Policy;


    Pid    : Process_ID;
    Sched  : Scheduling_Parameters;

begin
    -- Read current process unique identificator
    Pid:= Get_Process_Id;

    -- Display the default priority and scheduling parameters
    -- of a process in the current operating system
    Sched := Get_Scheduling_Parameters (Pid);
    Put ("Default priority/policy on this POSIX operating system : ");
    Put ( Get_Priority (Sched));
    Display_Policy (Policy => Get_Scheduling_Policy (Pid));
    New_Line;

    -- Change both priority and policy
    -- Apply SCHED_FIFO with a priority level of 10
    Set_Priority (Parameters => Sched,
                   Priority    => 10);
    Set_Scheduling_Policy (Process    => Pid,
                           New_Policy => SCHED_FIFO,
                           Parameters => Sched);
    Set_Scheduling_Parameters (Process    => Pid,
                               Parameters => Sched);

    -- Display the updated priority and scheduling parameters
    Put ("Updated priority/policy : ");
    Put ( Get_Priority (Sched));
    Display_Policy (Policy => Get_Scheduling_Policy (Pid));
    New_Line;
end Posix_Scheduling_Example;
```

Handling shared resources

We have now seen how to implement a periodic process and how to run it with a given priority under a particular scheduling policy. Package **POSIX.Semaphores** provides semaphores that can be used to implement shared resources. We can use these semaphores to provide communication and synchronization between processes. If the threads extension is supported, semaphores may also be used with threads.

Section 4.7.1 provided a brief description of the semaphore and how it might be implemented as a protected object. In Section 7.3 we used the semaphore in our descriptions of protocols for accessing shared resources. POSIX semaphores provide the necessary tools for implementing the Priority Ceiling Protocol (PCP).

POSIX **mutexes** and **condition variables** provide a second means of controlling access to resources shared by threads. They are more efficient than semaphores and thus recommended when using POSIX threads. See Gallmeister (1995) for more information on sharing resources with POSIX.

8.8 POSIX implementation of the car application

As our final POSIX example, we return to our car application of Chapter 7. On page 304 we presented an Ada solution based on periodic tasks. Now we'll write an equivalent program using periodic POSIX processes. We use the same task characteristics listed on page 304.

We take a similar approach to our earlier solution of using a generic unit as a pattern for our three different periodic jobs. Rather than use a generic package containing a task type, our POSIX implementation is based on a generic procedure that implements a periodic process. Here is its specification:

```
with POSIX;
with POSIX.Process_Scheduling;  use POSIX.Process_Scheduling;
generic
    with procedure Run;
    Priority_Parameter  : Scheduling_Priority;
    Policy_Parameter    : Scheduling_Policy;
    Nanosecond_Period   : POSIX.Nanoseconds;
    Second_Period       : POSIX.Seconds;
procedure Generic_Periodic_POSIX_Process;
-- This procedure contains an "infinite loop" that calls
-- procedure Run (the job of the process) once every period
```

This specification includes five parameters. Parameter **Run** is the procedure that contains the code we want executed periodically. The remaining four parameters specify the process priority, the scheduling policy, and the period. The period is expressed in seconds and nanoseconds.

The body of our generic procedure uses the constructs for periodic release and scheduling priority and policy developed in our previous two examples.

```
with POSIX;                           use POSIX;
with POSIX.Signals;                   use POSIX.Signals;
with POSIX.Timers;                    use POSIX.Timers;
with POSIX.Process_Identification;    use POSIX.Process_Identificatio
with POSIX.Process_Scheduling;        use POSIX.Process_Scheduling;
```

procedure Generic_Periodic_POSIX_Process **is**

```
Info          :  POSIX.Signals.Signal_Info;
Waited_Set    :  POSIX.Signals.Signal_Set;
Event         :  POSIX.Signals.Signal_Event;
Timerid       :  POSIX.Timers.Timer_Id;
Timerdata     :  POSIX.Timers.Timer_State;
Options       :  POSIX.Timers.Timer_Options;

Pid       :  Process_ID;
Sched     :  Scheduling_Parameters;
Period    :  POSIX.Timespec;
```

begin

```
-- Set up signal management
POSIX.Signals.Set_Signal (Event => Event,
                          Sig   => SIGUSR1);
POSIX.Signals.Set_Notification
     (Event  => Event,
      Notify => POSIX.Signals.Signal_Notification);
POSIX.Signals.Delete_All_Signals (Waited_Set);
POSIX.Signals.Add_Signal (Set => Waited_Set,
                          SIG => SIGUSR1);

-- Create and initialize the timer to the period
Timerid := POSIX.Timers.Create_Timer
               (Clock => POSIX.Timers.Clock_Realtime,
                Event => Event);
Period := POSIX.To_Timespec (S  => Second_Period,
                             NS => Nanosecond_Period);
POSIX.Timers.Set_Initial
   (State   => Timerdata,
    Initial => Period);
POSIX.Timers.Set_Interval
   (State    => Timerdata,
    Interval => Period);
POSIX.Timers.Arm_Timer
   (Timerid, Options, Timerdata);

-- Change priority and policy
Pid    := Get_Process_Id;
Sched  := Get_Scheduling_Parameters (Pid);
Set_Priority (Parameters => Sched,
              Priority    => Priority_Parameter);
Set_Scheduling_Policy (Process    => Pid,
                       New_Policy => Policy_Parameter,
                       Parameters => Sched);
Set_Scheduling_Parameters (Process    => Pid,
                           Parameters => Sched);
```

```
    -- The periodic process
    loop
        Run;  -- Call the procedure with the code for this job
        Info := POSIX. Signals. Await_Signal (Waited_Set );
    end loop;
end Generic_Periodic_POSIX_Process;
```

Finally, here is the program that makes use of the generic procedure to create and run three POSIX processes.

```
with POSIX;        use POSIX;
with POSIX. Process_Scheduling;
    use POSIX. Process_Scheduling;
with POSIX. Process_Identification;
    use POSIX. Process_Identification;
with POSIX. Unsafe_Process_Primitives;
with Ada. Text_IO;     use Ada. Text_IO;
with Generic_Periodic_Posix_Process;
procedure Posix_Car_Example is

    -- The following three parameterless procedures are stubs for
    -- the actual code that runs in the car

    procedure Read_Speed is
    begin
        Put_Line (" Tspeed reads speed sensor" );
    end Read_Speed;

    procedure Monitor_Engine is
    begin
        Put_Line (" Tengine performs engine monitoring algorithm" )
    end Monitor_Engine;

    procedure Display_Speed is
    begin
     Put_Line (" Tdisplay displays the speed of the car" );
    end Display_Speed;

    -- Instantiate an " infinite loop" procedure
    -- for each of our three processes

    procedure Tdisplay is new Generic_Periodic_POSIX_Process
        ( Run                    => Display_Speed ,
          Priority_Parameter => 12,
          Policy_Parameter   => SCHED_FIFO,
          Nanosecond_Period  => 1_000_000 ,
          Second_Period      => 0);
    procedure Tspeed is new Generic_Periodic_POSIX_Process
        ( Run                    => Read_Speed ,
          Priority_Parameter => 11,
```

```
         Policy_Parameter     => SCHED_FIFO,
         Nanosecond_Period    => 2_500_000,
         Second_Period        => 0);
procedure Tengine is new Generic_Periodic_POSIX_Process
    (Run                  => Monitor_Engine,
     Priority_Parameter => 10,
     Policy_Parameter     => SCHED_FIFO,
     Nanosecond_Period    => 5_000_000,
     Second_Period        => 0);

Pid  :  Process_ID;
Sched   :  Scheduling_Parameters;

begin

    -- Priority for "environment procedure"
    -- (for main POSIX process)
    Pid    := Get_Process_Id;
    Sched := Get_Scheduling_Parameters (Pid);
    Set_Priority (Parameters => Sched,
                   Priority    => 20);
    Set_Scheduling_Policy (Process      => Pid,
                           New_Policy => SCHED_FIFO,
                           Parameters => Sched);
    Set_Scheduling_Parameters (Process      => Pid,
                               Parameters => Sched);


    -- The main process creates a new child process
    Pid := POSIX.Unsafe_Process_Primitives.Fork;

    if Pid = Null_Process_ID then -- the child process?
        Tengine; -- Execute the engine process
    else
        -- The main process creates a second child
        Pid := POSIX.Unsafe_Process_Primitives.Fork;

        if Pid = Null_Process_ID then -- the child process?
            Tdisplay; -- Execute the display process
        else
            -- The main process creates a third child
            Pid:= POSIX.Unsafe_Process_Primitives.Fork;

            if Pid = Null_Process_ID then -- the child process?
                Tspeed;    -- Execute the speed process
            end if;
        end if;
    end if;
end if;
```

```
-- All child processes start to work after the
-- higher priority main process completes!
Put_Line ("Processes will start after " &
          "the main process completes!");
end Posix_Car_Example;
```

Creating POSIX processes is more complex than creating Ada tasks. The first set of statements in this program assigns high priority level to the process. Then, a call to the POSIX function **Fork** is performed. This function creates a new *child* process. The child process executes the same code as its parent beginning with the statement that follows the call to function **Fork**. So after the child process is created, the child and its parent both execute the if statement that tests the value of variable **Pid**. This if statement allows a process to determine if it is the child or the parent. In the child process, function **Fork** returns a value of **Null_Process_ID**. In the parent process, function **Fork** returns the process ID of its child — a value not equal to **Null_Process_ID**. The child process then calls procedure **Tengine** while the main process makes a second call to function **Fork**. The same logic is used to differentiate between the second child and its parent. The second child calls procedure **Tdisplay** while the main process makes a third call to function **Fork**. The logic is repeated with the third child calling procedure **Tspeed** while the main process displays a message and finishes.

Each process run is one of the three instantiated procedures implementing a periodic task with a given priority and scheduling policy. Similar to the Ada tasking implementation, we choose to assign priority level 20 to the main process. This higher priority level ensures that the three processes will not start running before the main process has completed. Again, this approach makes our program compliant with the critical instant assumption.

8.9 Ada tasks versus POSIX processes

Both Ada and POSIX provide compliance with real-time scheduling theory. In this section, we briefly compare these two approaches to writing real-time applications.

POSIX has two major advantages. It is supported by a large number of real-time operating systems. And, as it is language-independent, it allows us to combine processes written in different languages. Unfortunately, writing real-time applications with POSIX has some drawbacks. POSIX scheduling was intended for process or thread scheduling and we saw that POSIX scheduling may be implemented differently in several operating systems. As we saw in our car application, we must do far more work to write a periodic POSIX process than we do for an Ada task. The Ada compiler is responsible for expanding our tasks into the API calls we have to make ourselves when using POSIX (see Section 9.1 for more information on expansion).

Both POSIX and Ada are intended to write portable programs. But since many of the necessary POSIX constructs are optional, we expect that Ada achieves a higher level of portability.

The relationship between Ada tasks and POSIX processes is implementation-defined. So it is best to not mix Ada tasks or protected objects with POSIX processes and threads. With all of the negative aspects of POSIX, we might question if Ada programmers should use the POSIX Ada binding to write their real-time applications. The answer is yes, if no Ada 2005 compliant run-time and compiler is available for the underlying hardware and run-time system.

In Chapter 9, we discuss run-time systems and some tools that are available to write and verify concurrent real-time Ada applications.

Summary

- Two standards are available for programmers to write real-time Ada applications that can be compliant with the real-time scheduling theory: Ada 2005 and POSIX 1003.1b.

- With Ada:
  - Periodic task release times must be implemented with the `delay until` statement.
  - A task has a base priority and an active priority.
  - Base priorities of tasks and priorities of protected objects are defined with the `Priority` pragma.
  - Scheduling of tasks is specified by dispatching policies. Ada provides several dispatching policies.
  - The real-time scheduling theory compliance of an Ada program can be enforced by the Ravenscar profile.

- With POSIX:
  - The scheduling model is similar to Ada.
  - POSIX timers may be used to implement periodic task release times.
  - POSIX is flexible: it allows an Ada program to adapt itself to the underlying operating system.
  - We do not handle tasks but processes or threads.

- The portability level of an Ada program written with POSIX may be less than an Ada program written with Ada 2005.

Exercises

8.1 Contrast type `Time` in package `Ada.Calendar` to type `Time` in package `Ada.Real_Time`.

8.2 List what mechanisms enforce real-time scheduling compliance.

8.3 Explain the difference between cumulative drift and local drift with respect to periodic tasks.

8.4 Why should we use the `delay until` statement instead of the `delay` statement?

8.5 Write an Ada program that displays the following values defined in the package `System` (see page 301) on *your* computer.

- `Max_Priority`
- `Max_Interrupt_Priority`
- The lowest value of subtype `Any_Priority`
- The highest value of subtype `Any_Priority`
- The lowest value of subtype `Priority`
- The highest value of subtype `Priority`
- The lowest value of subtype `Interrupt_Priority`
- The highest value of subtype `Interrupt_Priority`

8.6 What pragmas must we include in an Ada program to be compliant with fixed priority scheduling and ICPP?

8.7 What is the major advantage of using the Ravenscar profile? Describe at least one disadvantage of using this profile.

8.8 In this exercise you will practice with POSIX 1003 scheduling policies. We assume a Linux operating system that implements the POSIX 1003 standard with a scheduling model with 100 priority levels (from 0 to 99, with 99 being the highest priority). Priority level 0 is devoted to time-sharing processes. All processes that have a 0 priority level are scheduled according to the `SCHED_OTHER` policy. The Linux `SCHED_OTHER` policy schedules tasks according to how long it has been since they last had the processor. The process dispatched first from the queue at priority level 0 is the one that has waited the longest for the processor. This waiting time is not just their waiting time in the ready queue for priority 0. It includes the time that the process may have been blocked for a resource or for input or output. Processes which have a priority level between 1 and 99 are scheduled either with `SCHED_FIFO` or `SCHED_RR`. Of course, the processes in priority queues 1 through 99 are dispatched before any processes in the lower priority queue 0. We assume a quantum of one unit of time for the `SCHED_RR` policy. The scheduling is preemptive.

Given the following process characteristics:

Name	Capacity	Release time	Priority	Policy
other1	8	0	0	SCHED_OTHER
rr1	5	2	3	SCHED_RR
rr2	5	2	3	SCHED_RR
fifo1	3	4	5	SCHED_FIFO
fifo2	3	3	2	SCHED_FIFO
fifo3	2	4	5	SCHED_FIFO

Fill in Figure 8.5 of the schedule from time 0 to 25 by darkening in the squares where a particular process is running on the processor.

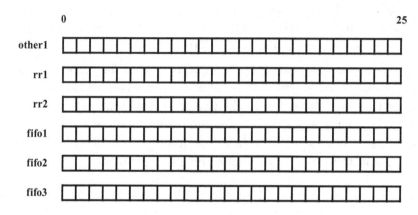

Figure 8.5 Drawing to fill

8.9 What are advantages and disavantages of using Ada tasks or POSIX 1003.b processes to implement real-time applications?

8.10 In this exercise you will practice with POSIX 1003 scheduling policies. We assume a system composed of two periodic processes T_1 and T_2 defined with $S_1 = 0, S_2 = 2, C_1 = 1, C_2 = 2, P_1 = 8$, and $P_2 = 7$. We also assume that the process deadlines are equal to their periods ($\forall i : D_i = P_i$).

The operating system is a POSIX 1003.1b operating system with 32 priority levels (priority levels ranging from 0 to 31). Priority level 31 is the highest priority level. This operating system provides POSIX 1003.1b SCHED_FIFO, SCHED_RR, and SCHED_OTHER policies. In the case of the SCHED_RR, the quantum is about one unit of time. SCHED_OTHER implements a time-sharing scheduling. The scheduling is preemptive.

1. Check the schedulability of the periodic process set.
2. Besides T_1 and T_2, the processor owns a set of aperiodic processes defined as follows:

Name	Capacity	Release time	Priority	Policy
fifo1	4	5	20	SCHED_FIFO
other1	5	0	0	SCHED_OTHER
fifo2	3	4	5	SCHED_FIFO
rr1	3	3	7	SCHED_RR
rr2	3	4	7	SCHED_RR

3. Assign a priority level to processes T_1 and T_2 which allows these periodic processes to meet their deadlines and which is compliant to the operating system properties (related to POSIX 1003.1b scheduling model). Explain your choice.
4. Draw the scheduling of all processes (both periodic and aperiodic processes) from time 0 to time 30.

8.11 In the implementation of the `Generic_Periodic_Task` package on pages 303 and 304, each synchronous periodic task computes its own first release time by a local call to the `Clock` subprogram. When the number of tasks is large, the resulting scheduling of this set of synchronous periodic tasks may be different from the one we can expect. Why? Propose an adaptation of this package to solve this problem.

9

Tools for building and verifying real-time applications

In the previous chapters, we introduced both Ada concurrency features (tasks, protected objects, and rendezvous) and advanced features to support real-time constructs (notion of priority, protocols to bound priority inversion, and task dispatching policies). Our Ada applications do not run alone. They execute within a run-time configuration. A **run-time configuration** consists of the processor that executes our application and the environment in which that application operates. This environment includes memory systems, input/output devices, and operating systems.

An important early design goal of Ada was to provide a compilation system that can create from one Ada program different executables that run in an equivalent way within a wide variety of run-time configurations. With little or no modifications to the Ada code, the same program should run on a variety of platforms — from small embedded platforms, such as those based on 8-bit micro-controllers and PDAs, to single processor microcomputers, multi-core processors, and multiprocessor systems. The run-time configuration may include no operating system; may include an RTOS (real-time operating system) like VxWorks™, LynxOS™, ORK+, MaRTE OS, and RTEMS; or may include a complete general purpose operating system such as Linux, Windows™, and Mac OS™.

In this chapter, we detail how Ada concurrency constructs are supported by the Ada run-time environment. We first introduce a generic architecture for mapping Ada constructs onto an operating system. Then, we examine three different run-times for the open-source Ada compiler GNAT. The run-time environment plays a large role in the timing and scheduling of tasks. In our final section, we discuss how to validate the schedule of our application.

9.1 Ada run-times to implement real-time applications

A run-time or **run-time system** (RTS) is a collection of code designed to support the execution of an application. A run-time system provides services for common operations (such as input and output) and the implementation of complex programming language features (such as the automatic managing of controlled types, exceptions, and tasking). The run-time system provides an abstraction that hides the complexity and variability of services offered by different operating systems. When we compile our application, the compiler inserts calls to run-time system functions and procedures that implement services and language features for a particular run-time configuration.

In this section, we discuss how the run-time system supports Ada constructs in a portable way. Let us imagine that we want to write an implementation of the Ada run-time system. We'll begin this thought experiment with some questions to help us see how to build it.

Question 1: How are Ada features handled?

The Ada compiler translates our Ada program into machine language that is later run on the target computer. This translation is a complex process that usually involves many intermediate steps. Each step translates abstract constructs into one or more simpler steps. Even a seemingly elementary construct like an assignment statement may map to a number of different machine language instructions to carry out the mathematical operations and conditional logic to handle potential range violations. Such translation of abstract to concrete is common in other domains. In Section 1.1.2 we developed several sets of actions for cooks in a kitchen. The human cooks will later refine these steps into simpler actions (taking an object, using it, cleaning it, taking another one, etc.).

In Chapter 3 we introduced the task life cycle. Translating a task declaration and body into machine language is a complex process. The compiler will create the necessary code to implement the task. This code will include calls to functions and procedures in the run-time system to carry out the creation, activation, execution, and finalization of the task.

Consider this simple piece of Ada code:

```ada
procedure Simple_Task is
    task A_Task;
    task body A_Task is
    begin
        null;
    end A_Task;

begin
    null;
end Simple_Task;
```

The GNAT Ada compiler allows us to view the intermediate steps of the compilation process. The compiler can produce a pseudo-source listing of the expanded code.[1] Here is a *portion* of the expanded code generated by the GNAT compiler for procedure `Simple_Task`:

```
-- A pseudo-source listing of expanded code produced
-- by the Ada compiler
with system.system__parameters;
with system.system__tasking;
with system.system__task_info;
with ada.ada__real_time;
--   ...
procedure simple_task is

    procedure simple_task___clean is
    begin
        --   ...
        return;
    end simple_task___clean;
begin
    system__soft_links__enter_master.all;
    _chain : aliased system__tasking__activation_chain;
    --   ...
    task type simple_task__a_taskTK;
    --   ...
    type simple_task__a_taskTKV is limited record
        _task_id : system__tasking__task_id;
    end record;
    --   ...
    procedure simple_task__a_taskTKB (_task : access
       simple_task__a_taskTKV) is
    begin
        --   ...
    at end
        simple_task__a_taskTK___clean;
    end simple_task__a_taskTKB;

    a_taskTKE := true;
    $system__tasking__stages__activate_tasks
        (_chain'unchecked_access);
    null;
    return;
at end
    simple_task___clean;
end simple_task;
```

This listing is only a small portion of the pseudo-source code that is generated. The purpose of the code generated is to perform each of the actions

---

[1] By using the -gnatDG compilation flag.

discussed when we introduced the life cycle of a task in Chapter 3. This expanded code has dependencies on the **Ada** and **System** package hierarchies. The latter is dedicated to implementation-specific source code to support Ada constructs and provides a major portion of the run-time system.

Similar code is generated to support protected objects, rendezvous, controlled types, to add range checks on arrays or arithmetic operations, pointers, etc.

Question 2: Do I need to use the operating system scheduling services?

As we have seen in the previous section, the compiler expands source code into simpler elements — a task is expanded into a number of data structures and subprogram calls. The operating system may provide some support for task creation, management, and termination. In Section 3.5, we mentioned that the Ada run-time relies on the operating system concurrency mechanisms, but did not justify this choice. You may wonder at first if this support from the operating system is needed. Ada has specific semantics such as the priority range of tasks, the numerical value of the highest priority level, and support of scheduling policies that may be different from the target operating system. Why can't the Ada run-time system simply provide these semantics directly?

We will use an example to illustrate why the Ada run-time system cannot always provide our task scheduling. Imagine the following run-time system design. Each Ada task is managed as a specific data structure maintained by the Ada run-time system. Each task is "scheduled" by the Ada run-time system — it is given processor time whenever required (e.g. upon a timing event). The run-time system maintains its own ready queues and entry queues. To support context switching between tasks, all we need is a way to store the current task's context (typically the current value of all the processor registers) and load the context of the next task in the ready queue.

Now consider the following application:

```
with Ada.Text_IO;  use Ada.Text_IO;
procedure Process_Blocking is

    task Hello;

    task body Hello is
    begin
        loop
            Put_Line ("Hello");
            delay 0.5;
        end loop;
    end Hello;
```

```
task Wait;

task body Wait is
    C : Character;
begin
    Get (C);
    Put_Line ("Got " & C);
end Wait;

begin
    null;
end Process_Blocking;
```

This program has two simple tasks: `Hello` periodically displays a string. `Wait` waits for the user to enter a character and hit the "return" key. What happens when we run this program? We expect the string "Hello" to be displayed periodically and whenever a character is entered, the text "Got" and the character is displayed.

Now, let us imagine we compile this code with our Ada run-time system we just described. Each task is replaced by a procedure that is executed from time to time. Suppose when we execute the program that the run-time system first schedules task `Hello`. This task displays its greeting and then executes its delay statement. The run-time system saves the context of task `Hello`, finds task `Wait` in its ready queue, and loads its context. Task `Wait` executes a call to procedure `Get`. Input is handled by the operating system. The operating system will halt our program until the user enters a character. When the program is blocked, its run-time system cannot execute and schedule another ready task. The whole program seems stuck until the user inputs some data. Only when the user enters a character will our program be unblocked and the character displayed. As the program is no longer blocked, our run-time system can handle the completion of task `Wait` and schedule the next execution of task `Hello`.

This is not the behavior we expected of our program. We expected task `Hello` to continuously display its message while task `Wait` waited for input. The problem is that the operating system sees our program as a single process that *it* schedules to run or not. The operating system is not aware of the run-time system code within the program that provides scheduling of the Ada tasks.[2]

When running a concurrent Ada program under a general or real-time operating system,we must make our tasks visible to the operating system

---

[2] For more details, see Anderson *et al.* (1992).

and allow it to schedule them. We can, however, run a concurrent Ada program on a target without an operating system — what are called *bare board* systems. In this case, the tasking semantics must be included in the run-time system.

Question 3: How are portability issues handled?

The Ada language defines uniform semantics for all its constructs, including concurrency. In some cases, the target operating system may not support all the concurrency features available in Ada. Ada is a modular language. In Section 8.6, we briefly introduced the **restriction** mechanism that allows us to reduce the constructs allowed.

These restrictions allow us to indicate that a specific Ada run-time support needs only a subset of the available concurrency mechanisms. Furthermore, some elements of the language are designated as being optional. For example, a compiler vendor need not supply or support Annex D, which is necessary to build real-time applications. Since concurrency constructs are part of the language, the Ada compiler can detect the use of unsupported features, and reject programs that cannot be executed on the target system.

We sometimes need to know the limits of some types such as priority ranges or the precision of time-related types. The Ada standard requires that all of this information be defined in the two packages **System** and **Standard**. Here are some excerpts from these two packages.

```ada
package System is

   --  Excerpt from the System package, for Mac OS X target

   Max_Interrupt_Priority : constant Positive := 63;
   Max_Priority : constant Positive := Max_Interrupt_Priority - 1;

   subtype Any_Priority is Integer range 0 .. Max_Interrupt_Priori
   subtype Priority is Any_Priority range 0 .. Max_Priority;
   subtype Interrupt_Priority is Any_Priority
      range Priority'Last + 1 .. Max_Interrupt_Priority;

   Default_Priority : constant Priority :=
      (Priority'Last - Priority'First) / 2;
end System;

package Standard is

   --  Excerpt from the Standard package, as shown for Mac OS X

   type Duration is delta 0.000000001
      range -((2 ** 63 - 1) * 0.000000001) ..
            +((2 ** 63 - 1) * 0.000000001);
```

```
    for Duration'Small use 0.000000001;
end Standard;
```

These types define some implementation limits as bounds on Ada types. By carefully using all this information, it is possible to write Ada programs that remain portable across different implementations of the Ada run-time system. Should we exceed the capabilities of a particular run-time configuration, the Ada compiler will inform us.

Question 4: How do I write an Ada run-time?

From our answers to the previous questions, we come to the conclusion that the Ada run-time system is based on two levels of facilities:

1. A set of low-level routines and data structures that support the semantics of Ada constructs. The Ada compiler will map each element (task, protected object, etc.) to a set of statements that will use these routines and data structures.
2. A library supporting concurrency, provided with the target operating systems to support the concepts of threads (independent flows of execution), locks (to protect data against concurrent access), and semaphores.

Writing the expander inside a compiler is a large challenge. We need to understand precisely how the Ada source code is represented internally, and how to map it onto elementary low-level routines. A typical approach taken when writing a compiler is to isolate run-time configuration specific elements so as to maximize code reusability when porting the compiler to new run-time configurations. In addition, the low-level routines must rely on the operating system library for mapping tasks or protected objects onto lower-level mechanisms.

A good compiler design clearly separates the expansion phase from the run-time system. Figure 9.1 illustrates such a design. Application code and the code derived through expansion interact with a generic Ada run-time. This generic run-time system provides services to build all constructs. The generic run-time interacts with a target-specific library that hides all implementation details necessary to interact either with the concurrency library or directly with the operating system.

9.2 Some variants of the GNAT run-time

In this section, we explore different implementations of the GNAT run-time. GNAT is an Ada compiler, initially started as a project at the New York

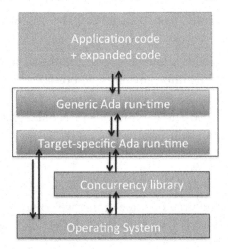

Figure 9.1 Layered design of an Ada program

University (see Schonberg and Banner, 1994, for the seminal work on the project). This compiler is now fully integrated in the GCC[3] collection of compilers, and supported by AdaCore.[4] We selected this compiler for our discussions because it is fully open source. We can analyze the source code of both the compiler and the run-time system.

Before we begin our discussion of GNAT run-times, let us mention that Ada and its real-time features are implemented and supported by numerous vendors. Aonix provides the ObjectAda compiler and support for the Ravenscar profile through its RAVEN[TM] line of run-time systems and compilers. IBM Rational's Apex Ada gives you a choice of three run-time systems: Wind River Tornado[TM], LynxOS[TM], and their own Rational Exec. Green Hills Software's Ada has three different versions of their Integrity[TM] RTOS. Irvine Compiler Corporation's Ada supports a variety of bare machine and RTOS environments. In addition to the three open source GNAT run-times that we discuss, AdaCore provides a variety of commercial run-time systems for embedded, real-time, and safety-critical applications.

9.2.1 Architecture of the GNAT run-time

The GNAT compiler targets a wide variety of operating systems, from bare board systems (without target operating systems) to large servers. GNAT supports more than 60 run-time configurations.

---

[3] A free software compiler, part of the GNU project, see `http://gcc.gnu.org`.
[4] See `http://www.adacore.com`.

To reduce portability cost and enhance maintainability, the architecture of the GNAT run-time follows the elements we outlined in Section 9.1. The run-time is made of two layers (see Giering and Baker, 1994, for some historical background on the design):

- **GNARL: the GNU Ada Run-time Library** is the upper layer. The higher level Ada constructs are expanded into calls to GNARL. Once expanded, the code of GNARL is treated as regular Ada code.
- **GNULL: GNU Low-Level interfaces** is the lower layer. It holds the portability layer that provides the interface to the host operating system. On a bare board system, GNULL provides all the necessary low level support of Ada semantics.

The combination of these two layers provides:

1. Support of Ada semantics: GNARL completes the host operating system constructs so as to support full Ada semantics precisely. Whenever possible, GNARL supports the Real-Time Systems Annex (see Chapter 8).
2. Separation of concerns: defining the run-time as a set of Ada packages called by the compiler allows one to separate compiler techniques from run-time concerns, easing the implementation of the run-time systems on a new operating system. It also allows incremental implementation — one may first implement a basic run-time, without concurrency, and then extend it to support a restricted tasking profile then full tasking capabilities.
3. Portability: an initial requirement of GNAT was that it was to be written in Ada as much as possible. This requirement was meant to provide a proof of concept of the compiler — it should be able to compile itself.[5] A second reason for this requirement was that all Ada checks are made on the Ada run-time itself. Target-specific code is isolated in the GNULL and kept as small as possible.
4. Efficiency: the run-time should be as efficient as possible and tailorable whenever possible. The run-time should avoid dependency on complex code patterns to ease analysis, required to meet the requirements of complex, critical applications.

In the following sections, we discuss three GNAT Ada run-times. We selected these particular run-times for two reasons. First, they are all part of open source projects so we can inspect the source code. Second, they illustrate the complete range of run-time system support of Ada constructs.

---

[5] This process is known as bootstrapping.

1. ORK+, a bare board Ravenscar run-time for mission-critical space systems based on the LEON2 processor.
2. MaRTE OS, a full Ada run-time and a companion RTOS that supports advanced scheduling algorithms for bare board x86 targets.
3. RTEMS, a full Ada run-time, based on a C RT-POSIX RTOS that supports a wide variety of processors and advanced tools like NFS or HTTP server, and a shell.

The distinction between bare boards and "regular" operating systems is thin. Usually, a bare board provides the minimum resources to schedule tasks. An RTOS adds some drivers and libraries but runs only one application. A full-fledged operating system like Linux allows us to run multiple programs. An RTOS is usually divided up into a core scheduler and additional services, hence a bare board system and libraries. A complete operating system like Linux boots up as a bare board, and then launches one particular service (called `init`) that allows it to spawn multiple processes.

9.2.2 ORK+, a bare board run-time

The Open Ravenscar Real-Time Kernel (ORK+)[6] is an open-source real-time kernel. ORK is an Ada run-time of reduced size and complexity used to develop high-integrity real-time applications in a subset of the Ada 2005 language compatible with the Ravenscar profile. ORK was originally developed under contract with the European Space Agency (ESA). It was based on Ada 95 and targeted to the ERC32 processor. The current version, ORK+, supports the Ada 2005 standard and the LEON2 processor.

The ERC32 and the LEON2 processors are two derivatives of the SPARC family of processors chosen by the European Space Agency. ESA selected this platform for its on-board mission systems. Because these systems operate outside of the Earth's atmosphere, these processors have been strengthened to resist radiation. The SPARC architecture permits the addition of mechanisms to recover from errors in memory induced by ionizing or electromagnetic perturbations.

ORK+ (see de la Puente *et al.*, 2000) is integrated as the lower-level interface of the GNAT run-time. The kernel and a modified run-time library are packaged together with the compiler and other tools into a comprehensive package. Hence, one can generate a full binary, ready to deploy, in one compilation step. The binary can be executed on either a real platform or a simulator.

[6] See `http://polaris.dit.upm.es/~ork/`.

ORK+ implements only the elements required to support the Ravenscar profile on a monoprocessor system. The Ravenscar profile greatly reduces the set of available Ada constructs (see Section 8.6 for a detailed description). The benefits are twofold. First, it allows for deterministic concurrency. Second, it allows for an efficient implementation. The GNULL of ORK+ has only 2,000 SLOC[7] fully written in Ada, plus some assembly code for low-level code such as context switch procedures. This reduced kernel is amenable to the thorough code analysis and inspection required to ensure quality of the code. The small size also makes it easier to make the necessary timing measurements of capacity required to perform the scheduling analyses discussed in Chapter 7.

This small size is a result of limiting the kernel to a small set of operations. Tasks are created only at elaboration time; they cannot terminate. Furthermore, there is no rendezvous allowed. All communications are performed through protected objects, and they all follow the simple-to-implement Priority Ceiling Protocol (PCP) that we discussed in Chapter 7.

In addition, ORK+ provides drivers to support serial communications and the SpaceWire spacecraft communication network (ESTEC, 2003) derived from the Firewire protocol.

Let's look at a small example for the ORK+ run-time. The first file, named **gnat.adc**, configures the compiler to enforce all compile-time checks required by the Ravenscar profile. This file contains the single line:

```
pragma Profile (Ravenscar);
```

Our program contains a single task that periodically outputs the string "ping!". To comply with the Ravenscar **No_Task_Hierarchy** restriction, all tasks must be defined in a separate package — they cannot be nested within the main subprogram. Here is the specification and body of the package that contains our periodic task.

```
package Task_1 is
   task Task_1 is
      pragma Priority (10);
   end Task_1;
end Task_1;
```

```
with Ada.Real_Time; use type Ada.Real_Time.Time;
with System.IO;
package body Task_1 is
   task body Task_1 is
      Start_Time : Ada.Real_Time.Time := Ada.Real_Time.Clock;
```

---

[7] SLOC: source lines of code, i.e. only code statements, no blank lines or comments are counted.

```
   begin
     loop
        System . IO . Put_Line ("ping!");
        Start_Time := Start_Time
          + Ada . Real_Time . Milliseconds (500);
        delay until Start_Time;
     end loop;
   end Task_1;
end Task_1;
```

Here is our main subprogram:

```
with Task_1;
with Ada . Real_Time;
procedure Simple_ORK is
begin
   -- Suspend the environment task forever
   delay until Ada . Real_Time . Time_Last;
end Simple_ORK;
```

The main subprogram `Simple_ORK` delays itself forever. The task defined in our package provides all of the functionality of this program.

GNAT Pro High Integrity[TM] is a commercially supported run-time for GNAT, derived from the original ORK+ and supported by AdaCore. It is being used by the Ocean & Land Colour Instrument (OLCI) project. This project is currently being developed by Thales Alenia Space and GMV, under contract of the European Space Agency, for the Sentinel-3 mission. Sentinel 3 is a scientific observation mission that will routinely monitor ocean and land surfaces.

Within the OLCI project, the Instrument Control Module (ICM) software is a critical component responsible for interfacing with the Satellite Management Unit — the central satellite control computer. The ICM also controls the rest of the instrument units. The Ada run-time for this critical software must be qualified to space standard ECCS-E-40B level B on the target processor. In the context of space systems, qualification requires the testing of every possible execution path in the system. Such exhaustive path testing of a run-time system is only possible in small run-times like ORK+ and GNAT Pro High Integrity[TM].

9.2.3 MaRTE OS, a minimum POSIX run-time

MaRTE OS (Rivas and Harbour, 2001) is a Hard Real-Time Operating System for embedded applications that follows the Minimal Real-Time POSIX subset.[8] Unlike ORK+ which supports only Ada, MaRTE OS provides support for mixed language applications written in Ada, C, C++, or Java. It also provides libraries for POSIX mechanisms (threads, mutexes, condvars) and a deterministic memory allocator. It fully supports the Ada 2005 Real-Time Annex and includes a wide range of schedulers, including application-defined scheduling and EDF.

MaRTE OS acts as a particular instance of GNULL. It is an x86 kernel written in Ada with more than 16,000 SLOC. This code is also exported as C functions to allow the construction of mixed language applications. Compared to ORK+, MaRTE OS provides a wider range of drivers: serial communication and various network protocols (Ethernet, CAN, RT-EP, etc.). In addition, the PolyORB middleware has been adapted to run on MaRTE OS and take advantage of its drivers.

MaRTE served as the test bench for the new scheduling features of Ada 2005 — application-driven scheduling and EDF. Both of these schedulers rely on a dedicated API to control the dispatching parameters associated with each task.

The package **Ada.Dispatching.EDF** provides the API to control the deadline associated with each task.

```ada
with Ada.Real_Time;
with Ada.Task_Identification;
package Ada.Dispatching.EDF is
   pragma Preelaborate;

   subtype Deadline is Ada.Real_Time.Time;

   Default_Deadline : constant Deadline := Ada.Real_Time.Time_Last;

   procedure Set_Deadline
      (D : Deadline;
       T : Ada.Task_Identification.Task_Id :=
             Ada.Task_Identification.Current_Task);

   procedure Delay_Until_And_Set_Deadline
      (Delay_Until_Time : Ada.Real_Time.Time;
       Deadline_Offset  : Ada.Real_Time.Time_Span);

   function Get_Deadline
      (T : Ada.Task_Identification.Task_Id :=
             Ada.Task_Identification.Current_Task)
         return Deadline;
end Ada.Dispatching.EDF;
```

To select the EDF dispatching protocol, simply configure the run-time by specifying the task dispatching policy with

---

[8] See http://marte.unican.es/.

pragma Task_Dispatching_Policy (EDF_Across_Priorities);

Using EDF or any API-based dispatching policy requires a good understanding of the policy itself and its interaction with the run-time system. While EDF was defined in 1973 by Liu and Layland (1973), the complexity needed to implement it in a run-time took considerably longer. It was first integrated into Ada in 2005.

9.2.4 RTEMS, a complete POSIX run-time

RTEMS is the Real-Time Operating System for Multiprocessor Systems.[9] It is a full featured RTOS that supports a variety of open API and interface standards including the Real-Time Executive Interface Definition (RTEID) and the Open Real-Time Kernel Interface Definition (ORKID). RTEMS includes support for POSIX threads and real-time extensions. It also includes a TCP/IP protocol stack, several networking clients and servers (web server or remote file systems), and a small shell to load/unload application code. RTEMS supports multiple languages including C, C++, and Ada. RTEMS is written in C. It targets around a dozen CPU platforms.

The POSIX interface of RTEMS serves as the basis of the GNULL part of the Ada run-time. However, RTEMS is more complicated to configure than the previous run-times. It relies on a series of C macros to configure part of its internals. Here are some examples of these macros. The full source is available on our web site.

```
/* configuration information */

#define  CONFIGURE_TEST_NEEDS_CONSOLE_DRIVER
#define  CONFIGURE_TEST_NEEDS_CLOCK_DRIVER

#define  CONFIGURE_MICROSECONDS_PER_TICK
         RTEMS_MILLISECONDS_TO_MICROSECONDS(1)

#define  CONFIGURE_POSIX_INIT_THREAD_TABLE

#define  CONFIGURE_MAXIMUM_SEMAPHORES 10
#define  CONFIGURE_GNAT_RTEMS

#define  CONFIGURE_INIT
```

Some of these declarations define different macros used to activate parts of the RTEMS libraries. Others configure the number of RTEMS tasks and semaphores used to support Ada tasks and protected objects. These macros

---

[9] See http://www.rtems.org.

are preprocessed before compiling the code. Since Ada does not provide a preprocessing mechanism, we must write some C code to write Ada code! Writing some C code to tailor the RTOS for our Ada application is common for RTOSs written in C.

RTEMS is being used in a large variety of projects written in both Ada and C.[10] The Avenger Air Defense System is one project that uses Ada.

9.3 Validating scheduling of a system

In the previous chapters, we discussed the Ada constructs that support concurrency and the extensions for real-time systems. In this chapter, we have presented different run-time architectures that support these constructs. Meeting deadlines is a requirement for real-time applications. In Chapter 7 we discussed real-time scheduling theory and different methods to determine whether or not scheduling constraints can be met. In Chapter 8 we showed how to write Ada code compliant with this theory.

In this section we complete the discussion by showing how we can ensure that our application will meet all of its deadlines. We need to tie together the impact of the run-time on scheduling (such as latency, jitter, and overhead), information on the application code, and an appropriate analytical framework.

9.3.1 Impact of the Ada run-time

The Ada standard goes well beyond the definition of the language. It also defines how to tailor the language to meet specific needs through restrictions and dedicated run-times.

Annex M.1 of the Ada Reference Manual, titled *Specific Documentation Requirements*, defines the key elements that make up a run-time configuration. In particular, this annex includes metrics associated with aspects of the run-time such as interrupt handlers, package `Task_Attributes`, procedure `Set_Priority`, setting the priority of a protected object, aborts, package `Real_Time`, delay statements, entry-less protected objects, execution time, and timing events.

These metrics are measured on particular test benches. Obviously, they depend on the architecture of the run-time, the processor being used, the release of the compiler, and the compilation options used. For example, Vardanega *et al.* (2005) have provided a full analysis of one version of the

---

[10] See `http://rtems.org/wiki/index.php/RTEMSApplications` for more details.

ORK+ run-time to evaluate how the number of tasks or protected objects impact each of the parameters defined in Annex M.1 and derive analytical formulas to compute each metric based on these run-time elements.

Compiler vendors may provide direct support to compute these metrics, but this is not a mandatory obligation: computing metrics is a costly process that implies using a dedicated test bench. This is done only when this is required for a specific contract or project.

9.3.2 From source code to analyzable systems

Of course the user-provided source code itself plays the major role in evaluating scheduling. Concurrency entities animate user code and the code itself takes time to execute. The complexity of the source code (measured by such metrics as Big-O notation, cyclomatic complexity, etc.) provides some general measure of efficiency and understandability of our code. It is the role of the software designer to clearly evaluate the algorithms and their impact on the execution time of the system.

Another point is to correctly use Ada constructs so as to minimize uncertainty. The careful use of patterns is important. By using regular patterns for periodic and sporadic tasks and protected objects, the code becomes aligned with the analytical framework we introduced for fixed priority scheduling. Reusing the same set of patterns allows an easy mapping from Ada code to task sets. In Chapter 8 we presented a generic package that provides a pattern for periodic tasks that we used to create the three tasks of our car application.

It is important to be able to compute an upper bound on the time taken by each function so we can calculate the capacity of each task. These capacities are needed to evaluate the various feasibility tests described in Chapter 7. We will discuss the determination of worst case execution times in Section 9.3.4.

9.3.3 Applying scheduling analysis

In Chapter 7 we discussed a number of techniques for determining whether or not all the tasks in an application could meet their deadlines. As these analyses were algorithmic in nature, it should not be a surprise that tools exist to support the work we did manually in that chapter. Using a model of our application, scheduling analysis tools allow us to run the various feasibility tests.

In some cases the system might be too complex for such tools. For example, most tools cannot directly handle interactions with the environment.

In such situations, it is important to explore other possible approaches to scheduling analyses such as model checking or simulation. There are formal methods with different schedulability analysis approaches based on Petri Nets, timed automata, or process algebra. These formal languages lead to the development of various simulators or model-checkers that can be used for schedulability analysis. TIMES (Fersman *et al.*, 2006), VESTA (Clarke *et al.*, 1995; Philippou and Sokolsky, 2007), and various Petri Net tools (Berthomieu and Vernadat, 2006; Hamez *et al.*, 2006; Wells, 2006) are examples of them. There is no "one-size-fits-all" analysis technique. A real-time multimedia system requires simulation because of the uncertainty of the run-time environment, whereas a critical system in a spacecraft will probably require an analytical framework that provides a definitive yes/no answer.

MAST[11] (Harbour *et al.*, 2001, University of Cantabria) and Cheddar[12] (Singhoff *et al.*, 2004, University of Brest) are two open source scheduling analysis tools. There are also some commercial tools such as Rapid-RMA from Tri-Pacific (2003) and TimeWiz from TimeSys (2002). All of these tools implement state-of-the-art analysis techniques to compute:

- Processors/tasks: worst/best/average response time, number of context switches/preemptions, missed deadlines, etc.
- Shared resources: worst/best/average shared resource blocking time, priority inversion, and deadlock, etc.
- Buffers: maximum/average message waiting time and maximum/average number of messages, etc.

Note that each tool implements only a subset of these analyses, so you have to select the tool that matches your requirements.

In Chapter 7 we presented a number of ways to compute the schedulability of a set of tasks. Before starting any computations, we must be careful to ensure that the hypothesis of the underlying theory holds. Furthermore, the computation itself is rather tedious, often requiring many steps. Software engineering tools help us by (1) requiring us to determine the scheduling parameters of each task in order to model it in the tool and (2) computing the results.

Modeling is usually the first step in building a complete application. Its importance is often underestimated by software engineers. By carefully modeling your system, you have a clearer view of what you intend to build. This modeling process is supported at different levels by each tool.

---

[11] See `http://mast.unican.es/`.
[12] See `http://beru.univ-brest.fr/~singhoff/cheddar/`.

There are many modeling tools available today for designers of real-time systems. Some of them provide Ada support. Modeling tools usually provide a means to graphically design the architecture of a real-time system. These tools may interact with other software engineering tools by model exchange to generate source code of the system, to produce documentations, or to perform various analyses (including schedulability analysis).

Modeling activities assume the use of a language that is able to model real-time features: we should be able to design a model of a real-time system composed of tasks, shared resources, and any other components of a real-time system, with all parameters presented in Chapter 7. Examples of real-time system modeling languages are various UML profiles such as MARTE[13] (Frédéric *et al.*, 2006; OMG, 2007), the SAE AADL standard (SAE, 2009), HOOD-HRT (Burns and Wellings, 1994), EAST-ADL (Debruyne *et al.*, 2005), or PPOOA (Fernandez and Marmol, 2008). Some of these languages are proprietary; others are international standards. Modeling languages are the link between modeling tools, source code generators, analysis tools, and many others. Use of standardized modeling languages may increase tool interoperability.

Stood (Dissaux, 2004) from Ellidiss Technologies, Rational Rhapsody (Chadburn, 2010) from IBM, and Artisan Studio from Atego (2009) are modeling tools available for Ada practitioners. Stood supports both AADL, HOOD-HRT, and UML. The others are mostly UML oriented.

Cheddar allows you to model your Ada tasks and some communication aspects to evaluate its schedulability. Cheddar is composed of a graphical editor and a library of processing modules written in Ada. The designer uses the editor to model their real-time systems. Cheddar has its own modeling language. A real-time system is modeled by a set of tasks, processors, shared resources, buffers, and address spaces. The modeling features of Cheddar are limited to real-time scheduling. Designers need to use separate modeling tools to perform the other aspects of the modeling activity. Cheddar has been directly coupled with Stood using the AADL language to link the two. This coupling allows real-time systems designers to easily apply schedulability analysis of the models they prepared with Stood.

The Cheddar library implements many feasibility tests and classical real-time scheduling algorithms (all the feasibility tests and algorithms presented in Chapter 7). This library also offers a domain specific language together with an interpreter and a compiler. This language is used for the design and analysis of schedulers that are not implemented into the library.

---

[13] Do not confuse MARTE (Modeling and Analysis of Real-Time and Embedded systems) with the MaRTE OS discussed in Section 9.2.3.

In Section 7.2.1 we presented the example of a car application with three periodic tasks. Given the period, capacity, and deadline of each of these tasks, we performed a set of computations to conclude that the system is actually schedulable. Let's use Cheddar to carry out these computations for us. Figure 9.2 shows the window for entering the scheduling parameters that we defined in Chapter 7. These parameters include priority, capacity, deadline, period, start time, and jitter. Cheddar will use the parameters to model each task.

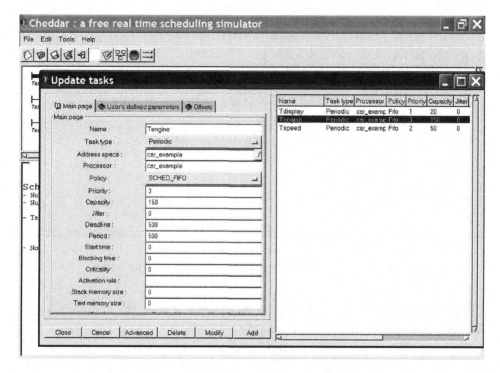

Figure 9.2 Characterizing the parameters of a task with Cheddar

Figure 9.3 shows the results of running the feasibility tests detailed in Chapter 7. The results of both the processor utilization factor and worst case response time feasibility tests are displayed. The feasibility tests provide a quick answer based on the recursive computation developed in Chapter 7. The result is a yes or no and provides a *theoretical* upper-bound value for the response time.

Figure 9.4 shows a simulation of the car application over the hyper-period of the tasks. Only a *portion* of the hyper-period is visible in this figure. As there is no interaction between tasks and no external source of events

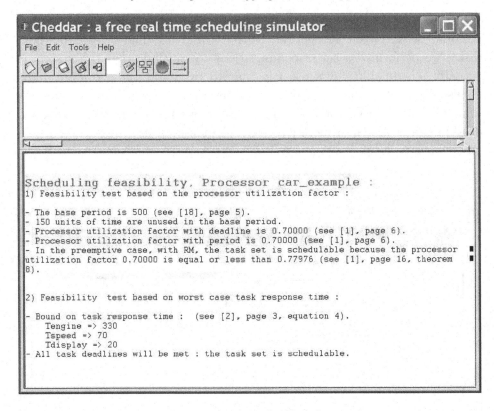

Figure 9.3 Output of the Cheddar tool: feasibility tests

(for example the input of a driver) in this *simple* model, the simulation and feasibility tests return the same results.

This simulation performs a step-by-step execution of the system as we did manually to fill in Figure 7.6 on page 271. At each simulated instant, the simulator computes the task to be dispatched based on the priority and running state information of each task. This simulation allows us to see accurately how the system behaves. It tells us how many context switches occur and, if there are shared resources, when mutexes (locks) are seized. This information provides a good estimation of the resource usage in the system. We can feedback the overhead incurred by the context switches to the processor utilization calculations and refine the priority ceiling value of the shared resources.

While schedulability analysis tools may provide *easy* answers, one should be careful when using them — they all require accurate modeling to avoid misinterpretations of the actual behavior of the application. Poor modeling can lead to false, non-representative, results. Real-time scheduling theory

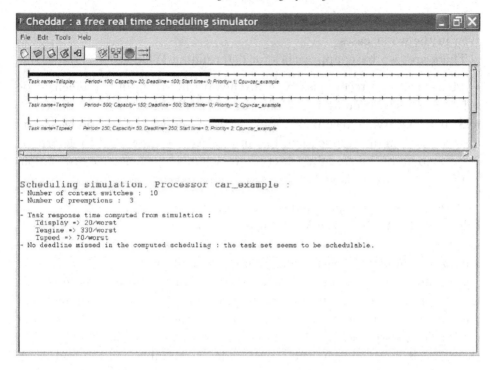

Figure 9.4 Output of the Cheddar tool: simulation

is not always easy to apply (Singhoff *et al.*, 2009). Remember that each feasibility test requires that the target real-time system fulfills several assumptions (e.g. critical instant, requests on deadlines, etc.). Thus, it may be difficult to choose the relevant feasibility test. The current generation of modeling languages and their software engineering tools provide very limited support for the *automatic* application of real-time scheduling theory. Still, schedulability analysis tools play an increasing role in software engineering and are used for increasingly more complex designs.

9.3.4 Computation of the worst case execution time (WCET)

All of the techniques discussed in Chapter 7 for determining whether or not a set of tasks will meet their deadlines required an estimate of the capacity of each task. The **capacity** of a periodic task is the amount of execution time required for one iteration. Although the actual amount of time a task requires for a particular iteration can vary, we always use the worst case execution time in our scheduling analysis to ensure that deadlines are met even in the worst cases.

There are two basic approaches for determining WCET:

- **Measurement** techniques typically involve inserting measurement code into the tasks, running them, and recording the time.
- **Static Analysis** techniques are based on models of the processor on which we run our application. Essentially, we use the model to determine the amount of time required to execute each machine language instruction. We then sum the times for the instructions in our task.

Both approaches require tedious and error-prone work. Tools do exist to help compute WCET (see Wilhelm *et al.*, 2008, for details). RapiTime™ is a tool for analyzing the WCET of Ada programs. It provides a hybrid approach combining measurement and static analysis.

Both measurement and static analysis techniques require us to determine the longest path of execution in each task. Once we have determined that path we can instrument our code or calculate the time from our processor model. Obviously, these paths must exist, but it may not be "easy" to find them. Tools may help analyze source code or assembly code to find worst case scenarios. Such determinations require a good understanding of Ada semantics. Some constructs such as pointers to subprograms, unbounded loops, run-time checks, exceptions, etc. complicate the longest path determination. We may decide to forbid such constructs to simplify our work.

In physics, the term *observer effect* (or Heisenberg effect) refers to changes that the act of observation will make on the thing being observed. It is possible that adding measurement code to our tasks may affect the time it takes the code to execute.

Static analysis requires a good understanding of how source code is executed. We need to know how the Ada code is translated into machine instructions for both simple constructs (like assignment, decision, and loop statements) and abstract ones (like tasks and protected objects). We usually require cooperation from the Ada compiler to obtain such information.

Modern processors present many challenges to static analysis of WCET. Patterson and Hennessy (2008) discuss the architecture of processors in depth. The common use of complex memory architectures is a major problem in modeling a processor. By providing multiple levels of different speed memories, cache memory provides faster *average* access to data and instructions. Different processors use different heuristics to locate items in the memory hierarchy. Since the location of data and instructions depends on past execution, all these heuristics have one property in common — the introduction of non-determinism. A study by Bernat *et al.* (2008) showed that cache memory heuristics introduce a large dispersion (around 20%) around a mean value. For hard real-time systems where determinism is crucial, it is usually advised to disable cache, or use it conservatively.

Furthermore, processors use different mechanisms to "predict" the next instruction to execute. Again, this introduces variability in the execution time. Hence, it is difficult to create a faithful model of the processor necessary to statically compute how much time each statement actually consumes.

The determination of WCET is complex, requiring the mastering of many algorithmic, architectural, and software engineering techniques. But it is a price we must pay to make sure that our planes, rockets, and trains never miss their deadlines. From its beginnings, Ada was designed to allow such analysis in as easy a way as possible.

Summary

- The role of the Ada compiler is to map constructs from simple arrays to tasks and protected objects onto elementary code (machine language) that is run on the target processor.
- The Ada compiler relies on a run-time system library to support some of the more complex constructs such as tasking. It maps such constructs onto calls to this library.
- A well designed run-time library maximizes portability to ease maintainability. The design should separate target-independent code from operating system and target-specific code.
- We introduced some elements of the GNAT run-time. The GNAT run-time separates concerns to maximize portability on a wide variety of platforms. GNARL provides the target-independent portions of the run-time system while GNULL provides the target-specific support.
- We introduced three different run-times supported by GNAT. The mechanism to support other operating systems is similar — isolate in GNULL the operating system specific code.
- By limiting the use of certain Ada constructs, the size and complexity of the run-time system can be reduced.
- ORK+ is an Ada Ravenscar run-time for SPARC platforms. Thanks to the restrictions imposed by the Ravenscar profile, its architecture has been highly optimized to reduce resource consumption, but also to enhance analysis.
- MaRTE OS is an Ada run-time for x86 platforms. It supports the Minimum POSIX Profile, and thus provides a range of scheduling algorithms, including EDF and application-defined scheduling.

- RTEMS is a C RTOS that supports a large variety of CPUs. RTEMS is highly configurable. However, the need to write a C adaptation layer to configure the required components makes the construction of an Ada program more complex.

- A knowledge of the architecture of the Ada run-time and the supporting operating system is often necessary to perform scheduling analysis of the system. The Ada Reference Manual defines the set of metrics to perform such analysis. These metrics are usually not provided with the compiler, but tool vendors may provide support to compute them for a particular platform.

- By using stringent coding rules, you may align your source code to the formal task set required to perform scheduling analysis, or some other modeling approach to check that your system meets all its real-time deadlines.

- Different tools support a wide variety of techniques, from analytical frameworks to partial analysis of all states through simulation, to complete analysis of all states through model checking. The selection of one method or another depends on the complexity of your system, and the applicability domain of each tool.

- The determination of worst case execution time is an important step in the analysis of the schedulability of a set of tasks. WCET may be determined by measurement or static analysis.

Exercises

9.1   Locate the Mac OS definition for type **Duration** in package **Standard** on page 338. This definition uses the attribute definition clause 'Small. Look up this attribute definition clause in the Ada Reference Manual and discuss its use in the definition of type **Duration**.

9.2   Explain why it is recommended to use fixed-point types for **Duration**.

9.3   In some cases, like RTEMS, the Ada run-time uses the POSIX concurrency library instead of an available lower-level one. The latter may be faster or use less resources. Explain why it is still reasonable for the Ada run-time to use the less efficient POSIX library.

9.4   Download the GNAT compiler. The tool **gnatls** allows you to locate the path to the run-time library using the -*v* flag. Locate these files, and review the corresponding Ada code. Pay attention to the children of **System**; they host the definition of protected objects, tasks, etc.

Try to isolate GNARL and GNULL elements.

9.5 We claimed that the support of the Priority Ceiling Protocol is trivial in the context of the Ravenscar profile for the ORK+ run-time. Explain why.

9.6 What are the restrictions to support the Ada Real-Time Annex on a GNU/Linux system? You may check the GNAT Reference Manual for more details.

9.7 Download Cheddar or MAST and model the examples and exercises from Chapter 7. What additional information would you need to perform more accurate analyses? Can you obtain any of that information from the Ada Reference Manual?

9.8 Install ORK+ or MaRTE OS and implement an example that you analyzed in the previous exercise.

9.9 Read the documentation for ORK+ or MaRTE OS. Evaluate the complexity of implementing a fixed priority scheduling with Rate Monotonic priority assignment or an Earliest Deadline First-based system.

9.10 Explain why using pointers to function makes the WCET analysis more complex. Explain why limiting run-time checks is often desirable for WCET analysis.

References

Amdahl, G. M. 1967. Validity of the single processor approach to achieving large scale computing capabilities. Pages 483–485 of: *AFIPS '67 (Spring): Proceedings of the April 18–20, 1967, Spring Joint Computer Conference.* ACM.

Anderson, T. E., Bershad, B. N., Lazowska, E. D., and Levy, H. M. 1992. Scheduler activations: effective kernel support for the user-level management of parallelism. *ACM Transactions on Computer Systems (TOCS)*, **10**(1), 53–79.

Atego. 2009. *Artisan Studio Architect Enterprise Edition.* White paper.

Audsley, A. N., Burns, A., Richardson, M., and Tindell, K. 1993. Applying new scheduling theory to static priority pre-emptive scheduling. *Software Engineering Journal*, **9**(5), 284–292.

Baker, T. P. 1991. Stack-based scheduling for realtime processes. *Journal of Real Time Systems*, **3**(1), 67–99.

Baker, T. P., and Cirinei, M. 2006. A necessary and sometimes sufficient condition for the feasibility of sets of sporadic hard-deadline tasks. Pages 178–190 of: *Proceedings of the 27th IEEE International Real-Time Systems Symposium.* IEEE.

Baker, T. P., and Oh, D.-I. 1997. Ada bindings for C interfaces: lessons learned from the florist implementation. Pages 13–22 of: Hardy, K., and Briggs, J. S. (eds), *Ada-Europe.* Lecture Notes in Computer Science, vol. 1251. Springer.

Barnes, J. 2003. *High Integrity Software, The SPARK Approach to Safety and Security.* Pearson Education Limited.

Barnes, J. 2006. *Programming in Ada 2005.* Pearson Education Limited.

Ben-Ari, M. 1982. *Principles of Concurrent Programming.* Prentice Hall International.

Ben-Ari, M. 2009. *Ada for Software Engineers.* 2nd edn. Springer-Verlag.

Bernat, G., Colin, A., Esteves, J., Garcia, G., Moreno, C., Holsti, N., Vardanega, T., and Hernek, M. 2008. Considerations on the LEON cache effects on the timing analysis of onboard applications. In: *Proceedings of the Data Systems In Aerospace Conference (DASIA'08).* ESA Publications.

Berthomieu, B., and Vernadat, F. 2006. Time petri nets analysis with TINA. In: *Proceedings of 3rd International Conference on The Quantitative Evaluation of Systems (QEST 2006), IEEE Computer Society.* IEEE.

Blaha, M. R., and Rumbaugh, J. R. 2004. *Object-Oriented Modeling and Design with UML.* 2nd edn. Pearson Prentice Hall.

Blair, M., Obenski, S., and Bridickas, P. 1992. *Patriot Missile Defense: Software Problem Led to System Failure at Dhahran, Saudi Arabia.* Tech. report GAO/IMTEC-92-26. United States General Accounting Office.

Briand, L. P., and Roy, D. M. 1999. *Meeting Deadlines in Hard Real-Time Systems, The Rate Monotonic Approach.* IEEE Computer Society.

Burns, A., and Wellings, A. J. 1994. HRT-HOOD: a design method for hard real-time systems. *Real Time Systems Journal,* **6**(1), 73–114.

Burns, A., and Wellings, A. 1998. *Concurrency in Ada.* Cambridge University Press.

Burns, A., and Wellings, A. 2007. *Concurrent and Real-Time Programming in Ada.* Cambridge University Press.

Burns, A., and Wellings, A. 2009. *Real-time Systems and Programming Languages.* 4th ed. Addison Wesley.

Buttazzo, G. 2003. Rate monotonic vs. EDF: Judgment day. *In Proceedings of 3rd ACM International Conference on Embedded Software.* ACM

Carey, R. W., Van Arsdall, P. J., and Woodruff, J. P. 2003. The national ignition facility: early operational experience with a large Ada control system. *Ada Letters,* **23**(1), 11.

Carlow, G. D. 1984. Architecture of the Space Shuttle Primary Avionics Software System. *Communications of the ACM,* **27**(9).

Chadburn, F. 2010. *Exploiting UML2 code generation with IBM Rational Rhapsody in Ada.* White paper.

Clarke, D., Lee, I., and Xie, H. 1995. VERSA: a tool for the specification and analysis of resource-bound real-time systems. *Journal of Computer and Software Engineering,* **3**(2).

Cohen, N. 1996. *Ada as a Second Language.* McGraw-Hill Series in Computer Science. McGraw-Hill.

Cottet, F., Delacroix, J., Kaiser, C., and Mammeri, Z. 2002. *Scheduling in Real Time Systems.* John Wiley and Sons Ltd.

Coulouris, G., Dollimore, J., and Kindberg, T. 2005. *Distributed Systems: Concepts and Design.* 4th edn. Addison-Wesley.

Dale, N., and McCormick, J. 2007. *Ada Plus Data Structures: An Object-Oriented Approach.* 2nd edn. Jones and Bartlett.

Dale, N., Weems, C., and McCormick, J. 2000. *Programming and Problem Solving with Ada 95.* 2nd edn. Jones and Bartlett.

de la Puente, J. A., Ruiz, J. F., and Zamorano, J. 2000. An open Ravenscar real-time kernel for GNAT. In: *Proceedings of the Reliable Software Technologies. Ada-Europe 2000.* Lecture Notes in Computer Science, 1845. Springer Verlag.

Debruyne, V., Simonot-Lion, F., and Trinquet, Y. 2005. EAST-ADL – an architecture description language. Pages 181–195 of: *Book on Architecture Description Languages, IFIP International Federation for Information Processing.* Springer Verlag.

DeRemer, F., and Kron, H. 1975. Programming-in-the-large versus programming-in-the-small. Pages 114–121 of: *Proceedings of the International Conference on Reliable Software.* ACM.

Dijkstra, E. 1968. Cooperating sequential processes. Pages 43–112 of: Genuys, F. (ed), *Programming Languages.* Academic Press. Reprinted from the original Technological University, Eindhoven, The Netherlands, September 1965.

Dissaux, P. 2004. Using the AADL for mission critical software development. *2nd European Congress ERTS, EMBEDDED REAL TIME SOFTWARE.*

Dobing, B. 1999. The Ravenscar profile: experience report. *ACM SIGAda Ada Letters*, **19**(2), 28–32.

Douglass, B. P. 1998. *Real-Time UML: Developing Efficient Objects for Embedded Systems*. 2nd edn. Addison Wesley Longman.

Duff, R., Hugues, J., Pautet, L., Quinot, T., and Tardieu, S. 2010. *PolyORB 2.7.0w User's Guide*. http://www.adacore.com/wp-content/files/auto_update/polyorb-docs/polyor%b_ug.html/.

Eisenstadt, M. 1997. My hairiest bug war stories. *Communications of the ACM*, **40**(4), 30–37.

English, J. 2001. *Ada 95: The Craft of Object-Oriented Programming*. http://www.it.bton.ac.uk/staff/je/adacraft/.

ESTEC, ESA. 2003. *ECSS-E-50-12A SpaceWire – Links, Nodes, Routers and Networks*. Tech. rept. European Space Agency.

Fernandez, J. L., and Marmol, G. 2008. An effective collaboration of a modeling tool and a simulation and evaluation framework. In: *18th Annual International Symposium, INCOSE 2008. Systems Engineering for the Planet*. INCOSE.

Fersman, E., Mokrushin, L., Pettersson, P., and Yi, W. 2006. Schedulability analysis of fixed-priority systems using timed automata. *Theoretical Computer Science*, **354**(2), 301–317.

Flynn, M. 1974. Some computer organizations and their effectiveness. *IEEE Transactions on Computers*, **C-21**, 948–960.

Frédéric, T., Gérard, S., and Delatour, J. 2006. Towards an UML 2.0 profile for real-time execution platform modeling. In: *Proceedings of the 18th Euromicro Conference on Real-Time Systems (ECRTS 06), Work in progress session*. IEEE.

Gallmeister, B. O. 1995. *POSIX 4: Programming for the Real World*. O'Reilly and Associates.

George, L., Rivierre, N., and Spuri, M. 1996. *Preemptive and Non-Preemptive Real-time Uni-processor Scheduling*. Tech. rept. INRIA.

Giering, III, E. W., and Baker, T. P. 1994. The GNU Ada runtime library (GNARL). Pages 97–107 of: *WADAS '94: Proceedings of the Eleventh Annual Washington Ada Symposium & Summer ACM SIGAda Meeting on Ada*. ACM.

GNAT. 2010. *GNAT Reference Manual*. AdaCore.

Hamez, A., Hillah, L., Kordon, F., Linard, A., Paviot-Adet, E., Renault, X., and Thierry-Mieg, Y. 2006. New features in CPN-AMI 3: focusing on the analysis of complex distributed systems. Pages 273–275 of: *6th International Conference on Application of Concurrency to System Design (ACSD'06)*. IEEE Computer Society.

Harbour, M. G., Moyano, J. M. D., Rivas, M. A., and Fernández, J. G. 1997. Implementing robot controllers under real-time POSIX and Ada. Pages 57–64 of: *IRTAW '97: Proceedings of the Eighth International Workshop on Real-Time Ada*. ACM.

Harbour, M. G., Garcia, J. J. G., Gutiérrez, J. C. P., and Moyano, J. M. D. 2001. MAST: Modeling and Analysis Suite for Real Time Applications. Pages 125–134 of: *Proceedings of the 13th Euromicro Conference on Real-Time Systems (ECRTS 2001)*. IEEE Computer Society.

Heitmeyer, C., and Mandrioli, D. 1996. *Formal Methods for Real Time Computing*. John Wiley and Sons Ltd.

Hugues, J., Pautet, L., and Kordon, F. 2003. Contributions to middleware architectures to prototype distribution infrastructures. Pages 124–131 of: *Proceedings of the 14th IEEE International Workshop on Rapid System Prototyping (RSP'03).* IEEE.

Joseph, M., and Pandya, P. 1986. Finding response time in a real-time system. *Computer Journal,* **29**(5), 390–395.

Klein, M. H., Ralya, T., Pollak, B., Obenza, R., and Harbour, M. G. 1994. *A Practitioner's Handbook for Real Time Analysis.* Kluwer Academic Publishers.

Kleinrock, L. 1975a. *Queueing Systems: Computer Application.* Wiley-interscience.

Kleinrock, L. 1975b. *Queueing Systems: Theory.* Wiley-interscience.

Knoll, K. T. 1993. *Risk Management In Fly-By-Wire Systems.* NASA STI/Recon. NASA.

Koren, G., and Shasha, D. 1992. *D-Over, an optimal on-line scheduling algorithm for overloaded real time systems.* Tech. rept. INRIA technical report number RT-0138.

Laplante, Phillip. 2004. *Real-Time Systems Design and Analysis.* Piscataway, New Jersey: IEEE Press.

Liu, C. L., and Layland, J. W. 1973. Scheduling algorithms for multiprogramming in a hard real-time environment. *Journal of the Association for Computing Machinery,* **20**(1), 46–61.

Lyu, M. R. 1995. *Handbook of Software Reliability Engineering.* McGraw-Hill.

Mauro, J., and Dougall, R. 2001. *Solaris Internals: Core Kernel Architecture.* Prentice Hall.

McCormick, J. 1997. Forum letter. *Communications of the ACM,* **40**(8), 30.

McHale, Ciaran. 2007. *CORBA Explained Simply.*

Nyberg, K. 2007. Multi-core + multi-tasking = multi-opportunity. *Ada Letters,* **27**(3), 79–81.

OAR. 2004. *RTEMS Ada User's Guide.* OAR Corporation.

OMG. 2001. *Ada Language to IDL Mapping v1.2.* OMG.

OMG. 2004. *The Common Object Request Broker: Architecture and Specification, Revision 3.0.3.* OMG. OMG Technical Document formal/2004-03-12.

OMG. 2007. *A UML Profile for MARTE, Beta 1.* OMG Document Number: ptc/07-08-04.

Panwalkar, S. S., and Iskander, W. 1976. A survey of scheduling rules. *Operations Research,* **25**(1), 45–61.

Patterson, D. A., and Hennessy, J. L. 2008. *Computer Organization & Design: The Hardware/Software Interface.* 4th edn. Morgan Kaufmann.

Pautet, L., and Tardieu, S. 2000. GLADE: a framework for building large object-oriented real-time distributed systems. Page 244 of: *ISORC '00: Proceedings of the Third IEEE International Symposium on Object-Oriented Real-Time Distributed Computing.* IEEE Computer Society.

Pautet, L., Quinot, T., and Tardieu, S. 1999. CORBA & DSA: divorce or marriage? In: *Proceedings of 4th International Conference on Reliable Software Conference.* Springer Verlag.

Pease, M., Shostak, R., and Lamport, L. 1980. Reaching agreement in the presence of faults. *Journal of the ACM,* **27**(2), 228–234.

Philippou, T. A., and Sokolsky, O. 2007. Process-algebraic analysis of timing and schedulability properties. In: *Handbook of Real-Time and Embedded Systems.* Chapman and Hall/CRC.

Riehle, R. 2003. *Ada Distilled: An Introduction to Ada Programming for Experienced Computer Programmers.* Tech. rept. AdaWorks Software Engineering.

Rivas, M. A., and Harbour, M. G. 2001. MaRTE OS: an Ada kernel for real-time embedded applications. In: *Proceedings of the International Conference on Reliable Software Technologies, Ada-Europe-2001.*

SAE. 2009. *Architecture Analysis and Design Language (AADL) AS 5506.* Tech. rept. The Engineering Society For Advancing Mobility Land Sea Air and Space, Aerospace Information Report, Version 2.0.

Schonberg, E., and Banner, B. 1994. The GNAT Project: A GNU-Ada 9X Compiler. Pages 48–57 of: *TRI-Ada.* ACM.

Sha, L., Rajkumar, R., and Lehoczky, J. P. 1990. Priority inheritance protocols: an approach to real-time synchronization. *IEEE Transactions on Computers,* **39**(9), 1175–1185.

Shen, S., and Baker, T. P. 1999. A Linux kernel module implementation of restricted Ada tasking. *ACM SIGAda Ada Letters,* **19**(2), 96–103.

Singhoff, F., Legrand, J., Nana, L., and Marcé, L. 2004. Cheddar: a flexible real time scheduling framework. Pages 1–8 of: *SIGAda '04: Proceedings of the 2004 Annual ACM SIGAda International Conference on Ada.* ACM.

Singhoff, F., Plantec, A., Dissaux, P., and Legrand, J. 2009. Investigating the usability of real-time scheduling theory with the Cheddar project. *Journal of Real Time Systems,* **43**(3), 259–295.

Sprunt, B., Sha, L., and Lehoczky, J.P. 1989. Aperiodic task scheduling for hard-real-time systems. *Journal of Real Time Systems,* **1**, 27–60.

Spuri, M. 1996. *Analysis of Deadline Scheduled Real-Time Systems.* Tech. rept. RR-2772. INRIA.

Stankovic, John. 1988. Misconceptions about real-time computing. *IEEE Computer,* **21**(10): 10–19.

Taft, S. T., Duff, R. A., Brukardt, R. L., Ploedereder, E., and Leroy, P. 2006. *Ada 2005 Reference Manual. Language and Standard Libraries. International Standard ISO/IEC 8652/1995(E) with Technical Corrigendum 1 and Amendment 1.* LNCS Springer Verlag, number XXII, volume 4348.

TimeSys. 2002. *Using TimeWiz to Understand System Timing before you Build or Buy.* Tech. rept. TimeSys Corporation.

Tindell, K. W., and Clark, J. 1994. Holistic schedulability analysis for distributed hard real-time systems. *Microprocessing and Microprogramming,* **40**(2-3), 117–134.

Tri-Pacific. 2003. *Rapid-RMA: The Art of Modeling Real-Time Systems.* Tech. rept. Tri-Pacific Software, Inc.

Turley, J. 1999. Embedded processors by the numbers. *Embedded Systems Programming,* **12**(5), 99.

Vahalia, U. 1996. *UNIX Internals: the New Frontiers.* Prentice Hall.

Vardanega, T., Zamorano, J., and de la Puente, J. A. 2005. On the dynamic semantics and the timing behavior of Ravenscar kernels. *Real-Time Systems,* **29**, 59–89.

Vinoski, S. 2004. An overview of middleware. Pages 35–51 of: *Proceedings of the 9th International Conference on Reliable Software Techologies Ada-Europe 2004 (RST'04).* Springer Verlag.

Wells, Lisa. 2006. Performance analysis using CPN tools. Page 59 of: *Valuetools '06: Proceedings of the 1st International Conference on Performance Evaluation Methodolgies and Tools.* ACM.

Wikibooks. 2010a. *Ada Programming*. http://en.wikibooks.org/wiki/Ada_
    Programming.

Wikibooks. 2010b. *Ada Quality and Style Guide.* http://en.wikibooks.org/wiki/
    Ada_Style_Guide.

Wilhelm, R., Engblom, J., Ermedahl, A., Holsti, N., Thesing, S., Whalley, D.,
    Bernat, G., Ferdinand, C., Heckmann, R., Mitra, T., Mueller, F., Puaut, I.,
    Puschner, P., Staschulat, J., and Stenstrm, P. 2008. The worst-case execution
    time problem – overview of methods and survey of tools. *ACM Transactions
    on Embedded Computing Systems*, **7**(3), 36–53.

Wind River. 1997. *VxWorks: Programmer's Guide.* Wind River Systems.

Index

Printed in the United States
By Bookmasters